Reflections on Modern History

Reflections on Modern History

The Historian and Human Responsibility

HANS KOHN

GREENWOOD PRESS, PUBLISHERS
WESTPORT, CONNECTICUT

Library of Congress Cataloging in Publication Data

Kohn, Hans, 1891-1971.
   Reflections on modern history.

   Reprint of the ed. published by D. Van Nostrand,
Princeton, N.J.
   Includes bibliographical references.
   "Books by Hans Kohn from 1922 to 1963
(in chronological order)": p.
   1. History, Modern--Addresses, essays, lectures.
I. Title.
[D7.K73 1978]   909.08   77-28495
SIBN 0-313-20232-X

Copyright © 1963, by D. Van Nostrand Company, Inc.

No reproduction in any form of this book, in whole or in
part (except for brief quotation in critical articles or reviews),
may be made without written authorization from the publishers.

Reprinted with the permission of Yetty and Immanuel Kohn

Reprinted in 1978 by Greenwood Press, Inc.
51 Riverside Avenue, Westport, CT. 06880

Printed in the United States of America

10 9 8 7 6 5 4 3 2 1

Preface

History has a twofold meaning. First of all it is a sequence of events, of what happened, a connotation characteristic of the German word *Geschichte* and of the Latin use of the word *historia* or *historiae*. In that sense our word story is connected with the word history. But the original meaning of the Greek word *historia* is inquiry, not so much the narrative of events but their interpretation and a study of their character and significance. History in the first sense is the work of princes and statesmen, of peoples and movements; in the second sense, it is the work of historians.

History in the first sense consists of events. An event, an e-ventus, is a fact or incident, that comes out from somewhere. The historian deals with the "somewhere." The world in which we have lived since the end of the Second World War is significantly more eventful than most preceding periods of history. This book is intended as a contribution to an understanding of some of these events and of the role of the historian in our time, a time in which relatively new goals of individual liberty, of national independence, and world-wide interdependence are agitating man's mind in many lands.

History implies both continuity and change. The present is an accumulation of the past, but it is always something more than that. The world which we face in 1963 bears little resemblance to that of 1914, of 1938, or even of 1945. In many lands events have happened which several decades ago few historians if any would have predicted. This character of change and of the possibility of change establishes, within certain limits set by human nature and by the trends of the past, man's liberty and above all his personal responsibility. In an age of democracy and of mass participation in the political, social, and cultural life, this responsibility is shared by everyone. But perhaps it weighs most heavily upon the historian. In that sense the historian should represent on the one hand the consciousness, the self-awareness of an epoch or a people, and on the other hand its conscience.

After having lived in many lands—under the Habsburg monarchy before the First World War, and in Russia, France, England, and Palestine for the following twenty years—the author has taught history, and written about it, in the United States for the past twenty-nine years. The addresses and essays collected in this volume indicate how he regarded his task as a historian and as a teacher and how he interpreted the events of these years and their background of liberalism, nationalism, and steep and difficult ascent to a supranational order. For this reason, no attempt was made to update the articles.

The book would not have appeared without the initiative and active sympathy of some of the author's friends. It is dedicated to them in joyful recognition of the deep and lasting value of their friendship.

HANS KOHN

Foreword

The career of Hans Kohn predestined him to become a historian of nationalism. Born in Prague in the province of Bohemia on September 15, 1891, he was reared in an atmosphere of explosive nationalism. Since 1848 attempts have been made to assert the independence of Bohemia in the old Austro-Hungarian Empire. The Bohemian question was eventually solved by the collapse of the Habsburg monarchy during the First World War and by the success of the Czechoslovak movement. The young man who witnessed this development and understood it eventually became one of the world's distinguished historians of nationalism.

Thrown into a prisoner-of-war camp in Siberia during the First World War, Kohn organized a series of lectures and cultural activities to exercise the minds of prisoners endangered by apathy and ennui. It was a typical gesture. This exuberance and enthusiasm for the intellect never waned in succeeding decades as he fashioned an extraordinary *Lebenslauf*. He lived successively in Paris, London, and Jerusalem, traveled widely in Europe and in the Middle East, and finally became a teacher on the American scene.

The professional life of Hans Kohn is best expressed in capsule form in three words—historian, humanist, humanitarian.

As historian, Hans Kohn has won the respect and friendship of his colleagues not only in his department at The City College of New York but throughout the United States. Here is the classic example of the twentieth-century mind working within the best traditions and high standards of modern scholarship. Hans Kohn has always remained the unbiased historian (*wie es eigentlich gewesen ist*), never the historicist seeking to use history for political purposes (*durch die Geschichte politisch zu wirken*).

Behind the Kohn technique of historical writing is a vast knowledge of sources and literature, a familiarity amazing in its diversity. Primarily the intellectual historian, the historian of ideas, he is one of the few scholars working in this discipline who knows the range of German, Slavic, French, Italian, and English literature and historiography in the original languages.

The range of Hans Kohn's interests is wide. Vigorous and thought-provoking, he is at all times in control of his subject, equally at ease with the history of Germany, Russia, England, or France. His judgments are penetrating and stimulating. Unimpressed by monistic interpretations of historical development, he sees history as pluralistic and operating on several levels, a vast, three-dimensional pattern always changing in a complex variety of lights and shadows. Above all, he reveals historical continuity—*Kontinuitätslehre*—opposed to the theory of catastrophe as motivating in historical change.

There are scholars and scholars. One well-known type—the master of the minuscule or the ferret scholar—spends a lifetime of concentrated effort pouncing on the obscure footnotes of professional colleagues and joyously coming up with a typographical slip or an incorrect date, which is then endlessly beaten into submissiveness. Hans Kohn, on the other hand, knows how to sort the significant from the unimportant in the ocean of facts. His books and lectures, are exercises in clarity, compact in outlining and organization, rich in interpretation.

Secondly, Hans Kohn as a humanist is the contemporary successor to those who brought the Greek and Roman classics into new vogue during the Renaissance. He has helped bring to a wide audience a new appreciation of literary beauties and varieties of subjects of the past. He has done much to popularize the free spirit so characteristic of the humanist approach. For him humanity has remained the central object of interest. He operates in an intellectual climate in which man is master of his environment.

Thirdly, the best word to describe Hans Kohn is humanitarian, the human being who reveals by his actions a deep regard for the interests of mankind. In value judgments he is invariably on the side of justice, toleration, decency. All who know him are aware of his sense of tone, tact, and taste. He is, above all, a kind and gentle man, the essence of the gentleman. This is the instinctive reaction of his students—among the most important people in his life. Many young scholars, recognizing the historian and teacher, impressed by his enthusiasm and energy, have turned to the discipline of history as a career. Young people are fascinated by his intellect, the *sympathisch* personality, the scholarly integrity.

In a recent musical program honoring Professor Kohn at the time

Foreword

of his retirement, the students of City College expressed their own reactions in these fine words:

> To Hans Kohn:
> —For your services to the school and the students,
> —For liberally sharing the knowledge of a scholar,
> —For conveying a belief in the democratic process,
> —For your optimism in a world of pessimism and doubt,
> —And for your faith in man as a rational being,
>   This program is humbly dedicated.

This collection of essays and speeches epitomizes the thinking of Hans Kohn during the last decade and a half. The varied pieces reflect many facets, but there is coherence to the whole. Here we learn how he regards the profession of the historian, how he interprets the events of his active years, and how he applies his understanding of liberalism, nationalism, and the contemporary supranational order. This is the historical diagnostician at his best, the elucidator and commentator alive to his calling.

The subjects in this book are grouped under four major headings. The first, on the historian and human responsibility, reveals the liberal historian in intellectual action. Six selections give a creed for our times. Kohn tells us that historians have responsibilities, not to nations or classes, to dogmas or creeds, but to truth and humanity. He warns against emotional prejudices and group interests. He states in admirable terms the ethos of discipline.

History, in Hans Kohn's view, takes a most important place in liberal education. It is the teacher's task to convey an understanding of history's relentless struggle to his students, without interpreting it in too soft or sentimental a way. History, like life itself, is hard and exciting. Moreover, the way the teachers function in a liberal society is vital. To Kohn the idea of academic freedom, in an era when liberalism itself is threatened, is no longer a professional fight for a principle; it is a fight for survival. Academic freedom is all-important precisely because it is a part of the educational structure. All our intellectual and moral resources must be devoted to creating a new world in which "the dignity of the individual shall be respected, the equality of men and races recognized, and the freedom of all safeguarded." Our college youth, Kohn says, are aware today of the values of Western civilization and of free society. "In the years ahead, the liberty of the individual and the spontaneous growth of our spiritual heritage will be values which will be felt poignantly. College youth will have to understand and sustain them."

In the final essay of this opening section, Kohn gives his view of a world based on freedom and diversity, a society which mirrors the interdependence of civilization, and one in which no one people can regard itself as exclusive possessors of the one, true way.

The unit sums up Kohn's concept of the *open society*, a phrase which runs as a theme through his books and articles. He describes its phases—liberalism, democracy, parliamentarianism, constitutionalism, civil rights, tolerance—in short, the ideas of the Western Enlightenment. At the same time, Kohn points out the shortcomings of the *closed society*, with its totalitarianism formulae, its dictatorships, its prisons and concentration camps, its accent on compulsion, indoctrination, and coordination, its suffusion with tyranny and terror. Kohn regards it as the historian's responsibility to show the aims, motives, and actions of the open society as contrasted with its opposite. In this sense, as chronicler, analyst, and interpreter, he helps safeguard the values of our civilization.

The second major section is devoted to the ideas of three great English political thinkers—Walter Bagehot, Lord Acton, and James Bryce. No advocate of Carlyle's great man theory of history, Kohn, nevertheless, recognizes the importance of individuals in history as initiators and carriers of ideas. These Englishmen he regards with empathy for he shares their ideas—Bagehot and his sense of "animated moderation," the man "who would rather be a subject of a humble commonwealth in the Alps than a subject of the superb autocracy that overshadows half of Asia and Europe"; Lord Acton, apostle of human liberty and human dignity who refused to share the easy, illusionary optimism of his era; and James Bryce, whose classic work on *The Holy Roman Empire,* one of the most remarkable studies in the history of ideas, gave direction to Kohn's own work as historian. It is a great trio of ideas—Bagehot's tolerance and "live and let live," Acton's sense of human liberty, and Bryce's love of the democratic way of life.

The major body of the book is devoted to that subject which has brought recognition to the author—nationalism. Before the First World War Norman Angell described nationalism as "the most important thing in the world, more important than civilization, humanity, decency, kindness, pity; more important than life itself."

Foreword

The contributions of Kohn on this vital subject are of enduring significance.

The chapters are uniformly excellent. Napoleon is portrayed as an anachronism in the age of nationalism, a romantic alone against the world, whose violent career aroused emotions hostile to the Enlightenment and stimulated entire peoples to follow his career of conquest. In a strikingly original essay, Kohn shows France after 1815 caught in an attitude of attraction and repulsion between Britain and Germany, with necessity and common traditions turning her westward for support and survival, but with her intellectual fascination turned longingly eastward.

Always in search of the significant in ideas, Kohn finds typical nationalist Russian Messianism in the writings of Dostoevsky and Danilevsky, both of whom were "less concerned with individual liberty than with Russian national power and destiny." In "Toynbee and Russia," the author sees important light for an understanding of the underlying causes of the anti-Western attitude of Russia against the historical background of civilizations. Toynbee's mind, different from Danilevsky's or Spengler's, is not obsessed by irrational fears of war. "Toynbee rightly refuses to act as a prophet." Kohn refuses to join the parade of those who see nothing but nonsense in Toynbee. He is critical of the British historian, but his criticism remains on a high, intellectual level.

In the other chapters on nationalism Kohn shows how three Central European non-Slavic movements—German romantic nationalism, the drive for German unification, and the Austro-Hungarian compromise—contributed much to the rise of Pan-Slavism. He pays eloquent tribute to the courage and honesty of Thomas G. Masaryk, liberator and first president of Czechoslovakia, and apostle of the open society. He sees the Jewish problem, which he analyzes in some detail, as a part of the human problem. He regards war as the normal and welcome concomitant of the totalitarian philosophy of life. He evaluates tensions between Yugoslavia and Soviet Russia. And, finally, he expresses his belief that the chances for a free Germany in the Western sense of the word, working for human liberty and humanitarian civilization, seem better today than at any time in the last century, despite the existence of vestigial remains of the older forms of German nationalism.

In his concluding section, Kohn surveys the contemporary world in which we live. He comments on the central problems of our time

—the cold war, the United Nations, the Atlantic Community, and Germany. He speaks as an American citizen, as a citizen-of-the-world who sees salvation in a world society, and as a historian familiar with the nuances of the past.

"One World?" was written shortly after the end of the Second World War. To Kohn, this war proved that no single totalitarian faith could impose itself on or undo the plurality and diversity of mankind. He calls for an end to fanatical ideology and for the introduction of a broader spirit of tolerance and compromise—an international society reflecting common human values and individual personal independence. The historian of nationalism recommends an end of a narrow self-centered nationalism and the introduction of a tolerable world society under the restraint of law.

As early as 1946 Kohn appealed for the reintegration of Germany into Western civilization. One of the first historians to call attention to Germany's tragedy—her unceasing oscillation between the ideals of the liberal West and an ego centered Germanophilism—he sees the new Germany as no longer the spearhead of struggle against the West. He believes the Bonn Republic to be a potentially vital force added to the intellectual strength and democratic security of the West. He welcomes Germany to the North Atlantic Community and sees in her close collaboration with her fellow members of the Western community one lasting gain out of the catastrophe which Hitler brought to Germany and Europe.

Kohn calls on the United States to seek constructive solutions for our many urgent problems, but always within the framework of the ideals of the United Nations, "which, after all, are only the application of the principles of modern Western civilization to an international community in which the West no longer plays the dominant role." He sees in the North Atlantic Community a will to defend the common spiritual and moral values of Western civilization. The cold war, he says, forces the West not only to seek greater unity, but also to grow beyond the confines of the nation-state, as well as into an awareness of its own principles of liberty for all and an earnest effort to apply them.

Taking the historian's view of Russian foreign policy, Kohn sees a hot war as improbable, because of the nature of the new armaments and the growth of world public opinion. He believes that the cold war will go on without deteriorating into a hot conflict. "Peaceful co-existence," he warns, "is only a pleasanter name for cold war."

Finally, Kohn pays a tribute to the United Nations which is "beginning to mitigate, through the Western method of discussion and compromise, the complex tensions which are inseparable from a world situation in which democracy and communism face each other." The United Nations must safeguard the principle of self-determination in the true sense of the word. This, in the long run, can defeat the threat of Communist or Fascist totalitarianism.

We find much in these thirty-two papers which will stimulate our thought and broaden our understanding. It is worthwhile to listen to the voice of a scholar who upholds the enlightened forces of civilization in the unending battle against human inertia, self-centered group egoism, and tyranny.

Louis L. Snyder

Table of Contents

PART ONE: THE HISTORIAN AND HUMAN RESPONSIBILITY

1. The Historian's Responsibility in Our Time — 3
2. History: Its Place in a Liberal Education — 10
3. Academic Freedom in Our Time — 22
4. Education for the Coming Era — 27
5. The Promise of This Generation of College Youth — 34
6. The Interdependence of Civilization — 43

PART TWO: THREE ENGLISH POLITICAL THINKERS

7. Walter Bagehot, Victorian — 51
8. Lord Acton and Human Liberty — 60
9. James Bryce and the Holy Roman Empire — 71

PART THREE: ASPECTS OF NATIONALISM

10. Napoleon and the Age of Nationalism — 89
11. France between Britain and Germany — 112
12. Dostoevsky and Danilevsky: Nationalist Messianism — 130
13. Toynbee and Russia — 149
14. The Impact of Pan-Slavism on Central Europe — 164
15. The Heritage of Masaryk — 174
16. Zion and the Jewish National Idea — 179
17. The Totalitarian Philosophy of War — 212
18. The Soviet-Yugoslav Controversy: Nationalism and Communism — 227
19. The Problem of German Nationalism — 235

PART FOUR: THE WORLD IN WHICH WE LIVE

20. One World? — 243
21. Germany and Russia: Old Dreams and New Realities — 251
22. Germany between East and West — 260
23. Germany in the New Europe — 269
24. Germany and Russia — 274
25. The United States and a United West — 281

26. The French Rightest Revolution 289
27. Western Europe and Atlantic Unity 296
28. The Atlantic Community and the World 303
29. United States Policy in the Cold War 313
30. Khrushchev's Foreign Policy 321
31. The United Nations and National Self-Determination 327
32. Germany in World Politics: 1963 345

PART ONE

*History and
Human Responsibility*

1

The Historian's Responsibility in Our Time*

The historian is a man who tries to find out what has happened in the course of time and to correlate the events, within the limits of the available material on the one hand and of his intelligence, imagination, and ethical understanding on the other, into a meaningful sequence. Only when correlated into the pattern of the onrushing and all-inclusive course of time do events become history. Time and its irreversibility is a fundamental and tragic aspect of human life and of history, the source of all ultimate frustration. The escape from time and history into timelessness, into eternity, into the end of history, the *eschata,* the ultimate time, the final day and the final reckoning, is a religious and secular utopian hope for an end of this fundamental tragedy. Such eschatological hopes are a historical fact, but except in their effects, they are not the concern of the historian. He is concerned with survival in the world of human contingency; past events, otherwise lost in the stream of time, are revived by him in the stream of human consciousness and enter into a relationship with our present life either by satisfying our playful curiosity or by enriching our pure knowledge in a disinterested way, or by broadening our understanding and guiding our actions in a utilitarian way.

Writing history, therefore, does not mean to regard events as isolated phenomena but to put them into the context of time. From this point of view everything can become the object of history: the doings of a man or of a nation, the development of our planetary system, the working of any branch of human activity. Though, due to the limitations of men and material, each historian deals with only

* Reprinted with permission of the Duke University Press from the *South Atlantic Quarterly,* Vol. LII, No. 3, July 1953, pp. 341-348. Originally published under the title, "A Historian's Creed for Our Time."

a small segment of history—one period, one branch of art, one nation —he must do it in the spirit of universal history, of viewing his segment in the light of what preceded it and at the same time in the context of all other human societies and activities. All writing of history, even of the most minute period or branch, should be part of universal history.

Historical consciousness of this sort is a rather recent phenomenon in the long development of the human species; it distinguishes modern civilization from all the rest of living nature. A-historic peoples, aptly called in German *geschichtslose Völker,* peoples without history, lived in the timelessness of natural time. Their stories begin with *"Es war einmal,"* "Once upon a time," which means, "It will always be so." Perhaps the ancient Hebrews were the first people strongly conscious of history: the past history of their tribe is to them always vividly present and continuous; at the same time tribal history broadens into the context of universal history. Probably it is only at this stage of time-awareness that we meet the phenomenon unknown to the rest of living nature, fear of death, and, corresponding to it, the promise of eternal life, of a new birth, of survival. But we should note that the message of comfort brought by Buddha is that of a death which will not be followed by new birth.

In the nineteenth century historical consciousness came fully into its own and became the dominant trait of the period. The revolutionary character of the period which started with the French Revolution and the rapid changes brought about by constant new discoveries and the unprecedented progress of technology created a new consciousness of time as a dynamic and moving force. While the Indian felt at home in timelessness and the Greek believed in the fundamental identity, the *semper idem,* of historical events, modern man became a conscious wanderer through time. Excavations and the interpretation of myths opened to him new dimensions of time. Through the law of evolution everything became subject to time, and thereby to history: religion, language, literature, art, institutions, science. This new historical consciousness came upon men in such a sudden and overwhelming fashion that the Germans developed it into a philosophy of its own, a *Weltanschauung,* historicism, which, in spite of its great achievements, brought great dangers. It led in Hegel and his disciple Marx to a metaphysicization of history, according to which theory the historical process itself is a revelation of the divine; the divine is no longer the law and limit of everything historical but is identical with history. Everything now becomes historically necessary. The German philosopher, Martin Heidegger, greeted in 1933 the National Socialist totalitarian state as historically inevitable, as *seinsgeschichtlich,* and stressed that the philosopher, *"der Wissende,"* must therefore avoid moral indignation as inappropriate. Lately Heidegger has taken a similar attitude toward Communism.

The other danger, closely connected with the one pointed out, is what might be called the historization of metaphysics, whereby everything becomes relative, valid in itself. Whereas the first attitude raises historical categories to absolutes, the second easily leads to nihilism, to the rejection of any absolute standards or values. Historicism in our own time has led to two other consequences: the abuse of the past (often in a misrepresented form) to justify present or future claims of nationalism; and the fascination of prehistory, enticing us to praise instinct and myth at the expense of reasonableness and common sense.

In spite of these inherent dangers, the new historical consciousness and the ensuing historiography have had beneficial effects. History, rightly studied, can sharpen man's critical insight into human relationships and personality; it makes him more conscious of his limitations and therefore more humble but also teaches him to regard the future as open, containing potentially new developments. True, the present is a product of the past; retrospectively, the historian can show how the present grew out of the past. But the present is also always something new and is itself pregnant with future developments. Though historians can show retrospectively, if without agreement among themselves, how the present has come about so that it almost appears as a necessary outcome of the past, historians at no moment in the past could have predicted the future development tending towards the present. In 1918, for example, there were several possibilities before Germany, but nobody in 1918 could have predicted the course of events of the 1930's. It might have been guessed as a possibility; it could never have been predicted as a certainty. It could have been assumed as a future possibility only in the Germany of 1918, not, for instance, in the United States of 1932 or even the France of 1934, because, though the past does not determine the future, it sets certain limits within which future developments can take place. Though by means of their intelligence, imagination, and moral understanding men at any given moment can decide freely among several possibilities, thereby establishing and affirming their humanity, they decide within the limits of a concrete situation, the result of past developments. Only by recognition of the conditions created by the past and thereby of the true nature of the concrete problem can men find an answer which is neither destructive nor utopian but which is, to use a famous expression of Toynbee, a response to the challenge, a responsible answer to the concrete situation. Such a response demands historical understanding and also ethical standards which are above and beyond all historical understanding but cannot be fruitfully applied without it.

Ranke's famous saying that it is the task of the historian to find out and to narrate "how things really happened," *"wie es eigentlich gewesen,"* can be accepted as basic. The first task of the historian is to find out by patient and painstaking research the true facts of the past. From this point of view history is scholarly research and, like all scientific endeavor, carries its reward in itself, in the joy of discovering unknown facts, of finding new interpretations, of shedding light on obscure relationships. Such history serves knowledge and not society. Its responsibility is to find out how it was, not how it should have been. Yet no historian can know the whole past, not even the full story of one man, of one year, or even of one day. From the infinity of facts we are always forced to select within the limits of surviving documentation and those imposed by our intelligence and our intentions. We select according to our set of principles, which, like a searchlight, illumines in the immensity of any past time that part which seems to us relevant. Therefore no work of history is ever finished, and there can be in the true sense of the word no definitive work of history. History, which is in its findings and conclusions always approximate and tentative, ever to be verified by fresh discoveries and above all by new experiences and insights, is a science and not an art, because art produces definitive creations which no new experience and no new discoveries can alter in their permanent validity.

Yet history—and in this it differs from the sciences—contains an essential element of art too; therefore great books by historians retain their permanent value—and not only for the historian of historiography—even though many single facts or whole interpretations have been found to be erroneous. For history, though it does not serve society, serves man—beyond enriching his knowledge—by equipping him with a deeper understanding of himself, of his fellow men, and of the situations in which men are put. It can tell us as much about man and the human condition as the best novel or the greatest drama. In this way too, then, history has much in common with art. Beyond this function, it should give us a critical awareness of ourselves and of our own time by providing perspective through comparison and distinction. Persons, events, and situations are always different and never the same: but they are never entirely new or unique. That is the truth, the partial truth, in the Greek attitude towards history, which saw in history a morphology of human behavior, or as Florus, the Roman historian of the time of Trajan and a disciple of Livy, put it pithily, *"ut qui res eius legunt, non unius populi, sed generis humani facta discant"* ("so that those who read its story, do not learn the facts about one people but about the whole human kind").

This view of the recurrent character of history, revived in our period by Rückert and Danilevsky, Nietzsche and Spengler, has been opposed by the view which sees in history one continuous development. This latter view has been generally accepted in the West since Augustine. The Judeo-Christian understanding of history as a meaningfully directed process of salvation, *Heilsgeschichte,* was secularized in the eighteenth century into the conviction that history is an infinite progress from darkness to ever-greater light, from the night of the past either to the bright day of the present, as the optimistic Enlightenment saw it, or to the even brighter day of the near future, as Marx, overstressing the dark shadows in the picture of the present, later proclaimed. This faith in progress, absolutized and vulgarized in Communism, has lately given way to another mythical interpretation of history, which regards at least modern history not as the story of progress and salvation but as the story of decay and doom. This concept was not unknown in antiquity, when it was immortalized in Hesiod's "Iron Age," and it has become fashionable in the last decades, which, in opposition to the promise of the bright day of Enlightenment, glorified the more "profound" view of man groping in the darkness of night and caught in the blindness of myth.

The naïve exaggerations of the men of the Enlightenment have been matched recently by these equally naïve laments of doom from our latter-day prophets. It is remarkable that our age of burning vitality and—in spite of its black spots—manifold promise should give rise to this kind of mournful pessimism. It is fashionable today to speak of an unprecedented "crisis," a crisis in everything. Historical insight could have tempered much the optimism of the eighteenth century; it can help us see today's crisis in perspective. The historian knows that throughout most of history men have lived in critical times. He might mention only a very few examples and take them from the Middle Ages, to whose supposedly "organic" character many romantics today look longingly back: Francis of Assisi and his followers led a saintly life because they were convinced that the world was sinking in an unprecedented moral crisis, in a morass of corruption, and could not go on in that way. The Black Death which swept Europe in the middle of the fourteenth century destroyed proportionally more lives than atomic bombs would have and left, quite understandably, a feeling of complete insecurity, of total abandonment, *Ausgeliefertsein,* as the existentialists call it today. A moral crisis of unsurpassed intensity is revealed to anyone who studies the years when Alexander Borgia was sitting on the papal throne and Savonarola was preaching in Florence. But even in the apparently so quiet late Victorian age, around 1880, the feeling of a deep moral crisis is reflected in the novels and periodicals of the day: the conflict of religion and science, the rise of unskilled labor, the emancipation of women, troubled moral minds. Everything appeared uncertain; foundations seemed to crumble and attitudes to change rapidly, and yet, retrospectively, the period seems blissfully quiet. The unspeakable savagery exercised today by man against man in some places and the frightening moral perversions have been matched in many preceding ages. What makes us speak today of a crisis is not the greater intensity of our suffering compared with that of former centuries but our greater consciousness of it, due to popular journalism and other factors, and, above all, our heightened moral sensitivity. Today we abhor cruelty which other ages accepted without widespread protest.

But an historian is not only a scholar and, to a certain extent, an artist; he should also be a teacher. In fact, most historians are primarily engaged in teaching: teaching not only their students, future historians, and future teachers but trying also to instruct their fellow men; in a democratic age history has become the concern of everybody, and the right teaching of history may be fundamental to the moral and political wisdom of peoples. Historical perspective may help in the rejection of both the utopias of enthusiasm and the utopias of despair; it may help to regard the present as not too bad and not to expect too much from the future. In spite of the imperfections and limitations inherent in the nature of man and the nature of things, of which the historian should be painfully conscious, he should nevertheless see that during the relatively short time of 3,000 years frail and fallible man has learned much through an ever-renewed and maintained effort, has set lasting examples, and has built a widely accepted ethical tradition. Historians can teach us not to look on nations and classes as isolated phenomena but to see and to judge them in a universal context in the light of this ethical tradition. This tradition continues to grow, and people are always able and sometimes willing to learn from experience. Thus each generation rewrites history, not by adjusting facts to an alleged need of the hour, but by changing its viewpoints, as an old man looking back on some period of his youth, though he has achieved no greater factual knowledge, arrives at a different judgment as a result of his experience. If people did not learn from living, life would become useless, but they do. Consequently age has had and should have a greater voice in determining courses of action than youth. Because of this possibility of learning by living, history remains a hopeful process. Past mistakes can be avoided, and new ways can be found.

Two recent examples may illustrate the hopefulness of history. The American people have learned from the experience of the first half of the twentieth century to turn away from isolationism; whereas some years ago a candidate for the presidency had to affirm his rejection of international co-operation, now such a candidate must declare his rejection of isolationism. An understanding of world responsibility and of the nature of a movement as totally alien as totalitarianism has come to Americans in recent years. But they are not the only ones who have learned by sad experience. After the catastrophe of 1945 German historians started to re-examine German history—a task which they unfortunately did not essay after 1918, as the Americans did not then turn away from isolationism—to re-examine the trends and ideas dominating the recent German past, the dangerous elements not only in the rise of Hitler but also in Bismarck's triumph and in the generally accepted Germano-centered and state-centered view. German historians are asking themselves whether the path followed by their craft since Ranke has not been wrong, not on account of the facts presented but on account of the value judgments involved. For as historians may find wrong facts, they may also be guided by wrong values; acceptance of either involves great dangers.

Historians have responsibilities, not to nations or classes, to dogmas or creeds, but to truth and to humanity. Their training can help them to understand the genesis of events and movements and to evaluate their relative worth and importance by comparison with similar attitudes in other peoples, climes, and periods. That should make their approach more critical and more cautious, especially as regards their own emotional prejudices and group interests. No sharp distinction is possible between political historians and historians of ideas; ideas and politics are closely interlinked and interdependent. So are facts and values. History, whether as scholarship or as art or as teaching, represents the meeting, the interaction, the interrelationship of objective and subjective factors. The facts of the past present the objective material; the ethos and the personality of the historian present the subjective factor without which the facts of the past and the past itself remain dead.

2

History: Its Place in a Liberal Education*

History is a foundation for the study of all liberal arts, including the classical ones. Carlyle said that history is not only the fittest study, but the only study, and includes all others; it is a true epic poem and the universal divine scriptures. I wouldn't go so far as Carlyle in claiming history as the foundation of everything, but history is fundamental because nothing can influence a student as a future member of society so much as the history and political science teacher. On the high school level history and political science are mostly combined into what we would call civic education—*paideia*, in the Greek sense, the formation of a responsible partner in the *polis*, the community of men.

If we ask ourselves how it could happen that the Second World

* An address delivered in 1943 before the Conference of Administrative Officers of Women's Colleges.

War came about, I think a very great responsibility for it rests upon the teachers of history and political science in Great Britain and in this country. For twenty years they had been leading the trend toward misunderstanding history, which so much weakened the democracies' discerning judgment and their determination to act that they allowed a situation to develop which resulted in the war. We were in a period of debunking history in which we took out of history all its meaning and essence, so that people forgot what history really is and what it demands of man.

History can be regarded as the fundamental science, if I may call it so, of men and society, of their growth and their development. Here we see man as a being between two worlds—on the one hand perishable and passing like grass, subject to any accident or incident, and on the other hand endowed with the great dignity of the laws of ethics. Human destiny can be realized only by man in history; this ephemeral being is the volitional center of all spiritual reality.

Our dependence upon accidents teaches us humility and the consciousness of human limitations. Man proposes, God disposes—history is a process influenced by forces beyond man's grasp. Let us look at the great tragedy of modern European history—the creation of Bismarckian Germany, of a German Empire that became a menace to the world. This was not understood in 1919; the Anglo-Saxons did not insist upon a complete transformation and change of heart in Germany. The problem of peace in our world cannot be solved by solving all the secondary problems like the problem of Transylvania—whether it should belong to Hungary or to Romania. This problem in itself will never cause a World War. The fundamental problem of peace at present is simple: to confine Germany and to confine Japan into a position of inability to threaten or wage war— which we did not do in and after 1919—and peace could be securely established. But if I say modern Germany has been and is a menace to the world, I do not say Germany is necessarily a menace to the world. That Germany has become the present chief menace is a result of historic development, not of anything unchangeable, not of anything innate in German "nature" which is beyond the hope of change. And this historic development was partly the result of accidents.

One example will show how accidents—biological accidents—play a role in shaping the destiny of a nation and therefore of the world, if the nation is as powerful a nation, as efficient a nation, as intelligent a nation as the German nation is. The great misery of Europe was produced by the success of Bismarck. If the Bismarckian Empire had not been created, the trend of European and of world history would have been different. Bismarck came to power in September, 1862. He was called to office by King William I, the then King of Prussia, who was ready to abdicate because he was unable to carry out his army reform through the Prussian Parliament. The King called his son, the Crown Prince Frederick. The Crown Prince Frederick was a *rara avis*—a very rare bird, a liberal Hohenzollern, who under the influence of his wife, the daughter of Queen Victoria, had acquired western humanitarian and progressive ideas. But Frederick was a timid liberal; instead of accepting the crown and building a liberal Germany, he implored his father not to abdicate, and refused the responsibility.

Looking for somebody to carry out the army program against the Parliament, the King called Bismarck, and Bismarck with an iron fist was able to realize the dream of William I, and much more than that. He used the instrument of the Prussian Army and was himself its most perfect and successful instrument. He created a Germany which was not a Germany, but an aggrandized Prussia, living and growing with the army as its backbone and soul.

Crown Prince Frederick, the future Frederick III, was deeply unhappy about that. He hated Bismarck, his work, and all his reactionary tendencies. Frederick may have wished many times that he had been less timid in 1862, but he and his wife lived in the hope of being able later to bring Germany back to more liberal and civilized ways. The King was by this time very old; he would die and then Frederick would dismiss Bismarck and liberalize Germany—make Germany a real member of the European society.

But these reasonable hopes were thwarted by accidents which nobody could foresee. William I lived to be ninety-one. The tragedy of many Crown Princes comes in waiting for the death of the men whose longevity deprives them of the opportunity to do their life work. Frederick's hope was thwarted by a biological accident; no one needs to live to become ninety-one.

William I died in March, 1888, and Crown Prince Frederick was called to become King of Prussia and German Emperor. He had an immense program before him to realize the dreams of the generation of 1848 in Germany. But at the moment he was finally called to the throne he was suffering from the last stages of cancer of the throat;

History: Its Place in a Liberal Education

he was a dying man. He ruled for three months, unable to speak, unable to change anything. He died and was followed by his son, William II, who hated his parents and everything they stood for. William II shared Bismarck's arch-reactionary attitude, his hatred of liberalism and of the rights of man, his glorification of and reliance upon armed force, his contempt for all humanitarianism and democracy; but he lacked Bismarck's steadiness, sagacity, and moderation. That William II came to power in 1888, was again the result of a biological accident. Thus is the web of history interwoven with accidents.

Without a real knowledge of history we cannot understand our own situation and task. For the present contains the past and man is the heir of the centuries. But there is another point to which I wish to draw your attention, that the deeper insight into our present conditions makes us understand the past better in that we re-interpret the past in the light of the present. There are many among us who now think differently about many things of the last twenty years than they thought three or four or ten years ago. We learn by experience, by the experience of our life and of our time, an experience, often dearly paid for. And that makes the teaching of history in schools difficult. History is something which cannot be understood without experience. A person who has not lived a full life, who has not suffered and struggled and thought about the world, cannot understand history. To give young people the sense of history is very difficult. Personally, I find it so much easier to talk to mature groups who have graduated from college into life than to students about history; not about the method of history, not about research, but to give them the feel of the essence of history.

Don't forget, for instance, that what is to you and me still a reality of our lives—Armistice Day, 1918—is something like a legend to the student body of today. There is no one in the colleges today who was born, say, before 1922 or 1923 and there is no one in high school born before 1925 or something like that. All that has been living history for us is for them a distant past. And yet we are fighting today a war which is only a continuation of the war of 1914, its resumption after a long and false armistice. We are still in the midst of this "distant past." To make the past a part of the living present, to make the present a heritage and a survival of the past, demands a great effort on the part of the teacher. For history, to make it really live, you need the best teachers. And history gives the necessary background to, it is the connecting link of, all studies in the humanities and liberal arts.

Whoever teaches literature or art or philosophy must know history, because no artist or philosopher lives in a vacuum; he lives in his times. If we are discussing a man like Thomas Aquinas, we cannot discuss him abstractly, but from the whole Gothic background of his life. The same is true, of course, of Chaucer and of Gothic architecture. No one can teach literature without a background of history, and, on the other hand, no one will be a good history teacher who does not have a broad knowledge of literature, art, and philosophy. In all of them the development of the human mind is expressed. History is the necessary foundation and basis of all humanities, as philosophy is their highest synthesis. I always advise my students to take at least one course in philosophy, at least a survey of the history of philosophy. I would take nobody as a teacher of history who has not had a course in philosophy. For the study of history gains its full meaning from its essential connection with the whole development of the human mind and of human society.

In this country we have arrived in our educational system at two rather strange things. The first is that you can become a Ph.D.—which means a Doctor of Philosophy—without ever having read one philosophy book. I think our history suffers from that—and so do our history teachers. In other fields, too, the lack of knowledge in philosophy and history is regrettable; an English poet of the sixteenth or seventeenth century cannot be understood without a background of the thought of the period. So I would say that, rightly studied, history is the foundation and synthesis of all liberal arts and should be taught as a synthesis of the development of the human mind and human society throughout the ages so that the students become conscious of their share in man's heritage, in the heritage of five thousand years. To understand whence we came and to be more conscious of whither we go, it is necessary to stress the role of ideas in history, to learn to separate the essential from the nonessential, the temporary and accidental from the substance. Critical insight can destroy some harmful clichés which obscure our understanding of history, in our elementary schools.

The eighteenth century of our country is sometimes taught as if there had been a violent tyrant, something like Hitler, who was called George III, who had tremendously oppressed the American people, who then rose in righteous indignation and threw this tyrant out—something like the Yugoslavs liberating themselves, or the French, or the Poles, from Hitler. It has not often been pointed out that American love of independence and American democracy were a part of the common spiritual inheritance of England, of the unique tradition of liberty under law, of representative government and of individual rights, of Milton and Locke. The revolution was not against British oppression, but an expression of British rights. Thus an opportunity is lost to make clear the historical and ideological foundations on which democracy in America rests and their broadening under the influence of society in a new country and of the rational thought of the eighteenth century into something of universal importance and appeal, the foundation on which all America is built without exception and which became a guidepost for mankind.

This fundamental understanding of American history is being regained today under the stress of history. For the present is a great period for history teachers. At present it may be difficult to find teachers. That is a passing phenomenon. Certainly, in three or five years' time teaching will come again into its own as an alluring vocation of great promise and responsibility. And no teacher will be the worse off for the years spent in the war, or in the war effort, outside the sheltering walls of school. No one can be a good history teacher who has not lived, who is not a mature person, a person who understands life. History is nothing else but life on a higher and more conscious level. And rarely is life being lived on a more concentrated and conscious level than in periods of extreme national danger. What is happening in this time is that people who normally do not mind history—because if you live normally you don't mind your past, you don't get conscious of it; it lives in you, but subconsciously—become conscious of their past in moments of great danger.

I have read that people who are drowning live in the last second of their lives, so to speak, their whole life's history in an immense condensation. I don't know whether it is true or not. In any case, it is true in moments of extreme national danger; what happens in such a situation is an identification with one's whole past. One becomes conscious of one's past in hours of test and trial. In periods more religious than the present, a dying person or a person in extreme danger, thought about his whole past and drew a balance sheet in the critical moment when Heaven or Hell, survival or annihilation, were at stake.

That is what is happening at present to whole nations on earth, in a certain sense even to humanity. In a moment of supreme danger —supreme danger to national or civilized existence—there is the greatest intensity of historical consciousness. People never live as deeply as in moments of great danger, moments which they know to be decisive; then they identify themselves with the whole past consciously; the past which is always there with us, in us, as a heritage subconscious, becomes conscious and is revived; it is there before our eyes.

To use Thomas Paine's famous words, "These are the times which try men's souls"—in these trying times we integrate our whole story, not only our present, not only the short space of our lifetime, but our whole national story into a meaningful whole and so try to find strength and justification in a supreme struggle for national survival. That is what happened in England in 1940 when rationally or logically Mussolini, Pétain, and all sorts of people were convinced that England was lost. England's survival was due to her sense of history.

In that light we can understand Churchill's immense importance. I personally consider Churchill the man who almost single-handedly defeated Hitler's attempt at world domination and thereby saved mankind. When Churchill said, "The English will fight on if necessary for years, if necessary alone, against all chances," what spoke in him was not this individual Winston Churchill, it was the whole history of the English people. He became, in a decisive hour of history, the incarnation of history. The England of Cromwell, of Milton, of Wordsworth became alive in the insignificant English men and women of 1940.

More astonishing than "the miracle of England" to many people is that this very same identification with history happened in 1941 and 1943 in Russia. There a new Russian nationalism, anchored in the depth of the past, animates the masses under Stalin's leadership. If you look today at Russia, Stalin appears a Russian nationalist, though he was born a Georgian. For that reason even more he tries to be a Russian identifying himself with the whole Russian past, with the autocracy and the mission of imperial Russia. Stalin calls himself Marshal Stalin at present and appears in a marshal's uniform. I don't know how much you know of Lenin, but the idea that Lenin could have been called Marshal Lenin, or to envisage Lenin or Marx appearing in a marshal's uniform, is unthinkable.

Another thing Lenin would never have understood is the fact that all the trappings of Czarist militarism have been brought back and

When I studied in my college days, I didn't begin with history. As a student my interests were the history of religion and philosophy, political theory and philosophy. It was in the First World War, not on the battlefields—I think the battlefields do not teach much—but when I was a prisoner of war in Russia. I spent four years in Russia and witnessed in Russia the revolution and the counterrevolution and the civil war. There I felt historical reality in its elemental forces, men really stripped naked down to the essentials by the great winds of history. There I began to become interested in history and to understand history, to search in it for the meaning of events, to order and to master the chaos around me and the bewilderment within me. More and more history is becoming the fundamental study because people wish to understand where they are. True, people like to forget and to sink back into "normalcy." We shall have to see to it that they don't forget when the war is over because we know what happened after the last war when we tried to forget history. We were eager to go back to so-called "normalcy," which is comforting and seems easy, for "normalcy" takes us into the world of illusions, of make-believe, of evasions, to escape the stern verities, to forget history. And so, for twenty years history teaching, not all of it, but much of it, was filled with that cynicism, with that disillusionment which was characteristic of the period between the two wars, and which helped to prepare the present war.

If we ask how it came about that we are where we are, namely in the Second World War, after having defeated the Germans in the First World War; why are we and the Russians, the British, the French, who fought the Germans twenty-five years ago, fighting them again, the answer is: we have not lost the peace, we have abandoned and betrayed victory. In 1919 victory was ours and victory means two things: victory means first, that we had by great sacrifices gained the power to order and to lead the world and we abandoned that power. We and the British refused to exercise the responsibility involved; we refused to accept the great obligation. We withdrew, the British and we. And as there cannot exist any vacuum of power in the world, the Fascists put their power and their claim of leadership in the place relinquished by us. But something even more fundamental and tragic happened. What won in 1918 against Germany and her glorification of military autocracy was not only our power, it was our idea, and never has there been a greater force for the democratization that the highest military order created in Russia in this present war is called after General Suvorov, not after a revolutionary or proletarian fighter or hero. For General Suvorov was not a revolutionary, not a Marxist, not a worker, not a liberal. He was a reactionary, a Czarist general, a feudal aristocrat whose armies defeated the great peasant uprising of Pugachev and the armies of the French Revolution. This bulwark of Czarist reaction has become the symbol of present-day Stalinist Russia. The new attitude in Russia toward the Church does not mean that Stalin has become pious, he is as little religious as Mussolini was in making his peace with the Church. It means that the Russians in the supreme hour of national danger understood the role of the Orthodox Church in Russian history: that they feel one with everything in Russian history, with the whole heritage which included feudal warriors and General Suvarov, Ivan the Terrible and Peter the Great, the Orthodox Church and the Russian autocracy. All that is one in the great unfolding of Russia's life.

This identification with history, with the past, in hours of supreme danger—we find even in America today, though to a limited degree, because we don't feel the war in this country. We are now two years in the war, yet the number of Americans killed in this war so far is much smaller than the number of Americans killed in every single year in civilian life, in motor car or industrial accidents. We should be at least self-critical enough not to complain of our sacrifices too much. For so far the people of this country do not suffer at all by restrictions. We eat a little less butter and we don't drive cars so much—which can't do too much harm for we drove too much anyway. On the other hand, most Americans live in a period of great prosperity and high income and high living and fast spending. Therefore, we are not like the Russians or the English or the French in that respect. We don't live history as they do. And yet even we are stirred into growing more conscious of our history, of our heritage and the obligations it imposes. There has not been for a long time so much talk of Thomas Jefferson, so much talk of the forefathers, so much talk of the Puritans and of the American idea and dream. In any case, what we are living through now is that even we are touched by the great breath of history. The great winds of history are blowing over our heads. We feel it and we learn, for we cannot understand history without having lived history. We understand the French Revolution today much better because we are living through a revolutionary period.

of the world than the First World War; never has democracy achieved a similar success on a wider scale.

Think of how the world looked in 1918, 1919. The keenest dreams, the most daring expectations of nineteenth century liberals and democrats seemed realized. A new freedom had dawned. The common man seemed about to come into his heritage. The military monarchies—the Romanov, Hapsburg, Hohenzollern, the conservative, anti-liberal, anti-democratic monarchies—were gone. The great Central and Eastern European bastions against liberty and its progress had fallen. Republics came in their place, constitutional liberties —everybody got the vote, including women, in 1918 and 1919. Without the First World War the women might not have the vote even today. You may remember, some of you, what an uphill fight the suffragettes had to fight in 1910 to get a hearing in England or America; they didn't get it. In 1919 they got the vote everywhere, and that was only a small symbol. Everywhere the masses were awakened; workers got the eight-hour day; everywhere democracy was triumphant. Even Japan introduced general democratic suffrage in 1926. Japan was ready to go democratic in 1920. Why didn't Japan go on? People ask me sometimes why the Germans didn't remain democratic. Then I answer: "The fault is partly British-American because from 1920 to 1938 you could hear young people in America say, 'Democracy is obsolete; democracy is 19th century.' " The democracies became in 1919, at the very moment of democracy's triumph, cynical and disillusioned about democracy. Democracy seemed an "abstraction," a pretense, not a value or an inspiration. When the Germans heard the British and Americans say it, why should they remain democratic? It was here in America that there were people daring enough and silly enough to call fascism or communism the wave of the future. If Americans could do that, why should the Germans or the Japanese stick to something which was obsolete? If young people in this country and in Great Britain, if the Student Union in Oxford, declared it not worth while to fight for democracy or to fight for King and Fatherland, why should the Germans or Japanese remain democrats? We abandoned not only our power, we abandoned our idea which had been triumphant, and we did it out of our desire to evade all the true issues by inventing all kinds of excuses and creating myths about the war of 1914 and its causes and the peace of 1919 and its implications. Now we should beware again of sliding back into this easy way of cynicism, for our own sake and for the sake of the coming generation.

In concluding I wish to say something which has nothing to do with history alone, but with our whole educational system, the second shortcoming of our educational system of which I spoke some time ago. I mentioned the fact that history must teach our young people the responsibility and the seriousness of our human heritage. That brings me now to a fact that I deplore so much—all the efforts to make learning easy in the United States. Nothing is more dangerous for the student of history than not understanding the seriousness of life and history. There is no learning, in life or in school, but the hard way. What is worth while, must be paid for; the price is high, but high is the reward, too. We must be quite clear that in our schools of higher learning we train or should train an intellectual elite. After all, to us come the boys and girls who have the leisure to devote years to study, who can afford it and who can afford good teachers, and who must be made to understand that this privilege carries with it an obligation. And the role of our schools is in America more important than in any other country in the world because there is no country in the world in which what I would call the intellectual life is so much in the hands of women as in this country. What we train in our schools for young women, is a great proportion of the future intellectual leaders of this nation, not perhaps on the highest plane, but on the intermediary plane upon which the health of the intellectual life of the nation depends. I always advise my students, if they can afford it, not to go to Washington and not to go to New York. If there are girls from the cities and towns in the vastness of these states, I appeal to them to go back to their home towns because if our cultural education has any value for the nation at large, it is not to concentrate more highly intellectual girls in the few big leading cities, but to bring some of this intellectual life into the provincial towns and to raise there the level and the intensity of cultural life by sowing the seeds of an understanding of the passionate beauty and the unique dignity of the life of the mind. Above all, to know that learning does not end at graduation, but is a process going on throughout life. There is no end of learning as there is no end of living.

In any case, we as teachers have an immense responsibility not to make it so easy, but to uphold the dignity and the seriousness of learning. I always regret that the requirement of Latin—and I would go further, of Greek—has been dropped in so many schools. Of course, I don't say that everyone should study Latin and Greek, but our intellectual elite should, for it was from the fountain of classical antiquity that, at all decisive turning points, Western civilization was rejuvenated and revitalized. Nothing prepares us so well for an understanding of history and politics and language as the classics. Nowhere can we learn so well what learning means and has meant for so many generations. Nowhere are we so much in the great chain of the tradition of learning. In this country, even women should study the classics, for as I said, fortunately, or unfortunately, as you wish, the intellectual field is left here very largely to women. If we can compare the average graduates of our best men's and women's colleges twenty years after graduation, in eight out of ten cases the alumna will be intellectually more alert than the alumnus, and therefore in this country we should do our best and our utmost in the training of women. Our background is antiquity, Biblical and classical literature, and yet there are many students today who know neither the Bible nor classical literature. That makes it difficult for them to read any of the great poets of Europe. You can't study history, really, without at least some knowledge of Latin; you can't study, in my opinion, French, Spanish, English or any other language, without Latin and I would say without Greek. So many words are of Greek origin and so many students misspell "difficult" words because they don't know where the words come from.

I had the great good fortune to get an excellent elementary training in a Catholic monastery school in Prague where I was born. I was taught in elementary school by Piarist Fathers and I still remember with gratitude my teacher, Father Heski. He was a stern man in his sixties, requiring much and having no inkling of progressive methods. As a result, I knew more grammar in the fourth grade than a senior in a very good private preparatory school knows today. It saved me much work in the upper grades. I had later in the grammar and secondary school eight years of Latin, in the first two years eight hours a week and in the other years, six hours a week. But I learned very easily, because I had a very good preparation, and I owed it to Father Heski.

I would say that one of the most dangerous mistakes in our educational system is the lowering of requirements and standards, especially because some students are spoiled "brats," self-indulgent and pampered. Father and mother are so busy with so many things that there is no intellectual discipline in the home. An added responsibility falls to our schools and especially to the history teacher, to make students understand the dignity of the life of the mind, the passionate excitement which can be found in ideas, in the development, the realization, the struggle of ideas.

And the teacher can convey an understanding of history's relentless struggle in which man has to prove his mettle, the strength of his character, the integrity of his will. We should not try to interpret history in too soft or sentimental a way. History, like life, is hard and exacting. We must understand that history is not soft and men's lives are not soft, but hard and demanding. We must beware above all of softness of thinking, of accepting easy clichés. Students can't learn soon enough that a real understanding of history and of men's lives, the lives of the generations of which we are the heirs, the responsible heirs, is immensely demanding, and immensely rewarding because nothing is so exciting in many ways as history, nothing so exciting as ideas.

Men make history, and the students should understand the unique dignity to which they are called by being called to make history, each one in his place, and nobody can tell beforehand how great one's place will be in this process of five thousand years of human sufferings, victories and efforts. But there is a place for each one to fill.

3

Academic Freedom in Our Time[*]

Academic freedom in the present meaning of the phrase is a product of recent times. Originally academic freedom meant the administrative and judicial autonomy of the university corporation of

[*] Address delivered before the Annual Meeting of the American Association of University Professors in Chicago, in December, 1938.

teachers and students. It was one of the many "freedoms" upon which medieval life was based. It did not and could not imply *Lehrfreiheit*, a notion entirely alien to the Middle Ages and to early modern times. Academic freedom in the modern sense is a product of the epoch of the Enlightenment, of liberalism and rationalism, of the triumph of intellectual and moral individualism. Therefore we find academic freedom today—with the great Central European counter revolution against enlightenment, liberalism, and individualism—again being threatened in its existence.

Academic freedom is, above all, a duty of the teacher. It is, to use a word from Cicero, his duty never to say anything false and never to dare to withhold anything true. "Nam quis nescit primam esse historiae legem, ne quid falsi dicere audeat? Deinde ne quid veri non audeat?"[1] The teacher is expected to present to his students the whole truth, as he understands it in the light of his research and thought. He should put his whole individuality into his teaching with no guide but his individual conscience. Only in this way can he present to the student, and make the student share in, the dignity of spiritual and intellectual endeavor and the seriousness which it exacts. The teacher must be free to speak his mind; the student must experience his effort at truth. This is impossible in totalitarian countries where objectivity and, thereby, the dignity of the teaching profession are not recognized.

Academic freedom as a duty of the teacher is different from academic freedom as a right. This right is no professional right of the teacher alone; it is part of every citizen's general right to freedom —the freedom to think for himself and to express his thoughts by word and in print. The teacher does not possess more rights than other citizens; he only has greater duties. Everybody has the right to speak the truth. The teacher *must* speak the truth. This is the meaning of his calling.

Academic freedom is therefore conceivable only within a certain intellectual order; it is based upon that interpretation of man's nature and of his place in history which we call liberalism. This attitude is not a "natural" birthright of man. It is a product of a great historical struggle, which started in the seventeenth century and was won, at least for the time being and for Western humanity, in the nineteenth century. This struggle—waged by Milton and Locke, by Grotius and Condorcet, by the Encyclopedists and Kant—produced

[1] Cicero, *De Oratore*, II, 15.

all the liberties, which are fundamentally one liberty. Academic freedom is nothing in itself, no abstraction which can be invoked at will; it is an indissoluble part of the whole system of liberalism, of individual rights, of a rational order, and only conceivable within it.

There is much confusion today with regard to this point. Academic freedom, the right to free speech, and the right of free elections are today often invoked by those who do not believe in them and in their liberal foundations, and who wish to use them solely for the purpose of undermining and destroying these liberties and their foundation. Enemies of liberalism should not be allowed to claim and use the instruments of liberalism in their fight against it. It is characteristic that a writer on Italian fascism could say of Mussolini's paper, *Popolo d'Italia*, that "no other newspaper in Italy took such advantage of the freedom from legal and political responsibility which the Italian press enjoyed." It used its freedom to destroy that freedom entirely.

For all these freedoms are nothing when dissociated from their common root, which alone makes them possible. They are a corollary of a certain interpretation of the nature of man and his place in history. It is faith, to use the words of Thomas Jefferson, in the "illimitable freedom of the human mind," in universal reason, shared, at least potentially, by every human being, irrespective of his class or caste, faith or creed, birth or race. The faith without which all academic freedom and all rights of the individual become meaningless is a faith in the dignity and equality of all individuals as human beings. From this assumption alone we can arrive at the conclusion that men are able and entitled to think independently, that truth can be found by their efforts and common discussion.

This free discussion appears to us as the only way in which science and truth can be promoted. Scholarship can prosper only by an unhampered free intercourse above all the frontiers of states, creeds, races, and classes. A totalitarian order, whether based upon the absolutization of the race or of the class or of any other relative division of mankind, undermines the development of truth and of scholarship, where the contribution of every fellow man is welcome and to be judged only according to its intrinsic value.[2] Liberalism presup-

---

[2] There is an essential difference between communism and fascism. Communism destroys the foundations of scholarship, the possibility of human freedom and of human dignity. It restricts "man" to "proletarian." But ultimately communism believes in the abolition of all separating and dividing exclusiveness in one universal, rational order, although in a future which may never dawn. After all, communism is a grand-

poses the existence of a universal truth, of universally applicable laws. It accepts the objectivity of science and of the search for truth. The Communist or the Fascist will ask who you are, to which class or people you belong, before evaluating or accepting any contribution of yours in the field of scholarship. The liberal will ask what you have to say, and accept the contribution at its objective value in the universal and unceasing search for truth. Academic freedom and freedom of scholarship are only possible within the system of liberalism.

Thus academic freedom has been accepted in the Western world as part of the liberal order. Certainly there are everywhere failures to live up to it. Academic freedom, like all liberties, is never completely realized. Although we may not always live up to it, it remains before us as a regulative ideal, a demand, and a reproach. Even if liberties, in a liberal order, are denied again and again, they can be fought for, and those who in actual fact deny them, find themselves on the defensive. In theory, at least, they have to pay lip-service to them, to recognize their general applicability. The shameful situation in Russia, in Italy, in Germany, today does not consist in the fact that in some or many cases the freedom to speak one's thoughts is denied, but in that there is no battle being waged for it, that graveyard silence reigns, that the ideal as such, the objectivity of truth, is denied.

We see the results of this attitude in the press and literary productions of the totalitarian countries with their one-sided and distorted views, their ludicrous judgments on the forces at work in history and in the contemporary world. Of course foolish opinions can also be put forward in liberal countries, but here they can be combated and rectified—the public can make its choice. In totalitarian countries no defense exists against the dulling of the intellect, against obscurantism, against cutting loose from world currents. Today even the language used in the totalitarian countries has nothing in common with the language used outside of these countries. The same words in no way convey the same meaning.

Academic freedom is an indispensable part of the democratic, liberal order. But this order is denied today. A new interpretation

---

child of Hegel. Fascism, in all its forms, denies any future universal truth, while it strengthens, idealizes, and absolutizes the exclusive divisions of mankind with their different kinds of "truth." It thus proclaims the eternal anarchism of all values. Only its dynamism is univeral in the sense that it is unlimited and illimitable. Like Communism it will not and cannot rest until the whole of mankind acknowledges it.

of man and of his place in history wishes to impose itself upon the whole of mankind. (It is not a question of certain nations, although certain nations, for historical reasons, succumb to it more easily; it is not the problem of a fight against Italy or Germany, but against the fundamental attitude which denies the equality of men, the universality of truth, the dignity of reason.) This new attitude threatens all other freedoms. In such a situation the academic teacher has a greater responsibility, to be wide awake to the dangers threatening not only academic freedom but the whole liberal tradition which produced academic freedom. He has no right to withdraw into an ivory tower, to care only for academic freedom. Academic freedom lives and dies with the whole liberal order.

If we care for academic freedom we have to fight for freedom generally, in the universities and in all other walks of life, in the United States, and everywhere. The enemies of freedom by their tactics destroy one isolated position after another; they can do it because they do not encounter united opposition. The forces for freedom are divided, not only among nations but also among professions. The attack, however, is a totalitarian attack. The fight for academic freedom is today, when liberalism itself is threatened, no longer a professional fight for the factual realization of a generally acknowledged principle. It is part of a fight for the survival of the fundamental values of liberalism for everybody and everywhere. It is a special application of the most fundamental battle in which man can be enlisted, the fight centered around the interpretation of the values governing the life and history of man.

4

Education for the Coming Era[*]

Two thousand years and more ago, in a situation strikingly similar to the one in which we find ourselves today, a man of Greece, who saw more clearly and spoke more courageously than most of his contemporaries, uttered warnings against a military autocracy that threatened his country from without. His warnings were unheeded because they were unwelcome. That man was Demosthenes, the Athenian orator, who lived in a period when the citizens of Athens —leading democracy of the Greek city-states—seemingly secure in their prosperity and isolation, were oblivious to impending dangers. Perhaps they thought that the day of world empires was gone forever, whereas in reality the greatest of those empires were still to come. Athens was full of false prophets who circulated among the people, offering advice that rings familiarly in our ears today: "Athenians, mind your own business. Preserve your own peace. Let other peoples take care of themselves, work out their own problems, fight their own battles."

I wish to set before you here for your consideration half a dozen passages from various speeches of Demosthenes, delivered in the fourth century before our era. Change the names of places and of persons, and these same words might have been said in England or in France two years ago. With equal force they could and should have been said in the United States at least twelve months ago.

Read this:

> Men of Athens, I want you to know and realize two things: first, what an expensive game it is to squander your interests one by one: and secondly, the restless activity which is ingrained in Philip's nature, and which makes it impossible for him ever to rest on his laurels.[1]

---

[*] Address delivered before the American Association for Adult Education in New York in May 1940.

[1] *Demosthenes*, with an English translation by J. H. Vince (The Loeb Classical Library), p. 13.

And this:

Seriously, is anyone here so foolish as not to see that our negligence will transfer the war from Chalcidice to Attica? Yet if that comes to pass, I am afraid, men of Athens, that just as men who borrow money recklessly at high interest enjoy a temporary accommodation only to forfeit their estates in the end, so we may find that we have paid a heavy price for our indolence, and because we consult our own pleasure in everything, may hereafter come to be forced to do many of the difficult things for which we had no liking, and may finally endanger our possessions here in Attica itself.[2]

And then this:

The chief object, however, of his arms and his diplomacy is our free constitution: on nothing in the world is he more bent than on its destruction. And it is in a way natural that he should act thus. For he knows for certain that even if he masters all else, his power will be precarious as long as you remain a democracy; but if ever he meets with one of the many mischances to which mankind is liable, all the forces that are now under restraint will be attracted to your side.[3]

And this:

But if anyone mistakes for peace an arrangement which will enable Philip, when he has seized everything else, to march upon us, he has taken leave of his senses, and the peace that he talks of is one that you observe towards Philip, but not Philip towards you.[4]

And this:

Men of Athens, you have deserted the post in which your ancestors left you; you have been persuaded by politicians . . . that to be paramount in Greece, to possess a standing force, and to help all the oppressed, is a superfluous task and an idle expense; while you fondly imagined that to live in peace, to neglect all your duties, to abandon all your possessions and let others seize them one by one, ensured wonderful prosperity and complete security.[5]

Finally, consider this passage from the speech "For the Liberty of the Rhodians," in which Demosthenes pleads with the Athenians to

---

[2] *Ibid.*, p. 13.
[3] *Ibid.*, pp. 197, 199.
[4] *Ibid.*, p. 229.
[5] *Ibid.*, p. 295.

Education for the Coming Era

come to the aid of the Rhodian democrats and help them to resist the aggression of Philip and his fellow oligarchs:

> Seeing that Chios and Mytilene are ruled by oligarchs, and that Rhodes and, I might almost say, all the world are now being seduced into this form of slavery, I am surprised that none of you conceives that our constitution too is in danger, nor draws the conclusion that if all other states are organized on oligarchical principles, it is impossible that they should leave your democracy alone. For they know that none but you will bring freedom back again, and of course they want to destroy the source from which they are expecting ruin to themselves.[6]

What was the situation in Greece when Demosthenes was thus exhorting the Athenians to rouse themselves to the truth of their position and resist the impending peril to their democracy? At that time, the country was divided into small city-states, each isolationist in its political philosophy, each supposedly secure in its own strength against all the world. To the suggestion that these separate city-states might perish before the new techniques of aggression which were being developed by the great powers that moved beyond their borders, the Greeks willfully shut their minds. Fighting planes and dive bombers were still things of the distant future; nevertheless, the Macedonians were then perfecting methods of attack hitherto untried, and the question that the Greeks were forced to face was whether they should cling to the individual sovereignty and isolation of their cities or unify themselves for mutual assistance and protection.

History tells us what their answer was. They refused to join together, and ultimately they succumbed, all of them one by one, to Philip. Greek liberty was gone. Greek democracy had perished. Athens was no longer a city of free men; it had ceased to be the light for mankind.

* * *

I have said that the situation of the Greeks in the days when Philip threatened and Demosthenes warned was similar to our own today. I wish now to point out two important differences that we should not overlook. The first difference is that Greece was only a small part of the world. Beyond its limits lay whole continents, still unknown. In these lands there might be born—as there has been—a sort of

[6] *Ibid.*, p. 423.

liberty then undreamed of. Today, there are no undiscovered continents, no frontiers still waiting to be opened up. The whole world has become one, and its destiny is one. In the place of Greece as it was then stand today all the democracies and all hope for future freedom.

The second and more important difference between the fate that overtook the Greeks and the possibility that confronts us now lies in the nature of the threatening force. Alexander the Great, who realized, or tried to realize, the ambitions of his father, Philip, was not antagonistic to Athenian civilization. On the contrary, being a disciple of Aristotle, Alexander had come to venerate the culture of the Greeks; he felt himself to be a Hellene. More than that, he considered himself the instrument by which that culture was to be disseminated far beyond the country of its origin. In reality, as all students of history know, it was Alexander who pointed the way to the birth of Stoic philosophy, with its recognition of the universal brotherhood of men in a rational world, and so made possible the greatest flowering of ancient civilization.

The forces that threaten the democracies today are openly hostile to the democratic spirit; they do not look upon themselves as heirs or carriers of the traditions of western civilization. They are doing what Alexander never did; they are leading a revolution against our civilization; a determined and conscious attack upon all that is basic to it. If they are victorious, the form and spirit of our life—our social life, our personal life—will be changed. Everything that we call good will be called evil, and everything that we call evil will be called good.

If, now, we ask ourselves what is the real root of the present trouble that afflicts our world, we have to go back twenty years and reexamine the Treaty of Versailles. Without rehearsing the details, we can say that we had an opportunity, by means of the great promises contained in this peace treaty, to do the three things that would have given us a firm basis for building a new world. If the ideals of Woodrow Wilson had been realized and if the spirit of enlightened liberalism had prevailed, these three things for which the foundations were well laid in the Treaty of Versailles might have been accomplished.

The first was to break Prussian militarism, that incubus upon the German people which was a menace to all of Europe; the second was to liberate oppressed people and to give them a new sense of dignity and happiness; and the third was to form an association of the free peoples throughout the world for common protection—the League of Nations.

The tragedy is that none of these three goals of the Treaty of Versailles was attained. None of them was fulfilled, not because of the "wickedness" of the governments, but because of the unwillingness of the peoples of the world to shoulder the burden of the peace treaties. In their shortsightedness they believed that they were still living in the nineteenth century. They did not realize that in 1919 a period of history had come to an end and a new era had begun. When the war was over they relapsed into their old habits of thought, shrank back into isolation, and allowed themselves once more to be dominated by intense feelings of alleged self-interest and of nationalism.

In the United States, the decade of the 1920's was one of disillusionment, of "debunking" as it was called. It was also a period of wishful thinking during which the American people persuaded themselves that they had at last achieved complete security, and that no new forces would ever again upset the established scheme of things. They refused to see that, as the Greek city-state had outlived its effectiveness in the fourth century B.C., just so the isolated and sovereign state of modern times, which developed between the Renaissance and the years of the First World War, had lost the basis for its existence in a new world of rapid communication. Instead of recognizing this change and addressing themselves to the task of creating a new world for a new mankind, they persistently turned aside from any deeper understanding of the new forces, from any firm moral choice that would have involved the assuming of personal responsibility.

*   *   *

In this hour of crisis, we are face to face with the question that confronted the Greeks in the time of Philip—the question of choosing between isolation and unity. If, like the Greeks, we allow the decision on this vital issue to go by default, we risk not only the loss of our liberties, as they did, but the far greater disaster of the destruction of the spiritual, moral, and intellectual values which we and our forebears have cherished and for which our fathers fought.

During the postwar period, and even in the midst of the preparations for a new and infinitely more decisive war, we have chosen isolation. By "we" I do not mean only the people of the United States, although they were the first to slip back into isolation in 1919 and have been the last to awaken from its comfort. I mean the peoples of all the democracies, and in each democracy I mean the people as a whole. Isolationism was not the fault of any one class, as, for instance, the British Tories. It has been characteristic of all classes during the last twenty fateful years; many socialists indeed out-chamberlained Chamberlain. The task of trying to unite the peoples of the world has been blindly left by the democracies to the dictators. And the dictators are attempting to achieve this task, not by reason, but by brute force and the degradation of man; they are not working in the interests of human freedom and dignity, but are seeking everywhere to overthrow them.

How effectively have we educators come to the defense of reason and freedom? How fully are we living in this new world? Are not most of us still dwelling in an imaginary prewar world, fascinated and paralyzed, unable to comprehend the forces that are changing reality far beyond any parallel with 1914? What have we done through education to concentrate the mind of the rising generation upon the one essential problem of the twentieth century, upon a true understanding of history and its forces? Have we not rather filled the minds of our people with so great a diversity of things that they have been distracted from the effort to concentrate upon the essential? Have we not increased their sentimentalism and their belief that wishful thinking, through the intensity of its sincerity alone, will blossom forth into reality? Have we not failed to show them that in the long run no democracy or decent life at home is possible, under twentieth-century conditions, if it is not first and above all internationally secure? Have we in any way helped our people to realize that whatever happens anywhere on earth happens to them?

The consequence of our attitude was that in the fateful months of the summer of 1939 we had no true understanding of the situation which we were facing. The success of fascism during the fourth decade of the twentieth century was due to its profound recognition of the fact that the struggle to come was not to be about frontiers or about raw materials, about markets or about migrations, but was to decide the future of civilization everywhere. The world was to be united. The question remained whether the unification was to take place under the leadership of the liberal and democratic forces that had come to the fore as the result of the Anglo-Saxon and

French revolutions of the seventeenth and eighteenth centuries, or was to be imposed by the great counterrevolution represented by European fascism and Japanese militarism. The democratic peoples refused to shoulder the burden that the twentieth century put upon them; they are now paying the price for this refusal.

We were in no way prepared for the inevitable conflict. In September 1939 we and the smaller democracies in Europe believed that we could escape the struggle by simply ignoring its existence. We tried to hide ourselves behind a wall of cynicism, behind denial that moral values were at stake, behind the complacent hope that if we minded our own business somehow the conflagration would not spread and reach our shores. Everywhere those who had criticized Chamberlain now outdid him; and to justify their "neutrality" they found fault with the attacked and made excuses for the aggressors. Thus it happened that in the hour of supreme test, when the democracies were faced with the immense responsibility of deciding the future for themselves and for civilization, they were totally unprepared to meet the test.

The danger to democracy arose out of failure to comprehend the issues that were involved. The final realization of their danger shocked the democracies into action, sometimes when it was very late, always when it was later than they thought; but it did not in every case arouse them to a full awareness of the truth that a world revolution is now in progress.

It is imperative that without further delay we concentrate all our intellectual and moral resources upon the one task of freeing our people from lack of understanding, from the illusions and fears, that shackle them and make them undecided, hesitating, and panic-stricken instead of resolute and farsighted. We must help them to see clearly what they wish to do and thus to gain the strength that springs from understanding knowledge and from devotion to a constructive purpose. We must equip them to live and function in the world of the twentieth century, which will be, whether we wish it or not, a unified and intercommunicating world. Our responsibility is to see that in this new world the dignity and worth of the individual shall be respected, the equality of men and races shall be recognized, the freedom of all shall be safeguarded; in short, that it shall be a world in which democracy will grow and peace will be assured. Such a world cannot come in any easy way, not by soft living nor by minding our business; it can come only through a hard struggle, through many sacrifices, and through unflinching courage and devotion. Only thus can the great heritage of western civilization that springs from Athens and Jerusalem be preserved and transmitted to future generations, enriched and purified by the thought and toil, by the suffering and striving, of our generation.

5

The Promise of This Generation of College Youth*

Youth, after the Second World War, shows little of the "lost generation" feeling which characterized its parents twenty-five years ago. Yet the generation of the 20's faced a seemingly much more promising and prosperous scene both at home and abroad. Today it has become a trite though true commonplace that the United States, and the whole of mankind, is passing through a crisis. Scientists and moralists find ever-new adjectives to describe the multiple horrors which this crisis holds for the future. Escape into cynicism and dissipation would be timely under such circumstances, but instead, this generation of college youth has been sobered by the crises of the last fifteen years. It has started to reappraise America's heritage and its position in the world.

The unexpected threat of Hitlerism and the even more formidable and unexpected threat of Stalinism have shocked youth into thinking about fundamentals. It has become increasingly clear that these threats cannot be met by military armaments alone. Arms are indispensable to guarantee national survival, but it would be a mistake to think of the danger as, above all, military. Nor is the threat of national socialism, whether of the German or the Russian type, di-

* An address on the occasion of the Seventh Annual Honors Day, Brooklyn College, November 15, 1950.

rected solely against the free economic system, the only one so far that has succeeded in providing the masses with a high standard of living. Stalinism, like Hitlerism before it, challenges the whole fabric of liberal civilization. They deny and reject the very structure of the tradition which has grown up in western Europe and spread from there in the eighteenth century to the other shore of the North Atlantic. To this challenge the West has to find a response. Defense against an attack carried on by a fanatical faith is not easy. Is this generation of college youth prepared for it? Does the recent past supply spiritual arms for the necessary response which will demand a rethinking and a reinvigoration of the traditions of free men? Liberal arts colleges have to form the youth capable to do that.

Eighteenth century European philosophers and intellectuals saw in the unknown and distant English settlements in North America the possibility for the realization of their dreams of progress, the promised land, where virtuous men living in virgin nature would build the ideal society, fulfilling the hopes of the age of reason. But real nature was in no way as kind as eighteenth century Rousseauans believed. In the new continent, especially in New England, the settlers found a hard soil of scant fertility, immense primeval forests without roads or amenities, a wilderness which exacted an all-out effort to turn it into a place fit to live in. In this struggle against overwhelming odds, one side of human nature was developed to a degree unknown elsewhere, the man who builds and forges and constructs, the man who masters nature and gains proud confidence in his own self-reliant powers.

Thus America became the country in which the spirit of enterprise, of initiative, of an optimistic belief in the future of man, triumphed. It became the leading nation in technology, in applied science, in ever-new mechanical discoveries. But it paid the price. The American outlook became primarily utilitarian. Material conquests beckoned and brought ample and enviable rewards. But there was little time and little inclination for disinterested theory. The Platonic pursuit of matters of the spirit and of beauty seemed a luxury. The United States became a center and a model of economic creativeness and of technological progress beyond the dreams of preceding generations. It did not become a radiant center of spiritual energy. In the nineteenth century the western European intellectuals abandoned their expectations of American leadership. They began to despise or pity the pursuit of the dollar and the cult of the machine. Only Europe's down-trodden and impoverished masses continued to look on America as a promised land.

But the achievement of America was at no time purely economic. That the United States became technologically the most prosperous country on earth was less important than the fact that it was politically the freest and most advanced land. Here the traditions of English liberty, the heritage of Milton and Locke, of habeas corpus and tolerance, grew into a universal message for all men, not only those of English descent, into a free society based upon respect for the individual, giving him scope for unfettered and spontaneous development, unknown even in England. But American well-being and political liberty do no longer suffice. What is needed today, for the United States and for the Western world, is the assertion of the spiritual, non-utilitarian values on which, often without any articulate clarity, all American life from the days of the Founding Fathers until today has rested. These values alone have made the economic progress and the political liberty possible. They were inherited from the free societies on the other side of the Atlantic. In face of the challenges raised against these values, it is the task of the liberal arts college to prepare youth to meet this challenge and thus to re-establish firmly the foundation on which political liberty rests.

Higher education cannot exhaust itself in the preparation of young people for citizenship or for a place as well-adjusted useful members of society. This may be the purpose of all education. It is not the criterion of higher education. Useful knowledge is being imparted, and should be so to an ever increasing degree, in technical and professional schools. In liberal arts colleges, youth should pursue knowledge for its own sake. The higher intellectual and spiritual functions are disinterested functions. They do not lend themselves to any immediate practical use, but they open up higher forms of experience, they make men look out at ever wider horizons, they give profound and enduring pleasure and enlarge the understanding of life. They provide inner resources to face the trials and hardships, the frustrations and sufferings inherent in human life. Without them life would be infinitely poorer and ultimately meaningless.

The wrong attitude toward higher education manifests itself clearly in the approach to one of the foundations of all our civilized education. If one asks American students to study the classical languages and civilizations, one often receives the saddening answer, "Of what use can such a study be to me?" But liberal arts colleges fulfil their function only if they do not emphasize matters of immediate use or of so-called practical importance. To study languages, and in the first line the classical languages, is a most valuable discipline in itself, and as such to be welcomed, for nothing can be achieved in higher education without hard work, without disciplined dedication, without deep respect for intellectual values as such. In the closer acquaintance with classical civilization, which our Founding Fathers had, we are going to the roots of our civilization, to the sources from which its inspiration and its ability of regeneration has flowed throughout the centuries.

Instead of travelling this hard road to the sources, the present generation seems to rely more and more for its salvation on manipulating techniques. To the idolatry of technology has now succeeded the idolatry of social science and of psychology. Everybody is looking for peace of mind, or for panaceas to solve all the evils of the world through establishing well-adjusted averages. But higher education need not aim at creating too well-adjusted individuals instead of personalities whose minds and hearts continue to be agitated beyond the years of adolescence, not in an adolescent "idealistic" way but in a mature, critical and searching way. They should ask themselves troublesome questions without stipulating easy solutions or happy ends, knowing well that there are no answers, and certainly no ready-made answers, to many questions and many problems, no panaceas to the ills of the individual, of society, and of mankind. What Socrates did, we should all learn to do on our own small scale: to examine life with an open mind, weighing all the alternatives. In his never resting intellectual curiosity the old sage preserved his youth.

This is, however, no plea for eternal youth. Youth should leave the colleges as fully adult persons. There is no time any more for the protracted childhood, for the "kids" in their twenties, and the "boys and girls" in their thirties and forties, who people the American scene and adorn queerly the American language. Few among our college students will turn into scholars or artists or saints. The vast majority of them should not even try. But all of them should carry with them from the liberal arts college into maturity a keen understanding of, and a cheerful respect for, the disinterested pursuit of scholarship, the great works of art, the exemplary inspiration of saintly conduct. They should enliven and brighten American life with that gift of discrimination, which even without consciously expressed reasons makes them prefer a great tragedy to a musical show and a literary classic to the current best-seller. They should fully grow during their college years into the spiritual heritage of Western civilization, which in its origin has been a Mediterranean civilization, and in its modern form, since the seventeenth century, has become a North-Atlantic civilization.

The world events of the last decades have put an added responsibility upon the United States. Western Europe has shown during that time signs of spiritual fatigue. Fascism and Communism have spread their growing confusion of minds and hearts. The intellectual scene has been dominated by the feeling of frustration expressed in Franz Kafka; by the emphasis placed by Karl Barth on the fearful abyss separating men from God; by the nihilism animating the heroes or rather non-heroes in Aldous Huxley's "Point Counter-Point"; by fear which Martin Heidegger, the representative philosopher of contemporary Germany, regards as the dominating obsession of man; by the idealization of the disciplined militant worker, a technological robot, presented by Ernst Juenger, the greatest writer of contemporary Germany; by the nausea of which Sartre speaks; by the labor of Sisyphus, in which the most gifted French writer, Albert Camus, sees the symbol of human life. These are only a few examples taken at random from the vast and varied scenery of the waste-land into which Europe was transformed as a result of the disaster of the first World War. These developments found their climax in the annihilation of man in Communism and Hitlerism. There the individual became the mere object of historical or biological forces, ruthlessly sacrificed to the inexorable march of history and to deified abstractions like race or class.

More and more Europe will be looking across the Atlantic not for dollars nor for free elections but for a new vitality giving hope and strength to the spiritual life of the common Western civilization. Only a college youth deeply steeped in the values of this civilization, and courageously facing the realities and the difficulties of life ahead, will be able to help in this task. For the future will be very difficult. For many years to come, probably for the life-time of the present college generation, men will live in an insecure world with very little peace of mind. This world cannot be made more secure by wishful thinking or by moralistic preaching. It is useless, and often positively harmful, to believe that something is being achieved when well-meaning people exhort the nations to do away with greed or with distrust. These generalities avoid the concrete problems where all the difficulties lie to which we have to find an answer in the slow and hard way.

The number of misleading clichés which are thoughtlessly thrown around today is bewildering. We are told that in arms there is no security, which is true. But neither is there any security in disarming. Hitler and Stalin tried before 1940 to find security in armament and failed. Britain and we tried before 1940 to find security in disarming and failed. Panicky thinking helps as little as wishful thinking; an unbounded and unfounded pessimism which foresees the destruction of all life on this earth is as bad as an unbounded and unfounded optimism which believes in the sudden transformation of collective man into exemplars of wisdom and goodness. Both prevent clear thinking and timely action. There were prophets of doom who foretold the annihilation of all civilization as a result of the invention of airplanes before 1938; similar prophets of doom appeared in 1945 with the invention of the atom bomb; they are now vocal with the invention of the hydrogen bomb; their prophecy of doom will be repeated at any new invention of that kind. Mankind certainly could lead a highly civilized life without aircraft and without atomic energy. But the wailing over these inventions will not solve the slightest of the concrete problems which we have to clarify, without fear and without illusions. The dangerous times ahead force us to live on higher planes of consciousness and conscience than we have been accustomed to. Here again, it is the youth trained in liberal arts colleges who should take the lead.

In the last three years the American people have made great progress in responsible thinking about the world in which they have to live. From March 1947, when President Truman announced a new American policy of support for Turkey and Greece against outside aggression, they travelled the road to the Atlantic Pact and to the United Nations action in Korea in an astonishingly short time. But this amazing achievement is in itself not enough. The American people must learn, and are learning, that they have to plan not only for a passing emergency but for a new period of history which will be with them for any foreseeable future. They are now beginning to awake to the realization of this unforeseen and unprecedented situation and of the obligating nature of their spiritual and intellectual heritage.

Twelve or fifteen years ago American college youth had little understanding for the values of Western civilization and of free society.

The period of debunking had produced a cynical indifference to spiritual or moral issues which were regarded as clever rationalizations of corporate interest or individual greed. At an awful cost, Hitler has rendered us a service, by making us conscious of the danger threatening civilization. We have become conscious of its fragility and vulnerability. In normal or seemingly normal times—and who does not remember the return to normalcy after 1918—we are taking our individual liberty and the values of civilized life so much for granted that we do not pay any attention to them and hardly esteem them. Only the sudden and unexpected dangers to which they have been exposed these last decades have awakened us to the realization of their nature. Today we know that life without them is not life at all. Thus it goes with most indispensable elements which we take for granted. We do not think of air or its value in normal times. But if suddenly we cannot breathe we know that there is nothing more precious than air. Ever present as air seems time to youth and therefore of hardly any value, until suddenly at a late moment men awaken to the irreparable loss of what now seems the most valuable of possessions. The opera *Der Rosenkavalier* deals with this subject in the unforgettable words of the great Austrian poet Hugo von Hofmannsthal, when the princess realizes the approaching inevitable end of her affair with young Octavian. In the passage, unsurpassed in its musical poetry, the middle-aged and still beautiful woman becomes aware of the unique nature of time:

> "Time, that is a curious thing;
> If one just lives, it seems like nothing at all!
> But then suddenly one feels nothing but it.
> It is all around us, it is also within us.
> All my veins feel its throbbing,
> and between me and thee,
> it flows in silence, trickles like sand
>   in the hour glass."

Thus it happens with liberty and with the security which law gives to the individual in a free society. In normal times it seems like nothing at all, one takes it for granted, but then suddenly, when there is danger of the knock at the door by secret police in the stillness of night, one feels nothing but it. In the years ahead, the liberty of the individual and the spontaneous growth of our spiritual heritage will be values which will be felt poignantly. College youth will have to understand and to sustain them.

The United States is growing into the unsought role of the guardian of Western civilization. It has become a commonplace to say that the center of economic and political gravity in the western world has shifted to the United States. It is not yet always clearly seen that the chief responsibility for the spiritual invigoration of the Atlantic community, with its wealth of diversity within fundamental unity, has also devolved upon the United States. To higher education and to college youth goes the responsibility and the honor of creating the conditions which might allow Americans, humbly and in painful consciousness of their limitations, to assume their share in this common task of the Atlantic community. In that field, more even than in the economic or military one, the fullest collaboration with western Europe is indispensable and carries in itself a great promise and hope. It is a positive and lasting aspect of an interdependence which is in no way confined to the momentary needs of security or prosperity. The foundations of the common Atlantic civilization were laid in the eighteenth century, when the English in Britain and the English in North America and the French entered into and kept alive an uninterrupted cultural exchange and intellectual conversation. These efforts are coming to fruition in our time. Perhaps 1950 may be in some respects nearer to 1750 than it is to 1850, above all in the feeling of growing interdependence as against national and nationalist limitations.

The threat which Stalinism presents to the Western world is not only, and not primarily, one of impoverishment and lower standards of living, and even not of the destruction of liberty. Stalinism meant also in Russia impoverishment and loss of liberty, but Russia had always a low standard of living and liberty had there only a very short and precarious existence. Yet Russia, in the years before the seizure of power by Communism, offered the spectacle of a rich and spontaneous spiritual life, a marvellous growth of all the forms of beautiful art and searching thought which fertilized, in an uninterrupted stream of exchange, the writers and artists of the West. Stalinism put an end to it by pressing all intellectual life into an official straight-jacket. It destroyed contemplation and meditation, disinterested seeking and lonely daring, the foundations on which alone creative civilized life can rest. Wherever Stalinism spreads there descends like a blight a monotonous uniformity of all thought, an idolatry of purely utilitarian technology in the service of the state, an appalling poverty of intellectual discussion which has to conform to principles known beforehand, and of artistic imagination which has to conform to the mediocrity of philistine taste.

The spiritual threat of Stalinism challenges civilization. The response to this challenge cannot be found in economic prosperity; it can only be found in the ever-deepening and ever-broadening spiritual life of the Western world. This should be a powerful and alluring challenge to American college youth, worthy of their mature and informed thought, of their conscious and conscientious sense of obligation to the best in their heritage. The future is not known to man and pessimism is very widespread today, yet the future seems, in spite of great difficulties, to carry the promise of a richer life, if the new generation will accept the burden which the epoch they live in, the tradition they inherit and the privilege of education, lay upon it. In that sense this generation is happier than the preceding ones, who entered the wasteland of the first half of the twentieth century and found themselves helpless and discouraged before violent revolutions and devastating wars, before cynicism and brutality, nihilism and fanaticism. At the turn of the half century, however, at the bottom of despair, the awakening to a new affirmation of the values of Western civilization, in maturity and responsibility, in historical perspective and in mutuality with allied partners in the common civilization, may inaugurate a happier period, similar to the time of the Enlightenment when, as a fruit of the hopes of Western mankind, the American nation was born.

6

The Interdependence of Civilization*

Individuals grow and develop, spiritually and morally, by contact. The same holds true of nations and civilizations. In the primitive stage, peoples live as strictly separated entities. They jealously guard their "own" civilization, their "original" traditions, protecting them from "alien" influences. But with the progress of history barriers give way to growing cross-fertilization of civilization; meeting the challenge of other cultures they diversify their own and liberate it from limiting shackles by assimilating and adapting outside influences, often in a complex give-and-take process. The more open society grows, the further it advances toward unity of mankind.

Buddhism in its vitality spread its message to China and Tibet, to Japan and Thailand, to Ceylon and Bali, everywhere vivifying and transforming the native civilizations and permeating them with the same attitudes. Even more penetrating was the spread of Greek civilization after Alexander the Great, who in his brief career was inspired by the hope of uniting the peoples of the earth in a new peaceful order based upon the community of civilization. He bade Greeks and barbarians, as Plutarch wrote, "to consider as their fatherland the whole inhabited earth, and as akin to them all good men." The Stoics developed this attitude into a philosophy, and the Romans made the spread of a uniform civilization throughout the then-known world possible. This civilization was no longer Greek; it had absorbed Oriental and Roman elements, with a new emphasis upon *humanitas*, the human quality in every man and the essential oneness of mankind. This cross-fertilization of civilization made the spread of Christianity, and later of Islam, possible. The latter, originally the creed of desert Arabs, became a world factor by assimilating Greek and Persian civilizations.

The flowering of Christianity in the High Middle Ages, with its universities, poetry and chivalry, was an outgrowth of its closer contacts with the world of Islam. Arab philosophy transmitted to the West the wisdom of Greece; the court of Frederick II in Sicily, who

*Unpublished article, written in 1949.

admired Mohammedan civilization for the greater freedom of its intellectual atmosphere, showed the first symptoms of modern government; the Crusaders brought home from the Levant sometimes a deep respect for the wealth and form of the alien civilizations which they found there. It was this very recognition of the interdependence of civilization and the willingness to become open to the influence of alien cultures which made the great advance of the West possible. It was the increasing withdrawal from open contact and intercourse which weakened Islam and Eastern Christianity. Around the year 1000 the leadership had been theirs, by 1500 it had definitely shifted to the West.

In the following five hundred years this leadership became more pronounced by the growing eagerness to explore other civilizations, to become enriched by this contact, and to visualize the world more and more as an open society in which the intercourse of ideas and the flow of goods should be untrammeled and continuous. It began with the fifteenth century, when Western scholars eagerly learned from the Greeks who had left Constantinople after its fall to the Turks; it found a climax in the eighteenth century, when Far Eastern wisdom and art was joyfully and respectfully received in the West, and its intellectuals turned to the newly discovered "primitive" civilizations for inspiration. Nor did Western civilization tend to dissociate into closed entities proud of their "originality." Educated men found their cultural fulfilment in Latin or French; scholars and diplomats could meet in understanding without the help of translators. The great achievement of the West, the recognition of the individual liberty and free inquiry, was due to the interplay and interdependence of the Low Countries—where Grotius, Descartes and Locke wrote, and where Pierre Bayle launched in 1684 his *Nouvelles de la République des Lettres*—and England, with its Puritan and Glorious revolutions, of the Anglo-Americans in the virgin lands across the Atlantic, and of France, where the English concepts of the rights of the individual and the limitations of government were transformed into a universal message for every man and citizen.

Germany's greatest writer, Goethe, always stressed this interdependence of civilization. He acknowledged his deep indebtedness to "alien" cultures which to him were part of the one great patrimony. He had hardly any sympathy for, or interest in, the German struggle of his time for "liberation" from the French "invader." In his old age he expressed his admiration for French culture, and he created

The Interdependence of Civilization

the term *Weltliteratur,* world literature, as a meeting ground for the good in all civilizations and the nursery for the writers in all tongues. He did not confine himself to the West, though in many ways he was one of the representative men of Western civilization. His most mature poems were influenced by his reading of translations from Persian and Arabic authors. They can be found in his West-Eastern Divan, where these celebrated lines occur:

> Gottes ist der Orient!
> Gottes ist der Okzident!
> Nord und südliches Gelände
> Ruht im Frieden seiner Hände.
>
> God's own is the Orient!
> God's own is the Occident!
> Northern and southern lands
> Rest peacefully in His hands.

The other great Germans of his time, Kant and Beethoven, Lessing and Schiller, were equally devoid of any national exclusiveness. But only a few years later a new emphasis was placed on the "originality" and uniqueness of national civilizations, on the difference of cultures. The more distinct a culture was, the more it became faithful to its "own" origins and past and remained unaffected by alien influences, the more it was thought to be creative. This cultural self-sufficiency was also applied to the political field in the stress of undiminished national sovereignty, and to economic relations, in which national frontiers became ever mounting barriers. In his *Der geschlossene Handelsstaat,* the German philosopher J. G. Fichte suggested the creation of an ideal society in complete isolation from the rest of the world so that, by as little contact as possible with foreigners, it might develop its national character to the highest degree. While it would close its frontiers to all commercial exchange with foreign lands—thus establishing its own state as a great common work house guaranteeing work to every citizen—Fichte at least exempted scholarship from this extreme isolationism. Whatever belongs to the citizen, he wrote, is under the control of the state, but scholarship belongs to man and not to a citizen. In the authoritarian societies of the twentieth century this distinction was given up in the name of total self-sufficiency.

The nineteenth century, however, took on the whole a different course. Society became more and more an open market place of ideas and goods. Cobden and Bright fervently spread the gospel of free trade, not only as an economic doctrine but as a means to build the interdepedence of mankind in peaceful dependence: "In place of the old local and national institutions and self-sufficiency, we have intercourse in every direction, universal interdependence of all nations. And as in material, so also in intellectual production. The intellectual creations of individual nations become common property. National one-sidedness and narrowmindedness become more and more impossible, and from the numerous national and local literatures there arises a world literature."

This fertilization by interdependence enriched the civilizations which tore down the walls separating them. Peter the Great broke a first window in the wall which Orthodox Russia had erected in an attempt to isolate herself from Europe. A century later, a more open intercourse between the two civilizations slowly began to emerge, though it continued to be hampered by prohibitive passport regulations and the fear of contact predominant in the reign of Nicholas I. But even this incipient recognition of interdependence bestowed upon both civilizations a new spiritual energy and broadened their horizons to mutual benefit. The Russian educated classes began, under European influence, to strive for liberty under law after the Western model and to fight the traditional police state autocracy. Europe, on the other hand, drew a new inspiration from the human warmth and the deep searchings of the Russian literature, from Gogol to Dostoevsky, from Tolstoi to Chekhov. Russia's contact with Europe produced suddenly and almost without precedent a literature of the first magnitude: its influence radiated back to Europe, and in its turn fertilized the older literatures.

However, the fact that the interdependence of civilization releases unprecedented creative energies was not easily conceded. Many denied it, and Peter the Great's work formed in the nineteenth century the subject of much bitter controversy in Russia. An influential group of Russian patriots, often called the Slavophiles, regarded his opening-up of intercourse with Europe as a misfortune for Russia. It was believed to have hindered or destroyed a pure indigenous cultural and spiritual development with exclusive roots in the peculiar traditions of Russian character and history. The Slavophiles were convinced that the flowering of Russian culture demanded an isolation from contact with alien elements—Russian culture in itself, and only in itself, contained the seeds for world leadership and world salvation. This exclusive nationalism turned above all against Slavdom's Western neighbors, the Germans.

Yet this Slavophilism with all its claims to self-sufficiency was not an indigenous Russian growth. It had developed under the influence of German romantic thought by simply transferring the anti-cosmopolitanism and anti-intellectualism of German folk theories to the Slavs as the bearers of the true spirit. Thus even the most "independent" movements bear witness to the interdependence of civilization.

It has not always been clearly seen that the very insistence upon indigenous development and its unique and exclusive originality has been the product of cultural contact and of an erroneous interpretation of the past. Oriental nationalists have often rejected Western civilization as an expression of crude materialism contrasting it with their pure indigenous spiritualism; in this attitude they were influenced by Ruskin and other European critics of certain aspects of Western civilization.

The degree to which cultural isolationism weakens and destroys a civilization that refuses to recognize cultural interdependence in a community of nations, can be seen from the attitude of the Chinese at the beginning of the nineteenth century. They were then convinced that they alone had the correct doctrine and knew the true way, that all others had to learn from them, while they could gain nothing from alien guidance or influence. From the towering height of their uncritical self-confidence, which placed them in the very center of all civilized life, they built a wall of isolation around themselves and refused intercourse with other civilizations on a footing of equality. As a result, Chinese civilization, in spite of its venerable antiquity and its unsurpassed records of beauty of form and serenity of wisdom, became the model of fossil pedantry. Only more recently the intercourse with other civilizations eagerly sought by the educated youth, re-invigorated the Chinese civilization. A similar process in other Oriental countries, from Turkey to the Philippine Islands, inaugurated an entirely new period in the history of Asia.

Cultural intercourse was hampered in preceding centuries by distances and the scarcity of means of communication. All this has changed rapidly during the last hundred years. Ever new geographic discoveries and technical inventions have made the globe one world, thus realizing in space what has long been recognized by religion and science—the existence of one mankind. This geographic and biological unity of a common earth and a common blood finds its spiritual fulfilment, however, in a plurality and diversity of civilizations. Each of them has its specific contribution to make, and complements the other. None of them exhausts the spiritual potentialities of man. In the intercourse and interdependence they find the stimulating challenges preserving them from ossification and arousing them to the search for new responses to ever-renewed questions. Western civilization, with its emphasis on individual liberty and free inquiry, would have been much poorer without the recent meeting of the ascetic morality of Gandhi with the humanistic wisdom of Rabindranath Tagore, both the fruit of ancient India's contact with the West. The Mediterranean, once the center from which Western civilization radiated, has witnessed recently at its western and eastern extremities, efforts at re-invigoration of the civilizations of Spain and of Islam, which in the past have played great roles. All signs portend that an African civilization arising out of a strong virgin soil under the fertilization of older civilizations will soon take its place among these which in clearly recognized and desired interdependence make their contributions to an open society based upon freedom and diversity. Such a society presupposes co-operation in the spirit of tolerance. No civilization must think itself in exclusive possession of the true way and endowed with an infallible insight into the course of human history.

PART TWO

Three English Political Thinkers

7

Walter Bagehot, Victorian*

In the last years of the nineteenth century Woodrow Wilson wrote in appreciation of the English political writer and "seer," Walter Bagehot, that "ever since my boyhood, I have had a great enthusiasm for Mr. Bagehot's writings and have derived so much inspiration from them. . . . It would be a most agreeable good fortune to introduce Bagehot to men who had not read him. To ask your friend to know Bagehot is like inviting him to seek pleasure. . . . Bagehot saw the world of his days, saw the world of days antique, and showed us what he saw in phrases which interpret like the tones of a perfect voice, in words which serve us like eyes."

Woodrow Wilson, thus introducing a typical Victorian, was himself the last of the great American Victorians. Even before Wilson died, the public temper in both English-speaking countries turned against the Victorians and against Wilson's own thought. Lytton Strachey's widely read biographies set the tone in debunking the Great Victorians. But by the middle of the present century this mood has largely given way to a nostalgic appreciation of the Victorian era. The centenary of Wilson's birth is being widely celebrated in the United States, and the foremost British historian of the Victorian age, G. M. Young, could write: "Of all decades in our history, a wise man would choose the 1850's to be young in." It may be time again to introduce Bagehot to the many men who in the last decades have not read him.

Bagehot, who lived his young manhood in the very decade which G. M. Young recommended as the wisest choice, was born in 1826, the son of a well-educated Unitarian businessman of dignified virtue and warm affections. As a boy Bagehot was an insatiable reader and

* From the Introduction to Walter Bagehot, *Physics and Politics* (Boston: Beacon Press, 1956). Reprinted by permission.

received an excellent grounding in the classical languages. As a nonconformist he went in 1842 for his college training to London, to England's modern university which had been founded under the influence of Jeremy Bentham and which was free of the religious narrowness of Oxford and Cambridge. Young Bagehot graduated there with the highest honors in mathematics and in philosophy. But already as a student he was as much attracted by the political life of the capital as he was by books. He listened to Peel, Disraeli, and Gladstone speak in the House of Commons. He witnessed the agitation of the Chartists and of the Anti-Corn Law League, a period of unrest and social discontent which impressed many Continental observers so much that they predicted the near approach of a revolution in Britain. As a result of the lives led by the sons of George III, the royal family had lost much of its prestige, and some people thought seriously of a republic for England. All that changed in the 1850's. Suddenly England appeared as the most stable country in the world. Who now would have expected revolutions there like those which had swept Europe in 1848 or civil wars like the one approaching in the United States? The agitation of the "lower classes" had disappeared as a threat, and, thanks to the young Queen and her Prince Consort, the monarchy became more firmly rooted in the hearts of the people than ever before. The Great Exhibition in 1851, arranged by the Prince Consort, expressed a new feeling of security and unlimited progress; it marked the beginning of a period of halcyon bliss, which lasted until Disraeli in 1867 carried through Parliament the extension of the suffrage to the urban working class, a step which many contemporaries regarded as a dangerous leap into a dark future.

In that year Bagehot published *Physics and Politics,* the shortest and best known of his major works. He was then forty-one years old. His life had been happy and well balanced in what might be properly regarded as a typically Victorian fashion. His character and temper knew none of the deep shadows which darkened the life of Carlyle or of Dickens. A number of brilliant literary and biographical essays early established Bagehot's reputation as a writer and thinker. His standing as a banker and business leader was enhanced when he married the daughter of Sir James Wilson, a wealthy Liberal politician of the period. Bagehot's marriage was unusually harmonious and opened to him the most distinguished social and political circles of London. Sir James was the publisher of the weekly

Economist, and after his death in 1861 his son-in-law became director and editor of the influential paper. Both as a human being, in the circle of his family and friends, and as a political and economic writer, Bagehot combined to a rare extent sound stability of judgment with a keen imaginative sensibility. His first biographer stressed that the tenet which Bagehot consistently put into practice was "live and let live." He was tolerant and considerate of the opinions and feelings of others, however different they might be from his own. He allowed no personal predilections to override his reasoned opinions. His eloquence was always the outcome of sincere conviction and deep feeling.

Though Bagehot was a member of the Liberal party and four times on its behalf unsuccessfully contested a seat for the House of Commons, he was much nearer to the Liberal conservative than to the Liberal reformer. He welcomed reform, but only as far as it helped to produce greater stability. The preservation of society appeared to him as society's first duty. Though he never succeeded in entering the House of Commons, he had the highest respect for this "deliberate assembly of moderate and judicious men," as it emerged from the reforms of 1832. British society in the 1850's presented to him an ideal system of "removable inequality" and a happy balance between social stability and individual advancement, between traditional values and enterprising initiative, between gentleman and businessman. "The spirit of the country is quiet," he wrote, "but reasonable, undisposed to sweeping innovations and equally undisposed to keeping in the old Tory way everything which is because it is. The moderate members of both parties represent this spirit very fairly."

Bagehot was a distinguished stylist, a brilliant conversationalist, and a very clever writer who loved originality and the paradox; but he recognized the dangers of brilliance in political life and appreciated the moral strength of English dullness. "What we opprobriously called stupidity," he said, "though not an enlivening quality in common society, is Nature's resource for preserving steadiness of conduct and consistency of opinion." In his article "A Wit and a Seer," Woodrow Wilson explained "stupidity" as meaning common sense and rational forebearance. But Professor Irvine pointed out that stupidity and dullness meant to Bagehot more than sound judgment. They expressed his distrust of facile intellectual analysis that reduces tradition to absurdity and conscience to prejudice. Himself a man of brilliance, Bagehot was weary of men in public life who got easily intoxicated with their own cleverness and who liked to see everything in its most exciting and its most startling form. Bagehot believed that a nation was soundest which could discuss exciting subjects without excitement. In his mature work Bagehot always pleaded for a statesmanlike consideration and application of sober scientific thought to political life.

Fundamentally Bagehot shared with John Stuart Mill a faith in liberty and diversity, a cautious optimism about human abilities and about the educational power of individual freedom, a belief that the enlightened civilization of a freer society would make the individuals more attentive to reason and less subject to prejudice and caprice. "Thus despotism of custom," Mill wrote, "is everywhere a standing hindrance to human advancement; the only unfailing and permanent sort of improvement is liberty, since by it there are as many independent centers of improvement as there are individuals." Some impatient minds complained that British parliamentary government was too slow and too inefficient for thorough and rapid action. In its defense Bagehot opposed those who were "forever explaining that the present is 'an age of committees,' that the committees do nothing, that all evaporates in talk. Their great enemy is parliamentary government; they call it, after Mr. Carlyle, the 'national palaver'; they add up the hours that are consumed in it, . . . and they sigh [for a great man], an eager, absolute man [who] might do exactly what other eager men wish, and do it immediately." All these objections to slow parliamentarism "come from philosophers, each of whom wants some new scheme tried; from philanthropists, who want some evil abated; from revolutionists, who want some old institution destroyed; from 'new eraists,' who want their new era started forthwith. And they all [recognize] that a polity of discussion is the greatest hindrance to the inherited mistake of human nature—to the desire to act promptly, which in a simple age is so excellent but which in a later and complex time leads to so much evil."

The virtue of the polity of discussion is the central thesis of Bagehot's *Physics and Politics.* The book was written under the impact of Darwin's *On the Origin of Species,* which appeared in 1859, and of the unprecedented controversy which it aroused. New branches of scholarship—anthropology, ethnography, sociology, and psychology—were throwing light on the origin of human societies. Bagehot was familiar with them as he was with the older natural sciences. He combined his wealth of reading, thought, and observations to explain the evolution of societies and civilizations by the application of Darwin's theory of natural selection. How did progress in human history come about? How did a few societies succeed in breaking the yoke of custom which first had made civilization possible and in setting free the originality of man so that he became able to alter his condition and seek perfection?

Bagehot's answer can be summed up by the term "intellectual freedom" or, as he calls it, "government by discussion." In memorable words—even more memorable now than in the Victorian Age—Bagehot praised the free state, "call it republic or call it monarchy, in which the sovereign power is divided between many persons, and in which there is a discussion among those persons." "Once effectually submit a subject to that ordeal [of discussion], and you can never withdraw it again; you can never again clothe it with mystery, or fence it by consecration; it remains forever open to free choice and exposed to profane deliberation." If a nation has "gained the habit, and exhibited the capacity, to discuss these questions with freedom, and to decide them with discretion, to argue much on politics and not to argue ruinously, an enormous advance in other kinds of civilization may confidently be predicted for it." Discussion "gives a premium to intelligence." "Tolerance too is learned in discussion and, as history shows, is only so learned." "If we know that a nation is capable of enduring continuous discussion, we know that it is capable of practicing with equanimity continuous tolerance." Discussion tends not only to diminish inherited defects but also to produce a heritable excellence, which Bagehot calls "animated moderation," a union of imagination with soundness, of life with measure, of spirit with reasonableness.

It was in the continuation of Bagehot's tradition when a modern British historian, Professor Herbert Butterfield, recently wrote that "the system that we have inherited replaces a doctrinaire quest for the highest good by a more difficult search—which demands so much more austere self-discipline,—the pursuit of the highest practicable good. It implies even a reluctance to bring things to a decision until something like the general sense of the nation makes itself clear."

This concept of animated moderation is the central idea of Bagehot's thought. In it he reveals himself as a true Aristotelian. It establishes the link connecting Victorian and Athenian democracy, both based on the freedom of discussion. Yet that moderation which Aristotle demanded was frequently absent in Athenian democracy, and this absence was one of the causes of Athens destruction. On the other hand, animated moderation has formed the continuous strength of modern Britain. It could be applied in all walks of life. "If anyone were asked," Bagehot explained, "to describe what it is which distinguishes the writing of a man of genius who is also a great man of the world from all other writers, I think he would use these same words, 'animated moderation.' He would say that such writings are never slow, are never excessive, are never exaggerated; that they are always instinct with judgment, and yet that the judgment is never a dull judgment; that they have as much spirit in them as would go to make a wild writer, and yet that every line of them is the product of a sane and sound writer." "If you ask for a description of the great practical Englishman, you will be sure to have this, or something like it: 'Oh, he has plenty of go in him; but he knows when to pull up.' ... Probably he will hardly be able to explain why he stops when he does stop, or why he continued to move as long as he, in fact, moved; but still, as by a rough instinct, he pulls up pretty much where he should, though he was going at such pace before." "A strongly idiosyncratic mind, violently disposed to extremes of opinion, is soon weeded out of political life, and a bodiless thinker, an ineffectual scholar, cannot even live there for a day. A vigorous moderateness of mind and body is the rule of a polity which works by discussion; and, upon the whole, it is the kind of temper most suited to the active life of such a being as man in such a world as the present one."

The two other major works which Bagehot published, *The English Constitution* and *Lombard Street*, were both highly praised for their lucidity and regarded as standard works at the time. *The English Constitution* shows a profound understanding for the "theatrical" value of court and aristocracy—an observation fully borne out by the coronation of Elizabeth II—but also an aristocratic distrust of government catering to the passions of immoderate men and of the appeal by ambitious statesmen to the emotions of the masses. At the same time, however, Bagehot stressed that statesmen "must avoid, not only every evil, but every appearance of evil; while they have still the power they must remove, not only every actual grievance, but where it is possible every seeming grievance too; they must willingly concede every claim which they can safely concede, in order that they may not have to concede unwittingly some claim which would impair the safety of the country."

Lombard Street was translated into German half a century after its English publication under the significant title *Das Herz der Wirtschaft (The Heart of the Economic System)*, and introduced as "the classical book about the proceedings and the structure of the financial market of a great country." Both works will still be read today by the student with pleasure and profit, although they are dated for the very reason that many of the reforms which they suggested have been carried through. *Physics and Politics,* on the other hand, has preserved its appeal to the general reader and has in none of its parts become obsolete. It will remain a classic because it deals with fundamental psychological and social facts which are of as absorbing interest today as they were a century ago, with the rise and fragility of civilization, and with the historical laws underlying political progress.

Modern society, as it first developed in England, implied an entirely new attitude toward man, society, and history. "It was government by discussion," Bagehot wrote in his *Physics and Politics,* "which broke the bond of ages and set free the originality of mankind. Then, and then only, the motives which Lord Macaulay counted on to secure the progress of mankind, in fact, begin to work: *then* 'the tendency in every man to ameliorate his condition' begins to be important, because then man can alter his condition, while before he is pegged down by ancient usage; *then* the tendency in each mechanical end towards perfection begins to have force, because the artist is at last allowed to seek perfection, after having been forced for ages to move in the straight furrow of the old fixed way. . . . Liberty is the strengthening and developing power—the light and heat of political nature; and when some 'Caesarism' exhibits as it sometimes will, an originality, it is only because it has managed to make its own the products of past free times or of neighboring free countries; and even that originality is only brief and frail, and after a little while when tested by a generation or two, in time of need it falls away."

Bagehot also points out that free government, government by discussion, will protect men against rash action or over-activity. Such rash action is "inherited from times when life was simple, objects were plain, and quick action generally led to desirable ends. But the issues of life are plain no longer. To act rightly in modern society requires a great deal of previous study, a great deal of assimilated information, a great deal of sharpened imagination; and then prerequisites of sound action require much time; and, I was going to say, much 'lying in the sun,' a long period 'mere passiveness.' Even the art of killing men which at first particularly trained men to be quick, now requires them to be slow. A hasty general is the worst of generals nowadays; the best is a sort of von Moltke, who is passive if any man ever was passive, who is 'silent in seven languages.'"

Bagehot died in 1877 in the house where he had grown up as a child, in the ancient small English town of Langport, Somerset, where he had been born fifty-one years earlier. Feeling the approach of death, he left the town house which he had just acquired in London and which William Morris furnished and decorated for him to return with his wife to the beloved home of his parents to which he had remained attached throughout his life. He died at a time when his mental powers were at their best and a full creative life seemed to lie ahead of him; the end came painlessly after a very brief illness, a fitting conclusion to an unusually happy and active life. Did it come at a time when his own world was declining? He would have been perhaps less contented and less influential in the 1880's. Though Queen Victoria outlived Bagehot for almost a quarter of a century, the Victorian age was visibly drawing towards its end. Socialist agitation was rising among the intellectuals; unskilled labor was being organized and was starting a wave of strikes; serious trouble for the Empire began to grow in Ireland and South Africa; soon the problems of competitive armament were to obscure the optimistic horizon of the 1850's.

Yet even in these changed circumstances, in a world ruled more and more by the spirit of impatience and violence, the essential Victorian temper of animated moderation continued to guide British political life. Tradition and progress, faith and reason, have rarely become conflicting opposites in England as they did on the Continent. While logic threatened to separate conservative religion and radical reform, reasonableness harmonized them. "The greatest Liberal of all times," G. M. Young writes of Gladstone, "was penetrated to his innermost fibre with the veneration for all established things: Church, Universities, Crown. Even in twentieth-century England, Christianity survived as a living force in a secular age, aristocracy in a commercialized age, monarchy in a radical age."

Gladstone resigned from the leadership of the Liberal party in 1875, in his sixty-sixth year, to devote the rest of his life to the defense of the Christian religion against the advancing tide of unbelief. A few years later, he threw himself, as a result of moral indignation, wholeheartedly again into political life, to become Prime Minister on three more occasions and to guide the nation and the Empire for twenty more years toward radical new solutions, to prepare them to meet the needs of a new age in the old spirit. British conservatism in its main stream never became a deadening reaction, and the main body of British radicalism never degenerated into destructive revolution. As the French revolutionary syndicalist, Georges Sorel, rather ruefully remarked in his *Reflections on Violence,* the English were distinguished—as are the Americans—by extraordinary lack of understanding of the class war.

Twentieth-century Britain has continued in the wake of the Victorian age but without much of its insular smugness and stuffy provincialism. At mid-century Britain's external position has sharply declined from what it was a hundred years ago. The economic strength and the maritime control which were then hers have been irrevocably lost. Yet at the same time her horizons have been broadened, her cultural life has been quickened, and many more of her people participate in it. But in the midst of all these changes, the political life of the nation has preserved that mixture of "audacity and sobriety" which Bagehot meant when he spoke of moderate animation. Bagehot would have found himself in agreement with the praise of liberty by Lord Acton, his younger contemporary who survived Queen Victoria by one year: "By liberty I mean the assurance that every man shall be protected in doing what he believes his duty against influence of authority and majorities, custom and opinion. Beyond the limits of things necessary for its well-being, the state can only give indirect help to fight the battle of life by promoting the influences which prevail against temptation—religion, education, and the distribution of wealth. The most certain test by which we judge whether a country is really free is the amount of security enjoyed by minorities. Liberty is not a means to a higher political end. It is itself the highest political end. A generous spirit prefers that his country should be poor and weak and of no account but free, rather than powerful, prosperous and enslaved. It is better to be the citizen of a humble commonwealth in the Alps than a subject of the superb autocracy that overshadows half of Asia and Europe."

8

Lord Acton and Human Liberty*

The revival of liberalism since the Second World War has attracted new interest to the three leading figures of nineteenth century liberal thought: Alexis de Tocqueville (1805-1859), John Stuart Mill (1806-1873), and Lord Acton (1834-1902). Of the three, Acton is nearest to our times. He faced, often with melancholy clairvoyance, many of those problems which began to darken the sky at the turn of the century and whose full impact is still upon us today.

The three men differed widely in background and upbringing. Tocqueville and Acton were aristocrats and deeply religious Catholics; Mill was a utilitarian rationalist. Yet they were at one in their dedication to individual liberty. All three saw in the United States its most vigorous exponent and in many ways the model of the future.

Being deeply religious, Acton stood closer to Tocqueville than to Mill. For him, as for Mill, Tocqueville's *De la Démocratie en Amérique* was a classic. But unlike Mill, Acton shared with Tocqueville a deep concern for the relation between religion and liberty. Tocqueville had pointed out that, whereas in France the spirit of religion and the spirit of freedom were marching in opposite directions, in America they were intimately united. Only two years before his death he had written, as he recalled on his visits to the United States, "I found myself in a country, where religion and liberalism were at one, and I breathed freely. More than twenty years ago I expressed this feeling in the introduction to my *Démocratie*. I feel it today as strongly as in my youth, and I do not know whether there exists another thought which would have occupied my mind more constantly." Even more than Tocqueville, Acton dedicated his entire life and thought to reconciling liberalism and religion, the newly emerging free society and the Church.

On the other hand Acton shared with Mill a sanguine belief in social progress and reform. "Most of the great positive evils of the world are in themselves removable, and will, if human affairs continue to improve, be in the end reduced within narrow limits. Pov-

---

* From the Introduction to Lord Acton, *Renaissance to Revolution* (New York: Schocken Books, Inc., 1961). Reprinted by permission.

erty in any sense implying suffering may be completely extinguished by the wisdom of society combined with the good sense and providence of individuals. All the grand sources, in short, of human suffering are in a degree, many of them almost entirely, conquerable by human care and effort." This statement from Mill's *Utilitarianism* Acton made his own. He shared equally Mill's insistence on complete objectivity. "Improvement," Mill wrote, "consists in bringing our opinions into nearer agreement with facts; and we shall not be likely to do this while we look at facts only through glasses colored by those very opinions." As a historian Acton exercised this impartiality. If he was particularly severe in his strictures against the crimes of the Church, it was only because he expected more from the Church as the bearer of Christian morality.

Tocqueville and Mill have left us monumental works on the theory and history of liberty. Acton never finished the great history of liberty which he intended to write. But now when the belief in liberty, especially in Europe, has become the object of cynicism, Acton's life and thought bear witness to its strength. "He did not merely set out to write a history of liberty—he regarded the whole of history as the story of the enlargement of human liberty, which also meant the passing from the domination of force to the domination of ideas. He once asked, 'What is the way of Providence?' and answered, 'Towards liberty, its security, conception, enjoyment.' "[1]

* * *

No period of history is more congenial to Acton's mind than that which led from the Renaissance and Reformation to the American Revolution. For here his central themes—religion, power, and liberty—are more closely interwoven than ever before or since. Modern history for Acton began with the Renaissance which he, like Jacob Burckhardt, saw as a complete break with the preceding age and the foundation of a new order of things. The Ottoman conquest removed Byzantium from the main current of Western history. The end of the Italian wars and the sack of Rome by troops of Charles V removed Italy from European politics. Thereafter the triumphal rule of Charles V in alliance with the Church "roused the phantom of universal Empire. The motive of domination became a reigning force

---

[1] H. Butterfield, *Lord Acton* (London: The Historical Association, 1948), p. 11. The best study of Acton is by Gertrude Himmelfarb, *Lord Acton: A Study in Conscience and Politics* (Chicago: University of Chicago Press, 1952).

in Europe." Against this idea of power as right "the threatened interests were compelled to unite for the self-government of nations, the toleration of religions, and the rights of men. And it is by the combined efforts of the weak, made under compulsion, to resist the reign of force and constant wrong, that, in the rapid change but slow progress of four hundred years, liberty has been preserved, and secured, and extended, and finally understood." This, then, is the story Acton tells with freshness and vigor in this volume.

It was in the Netherlands that "the great transition was made, that religious change became political change, that the Revolution was evolved from the Reformation." On the road which started in the Netherlands, the Puritan Commonwealth was the second stage. "Seen from a distance the value of that epoch is not in that which it created, for it left not creations but ruins, but in the prodigious wealth of ideas which it sent into the world. And its ideas became efficacious and masterful by denying their origin." It was the point where the history of nations turned into its modern bed and the Englishman became its leader.

The English Revolution of 1688 was a great achievement because it was accomplished without bloodshed, without vengeance, without exclusion of entire parties, with so little definiteness in point of doctrine that the Act itself "was narrow, spiritless, confused, tame and unsatisfactory. It was perfectly compatible with the oppression of class by class. . . . No change took place in the governing class." The Revolution was strangely imperfect. The greater change was to come from Englishmen beyond the Atlantic. The American Revolution innovated upon the English. The Federal Constitution of 1787 was as strangely imperfect and unsatisfactory as the English Revolution of 1688. "And yet, by the development of the principle of federalism, it has produced a community more powerful, more prosperous, more intelligent, and more free than any other which the world has seen." With these words Lord Acton concluded his lectures on modern history before the undergraduates of Cambridge University in the year 1900.

Today we no longer look upon the Renaissance as the sharp break in history which it represented for Burckhardt and Acton. Instead we see a continuous development from the fourteenth to the seventeenth century. If there is any break we prefer to put it in the later seventeenth and early eighteenth century, when the spirit of liberty and the spirit of science took control of the human mind to a degree entirely unknown in the Renaissance and Reformation. From the seventeenth century on begins "this constancy of progress in the direction of organized and assured freedom" in which Acton saw the characteristic fact of modern history. In this successive deliverance and passage from uncritical subordination to critical independence modern historical science has played a great role. But, Acton warns, "history must be our deliverer not only from the undue influence of other times, but from the undue influence of our own, from the tyranny of environment and the pressure of the air we breathe."

* * *

John Emerich Edward Dalberg-Acton, later Eighth Baronet and then First Baron Acton, was born in 1834 in Naples, Italy. By inheritance he was an aristocrat, a Catholic, and a cosmopolitan; by personality he became a liberal, a moralist, and a scholar. His paternal great-grandfather, an Englishman, had embraced the Catholic faith and emigrated to France. His grandfather Sir John Acton (1736-1811) moved to Italy and became Commander-in-Chief of the Neopolitan navy and later prime minister of the kingdom, where he made himself intensely and rightly unpopular. The admiral's older son, Sir Richard, married the daughter and heiress of Emmerich Joseph Duc de Dalberg (1773-1833), a man of ancient German noble lineage who had entered the service of Napoleon and later of the Bourbons. From his uncle Karl Theodor von Dalberg (1744-1817), the last Archbishop-Elector of Mainz and Arch-Chancellor of the Holy Roman Empire, Emmerich Joseph inherited the family estate at Herrnsheim near Worms on the Rhine. When his daughter Marie Louise Pelline de Dalberg married Sir Richard, the latter assumed the additional name of Dalberg; and through this marriage the estates at Herrnsheim passed to Lord Acton, and were added to his English family estates in Shropshire. Thus he was from the beginning at home in Italy, England, and Germany. On both sides of his family he had high ecclesiastical connections. His father's younger brother Charles (1803-1847) was made a cardinal of the Church and Protector of the English College in Rome.

Soon the family moved from Italy to France where Acton's father died in 1837. Three years later his mother married the Second Earl of Granville (1815-1891) whose father was then British ambassador in Paris. Granville belonged to one of the great Whig houses. An amiable man, a Liberal and a Free Trader, who spoke French as well as

English, he filled many cabinet posts and was twice Foreign Secretary under Gladstone. Through the death of his father Acton became the eighth baronet at a very early age. He first went to school in Paris, and later to the Catholic Oscott College near Birmingham, whose president at the time was Nicholas Wiseman (1802-1865). Wiseman was a zealous ultramontane Catholic who became Cardinal and Archbishop of Westminster upon the re-establishment of the English Catholic hierarchy in 1850. Acton came under an entirely different influence when he went to Munich to study with Ignaz von Döllinger (1799-1890), Professor of Ecclesiastical History at the University. From this man, whose moral rectitude and courage matched the breadth of his scholarship and the strength of his faith, Acton learned to oppose Catholic intolerance and to insist on freedom of learning.

In 1859 Acton settled in England. For several years he edited Catholic periodicals and tried to impress upon them a spirit of impartial scholarship and high moral earnestness. His liberalism was censored by the Church, and the periodicals ceased publication. Acton turned to politics as a Liberal and a friend and supporter of Gladstone, but he felt as little at home there as in the Church. Like Gladstone, whom he deeply respected, he developed from more conservative to ever more liberal views. In 1869 he was raised to the peerage. He received honorary degrees from the universities of Munich, Cambridge, and Oxford. His reputation for vast learning was great. In 1895 he was made Regius Professor of Modern History at Cambridge, a post he filled until illness forced him to retire in 1901.

Despite his advantages of birth, connections, and education, Acton never achieved the goal he set for himself. He longed to influence Catholic thought, but was silenced by the Church. He hoped for a position in the Liberal cabinet or for an ambassadorial post. Neither came his way. He hardly played a role in political life. His prodigious learning and luminous style entitled him and his friends to expect great works from his pen. During his lifetime he published many articles, never a book. He left a great number of manuscript notes at the time of his death. They bear witness to his unusually wide reading and his illuminating insights, but they defy attempts at coherent organization. His fervent liberalism and his loyalty to the Catholic Church made him a lonely man. For the liberals, he was too Catholic; for the Catholics, too liberal; for both he was too impartial a historian, the keeper of man's conscience. The very qualities which made him lonely in the more complacent late Victorian age, have brought him recognition as a prophet in our perplexing and perplexed era of violence, of self-assured partisanship, and confident dogmatism.

* * *

Several years after Acton's death, his friends began to collect and publish his articles, letters, and university lectures in book form. By delving into his manuscript notes in the University of Cambridge library, scholars in our own time have revealed their infinite wealth and pertinence. A fuller image of Acton's personality and complex mind has emerged. The first of these publications was his *Lectures on Modern History*, which he delivered at Cambridge University in the academic years 1899-1900 and 1900-1901. They were published exactly in the form in which they were delivered by two of his admirers among Cambridge lecturers, John Neville Figgis and Reginald Vere Laurence. They first appeared in the fall of 1906 and were nine times reprinted, most recently in 1950.

Acton was not a systematic thinker. Yet there was unity in his thought because it revolved around three interrelated problems—liberty, power, and responsibility. He saw all three of them as a historian and he saw them critically, conscious of the complex tensions which each involved.

"Liberty, next to religion, had been the motive of good deeds and a common pretext of crime, from the sowing of the seed at Athens, 2460 years ago, until the ripened harvest was gathered by men of our race." Thus he began the lecture on "The History of Freedom in Antiquity," which he delivered in 1877. Later on in the lecture he defined liberty as "the assurance that every man shall be protected in doing what he believes is his duty against the influence of authority and majority, custom and opinion. The State is competent to assign duties and draw the line between good and evil in its immediate sphere. [Beyond these limits] it can only give indirect help to fight the battle of life by promoting the influences which prevail against temptation—religion, education, and the distribution of wealth." Liberty is an idea that "owes more to Cicero and Seneca, to Vinet and Tocqueville" than to laws and constitutions. It is "the only unity of the history of the world and the one principle of a philosophy of history." [2]

---

[2] Alexander Vinet (1797-1847) was a Protestant theologian in French Switzerland who stressed conscience as the seat of a moral individuality which nothing can rightly infringe. Hence he advocated complete freedom of religious belief.

At a time when people everywhere sacrifice liberty and truth to some supposedly higher ends, Acton reminds us that liberty is not a means to a higher political end. It is itself the highest political end. Because he thought that the American Revolution was fought for liberty as a pure principle, he overstressed its importance. In a review of James Bryce's *The American Commonwealth* he wrote: "Here or nowhere we have the broken chain, the rejected past, precedent and statutes superseded by unwritten law, sons wiser than their fathers, ideas rooted in the future, reason cutting as clean as Atropos." [3]

Acton quoted in agreement Lamartine's words: "La liberté est plus que l'esprit humain, c'est la conscience humaine" (Liberty is more than the spirit of man, it is his conscience). In summing up Acton's political philosophy Mr. Fasnacht wrote that his "center of interest is the common fortunes of mankind, his ideal a world of federal democracy, a world of real freedom based on the twin foundations of real comfort for the masses, and the sharing of a common moral ideal. It is the Christian alternative to Communism, an undenominational universalism, informed by the lessons of experience." [4]

Among Acton's manuscript notes there were the following: "There is no liberty where there is hunger. . . . The theory of liberty demands strong efforts to help the poor. Not merely for safety, for humanity, for religion, but for liberty." "Federalism . . . allows of different nationalities, religions, epochs of civilization to exist in harmony side by side. Capable of unlimited extension."

But Acton was no easy optimist about man or history. His faith was clear-sighted. He knew the strength of evil. His axiom that "Power tends to corrupt and absolute power corrupts absolutely," has been quoted many times. In his "Inaugural Lecture on the Study of History," he warned us to "suspect power more than vice." He distrusted great men more than little people. "Most assuredly, now as heretofore, the Men of the Time are, in most cases, unprincipled, and act from motives of interest, of passion, of prejudice cherished and unchecked, of selfish hope or unworthy fear," he wrote to Gladstone's younger daughter Mary. His anti-Machiavellian philosophy was best summed up in a manuscript note, "History is not a web

---

[3] Atropos was the inflexible of the three Greek Fates or Moirai, the one who cuts off the thread of life. Acton's judgment on the American Revolution is here much more radical than in his lectures on modern history. He overlooks both the dependence of the Revolution on the English tradition and the continuation of slavery.

[4] G. E. Fasnacht, *Acton's Political Philosophy* (New York: Viking, 1953), p. 200.

woven with innocent hands. Among all the causes which degrade and demoralize men, power is the most constant and the most active."

Power and untruth also corrupted the Church. Although a devout Catholic, Acton could not abide the doctrine of Papal infallibility promulgated by Pope Pius IX in 1870. Reviewing a book by Döllinger against Papal infallibility, Acton wrote in 1869 that, "the passage from the Catholicism of the Fathers to that of the modern Popes was accomplished by willful falsehood; and the whole structure of traditions, laws, and doctrines that supports the theory of infallibility, and the practical despotism of the Popes, stands on a basis of fraud." He bitterly attacked the Inquisition as the peculiar weapon of the Popes. "It is the principal thing with which the papacy is identified, and by which it must be judged," he wrote to Mary Gladstone. "That blot is so large and foul that it . . . eclipses the rest."

Acton was equally severe with the modern phenomenon of nationalism. His essay on "Nationality" (1862) has often been quoted.[5] The emphasis in any state on one race, one nationality or one religion, tends to diminish liberty in that state. "If we take the establishment of liberty for the realization of moral duties to be the end of civil society, we must conclude that those states are substantially the most perfect which . . . include various distinct nationalities without oppressing them." And in his manuscript notes Acton insisted that "the process of civilization depends on transcending Nationality. . . . Influences which are accidental yield to those which are rational. . . . The nations aim at power, and the world at freedom." The English historian George Macauley Trevelyan, who studied at Trinity College in Cambridge when Acton was there and later became its Master, wrote in his autobiography that he remembered Acton's saying to him that states based on the unity of a single race, like modern Italy and Germany, would prove dangerous to liberty. "I did not see what he meant at that time, but I do now!" [6]

[5] See Lord John E. Acton, *Essays on Freedom and Power*, ed. by Gertrude Himmelfarb (Boston: Beacon Press, 1948), pp. 166-195. This book also contains a bibliography of Acton's writings, compiled by Bert F. Hoselitz. See also on Acton and nationality, Hans Kohn *Prophets and Peoples. Studies in Nineteenth Century Nationalism* (4th Printing) (New York: Macmillan, 1957), Chapt. I.

[6] G. M. Trevelyan, *An Autobiography and Other Essays* (London: Longmans, Green, 1949), p. 18. There he also wrote about Acton's coming to Cambridge: "He at once created a deep impression in our somewhat provincial society. Dons of all subjects crowded to his oracular lectures, which were sometimes puzzling but always impressive. He had the brow of Plato, and the bearing of a sage who was also a man of the great world. . . . Though he was not a Protestant, he valued everyone's right to protest. Modern history was to him a record of the slow evolution of freedom and the rights of conscience, through a balance of rival forces."

Acton knew Germany and Italy well and therefore, unlike other British Liberals, had doubts about the value of German and Italian unification and the means employed. In his *Lectures on Modern History,* at the end of his lecture "On the Rise of Prussia," he insisted that the tremendous power, supported by millions of bayonets, established in Russia and Prussia, represented the greatest danger which Britain and the United States would have to face. He emphasized the difference in scope and goals of government as understood in St. Petersburg and Berlin, and as understood in London and Washington. To the first issue of the *English Historical Review,* which he helped to establish in 1886, he contributed an essay, "German Schools of History," in which he spoke of a phalanx of scholars, "the first classics of imperialism, a garrison of distinguished historians, that prepared the Prussian supremacy together with their own and now hold Berlin like a fortress." In those days it seemed an impregnable fortress, but, as in all fortresses, those within had a limited view of the outside world and a distorted perspective. Acton enjoyed a broader and truer perspective.

In this perspective Acton viewed not only nationality but also class. "The danger is not that a particular class is unfit to govern," he wrote. "Every class is unfit to govern." In one of his manuscript notes he insisted that in "the poorer class . . . their interests are the most sacred." If there is a free contract between capital and labor in the open market, as Liberal economists insisted, then, Acton wrote to Mary Gladstone in April, 1881, "It cannot be right that one of the two contracting parties should have the making of the laws, the management of the conditions, the keeping of the peace, the administration of justice, the distribution of taxes, the control of expenditure, in its own hands exclusively. It is unjust that all these securities, all these advantages, should be on the same side."

In one of the great passages of historical writing, which occurs early in his *Lectures on Modern History,* Acton rejects the adoration of success and the social Darwinism so characteristic of the later nineteenth century. "The passion for power over others can never cease to threaten mankind, and is always sure of finding new and unforeseen allies in continuing its martyrology. . . . Progress has imposed increasing sacrifices on society, in behalf of those who can make no return, from whose welfare it derives no equivalent benefit. . . ." The progress of civilization "depends on preserving, at infinite cost, which is infinite loss, the crippled child and the victim of accident, the idiot and the madman, the pauper and the culprit, the old and infirm, curable and incurable. This growing dominion of disinterested motive, this liberality towards the weak, in social life, corresponds to that respect for the minority, in political life, which is the essence of freedom." [7]

* * *

Acton saw it as the responsibility of the historian to be impartial and fair, swayed neither by the interests of, or preference for, nationality or class, religion or state. In the spirit of universal morality and comprehension, Lionel Kochan writes, "Many of Acton's aphorisms demand of the historian that he understand his opponents so much better than they do themselves as to be able to improve their case for them." Acton went beyond the general standards of fairness. "We estimate a historian," he wrote, "very much less by his own ideas than by the justice he does to the ideas which he rejects—not for his national, his religious views, but for his appreciation of nations, religions, parties not his own." When his old teacher and respected friend, Döllinger, found extenuating circumstances for the Inquisition in the spirit of its time, Acton disputed him. He wished "to judge by manifest canons and not by sympathy; to apply the canons equitably to friend and foe, leaving no room for favor, or privilege, or prejudice. For I observed that everybody is determined by likes and dislikes, by something in his own wishes and experience, and all this I knew must be shut out of conscientious history." [8]

As Acton turned against Döllinger for his leniency in judging the Inquisition, he turned also against Mandell Creighton, an Anglican historian, founder and editor of the *English Historical Review*. There Acton reviewed Creighton's *History of the Papacy During the Reformation* in a sharply critical way. In his letter to Creighton of April 5, 1887, Acton's famous and much quoted sentence about power occurs. It occurs in connection with the responsibility of the historian. "I cannot accept," he wrote, "that we are to judge Pope and King unlike other men, with a favorable presumption that they did no wrong. If there is any presumption, it is the other way against holders of power, increasing as the power increases. . . . The inflexi-

---

[7] The same thought recurs in many of his manuscript notes where he describes progress as "consideration for the individual, not for society; wounded and captive, accused prisoner; condemned convict; afflicted in body or in mind; indigent poor; the very old and very young; the sick man and the exposed."

[8] Lionel Kochan, *Acton on History* (London: A. Deutsch, 1954), pp. 61, 82 f.

ble integrity of the moral code is, to me, the secret of the authority, the dignity, the utility of history. If we may debase the currency for the sake of genius, or success, or rank or reputation, we may debase it for the sake of a man's influence, of his religion, of his party, of his disgrace." [9] When Gladstone turned to Acton, seeking confirmation of his stand for revealed religion, Acton reproached the man whom he revered more than any other political figure of his time "for exaggerating the moral superiority of Christianity over Paganism, for not taking seriously the Biblical criticism of Strauss and Renan, and for ignoring the fact that it took deists and unbelievers to sweep away 'that appalling edifice of intolerance, tyranny, cruelty,' by which Christians had hoped to perpetuate their belief." [10]

Acton was a genuine humanitarian in deep sympathy with democracy. In this respect he agreed with the most "progressive" urge of the nineteenth century. But he did not share the easy, illusionary optimism of his age. Since he knew the evil that persists in man, the cruelties and anxieties of the twentieth century could not have forced him to re-evaluate his liberalism. He would not have sought refuge in a call for religious revival, nor in doubt or condemnation of scientific or technological advance. As a historian he would have insisted that the ages of faith had certainly not been more respectful of human life and dignity than the present age.[11] For this reason Acton more than other nineteenth-century historians who have masterpieces of historical writing to their credit remains of living and immediate concern to our generation. What counts with him is not the work he completed but the spirit which animated him. It shone through his *Lectures on Modern History* and made them forever remarkable. They remain for us as for John Pollock, one of his students, "a wonderful work of art, such as in all likelihood will never again be witnessed."

---

9 Mandell Creighton (1843-1901) became in 1884 Professor of Ecclesiastical History at Cambridge and in 1897 Bishop of London, succeeding Dr. Frederick Temple when the latter became Archbishop of Canterbury and Primate of the Church of England. The Acton-Creighton correspondence is reprinted in Lord John Acton, *op. cit.*, pp. 357-373. The letters by both men are testimony to their high intellectual and moral standard.

10 Gertrude Himmelfarb, *op. cit.*, p. 167.

11 See Lionel Kochan, *op. cit.*, p. 139 f.; and Gertrude Himmelfarb, *op. cit.*, p. 240 f.

9

James Bryce and the Holy Roman Empire*

In a long, rich, and productive life James Bryce wrote only one book which can properly be called a historian's work. Yet this book immediately established itself as a classic. It has served until today—that is, for almost a century—as the main source from which students all over the world have gained deeper understanding of the ideas underlying the political thought of the Middle Ages. Although these ideas now belong to the past, yet, like so many other relics, they continue to exercise an often subterranean influence on the thought, emotion, and actions of peoples. Thus Bryce's *The Holy Roman Empire* not only informs the reader about the nature of the medieval mind and the continuation and transformation of the Roman idea as it survived in the Roman Church and the German Empire; it also sharpens his awareness of the survival of this idea, in adulterated forms, in some of the "modern" movements of our day.

Bryce's classic book was a work of his youth. It originated in a prize essay which the twenty-four-year old student, newly elected Fellow of Oriel College in Oxford, submitted in 1862. Two years later it was published as a slender volume of 170 pages. It was immediately hailed as one of the most remarkable studies in the history of ideas—comparable to *Die Kultur der Renaissance in Italien* which the then forty-two-year old Swiss historian, Jacob Burckhardt, had published four years before. In subsequent editions *The Holy Roman Empire* grew into a volume of more than 450 pages. It went through thirty-five printings—the latest in 1956—and was translated into many languages.

The changes and enlargements in the edition of 1873 and especially that of 1904 were made not merely to accommodate new scholarly insights. Under the impact of Bismarck's establishment of the Second German Empire, Bryce went further and added new chapters on the history of German nationalism, a subject hardly connected

* From the Introduction to James Bryce, *The Holy Roman Empire* (New York: Schocken Books, Inc., 1961). Reprinted by permission.

with the ideas underlying the Holy Roman Empire. For, in truth, the Holy Roman Empire was in origin and substance the representation of a non-nationalist age, in fact the very antithesis of nationalism. To confound it with later German nationalist developments obscured their true character and helped to bring about disastrous consequences. But when Bryce's book appeared in the 1860's, its analysis of the inner meaning and significance of the Holy Roman Empire attracted attention because of the almost simultaneous sequence of events through which Bismarck raised Prussia to a paramount position in Europe.

This new German Empire, whose creation and basic idea really ran counter to both German tradition and the nature of the Holy Roman Empire, was often identified in German historiography and public opinion with the Empire, which had existed for 1,000 years, from 800 to 1806. The identification gave rise to misleading myths and dreams. This "Second Empire" of Bismarck lasted less than half a century. It was followed, under Hitler, by a supposedly "Third Empire" or "Reich" which in a dangerous way mixed the most objectionable features of the "First" and "Second" Empires, while overlooking or rejecting whatever good features and traditions they possessed. Hitler's "Third Empire," which claimed that it would last for 1,000 years as had the "First Empire," collapsed after only twelve years of existence and buried in its ruins whatever remnants there were of the Holy Roman Empire or of Bismarck's Reich. Thus this collapse may have brought to an end the dangerous influence which the imperial idea, the idea of the Reich, exercised upon the German mind.

* * *

Burckhardt's classic treatise on the Renaissance stressed a sharp difference between the Renaissance, which inaugurated a new era, and the thought and society of the period which preceded it. Like Goethe, Burckhardt went back, beyond the Middle Ages and Rome, to the humanism of the Greeks, and celebrated its rebirth in fifteenth-century Italy. His book was not a narrative history of events, but an analysis of underlying ideas, of the intellectual and moral climate of the period. The same can be said of Bryce's treatise on the Holy Roman Empire. It is an essay on the history of ideas. However, Bryce's work is not limited, as is Burckhardt's, to one century and one country. It covers the long period from the Barbaric Invasions to the Napoleonic Age, and treats of lands and orders which have "almost wholly passed away from the world." To make his book more readily accessible to the student of history, Bryce rightly added some account of the great events and territorial shifts which marked the growth and decay of the idea of the Holy Roman Empire.

Burckhardt's and Bryce's approaches to the history of ideas differ also in another point: the former put emphasis on civilization and the arts, the latter on political systems and institutions. Burckhardt was fascinated by Greece; Bryce by Rome. Rome meant not a creative explosion of the arts and sciences as did the Greek city-states, but the cultivation of law and of political and administrative institutions which helped to unify its immense territory within an order of peace and justice.

This difference in interest follows indeed from the different backgrounds of the two scholars. Burckhardt was a burgher living a retired life in the small and quiet city-republic of Basel; Bryce was a citizen of a mightily expanding empire, himself actively interested in politics, law, and diplomacy, and holding high positions in the most varied fields. Burckhardt traveled extensively in Italy, which he loved deeply; her ancient art centers became his spiritual home. Bryce, too, loved Italy and Rome, but he traveled throughout the civilized world.

This typically British familarity with the world at large and with the ways and responsibilities of public office gave Bryce's writing a density and sustained interest seldom found in historical treatises. He was a master of English style. His language is lucid and often rises to passages of great beauty. Thus he succeeds in evoking for the student of today the importance in universal history of an idea whose power and fascination modern minds can scarcely apprehend.

* * *

James Bryce (1838-1922) was born in Belfast, Ulster province, of Scottish parents. His father was headmaster of the high school in Glasgow, and Bryce studied at the University of Glasgow. He excelled in classical studies as well as law and modern history. In 1857 he was elected to a scholarship at Oxford. This coincided with the start of a decade whose great intellectual and political transformations agitated the minds of mid-Victorian England. In 1859 Darwin's *On the Origin of the Species by Means of Natural Selection* appeared; its whole first edition was sold out on the day of issue. In 1867 the broadening of suffrage was widely discussed and, with the second Parliamentary Reform Bill, the age of democracy dawned in Britain. On all these issues Bryce took his stand on the side of liberalism and democracy.

In 1867 he contributed a chapter to *Essays on Reform,* the collective effort of a group of academic Liberals. When his opponents cited examples from ancient Greece, Rome, and contemporary France to point out the evils of democracy, Bryce replied by showing that the Greek republics were all slave states ignorant of the brotherhood of man. While England was closer to Rome than to Greece, Rome was never a democracy either. And as for contemporary France, he simply quoted Tocqueville's remark that "France did not demonstrate the evils of democracy but the evils of a democratic state of society without a democratic government." To exemplify the merits of democracy Bryce referred to the United States and Switzerland. Class government, he maintained, was inherently bad because it was inherently selfish. "The real danger of England now is not from the working class," he wrote, "for no working class in any country was ever more peaceably disposed than ours is, but from the isolation of classes." The century which has since passed has borne out his confidence in British democracy.

In 1870 Bryce was appointed Regius Professor of Civil Law at Oxford, a chair he held until 1893. That same year he made his first visit to the United States. In the late 1870's he wrote articles for the New York weekly, *The Nation,* then brilliantly edited by Edwin Lawrence Godkin, in which he attacked the foreign policy of Disraeli's Conservative government. Bryce bitterly castigated the Turkish persecution of the Armenians and followed his leader, Gladstone, in advocating Irish home rule.

In 1888 he was elected to the House of Commons and in later years joined several Liberal cabinets. He revisited the United States in 1881 and in 1883, and as a result of his studies and observations wrote his second great work, *The American Commonwealth,* published in 1888, half a century after Tocqueville's *Démocratie en Amérique.* The two men approached the subject in different ways. Tocqueville was less interested in the United States itself than in democracy in general, less in forms and institutions of government than in the conditions of social life. Bryce discussed social conditions only in the third volume of his work, where he analyzed the impact of public opinion and social institutions on politics. He was able, as Tocqueville was not, to discuss institutions in the United States from the viewpoint of a constitutional lawyer, for in contrast to Tocqueville he was deeply familiar with English history and the working of English institutions. He was rightly convinced that the whole American fabric was founded, in the first instance, upon English constitutional and legal traditions.

He went to the United States as a convinced democrat and his studies and experiences there confirmed his faith. "America marks the highest level," he wrote, "not only of material well-being but of intelligence and happiness, which a race has yet attained." He clearly saw the dangers in American democracy but remained confident about the outcome. "The Americans have fortunately the power of recognizing, trusting and following a strong and honest man. In this quality, coupled with that instinct for order, that sense of justice, that freedom from class bitterness which belong to the native American, we may perhaps find the best ground for hope for the future of the nation."

In 1907 Bryce was appointed Ambassador to the United States, the first nonprofessional diplomat to fill this coveted post. At his retirement in 1913 he was created a viscount. He availed himself of his experiences in the United States and his travels in Canada, Latin America, Australia, and New Zealand to publish in 1921, at the age of eighty-three, the two volumes of his *Modern Democracies*. After a general historical introduction, in which he also discussed Spanish America, Bryce devoted most of the book to an analysis of the forms of government in six countries—France, Switzerland, Canada, the United States, Australia, and New Zealand. In his concluding remarks Bryce expressed certain fears about the future of democracy: "Democracy has become, all over Europe, and to some extent even in North America also, desired merely as a means, not as an end, precious in itself because it was the embodiment of liberty. It is now valued, not for what it is, but for what it may be used to win for the masses. When the exercise of their civil rights has brought them that which they desire, and when they feel sure that what they have won will remain with them, may they not cease to care for the further use of those rights? . . . If that which the masses really desire should turn out to be the extinction of private property or some sort of communistic system, and if in some countries such a system should ever be established, the whole character of government would be changed, and that which is now called democracy would become a different thing altogether, perhaps an industrial bureaucratic oligarchy."

But these doubts in no way diminished his faith in the vitality and fecundity of American democracy. He firmly believed in the soundness of its institutions and in its future. He rejected, and tried to refute, the widespread belief in the tyranny and fickleness of the majority and in democratic incapacity for energetic action. He was in no way convinced that the higher education of the upper class was a safer guide in politics than the political sentiments of the masses who, though more slowly, arrive more frequently at the right decision.

During the First World War Lord Bryce, while taking his stand whole-heartedly on the side of democracy, adhered to the great liberal tradition of which he was one of the best representatives. In his Presidential Address, delivered to the British Academy on June 30, 1915, he warned that "time modifies our judgment as it cools our passions. Neither the friendships nor the enmities of the nations are exempt from change. It is better that nothing should be said today in an address to the Academy which any one of its members, to whatever country he may belong, would feel pain in reading ten or twenty years hence. Newspapers and pamphlets will convey to posterity sufficiently, and even more than sufficiently, the notions and fancies and passions of the moment." In another Presidential Address the following year, on July 14, 1916, he insisted that "the study of philosophy and history has done little for those of us who pursue it if it has not extended their vision beyond their own country and their own time, pointing out to them that human progress has been achieved by the united efforts of many races and many types of intellect and character, each profiting by the efforts of the others, and also reminding them that for further advance this cooperation is essential. To restore it is at this moment impossible. But let us at least do nothing to retard its return in happier days."

His love for the United States, his faith in democracy, his desire for peace inspired the course of his lectures on his last visit to America. He appealed to Americans "to take their share in the great task of raising international relations to a higher plane." He would not venture to prescribe the mode in which Americans should do it, for that must be left to them; but he asked them to take their share, each assuming his responsibility as the citizen of a great nation in helping to form public opinion. The lectures appeared in book form under the title, *International Relations,* in 1922, shortly after Lord Bryce's death.[1]

* * *

Most of Lord Bryce's great works, based on keen observation of political realities, bear out his training and experience as a British lawyer and politician. They may be called thoroughly practical in character. *The Holy Roman Empire* shares with them the erudite scholarship, the philosophic insight, and the judicial temperament of the author. But it deals less with the concrete workings of a state and its institutions than with a "wonderful" and, to the modern reader, perplexing "system of ideas." To the modern mind, which has been trained since the seventeenth century to think critically and practically, these ideas may appear absurd or fantastic. As far as this writer knows, there is no other work which brings to the modern student a similar grasp of the power of the ideas which dominated the medieval mind.

Medieval thinkers, enthralled by the majesty of their own theory, a theory which existed outside the sphere of fact, were not disturbed by fact inconsistent with it. Their conception of a universal Christian commonwealth was a part of that imaginative vision and mystic sense, on which even our own imagination, poetry, and legend still feed. It was founded upon the earlier reality of Roman domination. But more important even than the reality of Roman rule—although Bryce does not stress this sufficiently—was the assimilation by Rome of the Greek Stoic philosophy of cosmopolitanism. For under the impact of this philosophy the Roman Empire changed. Had it been dynastic or national or attached to its own center, it would have fallen with the destruction of the city or with the defeat of the ruling tribe; but it was not so limited or localized. "It was imperishable because it was universal; and when its power had ceased, it was remembered with awe and love by the races whose separate existence it had destroyed, because it had granted equal rights to all, and closed against none of its subjects the path of honorable ambition. When the military power of the conquering city had departed, her sway over the world of thought began. . . . The magic of her name remained, and she held sway over the imagination which the passing

---

[1] The standard biography *James Bryce* was written by H. A. L. Fisher (1865-1940), who, like Bryce himself, was an Oxford man, a Liberal, a historian and a man of letters, a member of the House of Commons and of the Cabinet. The book appeared in New York: Macmillan, 1927.

of century after century scarcely reduced. She had gathered up and embodied in her literature and institutions all the ideas and all the practical results of ancient thought. Embracing, organizing, and propagating the new religion, she made it seem her own. Her language, her theology, her laws, her architecture made their way where the eagles of war had never winged their flight."

The Middle Ages accepted the idea of the universal dominion of Empire and Papacy, based upon the imprescriptible rights of Rome, without regard to the actions of individual emperors or popes or the actual exercise of their power. The human spirit was then "prostrated before authority and tradition" and the exercise of private judgment "was impossible to most and sinful to all." Life, with its ferocity, violence, and disorder, was made bearable by the passion for unity. The modern insistence on verification, individualism, and pluralism was unthinkable.

It is the story of this persistence of the Roman idea within ever-changing historical contexts which Bryce unfolds with style and clarity. This idea shaped Europe, or at least Western Europe, until, contemporaneously with the settlement of the New World, there emerged the philosophy of life and government upon which the United States is based. That Bryce's penetrating vision could embrace both the Holy Roman Empire of the Middle Ages and the United States, which from its beginnings was the most modern nation, testifies to the catholicity of his education and understanding.

When the Roman Empire was destroyed by barbaric invasions, the conception of this Empire as a necessary part of the world's order did not vanish. The idea was admitted by the very conquerors who destroyed its representation on earth. It was accepted in its fullness by the Roman Church. It was cherished by the peoples who had formerly been vanquished by Rome and who now looked back upon it as a golden age of peace and order. The Dark Ages came to an end when, in 800 A.D., Charlemagne and the Pope restored the Empire in the West. Thereby they laid the foundation for the emergence of the Western world of Latins and Germans. This world remained the center of our understanding of history, until the eighteenth century, when Russia and the Near East entered into active partnership with it, and broadened its basis. Even this basis has become too narrow in our own day. The revitalization of Asia and Africa have transformed the idea of a single world history and world order, as envisaged by the Roman Empire, into an incipient reality.

James Bryce and the Holy Roman Empire

Yet within the very narrow frame of the Stoic Roman Empire and the Christian Western Empire the idea of unity and universal order shone with an all-pervasive splendor of which our age shows no trace. For then this idea had its foundation, it was believed, in the very nature of the divine universe, in which an exact correspondence of heaven and earth reigned. The Holy Roman Church and the Holy Roman Empire were one and the same thing, seen from different sides. Both rested upon the universality of Rome. Their mystic dualism corresponded to the two natures of the Founder of the Church, He who was born into His earthly existence by divine providence under the reign of Augustus, the founder of the Roman Empire. Accordingly, it was believed that men's souls were entrusted to the Pope; their bodies to the Emperor.

At no time did factual reality correspond to theory. But this discrepancy was characteristic of the age and was not felt as such. "At no time in the world's history," Bryce writes, "has theory, professing all the while to control practice, been so utterly divorced from it. Ferocious and sensual, the age worshipped humility and asceticism; there has never been a purer ideal of love, nor a grosser profligacy of life." Magnificent theories were proclaimed which no one attempted to carry out. "While everyone believed in the rights of the Empire as a part of divine truth, no one would yield to them where his own passions or interests interfered. Resistance to God's Vicar might be, and indeed was, admitted to be a deadly sin, but it was one which few hesitated to commit." At no time was the theory of the Holy Roman Empire more strikingly set forth than in the treatise *De Monarchia* which Dante, the greatest and most representative mind of the age, wrote at the very moment when the last shred of real power was torn from the imperial dignity.[2]

* * *

Even at the height of the Middle Ages the idea of one Empire and one Church, as glorified by Dante, hardly took note of the fact that the Roman Empire continued in Constantinople, the new or Second Rome, where Constantine I had transferred and consecrated the capital. The truly Holy Roman Empire was there, for its history started

[2] Dante's treatise is probably the most revealing single document of the medieval concept of the Empire. See James Bryce, *The Holy Roman Empire* (New York: St. Martins, 1956), pp. 278-284; and the translation by Herbert W. Schneider, *On World-Government* or *De Monarchia* by Dante Alighieri (New York: The Liberal Arts Press, 1950).

not with a pagan Rome but with a city consecrated by Christian bishops. This Eastern Roman Empire lasted for over 1,000 years, from the accession of Arcadius in 395, when the real separation of East and West began, to the conquest of Constantinople by the Turks in 1453. The civil and military administration of the Eastern Empire was much superior to that of its Western rival. Until recently scant attention was paid by Western thinkers and historians to the Roman Empire which continued in a legitimate line in Constantinople. Its advanced civilization has been carefully studied only since Bryce first published his book. After the fall of Constantinople the princes and people of Moscow, who were as much a religious as a political community, claimed the succession to the Eastern, or true, Roman Empire. Moscow was proclaimed the new or Third Rome, which was to stand to the end of history, for a Fourth Rome was regarded as inconceivable.

This Eastern Empire was not disturbed by the conflict which raged in the West, where in the thirteenth century each of three different parties asserted itself as the true source of the imperial office—the Emperor, the Pope, and the people of Rome. In the thirteenth century the papal and imperial claims reached their high points. With the fall of the Hohenstaufen dynasty the glory began to decline rapidly, never to recover. Fifty years later, the Pope removed the court from Rome to Avignon and this "Babylonian captivity" lasted for seventy years, to be followed immediately by the great Schism which lasted another forty years. The city of Rome has scarcely a building to commemorate this period; to her "they were times of turmoil and misery, times in which the shame of the present was embittered by recollections of the brighter past."

After the fourteenth century the Holy Roman Empire, in theory a world empire, became more and more a purely Germanic Empire. Yet the myth of its former glory survived as an illusion. The imperial dignity was extolled by writers whose imaginations were enthralled by the glories of a legendary past. "The Germans," Bryce writes, "had confounded the two characters of their sovereign so long, and grown so fond of the style and pretensions of a dignity whose possession appeared to exalt them above the other people of Europe, that it was now too late for them to separate the local from the universal monarch."

The most powerful of the Hohenstaufen emperors, Frederick Barbarossa, was believed to lie asleep deep down in the Kyffhäuser

Mountain in central Germany. If Germany were ever in need of a saviour, he would rise and lead her to the glory of a new golden age. Compared with this certainty of salvation, the actual events of German history and the realities of the world outside paled. In their hearts the Germans felt that their true ruler, the *heimliche Kaiser*, was ever ready to come to their rescue. Under the spell of such legends, Germans were sometimes in danger of losing sight of political realities and of abandoning themselves to wistful dreams.

The Reformation destroyed the very basis of an imperial idea which was founded on the assumption that the limits of Church and State were co-extensive. The united Christendom which the Empire was created to represent had now vanished. After exulting for centuries in the heritage of Roman rule, half of the Germans now turned against it to exult in Arminius, the barbaric prince who defeated the Romans. In the treaty of Westphalia of 1648, "the last link which bound Germany as a whole to Rome was snapped, the last of the principles by which the Empire had existed was abandoned." But the fiction and illusion continued for another 150 years.

The official end came in August, 1806, when the last Holy Roman Emperor resigned the imperial dignity. A new claimant to the imperial title had arisen: Napoleon Bonaparte, who regarded himself as Charlemagne's successor and as lawful emperor of the West. His imperial throne, based on the two capitals of Paris and Rome, seemed the first on earth. Like Charlemagne, he wished to found the empire in collaboration with the Roman Church yet without allowing it to be weakened by papal claims. To the Ecclesiastical Committee, Napoleon declared on March 16, 1811: "The present epoch carries us back to the time of Charlemagne. All the kingdoms, principalities, and duchies which formed themselves out of the debris of the Empire have been rejuvenated under our laws. The Church of my empire is the Church of the Occident and of almost the whole of Christendom." In 1811 this Empire, with its frontiers on the Elbe, the Ebro and the Adriatic Sea, was practically co-extensive with that of Charlemagne.

This new Empire of the West collapsed when it challenged the Empire of the East. The new Rome of Moscow turned back the new Rome of Napoleon. But the real victor was modern Britain. In the liberal nineteenth century a revival of Rome, whether in the West or in the East, was an anachronism. Napoleon's liberal opponent, Benjamin Constant, in his *De l'esprit de conquête et de l'usurpation dans leurs rapports avec la civilization européenne* (1813), saw in imperial wars the instrument of the past, and in commerce that of modern civilization. "Carthage, fighting with Rome in ancient times, had to succumb; it had the force of circumstances against it. But if the fight between Rome and Carthage were taking place today, Carthage would have the universe on its side. *Elle aurait pour alliés les moeurs actuelles et le génie du monde* [Carthage would have as her allies present-day morality and the spirit of the world]."

In 1806 the history of the Holy Roman Empire itself came to an end. Less than ten years later Napoleon's effort to assume its succession ended in disaster. At that point Bryce's original book ended, too. Yet the imperial glory of the past continued to haunt the three peoples—Germans, French, and Italians—who in various ways regarded themselves as its heirs. The century from 1850 to 1950 was filled with unfortunate attempts to revive the imperial idea, to fight the commercial spirit of the modern West on behalf of Roman virtue. The fascination of the myth of the past misled these peoples, and their attempts at revival ended in disaster. In two additional chapters Lord Bryce told, in the 1904 edition of his book, of the beginnings of this revival of the imperial idea. These two chapters, which are omitted in the present edition, no longer show the penetrating insight of the preceding chapters. They are filled with the spirit of an unfounded optimism about the trends which led to the renewal of the imperial idea, an optimism typical of British liberal thought in the second half of the nineteenth century as it contemplated developments on the European continent.

* * *

The forty years between the first publication of Bryce's book (1864) and its final revision (1904) witnessed the unification of Italy and Germany, the two countries in which the idea of the Holy Roman Empire had settled its terrestrial foundation. In one and the same year, 1870, Bismarck established the new German Empire on the victory of the Prussian army over imperial France, and the new Italian kingdom took possession of Rome, the ancient imperial seat with all its haunting memories. Bryce was in full sympathy with this trend of events. Without much hesitation he followed the official line taken at the time by German and Italian national historiography.

Bismarck's German Empire or Reich was, in spite of many differences, regarded by Bryce as being "in a real sense the representative" of the Holy Roman Empire. Bismarck's creation gave, according to Bryce, "a new and more cheerful meaning to all that has gone before. It is, in a moral and intellectual sense, the offspring of the old Empire." This was the theory then being proposed by the Prussian school of German historiography. Under the impact of the Prussian victories it was soon generally accepted, but it was an entirely new interpretation of German history and represented a break with the main line of German tradition.

This new interpretation shifted the center of German history from the West, that is, the Rhineland, to Prussia in the northeast. It made Protestantism its dominant and creative religion, and based this religion upon a strictly nation-centered concept. Its outlook was not only anti-Roman but anti-Western. It held that following the fall of the mighty Hohenstaufen, German history reached a new climax in the Prussian-led War of Liberation against France in 1813-1814 and a fulfillment in Prussia's victory over France in 1870. Speaking of Prussia's rulers, the German historian Johann Gustav Droysen declared in 1848: "To the Hohenzollern belongs the place which has been empty since the days of the Hohenstaufen."

At the time of the great flowering of the German mind in the second half of the eighteenth century no German historian or representative thinker would have accepted this thesis. Prussia then appeared alien to the German mind. Its garrison spirit was repugnant to the pacifist, cosmopolitan ideology of the average German intellectual. Travelling in southern Germany in the later years of the reign of Frederick the Great of Prussia, Friedrich Nicolai, the well-known Berlin bookseller and publisher, wrote that "these free people look down upon us poor people from Brandenburg as slaves." Eleven years before, Gotthold Ephraim Lessing, on August 25, 1769, wrote to Nicolai: "Don't tell me of your Berlin freedom of thinking and writing. It reduces itself exclusively to the liberty of saying as much nonsense about religion as one wishes. And by now the honest man must be ashamed to make use of this liberty. But let anyone in Berlin try to . . . tell the truth to the noble Court rabble there as Sonnenfels did in Vienna; let anyone in Berlin raise his voice for the rights of the subjects against exploitation and despotism, as is now being done even in France and Denmark, and you will soon learn which country is even today the most enslaved in Europe."

The great art historian, Johann Joachim Winckelmann, a Prussian subject, escaped to Rome and wrote in 1763 that he shuddered from head to foot whenever he thought of the Prussian despotism and of Frederick. This slave driver of peoples would transform his country into an abomination for men; "better to be a circumcised Turk than a Prussian." Another Prussian subject, Johann Gottfried Herder, advocated the dismemberment of Prussia for the happiness of its people and prophesied that Frederick's work would remain sterile and his Empire disintegrate.[3]

The paradoxical identification of Bismarck's Prussian Germany with the old Reich which had fascinated the imagination of the Middle Ages had dangerous consequences for German political thought. "It was the tradition of the glorious past when Germany led the world," Bryce writes, "that made the Germans again a united people, the central power of continental Europe." The consciousness of being heirs to the Reich made the Germans feel much superior to the other peoples of Europe, a feeling entirely unknown to Kant or Goethe. The Germans made the mistake of regarding the temporary superiority of Bismarck's diplomacy and of Prussian arms as something permanent, something inherent in the national character and its history. In reality it was a passing phenomenon and the feeling of superiority only helped to make it more passing. But when the Bismarckian Prussian Empire collapsed in 1918, the Germans not only clung to its fundamental concept of a Berlin-centered Reich— the republican constitution of Weimar maintained the official title Deutsches Reich—but also intensified it in proud defiance of the West.

The assumed heritage of the Roman Empire confused not only the Germans but also the Italians. It burdened the young and weak Italian nation with a legacy of the past which like a will-o'-the-wisp drew it from the patient mastering of reality to the world-embracing dreams of Roman ghosts. Giuseppe Mazzini, the prophet of Italian nationalist regeneration, wished to found it on the rock of eternal Rome. Twice Rome had guided mankind in the past, under the Caesars and under the Popes. Would not a Third Rome, the Rome of the People, rise to even greater heights in the future? Writing in 1871, Mazzini demanded the creation of a vast colonial empire over the southern shores of the Mediterranean. "The Roman standard did float over those lands in the days when, after the fall of Carthage, the

---

[3] On the interpretation of German history, see Hans Kohn, *The Mind of Germany* (New York: Charles Scribner's Sons, 1960); and *The Idea of Nationalism* (7th Printing) (New York: Macmillan, 1958), Chapt. VII.

Mediterranean was named our sea. We were masters of the whole of that region up to the fifth century." This identification of present-day Italy with the Roman past haunted many Italians until 1945.[4]

Bryce's contemporary, Lord Acton, recognized more clearly than did Bryce the dangers inherent in modern nationalism and the identification of this nationalism with past stages of history. In an article written in 1862 Acton warned that a state which identifies itself too closely with one nationality or one class tends to become absolute. Diversity, he wrote, is a corrective against intolerance. Deeply trained in the German method of scientific history which he helped to introduce in Britain, he had no illusions about the Prussian German Reich established in Berlin. Speaking of the Prussian government, he stressed its fundamental difference from the Western type of government. "Government so understood is the intellectual guide of the nation, the promoter of wealth, the teacher of knowledge, the guardian of morality, the mainspring of the ascending movement of man. That is the tremendous power, supported by millions of bayonets, which grew up in the days of which I have been speaking at Petersburg, and was developed by much abler minds, chiefly at Berlin; and it is the greatest danger that remains to be encountered by the Anglo-Saxon race."[5]

No finality can be claimed for any historical idea or any historical form of government. The collapse of the Third Reich in Berlin and of the Third Rome on the Tiber may have laid the ghost of the Holy Roman Empire to its rest. Its last two representations were unholy travesties of a great idea of the past. Today the myth of the Reich seems to have lost its fascination for the German mind. There is no longer a *Deutsches Reich* but a Federal Republic of Germany. The center of gravity has shifted from Prussia in the northeast, westward to the Rhine where it has traditionally belonged. The intellectual and social orientation of Germany is today no longer self-centered and turned against the West. Rather, Germany has again become part of the common Western development. The state of Prussia no longer exists and its former dominant class has been uprooted. The city of Königsberg, in eastern Prussia, where in 1701 the

---

[4] See Hans Kohn, *Prophets and Peoples: Studies in Nineteenth Century Nationalism* (4th Printing) (New York: Macmillan, 1957), Chapt. III; and Guido de Ruggiero, *The History of European Liberalism*, tran. by R. G. Collingwood (London: Oxford University Press, 1927), pp. 298-324.

[5] See Lord John E. E. Dalberg-Acton *Lectures on Modern History* (New York: Schocken Paperbacks, 1961), pp. 289 and 314.

Electors of Brandenburg assumed the newly created royal crown of Prussia, has been renamed Kaliningrad. Thus the last sentence with which Bryce concluded his book in 1864 can, in slightly varied form, be applied to the Germans of today. The Reich, the Holy Roman Empire, which to the Germans of 1860-1945 loomed so large on the horizon of the past, will to the Germans of today sink lower and lower as they journey onward into the future. But its importance for the past history of Europe, it can never lose.

PART THREE

Aspects of Nationalism

10

Napoleon and the Age of Nationalism*

A sincere patriotism, a deep attachment to the soil and people of France, inspired Robespierre. It provided a moving lyrical undertone to the tragic sternness of his reports: "Yes, this delightful land which we inhabit and which nature caresses with love is made to be the domain of liberty and happiness; this sensitive and proud people is truly born for glory and virtue. O my fatherland, if fate had caused me to be born in a foreign and distant country, I would have addressed heaven continuously with wishes for thy prosperity; I would have been moved to tears by the recital of thy combats and thy virtues; my attentive soul would have followed with a restless ardor all of the movements of thy glorious revolution; I would have envied the fate of thy citizens; I would have envied that of thy representatives. I am French, I am one of thy representatives. . . . O sublime people! Accept the sacrifices of my whole being; happy is the man who is born in your midst; happier is he who can die for your happiness." [1]

This feeling for France was unknown to Napoleon. At no time in his life had he the desire to die for the happiness of the French people. He knew patriotic sentiments in his youth: the rhetorical patriotism of a late-eighteenth-century adolescence which had been instructed by the classics and Rousseau. It was, however, a patriotism directed against France. Napoleon the Corsican shared his fellow-countrymen's hatred of their French conquerors and their admiration for Pasquale Paoli, the leader of the Corsican fight for independence in which he longed to join. What attracted him most to Jean-Jacques Rousseau in his early youth was the latter's idoliza-

---

*Reprinted from the *Journal of Modern History*, Vol. XXII, No. 1, March 1950, by permission of the University of Chicago Press.

[1] "Rapport sur les rapports des idées réligieuses et morales avec les principes républicains, et sur les fêtes nationales," 18 floréal, an II (1794), p. 6.

tion of primitive agrarian Corsica.² "My relatives, my country, and my veneration for Paoli and Rousseau were my only passion," Napoleon wrote later of this period of his life. When, at the age of ten, he entered the military school of Brienne, Napoleon knew little French. "As I still spoke French badly, and found it hard to accustom myself to a completely different mode of living, I generally kept away from my companions at first and preferred to occupy myself with my books. Extraordinarily sensitive as I was, I suffered infinitely from the ridicule of my schoolmates, who used to jeer at me as a foreigner. My pride and sense of honor would tolerate no insult to my country"—Corsica!—"or to the beloved national hero Paoli."

At the beginning of 1786 the young Buonaparte received his commission as a sublieutenant in the French garrison town of Valence. There his thoughts returned incessantly to his native land; the words which he wrote in May 1786 were characteristic of his feeling throughout the period: "What tragedy awaits me in my country! My fellow countrymen are loaded with chains! and have to bear, trembling, the weight of the oppressor's hand!"—the oppressor was the king of France, whose uniform Napoleon wore. "You Frenchmen! It is not enough that you have robbed us of what we love the most, you have even destroyed our manners and customs! What attitude shall I adopt, how shall I speak when I arrive in my country? When his country no longer exists, a good citizen should die. If one man could save my countrymen by sacrificing his life, I would at once rise and thrust the avenging sword into the breast of the tyrant in order to revenge my country and its injured rights." [3]

For the French people the Revolution meant a full awakening to nationalism; for Napoleon its influence was different. He abandoned his Corsican patriotism to embrace the Revolutionary cause. Was he swayed by the promise of liberty it held out to French and Corsicans alike? Political liberty soon came to have as little meaning for him as did nationalism, but he sensed the dynamic possibilities in this enthusiastic upsurge of a great people. Edmund Burke had wrongly believed that the Revolution dealt a mortal blow to French strength, leaving

---

[2] See Hans Kohn, *The Idea of Nationalism* (New York: 1944), pp. 253-54. Napoleon later wrote that, up to the age of sixteen: "I would have fought for Rousseau against all the friends of Voltaire. Today it is the opposite. Since I have seen the East, Rousseau is repugnant to me. The wild man without morals is a dog." (F. M. Kircheisen, *Napoleon's Autobiography: The Personal Memoirs of Bonaparte, Compiled from His Own Letters and Diaries*, trans. Frederick Collins [New York: 1931], p. 253).

[3] Kircheisen, *op. cit.*, pp. 13 and 17-18.

the country a great void. Mirabeau, in a memorandum which he sent in September 1792 by Comte de La Marck to Emperor Leopold II, remarked that Burke "has said something very stupid, for this void is a volcano, the subterranean agitations and approaching eruptions of which no one could neglect for a moment without imprudence." He predicted incalculable earthquakes and innumerable grave consequences from the streams of lava that were to pour down on neighboring countries. Even more clearly than Mirabeau, Napoleon understood the dynamism of the French Revolution, this immense release of energy, this gateway to ceaseless activity and boundless ambition. His personality was admirably suited to his time. In a period which exalted the individual and his opportunities, Napoleon, as Friedrich Nietzsche so clearly sensed, was an extreme individualist, for whom France and Europe, nation and mankind, were but instruments of his destiny.

The same quest for an efficient government that brought about the Revolution in 1789 helped Napoleon to power ten years later. The French longed for a strong man who would safeguard the main achievements of the Revolution in orderly security and stabilize the new frontiers and glorious conquests in peace. Of all the institutions of the young republic, the army alone possessed the prestige and the power to achieve this. Of its young generals, Buonaparte appeared the most promising. He did not disappoint the country's expectations. A man of rare vitality and capacity for work, of penetrating intelligence and prodigious memory, he proved a great administrator and organizer, continuing the line of enlightened monarchs of the eighteenth century and surpassing them by far, the last and the greatest of them. Like them, he did not understand and had no use for nationalism and the new popular forces. Like them, he believed in the state, in direction from above, in efficiency and rational order. But unlike the greatest of them, he did regard himself less the first servant of the state than its master. The state was the vehicle and instrument of his personal destiny. His primary end was not the welfare of his subjects or the *raison d'état* of France and not, except for brief moments, the perpetuation and glory of his dynasty. All these limited goals he accepted and from time to time promoted each one or all of them, but they did not satisfy or contain him. His ambitions knew no definite limits; his activities had no fixed and stable direction. He felt his will was strong enough to triumph over the nature of man and the nature of things alike. To him, the impossible was only "a phantom of the timid soul and the refuge of the coward." Despite his youthful Rousseauan nationalism, he was an eighteenth-century cosmopolitan for whom civilization was one and the world the stage; in other respects he anticipated the twentieth century. He set the earliest and greatest example in modern times for the potentialities of the cult of force that found so many adherents in the extreme movements of socialism and nationalism a hundred years after his death. The words of this eighteenth-century man of genius sound sometimes like pronouncements of our times: "There is only one secret for world leadership, namely, to be strong, because in strength there is neither error nor illusion: it is naked truth." "Succeed! I judge men only by the results of their acts." He was a dynamic force, for whom "the world is but an occasion to act dangerously." [4] Though his daring had ultimately to fail, it built much that lasted.

Unlike the typical eighteenth-century man, Napoleon did not know moderation, nor could his temperament accommodate itself to peace. He did not believe in harmony but in mastery, not in compromise but in struggle and decision. In 1803, after the Treaty of Amiens, France had everything it could desire, but Napoleon was unwilling for it to become a great state among other states and for himself to be a king equal to other kings. He had to be the first of all, the emperor of the Occident, the successor to Charlemagne and to Caesar; soon his ambitions went beyond the legacy of Rome, to Byzantium and to Asia. His triumphs he owed to the disunity of his adversaries, to their hesitation and half-measures. But his *hubris* drove him on until he succeeded in arousing the peoples, in overcoming the jealousies and pettiness of the rulers, in uniting Europe—not under his leadership but against him. He was repeatedly offered favorable peace conditions that would have left France in possession of many of its conquests; he rejected them. His stake was everything; the alternative was nothing. He could not resign himself to the French nation-state of the nineteenth century. He did not belong to the age of nationalism.

The constitutional liberties for which 1789 and the nineteenth century strove meant little to Napoleon. He did not deny them; he denatured them. He paid lip service to universal suffrage and deprived the people of any effective vote. With supreme contempt, he drew up many meaningless constitutions and had them confirmed by

---

[4] Georges Lefèbvre, *Napoléon* (Paris, 1935), pp. 65 and 58.

plebiscite. The people had no share in the government of their affairs; their public spirit was not encouraged. Yet in his declarations, he always took care to emphasize his wish to "rattacher les grandes autorités de l'état à la masse de la nation, d'où dérive nécessairement toute autorité nationale." But he admitted, no doubt, that as "l'élu du peuple" he alone represented the majority of the nation. He praised democracy if it was democracy on his terms—"true" democracy. Napoleon's effective coups d'état with their subsequent plebiscitarian endorsements did not strengthen French respect for constitutional legality. The order which he undoubtedly brought to France was not the animated coherent working of creative national forces; these were cowed and dormant, deprived of all spontaneity; what remained of movement was directed from above by an administrative system that insured quick obedience but did not allow any room for discussion or free co-operation. All public and intellectual life was closely supervised; the formation of parties or associations was prohibited; and though Napoleon was personally not cruel and his regime was devoid of brutality and mass executions in the twentieth-century style, it created an atmosphere of enforced silence, of distrust and denunciation, of arbitrary arrests and insecurity.

Napoleon's dictatorship differed from twentieth-century totalitarianism in another respect. In his contempt for public opinion, for *idéologues* and writers, he failed to know how to make use of them. He made little attempt to mold public opinion. He did not flood the country with newspapers and pamphlets, he did not spread popular reports of his great campaigns and victories, nor did he try to explain the virtues of his legislation. He distrusted even a controlled use of the printed word. The Revolutionary period had abounded in pamphlets and newspapers; in Paris, Napoleon allowed only nine papers to be published, which in the spring of 1803 had a combined circulation of less than twenty thousand copies, and one semiofficial newspaper in each department. As there was to be only one party in France and only one opinion, there seemed to be no need for diversified newspapers. But even the few that did appear had to be protected against "the spread of false news." They were threatened with suppression if they published "articles contrary to the respect due to the social pact, to the sovereignty of the people, and to the glory of the [French] arms." Even pamphlets praising the emperor and popularizing his soldiers were extremely rare. The number of printers was limited, too; they and the booksellers had to be licensed and were required to take an oath that they would not print or sell any publication which might conflict with "their duty to the emperor and the interests of the state." No less close was the supervision over the theater and over literature. Both became "official"; as a result, they were conventional in style and content, with the sources of creative inventiveness drying up.[5] While the armies of Napoleon carried French power to the furthermost limits of Europe, the French spirit was in danger of losing the leadership it had exercised for so long.

Similarly, Napoleon did not concern himself with promotion of elementary education or the education of women. His reforms confined themselves mainly to higher schools for the training of capable and loyal civil servants. "Public instruction," declared Pierre Louis, Comte Roederer, who was put in charge in 1802 of all affairs concerning it, "can and must be a very powerful machine in our political system. Through it the legislator will be able to re-create a national spirit and then to make use of it himself." The concern of the Enlightenment for education had evaporated; what remained was paternal care of good and useful subjects. Napoleon centralized education, as he centralized the state. The decree of March 17, 1808, organized the "University," the general corporation charged with the direction of the political and moral formation of French youth. Its bases were the teachings of the Catholic religion; loyalty to the emperor and the imperial monarchy, the depository of the happiness of the people, and to the Napoleonic dynasty, the preserver of the unity of France and of all the liberal ideas proclaimed by the constitutions; and obedience to teachers and parents. For Napoleon more and more only the official world existed, the armor of the state; for the nation and its intellectual life he had little use. He underestimated their importance, both in France and abroad.

In a speech to the senate, Napoleon said on July 9, 1810, "A new order of things now guides the universe." This order, though rational in its outline and efficient in its application, broke upon the one

[5] Napoleon treated painters in a similar way. They were attached as officers to the armies of the First Consul. "Militarized artists, submitted to the strictest discipline, they had nothing to paint but glorious battle scenes—which caused them to be called 'painters of victories'—and they could not paint them according to their inspiration; they could choose neither the day nor the hour nor the composition of the picture, and their talent was circumscribed by minute regulations worked out by offices which had little concern with art, even if one admits that it was not completely strange to them. They have left a considerable amount of work dispersed in various archives and museums and generally little known" (Louis Villat, *La Révolution et l'empire (1789-1815)* ["Clio, introduction aux études historiques," No. 8] [Paris, 1936], II, 114).

obstacle which it did not take into account: the human element, the popular reluctance to accept the imposed form. Napoleon's society was planned by a great strategist in the camp of a victorious army. Distrusting spontaneous manifestations of liberty, he regarded the order of the army and the discipline and *élan* of war as an antidote to social anarchy; he did not see that long wars in themselves threaten to produce anarchy and to destroy much of the substance on which every living order must be based. He tried to compensate the French with economic activity for the political immobility that he imposed.

Napoleon appealed to the ambitious self-love of the French that the success of the Revolutionary armies had fanned, to their feeling of superiority. He wished his rule to be a "dictatorship of persuasion based upon popularity." [6] To some, he promised to continue the gains and heroism of the Revolution; to others, he appeared as a conservative force. "So artfully was the system of Buonaparte contrived, that each of the numerous classes of Frenchmen found something in it congenial to his habits, his feeling, or his circumstances, providing only he was willing to sacrifice to it the essential part of his political principles. . . . To all these parties, Buonaparte held out the same hopes under the same conditions.—'All these things will I give you, if you will kneel down and worship me!' Shortly afterwards, he was enabled to place before them to whom the choice was submitted, the original temptation in its full extent—a display of the kingdoms of the earth, over which he offered to extend the empire of France, providing always he was himself acknowledged as the object of general obedience, and almost adoration." [7]

The dynamism of Napoleon's temperament did not allow him to formulate and follow a consistent foreign policy, conforming to the interests of the French state, as Cardinal Richelieu had done. His aspirations led him in too many directions. Everywhere he found England in his way, whether he tried to expand throughout Europe or to re-create the Mediterranean empire of the Romans that he, himself a Mediterranean, regarded as his legacy. From his earliest years, his glance had embraced distant lands and his plans mapped out roads for future adventure. When he started for Egypt in April 1798 as general-in-chief of the Army of the Orient, he carried with him a directive to "drive out the English from all their possessions in the

---

[6] A. Aulard, *Études et leçons sur la Révolution française* (9 vols.; Paris, 1902-24), VII, 146.

[7] Sir Walter Scott, *The Life of Napoleon Buonaparte, Emperor of the French* (3 vols.) (Philadelphia, 1827), I, 464.

Orient," to cut the isthmus of Suez and to take all necessary measures to assure the French Republic free and exclusive possession of the Red Sea. The daring march to the Pyramids and across the Sinai Desert was motivated not by the arbitrariness of a freebooter but by the logic of a great vision: to make Egypt the starting point, as it had been with Alexander and Caesar, for the conquest of Asia, for an advance toward India, for a decisive battle in the heart of the new British empire. Successful, Napoleon would have attained the triumph of vast land masses over sea power, the reopening and control of the ancient land routes to the East, the revival of the decayed civilizations and glories of the Levant and the Orient. This "mirage" of a renaissance of the lands long relegated to obscurity by the rise of oceanic sea power beckoned him on all his life. It was inextricably linked with his hostility to Britain, the mistress of the sea, and his jealousy of Russia, the empire of the East, for Napoleon himself vacillated between re-creating the empire of the West—and protecting it and its Mediterranean civilization against the threats from the north and the east—and the limitless horizons of the earth. In the twenty years of his career he had to confine himself to uniting Europe; he was stopped at the Channel and on the snow fields of Russia from going beyond. But at the beginning of the age of nationalism stands its denial in Napoleon's universal empire, a vision that was taken up again only at the end of the age by Lenin and Hitler.

When Napoleon in 1804 assumed the title of "Emperor of the French," many regarded this step as a betrayal of the Revolution. The Revolutionary hero seemed dead, buried under glittering uniforms and high-sounding titles, church incense and court ceremonial. Beethoven tore up the dedication of his *Third Symphony* to General Buonaparte and replaced his name by the lament, "To the memory of a great man." Stendhal, watching the coronation ceremonies in Paris, looked with disgust at the emperor as a new Caesar and called his accommodation with the pope "an alliance of all the charlatans." He "rinsed out the bad taste" in his mouth by reading Victor Alfieri, the revolutionary nationalist of eighteenth-century Italy.[8] In reality, Napoleon never ceased to incarnate truly one aspect of the French Revolution: its universalism and its quest for efficient government. To other aspects like nationalism and liberalism he often paid lip service, but he found little use for them in his actions. His own nature drove him to disregard or misinterpret the forces of liberty long

[8] Matthew Josephson, *Stendhal* (Garden City, N. Y., 1946), p. 122.

before he became emperor.[9] He did not revive the title of king, because it seemed to imply an abdication of popular sovereignty, while the title "Emperor" flattered the nation and its desire for glory without alarming it unduly. It preserved the feeling that national sovereignty was unimpaired—"My policy consists in ruling men according to the rule of the great majority. In this way I believe one recognizes the sovereignty of the people"[10]—and did not recall the struggle with the royal government for liberty.

The new title did not strike the French as strange or as incompatible with republican achievements. The same law that proclaimed Napoleon emperor charged him with the government of the French Republic. The term "empire" had been widely used in eighteenth-century France and by French republicans to connote a vast and prosperous land with a great future—as it had been by American patriots for the thirteen colonies and later for the young and growing United States. It was in no way contrary to liberty and it was full of the promise of human happiness. Napoleon, however, thought less of this modern meaning of the word than of its ancient and hallowed significance, the memory of the Roman Empire as the guarantor of peace and justice in a universal world order. When he married Marie Louise, the daughter of the last Holy Roman Emperor, this imperial succession meant as much to him as the practical advantages of an alliance with Austria and as the fact that the mother of his son was the niece of the last queen of France. In his renovation of the empire of the West, he naturally recalled Charlemagne, who like him had rebuilt the Roman Empire in the West and, as ruler of the Franks, had united Italy and Germany. Soon after Charlemagne the Western empire had disintegrated. Napoleon hoped to revive its greatness and force and to bring to a close the long struggle between French and Germans for its heritage. Like Charlemagne, he wished to found his empire in collaboration with the Roman church but without allowing it to be weakened by papal claims. No longer should the church have the power it possessed in the middle ages to war with the emperor for supremacy. The secular ruler should hold undisputed sway.

An eighteenth-century agnostic, Napoleon was willing to use the

---

[9] That he became one, while the "great leaders" of the twentieth century, Hitler and Stalin, did not, was due to the different circumstances of the two periods. In Napoleon's time nationalism had not yet sufficiently consolidated nations, nor was it possible to elaborate a doctrine for the masses or forge a mass party, so that a hereditary dynasty seemed the only guarantee of continuity.

[10] Kircheisen, *op. cit.*, p. 234.

church to support order and morality among his subjects and to solidify his reign. He regarded it as an institution of his empire and the pope as an imperial official. "Paris was to be the metropolis of Christendom, the center and guide of the religious as well as of the political world." [11] To the Ecclesiastical Committee he declared on March 16, 1811: "The present epoch carries us back to the time of Charlemagne. All the kingdoms, principalities, and duchies which formed themselves out of the debris of the empire have been rejuvenated under our laws. The church of my empire is the church of the Occident and of almost the whole of Christendom." He announced the convocation of a Council of the Occident in order that "the church of my empire be one in its discipline, as it is in its faith." When he annexed the Papal States on May 17, 1809, he did so on the strength of the theory that the secular domain of the pope had been a fief of Charlemagne, "Empereur des Français et notre auguste prédécesseur," and that the true sovereignty remained with the donor and his heirs, who could revoke or modify the gift. The expenses of the papal office were charged to the imperial budget, and the autonomy of the Gallican church of 1682 was extended to the church in the whole empire.

In 1811 this empire, with its frontiers on the Elbe, the Ebro, and the Adriatic Sea, was practically coextensive with that of Charlemagne. French prefects administered its affairs in Rome and Florence, Genoa and Turin, Antwerp and The Hague, Hamburg and Mainz, Trier and Cologne, Barcelona and Saragossa. In addition, it included the Illyrian provinces on the Adriatic coast, and the Kingdom of Italy with Milan as its capital. Around this mighty nucleus, there was an outer circle of closely controlled vassal states, Spain and Naples in the south, the Confederation of the Rhine, the Helvetic Confederation, and the Duchy of Warsaw in the east. By its hold on the Vistula and on the Ionian Islands, Napoleon's empire went far beyond that of Charlemagne, stretching out in the direction of the Orient, toward the reunion of Byzantium with Rome.

This empire of the West had two capitals, Paris and Rome, which on February 17, 1810 was proclaimed "the second city of the empire." The emperors, after their coronation in Notre Dame in Paris, were to be crowned once more before the tenth year of their reign in Saint Peter's. The pope was invited to reside where he pleased but preferably in Paris or Rome. The yet unborn heir to the throne

[11] *Ibid.*, p. 180.

received in 1810 the title "King of Rome," which all future heirs were to bear, an appellation recalling that of the uncrowned Holy Roman Emperors and of what infinitely greater majesty and promise than the title "Prince of Wales" borne by the heirs to the disputed realm of the sea! With the magnificence of the twentieth-century despots Napoleon set out to monumentalize his two capitals as centers of triumphant empire. An imperial palace was planned for the Capitol in Rome, and excavations were begun to lay bare the forums of antiquity, the focuses of ancient world order.

Napoleonic rule imposed upon the provinces and satellites of his empire new concepts and vitalized them with new life. Much of it quickly vanished after his fall, but something remained of his invigorating efficiency and ended many outworn traditions and institutions. Wherever Napoleon went, he brought with him rational reforms and administrative progress. When he started for Egypt, the decree of the Directory of April 13, 1798 charged him in Article IV "to improve by all means at his disposal the fate of the natives." He took with him a great number of carefully chosen scholars and scientists in all fields, and with their help he founded on August 22, 1798 the Institut d'Égypte, of which Gaspard Monge became the first president. Scientific research into the antiquity, the geography, the fauna and flora, and the present state of Egypt was eagerly promoted, to go hand in hand with the spread of enlightenment among its people. On October 2, 1798 the first issue of a literary and philosophical journal, *Décades égyptiennes,* appeared. The French hoped that through modernization Egypt would become the cradle of the regeneration of Islam and that civilization, science, and industry would return to the country that had once been their center. As this renascence developed under French inspiration, a close tie between France and the Middle East was to result: the spread of enlightenment would entail a growth of French influence.

Though Napoleon's rule in Egypt was short-lived, his hopes were not all disappointed. It is true that his progressive reforms did not reach the people and did not influence their lives. But modern Egyptology owes its origin to the work of his scholars and found its initial expression in the famous *Description de l'Égypte,* which in its nine volumes of text and twelve volumes of plates made the first survey of the antiquities, the natural resources, and the modern society of the land of the Nile. French civilization and language remained predominant in Egypt in the tiny educated upper class for well over a century; and when a few years after Napoleon's expedition the vigorous and ruthless Albanian soldier, Mohammed Ali, laid the foundation of the first modern Islamic state in Egypt, he did it partly under the inspiration of the legacy Napoleon's administration left in the ancient land.[12]

More immediately far-reaching were the effects of Napoleon's administration in the Belgian departments that the Convention had incorporated into France. Under the Directory they had merely felt bewildered and oppressed; under Napoleon they were infused with fresh energy and benefited from the new social order created by the Revolution. The ties with the traditional past of estates and provinces, castes and guilds, privileges and rights, still so potent in 1792, were definitely broken. When Napoleon's domination ended, no return to 1792 was any longer possible. His rule had not aroused a Belgian nationalism, for whatever national feeling had existed had been closely connected with the old regime and provincial autonomy, which were now no more than a distant memory. Napoleon succeeded only in preparing the soil for a future growth of a new Belgian nationalism. Meanwhile, "if one did not feel one's self French, one did not feel one's self Belgian either. One was satisfied to live by making the best of one's opportunities without considering them as good in themselves. Instead of a true national sentiment, there were only vague aspirations toward a better future which no one could define." [13]

The Belgians recognized the good qualities of the new administration, its useful innovations, and the security it afforded to the rising spirit of enterprise and individual advancement; but they suffered from a lack of civil liberties, and they felt the French administrators to be aliens. Napoleon carried out the program of enlightened absolutism that Joseph II had tried to implant in Belgium, and its reforms, rejected twenty years before, were now accepted. But the measures of frenchification of instruction and administration and the conflict with the Catholic church alienated many Belgians. Religious publications like the *Jerusalems herstelling* (1811) by the priest Stichelbaut kept love of the mother-tongue and devotion to the church alive. When the French occupation ended with the allied victories in the spring of 1814, the Belgians did not aid the French, nor

[12] See Napoleon's letters of Aug. 2 and 22, 1798, *Correspondance de Napoléon Premier, publiée par l'ordre de Napoléon III*ᵉ (Paris, 1858-70), IV, 224-25 and 534-37. See also P. G. Elgood, *Bonaparte's Adventure in Egypt* (London, 1931).
[13] H. Pirenne, *Histoire de Belgique* (Brussels, 1926), VI, 141.

did they, like the Dutch, rise against them. A return to the old regime was unacceptable to the younger generation grown up during the last twenty years; most of the people did not wish to abandon the achievements of the Napoleonic era; but the Belgians had no national program of their own, for Napoleon's regime nowhere directly encouraged the growth of spontaneous group activity and of national sentiment, though indirectly it prepared for it.

Napoleon was ready to use national aspirations as far as they seemed to fit into his system, without having any sincere desire to satisfy them. He never thought seriously of an indepedent Poland or an independent Italy, though from time to time he gave vague encouragement to those who believed in them. For him nations had no reality of their own. He created and dissolved new states incessantly and shifted frontiers and rulers restlessly. Nor did he encounter opposition from nationalism in the beginning. The people dissatisfied with his rule were less moved by national sentiments than by dislike of alien troops who stayed on and lived off the land and in many cases behaved without tact or restraint. They were motivated much more by loyalty to religion or to traditional ways of life than by nationalism. Only toward the end of his reign did Napoleon succeed, against his will and intention, in arousing nationalism in some of the people subject to or threatened by his rule. Thus indirectly and unwittingly Napoleon became a midwife to the birth of the age of nationalism on the continent of Europe.

At the end of 1811 Marshal Davout, the commanding officer in Hamburg, warned Napoleon of the mounting national sentiment in Germany and of the dangers to French rule that this growth of German nationalism involved. Napoleon rejected the warning; he did not believe in the possibility of nationalism and in his rebuke pointed to the peaceful character of the German people. Germany seemed to him quiescent and obedient. "If there were a movement in Germany, it would ultimately be for us and against the small princes." [14] Whatever understanding of nationalism there was in Napoleon's mind applied to Italy. He was the first to create an Italian republic and later a kingdom of Italy and thus to give a powerful impetus to the slowly awakening demands for Italian unity and nationhood. Later on, he was to say that he had planned eventually "to create a single state out of this great peninsula." Yet while he had the power, he divided up Italy arbitrarily and repeatedly, ac-

[14] *Correspondance*, XXIII, 45 (No. 18,300, Dec. 2, 1811).

cording to what he believed were the momentary interests of his empire and his dynasty. On behalf of these interests, he might, if his empire had survived, have crowned a second son king of Italy and united the country around his throne.[15]

Only when all hopes for empire and dynasty had vanished and Napoleon himself was a captive on St. Helena did he begin to build up consistently a legend about his intentions and plans to promote the liberty of nations and the happiness of Europe. This legend deeply influenced the thought of following generations and prepared the way for a brief rebirth of empire and dynasty. In a famous passage, he espoused simultaneously the cause of national unity for the four great continental peoples, the French, the Spanish, the Italians, and the Germans, and the cause of a united Europe where the same views and interests, laws and principles, would prevail throughout the continent. Even then, his words betrayed the vagueness of his thinking on these issues. His decisions were dictated by changing strategic needs. Against England and Russia, Napoleon wished at times to consolidate France, Spain, and Italy into a compact Latin bloc that would be an impregnable barrier against "all the nations of the north." He asked himself why no German prince had used the German demand for unity to his own profit. "Certainly, if heaven had willled that I be born a German prince, I would infallibly have governed thirty million united Germans; and from what I think I know of them, I believe that, once they had elected and proclaimed me, they would never have abandoned me, and I would not be here now."

Napoleon believed that he might have led a willing and obedient German nation to dominion over Europe. Little in these words betrays any attachment to France or to the happiness of peoples. But at the same time he sounded a different note: "Le premier souverain qui, au milieu de la première grande mêlée, embrassera de bonne foi la cause des peuples, se trouvera à la tête de toute l'Europe et

---

[15] Kircheisen, *op. cit.*, p. 236. On Napoleon's treatment of Italian patriotism see *Correspondance*, II, 63 (No. 1,099, Oct. 17, 1796), 157 (No. 1,258, Dec. 10, 1796), 223-24 (No. 1,349, Jan. 1, 1797), and 483 (No. 1,724, Apr. 12, 1797); III, 153 (No. 1,960, June 29, 1797) and 235 (No. 2,013, Aug. 16, 1797): "Les îles de Corfu, de Zante et de Céphalonie sont plus intéressantes pour nous que toute l'Italie ensemble. Je crois que si nous étions obligés d'opter, il vaudrait mieux restituer l'Italie à l'Empereur et garder les quatre îles, qui sont une source de richesse et de prospérité pour notre commerce. L'Empire des Turcs s'écroule tous les jours; la possession de ces îles nous mettra à même de le soutenir autant que cela sera possible, ou d'en prendre notre part"; XXVII, 11-12. (No. 21,063, Jan. 4, 1814); and XXXII, 386 (reported by Dr. Francesco Antommarchi as told to him on Jan. 26, 1821).

pourra tenter tout ce qu'il voudra." Napoleon III certainly remembered these words. Yet, even provided that the interests of the various nations and of the whole of Europe did not conflict, the leader of the peoples and of the whole continent might have discovered that it was difficult under any circumstances to attempt whatever he desired.[16] The cult of force and of limitless empire dominated Napoleon's mind to the last: his dream did not change on St. Helena. With greater sincerity he told Benjamin Constant a few months before he had to leave France: "I wished for the empire of the world, and to insure it unlimited power was necessary to me. To govern France alone, a constitution may be better." [17] The age of nationalism rejected the emperor of the world and demanded constitutions.

Concretely, Napoleon's European union, his Continental System, was a weapon in his struggle with England. "Let us be masters of the Channel for only six hours, and we shall be masters of the world." In this struggle, he claimed to represent the interests of mankind and to defend the liberties of all peoples. These peoples, however, did not agree: they feared Napoleon and the French much more than the English. The English employed the advantages of commerce and inspired jealousy; Napoleon used the means of wars and imposed tyranny. Napoleon's liberal opponent, Benjamin Constant, in his *De l'esprit de conquête et de l'usurpation dans leurs rapports avec la civilisation européenne* (1813) saw in war the instrument of the past, in commerce that of enlightened civilization.

> War and commerce are only two different means of arriving at the same goal—the possession of what one desires. Commerce is an attempt to receive by agreement what one no longer hopes to conquer by force. A man who would always be the strongest, would never think of commerce. It is experience which, in demonstrating to him that war—this is to say, the employment of his force against that of another—is exposed to various resistances and checks, leads him to have recourse to commerce—that is to say, to a more pleasant and certain way of compelling the interests of others to consent to what accommodates his own interest. . . . Carthage, fighting with Rome in ancient times, had to succumb; it had the force of circumstances against it. But if the fight between Rome and Carthage were taking

---

[16] *Correspondance*, XXXII, 304-6; Eng. trans. in Emmanuel, Comte de Las Cases, *Memoirs of the Life, Exile and Conversations of the Emperor Napoleon* (4 vols.; New York, 1890), IV, 104-8.
[17] Apr. 14, 1815, Henri Benjamin Constant, *Mémoires sur les Cent Jours*, Part II (Paris, 1829), pp. 19-24.

place today, Carthage would have the universe on its side. Elle aurait pour alliés les mœurs actuelles et le génie du monde.[18]

Napoleon showed some understanding of English liberty, but he rejected the possibility of its application in France.

> In the case of a nation like the English where everything is influenced by public opinion, even the actions of the Minister of State and the resolutions of Parliament, it will be easily understood that the press enjoys unlimited freedom. Our constitutions, on the other hand, do not require the interference of the people in state affairs. If the people were not satisfied with this, the existing organization would have to be completely altered; but it has been proved that such a force of public opinion produces nothing but confusion and excitement, so that a strict surveillance of the press would have to be set up.[19]

On St. Helena, Napoleon expressed himself more enthusiastically about liberty and the English model. Aware of the contradiction between his words and his acts, he pointed out.

> There is no comparison between my situation and that of the English government. England is able to work on a soil which extends to the very bowels of the earth; while I could labor only on sandy surface. England reigns over an established order of things; while I had to take upon myself the great charge, the immense difficulty, of conciliating and establishing. I purified the revolution, in spite of hostile factions. I combined together all the scattered benefits that could be preserved; but I was obliged to protect them with a nervous arm against the attacks of all parties; and in this situation it may truly be said that the public interest, the state, was myself.[20]

While Napoleon rejected liberty, he offered equality. "I have always been of the opinion that sovereignty lay in the people. The imperial government was a kind of republic. Called to the head of it by the voice of the nation, my maxim was 'La carrière ouverte aux talents' without distinction of birth or fortune." [21] He had no racial

---

[18] Henri Benjamin Constant, *De l'esprit de conquête* . . . (Paris, 1918), pp. 12 and 14, chap. ii, "Du caractère des nations modernes relativement à la guerre."

[19] Kircheisen, *op. cit.*, p. 238. Like Frederick II of Prussia, Napoleon permitted religious discussions but no political opposition. "Great freedom must be allowed in writings on religious questions, so that the publication of useful truths may not be strangled under the cloak of offense to religion. However, censorship will be inflexible in the case of documents directed against the state" (*ibid.*, p. 245).

[20] Las Cases, *op. cit.*, III, 255.

[21] Barry E. O'Meara, *Napoleon in Exile, or a Voice from St. Helena* (New York, 1853), I, 249.

prejudice. Repeatedly he suggested as the best way of establishing peace and civilization in the colonies the encouragement of intermarriage between whites and blacks. To that end he proposed to authorize polygamy, provided that every man took wives of different colors, so that the children of each, brought up under the same roof and upon the same footing, would from their infancy learn to consider themselves as equal and in the ties of relationship forget difference of color.[22] On St. Helena he regretted the expedition to Santo Domingo. "I ought to have negotiated with the black chiefs; I ought to have appointed Negroes as officers in their regiments, and made Toussaint l'Ouverture viceroy." [23] Not only did he give equality to the Jews, but he welcomed their influx into France. In his opinion they supplied good soldiers for the French army, and great wealth was brought to France through them. He was convinced that if his empire had lasted, many more Jews would have immigrated to France, for all the Jews would gradually have come to settle in a country where equality of laws was assured to them and where all honors stood open to them.[24] What Napoleon demanded was loyal and obedient subjects, useful to the state; as long as they were that, he did not inquire into their religion, race, or nationality.

This emphasis on equality made Napoleon plead strongly for military conscription. "An emperor puts his confidence in national soldiers, not in mercenaries." In a talk with an Englishman who objected to conscription, Napoleon maintained that universal military service wounded the pride of the English oligarchy because it fell upon all ranks. "Oh, how shocking that a gentleman's son should be obliged to defend his country, just as if he were one of the *canaille!* That he should be expected to expose his body, or put himself on the level with the vile plebeian! Yet God made all men alike." [25] Nevertheless, it is interesting to note that even under Napoleon conscription was far from all-inclusive. As in the days of the Convention or the Directory, only unmarried young men served, and the wealthy

---

[22] Hugh Fortescue, *Memorandum of Two Conversations Between the Emperor Napoleon and Viscount Eberington at Porta Ferrajo on the Sixth and Eighth of December, 1814* (London, 1823), p. 27. See also *Correspondence*, XXIX, 490-91; and Las Cases, *op. cit.*, III, 318.

[23] Kircheisen, *op. cit.*, p. 104. "Instead of sending troops, I ought to have left everything to the black men, or, at most, have sent a few white officials, for instance, a treasurer, and required that the white men marry Negro women."

[24] *Ibid.*, p. 181. See also *Correspondence*, XXXII, 316-17; and O'Meara, *op. cit.*, I, 113-14.

[25] O'Meara, *op. cit.*, II, 225. See also Las Cases, *op. cit.*, IV, 145.

were allowed to buy substitutes; the heaviest burden fell not upon France but upon the newly acquired provinces and vassal states. Yet conscription was very unpopular. In 1811 the number of evaders was estimated at one hundred and sixty thousand for France, and in formulating the appeal for 1813 the emperor himself expected one hundred thousand more. Bribery, self-mutilation, and marriages between very young men and very old women to evade service were not rare. When the Grand Army crossed the borders of Russia in 1812, Frenchmen formed less than half its numbers. The wars of Napoleon had ceased to be national wars; it was only in defense of French territory in 1814 and 1815 that something like the original national enthusiasm reappeared.[26]

Nationalism was at a low ebb in France when Napoleon returned from Russia. The nation was tired of wars and tired of glory. Napoleon fought on throughout 1813 with indefatigable valor on German battlefields. But even his retreat to the Rhine and his appeals to the memories of 1793 could not rekindle the burnt-out flame. The people had been deprived of initiative and activity, their true desires stifled, for too long. Glory had seduced many in whom the new liberty of 1789 had not yet taken root. But glory depended on success; when fortune deserted Napoleon, it was quickly forgotten in the bitter disappointment of the moment that he had carried the French banners to Madrid and Rome, to Berlin and Vienna; he was now held responsible for misfortune and defeat:

> Eh bien! dans tous ces jours d'abaissement, de peine,
>   Pour tous ces outrages sans nom,
> Je n'ai jamais chargé qu'un être de ma haine . . .
>   Sois maudit, ô Napoléon!
> Ô Corse à cheveux plats! . . .

The provisional government that Talleyrand formed on April 1, 1814 reminded the French people three days later:

> To end civil discord, you chose as your head a man who appeared on the world stage with the marks of greatness on him. You put all your hopes in him; those hopes have been betrayed; on the ruins of anarchy, he founded nothing but despotism. He should at least, out

---

[26] How much conscription was resented may be seen from the violent diatribe against "la loi homicide" in F.-A.-R. vicomte de Chateaubriand's "De Buonaparte et des Bourbons" (Mar. 30, 1814), *Œuvres complètes* (Paris, 1828), XXIV, 20-24; and in Édmond Gérard's journal for March 1814, quoted in H. F. Stewart and Paul Desjardins, *French Patriotism in the Nineteenth Century 1814-1833, traced in Contemporary Texts* (Cambridge, 1923), p. 120.

of gratitude, have become a Frenchman with you. That he has never been. . . . He knew not how to rule, neither in the national interest, nor in the interest of his despotism. He destroyed whatever he wished to create, and recreated whatever he wished to destroy. He believed only in force; today he is overthrown by force: just retribution for his insensate ambition.

Napoleon had wished to create an empire out of all proportion; it was time, many Frenchmen felt, that the nation recognized its limits and regained its proper measure. Only on such foundations could true grandeur for France be founded.[27]

A young Frenchwoman who had lived through the Revolution and the Empire observed in 1813: "All the peoples have found a patriotic energy to repel us, why did we lack it? What is the fatherland, if not love of long-standing habits, of family, of country and of quiet happiness? Alas! France at present is nothing more than a garrison where discipline and boredom rule. We will defend this garrison out of obedience, but the inhabitants will not identify themselves with the quarrel, and the conquest of France is but a military affair, threatening only the honor of the army."[28] Pierre Jean de Béranger, who felt the pulse of the city on March 31, 1814, the day when the victorious allies entered Paris, was convinced:

If the emperor had been able to read all their hearts, he would have doubtless recognized one of his greatest mistakes, one which the nature of his genius caused him to make. He had gagged the people; he had taken from them all free intervention in their own affairs and thus obliterated those principles that our Revolution had inculcated in us. From this resulted a deep torpor of the sentiments which are most natural to us. For a long time his success took the place of patriotism for us; but, as he had absorbed the whole nation within him, the whole nation fell with him. And, in our fall, we did not know, in the face of our enemies, how to be anything more than he had made us.[29]

[27] Stewart and Desjardins, *op. cit.,* pp. 130 and 131.
[28] Aimée de Coigny, *Mémoires,* ed. Étienne Lamy (Paris, 1902), p. 229. See also Mme de Staël, *Considérations sur la Révolution française,* Part IV, chap. xix.
[29] Pierre Jean de Béranger, *Ma biographie* (3d ed.; Paris, 1859), p. 162. See also the *Mémoires de la Comtesse de Boigne* (Adèle d'Osmond), ed. Marquise d'Osmond (Paris, 1921), I, 292: "It was no longer a public matter—one had no personal connection with it, and one was not allowed to inquire about it: the emperor had made such an effort to make it his affair and not ours, that one had finally taken him at his word. And, whatever people may have been saying about him for the last few years, in 1814 everybody, including his army and officials, was so tired that they asked for nothing but to be relieved from an effort that had ceased to be directed by a wise and reasonable will."

There still survived republican patriots who had fallen into disfavor with Napoleon because of their outspoken criticism. One of them was Lazare Carnot, who had voted against the establishment of a hereditary monarchy by Napoleon. In his speech on that occasion he emphasized that he could not consent to regard liberty, a good so superior to all others and without which the others were nothing, as but an illusion. "My heart tells me that liberty is possible, that a free regime is easy to maintain and that it is more stable than any arbitrary government." In spite of his refusal to sanction the destruction of liberty, he repeated that he was always ready to sacrifice his dearest affections to the interests of the fatherland.[30] The disaster of 1813 called him from retirement to the defense of his country. He offered Napoleon his services, was appointed commander of the garrison of Antwerp, and proved there "a faithful and incorruptible soldier." When Louis XVIII became king of France, Carnot addressed a memorandum to him in July 1814, in which he emphasized the need of nationalism to unite the French people. "Only a noble and strong passion can do it, and this passion can only be love of the fatherland. One must therefore insure its birth, one must create a national spirit; that is what we lack, and what we lack to such a degree that we can hardly conceive of it, so that scarcely one of us understands how one can sacrifice one's personal interest to the general interest, and forget oneself for the salvation and glory of one's country."

The French, Carnot went on to say, would hardly believe in the possibilities of patriotism if they had not seen its development in England, where all private fortunes were tied up with the common good and where, therefore, everyone was strongly interested in the general welfare. France must develop, he believed, a similar patriotism, though its focus would be different. "England makes it a point of honor to regard herself as the center of great maritime enterprises which unite all nations; France must make it hers to profit from the gifts with which nature has prodigiously endowed her." He demanded a loving attachment to French soil and its cultivation without any wish for rivalry with the British in foreign trade, supremacy in which was assured to the latter for a very long time by geographic position and the balance of power in Europe. Such a love of the fatherland, Carnot believed, would unite the various national forces

[30] Huntley Dupre, *Lazare Carnot, Republican Patriot* (Oxford, Ohio, 1940), p. 264.

in a common sentiment and task and preserve them from adventures and conquest.[31]

At the same time, two of the most influential thinkers of the coming generation, Claude-Henri Saint-Simon, the great visionary of early socialism, and Augustin Thierry, his disciple and the future historian, published in October 1814 *De la réorganization de la société européenne*, in which they regarded an Anglo-French alliance as desirable but impossible. Half a year later, in their *Opinion sur les mesures à prendre contre la coalition de 1815*, they proposed to found a new Europe on an alliance between the two nations. Such co-operation, they thought, was demanded by interest and necessity alike; and though the authors foresaw that the French would at present reject it, they were convinced that the time would come when such a union would put an end to French turmoil and ills. The two nations were in one respect complementary: Britain had at its disposal accumulated trade capital, France a fertile soil. More important was their community of political ideas. Britain had behind it one hundred and thirty years of the parliamentary government upon which the French were now embarking; the constitutional party in France would find in the British nation support against both the defenders of despotism and those of an extravagant liberty. France was the only nation on the continent of Europe, all the other states were only governments; between France and Britain nation could speak to nation and influence the governments to act according to the national will.

Therefore, the two authors demanded that the French nation, which Napoleon had convoked for June 1, 1815 to swear fidelity to the constitution on the Champ de Mai, reviving for that purpose the old name of the Frankish assembly, declare: "That the English people, by the conformity of our institutions with its own, by that affinity of principles and that community of social interest which are the strongest ties between men, is henceforward our natural ally; that the will of the French nation, that the interest of England and France, the interest of the whole of Europe, demand that this union be rendered more intimate, stronger and more regular by an accord between the governments; and that, therefore, the Assembly order the

---

[31] A. Aulard, "Les idées politiques de Carnot," *Révolution française*, XIV (1888), 640-58; and René Girard, "Carnot et l'éducation populaire pendant les Cent Jours," *Révolution française*, LII (1907), 424-48.

government that it was to create, to conclude an alliance with the British government." Saint-Simon and Thierry insisted that the making of the constitution of the French state should be adjourned until the war crisis of 1815 was averted, so that the nation could deliberate freely.[32]

Their hopes were not realized. The Assembly of the Champ de Mai adopted the Acte additionnel which Napoleon proposed to meet the demands for liberal reforms after his return from Elba. It was accepted without enthusiasm and without confidence: Napoleon did not like concessions so contrary to his personality and temperament, the people found them insufficient to safeguard liberty against the return of despotism. But whatever their feeling toward Napoleon, most Frenchmen were willing to fight. They resented the returning Bourbons and *émigrés* even more than they did Napoleon, they were eager to preserve the social gains of the Revolution, and they were bitter at the humiliation of France by the invading armies. For the first time genuine national feeling seemed to rally around Napoleon. It was too late. Waterloo brought the Bourbons back, and though the peace terms were generous and mild and France was preserved within its territorial frontiers of 1791, the fall from towerings heights of glory and power had been too steep not to leave its mark upon French national pride. Waterloo was regarded as an English victory, the outcome of the long wars of the Revolution as a British triumph; emotionally, French nationalism was to be directed for many years against England. Their common ideal of liberty did not, as Saint-Simon and Thierry had hoped, unite the two nations in the face of a Europe in which nationalism had either not yet awakened the peoples or had taken a definite turn away from the conception of a free society based upon rational law and rights of citizens to a romantic longing for originality and uniqueness and close communal ties based upon the call of the blood and the lure of the past.

Many Frenchmen, after having conquered and occupied foreign lands and dismembered states, remained deeply resentful for a long time of the peace treaty of 1815, which treated them much less harshly than they had treated others. A legendary interpretation of Napoleon revived his cult in France for a short while, and Jacobin fanaticism, with its exaltation of the common weal and engineering of the human soul, still has not died out in France. Nevertheless, in France the liberalism of 1789 has proved the most lasting heritage of

[32] Stewart and Desjardins, *op. cit.*, pp. 160-65.

all. It was only outside France that the essential Napoleonic traits were revived and then only after the nineteenth century, the age of the bourgeoisie and of nationalism, had ended in the German "spirit of 1914" and in Lenin's revolution, both opposed to the principles of 1789.

Napoleon's regime foreshadowed the twentieth-century totalitarians who "regarded weakness as ignoble, laws as superfluous subtleties, and despised parliamentary forms for their allegedly unbearable slowness. They preferred rapid and trenchant decisions as in war and thought unanimity of opinion as essential as in an army. Opposition they regarded as disorder, critical reasoning as revolt, the courts as military tribunals, the judges as soldiers who must execute the orders of authority, those who were suspect or accused as if they were enemies and convicted criminals, and the judgments of the courts as battles in the state of war into which they had transformed government." [33] Like Napoleon, they had little respect for the nature of man and of things and arrogantly and forcefully intended to regiment the human soul. Systematic imposition of a common pattern promised to facilitate government and to strengthen authority. Men thus reduced to similarity and equality afforded ready material for the engineering feats of the *hubris* of the leaders. In France, however, the imprescriptible rights of the Declaration of Rights of Man and the Citizen had taken too deep root to allow the sacrifices of the human personality to the collectivities which arose in the age of nationalism.

The nineteenth century was in the main a period of the growth of constitutional liberties and commercial intercourse. Toward its end, however, Nietzsche predicted the coming of a new and more "virile" age. "We owe it to Napoleon," he wrote, "that several warlike centuries, which have not had their like in past history, may now follow one another—in short, that we have entered upon the classical age of war, war at the same time scientific and popular." Nietzsche's expectation of "several warlike centuries" may be wrong; but he forecast correctly the character of the new era that began in August 1914 and November 1917, in which individual national life no longer formed the center of concern. "Inescapably, hesitatingly, terrible like fate, the great task and question approaches: how should the earth as a whole be administered? And to what end should man as a whole—no longer a people or a race—be raised and bred?" To

[33] Slightly paraphrased from Constant, *De l'esprit de conquête*, p. 25.

that end, Napoleon, as Nietzsche said, "wanted *one* Europe, which was to be the mistress of the world." [34]

Napoleon appeared as a "violent anachronism" in the age of nationalism; at its beginning, for the protection of their liberty, tranquillity, and diversity, the other peoples united against him and overthrew his new order of conquest and uniformity. Their resistance sealed his fate. In the first war of nationalities he perished. But his violence aroused dark passions hostile to the Enlightenment, which had formed the background of his own ideas. Napoleon was still a rational classicist whom Goethe and Hegel greeted as an embodiment of the world spirit, but the superman in him broke the bounds of the human and the humane. Romantically, a man alone against the world, he rose above the common law in the certainty of his historical mission. What would happen if a whole people followed his lead and—without the safeguards of respect for reason and the essential oneness of men of all classes and nations—also rose above the common law, ready to stand alone against the world, and bear this burden in equal certainty of historical mission?

11

France Between Britain and Germany[*]

In the intellectual history of eighteenth-century France Voltaire's *Lettres sur les Anglais* marked a milestone. They established England with its enlightened literature and freedom of life as a model for France. Mlle de Lespinasse (1732-1776) expressed this trend well in

[34] Friedrich W. Nietzsche, *The Will to Power*, trans. A. M. Ludovici (New York, 1924), Book IV, "On breeding: the masters of the world," No. 951; *The Joyful Wisdom*, Book V, "We fearless ones," No. 362; and *Genealogy of Morals*, first essay, "Good and evil, good and bad," No. 16.

[*] Read before the Tenth International Congress of Historical Sciences at Rome, Sept. 8, 1955; reprinted from *Journal of the History of Ideas*, Vol. XVII, No. 3, June 1956, pp. 283-299.

her letters, "Il n'y a que la gloire de Voltaire qui pourrait me consoler de ne pas être née Anglaise." This relationship persisted in spite of the wars which the two countries fought for hegemony on three continents. It changed, however, completely with the progress of the French Revolution after 1789. France was now convinced that she had achieved true liberty and had far surpassed England; this tremendous advance, accomplished by an unprecedented heroic effort, established France's undisputed claim to the leadership of mankind on the road to liberty as well as her moral superiority. In French eyes, France now represented the virtue of Rome, England the corruption of Carthage. The heroism of republican France was pitted against British perfidious plutocracy which defended the past, the age of despotism and barbarism. Napoleon expressed a widespread conviction when in his decree of October 26, 1806 he called the British not only "les éternels ennemis de notre nation" but also the disturbers of the peace of Europe and the tyrants of the sea.

In the exaltation of victory which the French poets began to celebrate in 1794, their wrath and their scorn was directed above all against England. Lebrun's "Hymne à la victoire" after the battle of Fleurus thanked God "who fought on our behalf" for "this vast coffin of Fleurus,"

> Où des rois expire l'orgueil,
> Où périt l'insulaire avare;
> C'est là qu'au fer de nos soldats,
> L'Anglais fourbe, lâche et barbare
> A payé ses assassinats.

In his "Ode nationale contre l'Angleterre" Lebrun predicted a few years later the complete annihilation of England:

> Tremble, nouvelle Tyr! un nouvel Alexandre
> Sur l'onde où tu regnais va disperser ta cendre:
> Ton nom même n'est plus.

And Chénier, glorifying the recapture of Toulon, had no doubt that "the insolent rival of a magnanimous people will everywhere be beaten down," for

> Le Français au combat marche avec la vertu,
> Et l'Anglais marche avec le crime.

The French were going to save mankind from English brigandage:

> L'Univers se soulève; il remet en nos mains
> Le soin de recouvrer le public héritage,
> Et les bras des nouveaux Romains
> Renverseront l'autre Carthage.

In 1797 Rouget de Lisle sang a "Chant des vengeances," a song of hate against England, which still refused to succumb to France:

> L'affreux brigand de la Tamise
> N'a point succombé sous nos coups! . . .
> Vengeance! Nous ferons justice
> À Londres, à nous, à l'univers.
> Artisan des malheurs du monde,
> Trop fier dominateur de l'onde,
> En vain crois-tu nous échapper:
> Sur les rochers inaccessibles,
> Le géant, de ses bras terribles,
> Va te saisir et te frapper.

These sentiments, strengthened during the Napoleonic Wars, explain the fact that the French feelings of bitter humiliation after 1815 and Waterloo turned against Britain much more than against Prussia. For decades French patriots hated Britain and longed for her punishment. When Michelet visited England in 1834, he was deeply mortified by his recognition that the collapse of Britain, which he had foreseen and desired, might after all not happen. All the monuments of London revolted him by evoking in him the memory of "Waterloo, Waterloo, partout!" [1] This anti-British feeling was hardly motivated rationally, for British statesmen had shown great moderation toward defeated France in 1815, whereas Prussian statesmen and German writers had insisted not only on a large French indemnity but also on the cession of Alsace and Lorraine, of Flanders and the Franche-Comté. German demands for annexation of French territories, already considerable in 1814, received great encouragement by the war of 1815. Field Marshall Gneisenau in his letter to Justus Gruner on July 7, 1815 insisted that France should pay not only an indemnity covering all costs of war, but that her payments should put Prussian finances on a new basis. In his letter to Prince Hardenberg of June 22, he reviled diplomacy in a most characteristic manner and de-

---

[1] See Hans Kohn, *Prophets and Peoples* (New York, 1946), 49 ff.

manded ruthless annexations. The British drew upon themselves the scorn of romanticists and liberals alike for becoming the jailers of Napoleon on a far off island, but Stein and Gneisenau had demanded Napoleon's execution. If they had prevailed, it would have deprived the fallen emperor of the opportunity of creating in his memoirs that legend which inspired so many youths during the Restoration.[2]

This remarkable change of attitude in nineteenth-century intellectual France toward England coincided with a sudden veneration for Germany which took the place held by Britain in the preceding century. In both cases it was "progressive" France and not the government that looked with admiration at the neighbor. In the new orientation, Madame de Staël's visit to Germany and her discovery of the intellectual life of the then hardly known country played the same rôle which Voltaire's visit to England and his report had played one hundred years before. To the newer French generation Madame de Staël communicated both her enthusiasm for German thought, for "la patrie de la pensée," and her misreading of the apparently peaceful and apolitical character of the Germans. In the cosmopolitan spirit of eighteenth-century liberalism she knew how to combine a profound and justified fascination for the surprising fertility of the German genius—which attained its greatest height at the time of Germany's greatest political weakness—with an unwavering loyalty "to the fortunate English constitution," the political guiding light for France and Europe. She knew that Britain owed the victory in the long struggle, in which that nation often stood alone, to the love of liberty, and that this traditional liberty was better founded than the revolutionary and absolute liberty of France. For the sake of the growth of French liberty she hoped for the closest cooperation between Britain and France.[3]

In this attitude Madame de Staël was not at all alone. In October

[2] See Georg H. Pertz and Hans Delbrück, *Das Leben des Feldmarschalls Grafen Neithardt von Gneisenau*, IV (Berlin, 1880), 568, 529, 542. Cf. also Karl Grievank, *Der Wiener Kongress und die Europäische Restauration 1814-15* (Leipzig, 1954), 340 f.

[3] Madame de Staël clearly recognized negative traits in German public life. Telling of an encounter between her son and a German captain, she writes: "Le capitaine lui avait répondu avec une brutalité qu'on ne saurait rencontrer que chez les Allemands; l'on ne rencontre aussi que là ce respect obséquieux pour le pouvoir qui succède immédiatement à l'arrogance envers les faibles." "Dix Années d'Exil," *Oeuvres Complètes* (Paris, 1838), II, 387. *De l'Allemagne* encouraged the Germans. Goethe wrote in a letter of Feb. 17, 1814: "In the present moment the book has a miraculous effect. If it had appeared earlier, one would have attributed to it an influence upon the present great events." *Goethes Briefe*, ed. Stein (Berlin, 1905), VI, 293.

1814 Saint-Simon and the young Augustin Thierry published an essay on "The reorganization of European society" in order to preserve peace and secure liberty, which would make the development of an industrial society possible. Saint-Simon suggested that Britain and France, both liberal and parliamentary states, should unite to form the nucleus of a future European federation. From such a union France would profit most, the two Frenchmen declared, because Britain had behind her one hundred thirty years of parliamentary government upon which the French were only then embarking, and the constitutional parties in France needed British support against the domestic threats of despotism on the one hand and of an extravagant liberty on the other hand. Saint-Simon demanded from his fellow-countrymen the recognition that the English people "by the conformity of our institutions with its own, by that affinity of principles and that community of social interests which are the strongest ties between men, is henceforth our natural ally." [4]

The French constitutional monarchy shared on the whole this point of view. The two Western governments cooperated closely during the period: in many ways they represented the liberalism of the rising middle class as opposed to the conservative absolutism of the Holy Alliance. But intellectual France was largely in opposition to the government and to its pro-British policy; to the heirs of Jacobin patriotism and Napoleonic heroism the government's policy seemed too peaceful, too sober, too commercial. July 1830 for a brief time raised the hopes of the "patriots." The Bourbons had been imposed in the wake of a defeat. Even their efforts to restore the national prestige by participation in the campaigns in Spain and for Greece, and the step which they took toward establishing the French-African empire by the invasion of Algeria, did not increase their popularity. Greater things were expected when the "King of the Holy Alliance" was replaced in 1830 by the "King of the Revolution," and the tri-

[4] Saint-Simon and Thierry went so far as to demand an Anglo-French Parliament, composed of two-thirds English and one-third French deputies because the French needed "the guidance of the experienced English." The text of Saint-Simon's proposal is now easily accessible in *De la Réorganisation de la Société Européenne* (Paris, 1925), and Saint-Simon, *Selected Writings* (New York, 1952). A German in Paris, Count Gustav Schlabrendorf (1750-1824), one of the early friends of the French Revolution, in 1814 rightly regarded England as the true home of liberty in the sense "as to allow everyone without being a hero and ever ready to fight for it, to live always as a free man and with dignity." But he was afraid that England might fall behind France if it did not take three decisive steps: the emancipation of the Catholics, the placation of Ireland, and the reform of Parliament. E. A. Varnhagen, *Denkwürdigkeiten des eigenen Lebens* (Leipzig, 1843), pt. III, 188 ff.

color again waved over France.⁵ But except for the brief interlude of 1840 Louis Philippe followed the peaceful policy of Louis XVIII. Yet the events of 1840 seemed to bear out the predictions of the French intellectual opposition: Britain and Russia combined to frustrate France's ambition in the Levant. Henrich Heine reported from Paris to the *Augsburger Allgemeine Zeitung* on July 27, 1840 that "mit Ausnahme der Legitimisten, die ihr Heil nur vom Ausland erwarten, versammeln sich alle Franzosen um die dreifarbige Fahne, und Krieg mit dem perfiden Albion ist ihre gemeinsame Parole." Two days later he wrote again of the "Ränke des perfiden Albions" and of the "Schlangenlist Karthagos." ⁶

Thwarted in his ambitions in the Mediterranean, Thiers turned toward the Rhine. There too he was stopped, not so much by the Great Powers as by the violent and, to the French, unexpected flareup of German national feeling which found its expression in the famous Rhine poetry of that year. Peace was preserved thanks to Louis Philippe; the government under Guizot returned to the policy of close cooperation with Britain. Like Charles Maurras later, though with a different emphasis, Michelet was convinced that England in the eighteenth century had plotted to undermine France and was now continuing the nefarious game. "Covering her sordid interests with political fictions in mendacious language in which she herself does not believe," he wrote, "England has long been working for the ruin of France, using in the eighteenth century the genius of France —Voltaire, Montesquieu, Mirabeau—to deceive her." Michelet suspected the British of designs on Cherbourg and of plans to annihilate France as they had, without direct conquest, annihilated the Dutch. "Strange and capricious insolence!" he exclaimed. "To wish to domineer over a country which in spite of its paltry government of that time was influencing and captivating the world by the power of the mind! To rule requires the right, and this right is an idea . . . I should like to see an English idea! A great and fruitful moral idea!

---

⁵ Lerminier, "Lettres Philosophiques addressées à un Berlinois," Letter 5, dated Paris, May 21, 1832 (*Revue des deux mondes*, VI, 580): "Quand vous songez à la France, monsieur, considérez avec respect les trois couleurs; elles sont l'image sacrée de notre religion politique, l'unique symbole qui, à nos yeux aujourd'hui, signifie quelque chose: glorie de la patrie, indépendance nationale, émancipation européenne, liberté et puissance de l'esprit humain, voilà ce que représente pour nous le drapeau tricolore. Non, je n'oublierai jamais l'enthousiasme qui passa dans mon coeur quand je le vis reparaître; c'était ma première joie patriotique, depuis qu'enfant, j'avais pleuré sur Waterloo, à côté de ma mère."
⁶ Heine, *Werke* (Hamburg, 1885), IX, 262, 264.

England never had, nor will she ever have, any great moralist or jurist."

Michelet in his history of the early years of the French Revolution predicted, as so many Continentals then did, that the England of his own day was doomed through its "lugubrious spectacle of juvenile misery," not only economically, but racially. "No remedy will cure this," he wrote in the 1840's, ". . . The whole hope of the aristocracy is that those millions of men who are dying and who are replaced by dying children, will die at least in silence and without any disturbance." He compared the brutish British working man with the French worker who, though he may be less well-fed, as Michelet conceded, nevertheless in handling the pickax knew that his father had handled the sword at Marengo and Austerlitz. And yet under Louis Philippe British capitalism was invading France. Michelet could hardly bear this spectacle. "Impious, thrice impious . . . is it to behold a Frenchman in France under the rod of an Englishman! The son of the Grand Army under a serf whose father made nothing but calico or something still more trivial! It is the Government's most sacred duty to stop these indignities. Economic interests, the freedom of industry, and all such grand words are of no use in this matter. The foreigner, they reply, brings us capital. But what if he takes away our honor!" [7]

Michelet shared a widely held view that the commercialization of French life after the English model would destroy France. Louis Blanc expressed similar views in his *Organisation du Travail,* first published in 1839. Depicting a doomed and decaying Britain with colors as gloomy as those employed by Michelet, he too attributed social disaster not only to a wrong economic system but also to moral depravity. Louis Blanc was convinced that England would expiate her sins to the full. Already now, in the middle of the nineteenth century, her power was fast waning. "L'empire de la mer lui échappe." [8] The fifth edition published before Louis Blanc was forced to seek refuge in England contained a chapter "La concurrence aboutit nécessairement à une guerre à mort entre la France et l'Angleterre." All the fallacies of the "economic" interpretation of history were assembled here: that commercial rivalry must lead to war—yet in the one hundred years since 1848, France and England did not fight each

---

[7] Michelet, *Historical View of the French Revolution from its Earliest Indications to the Flight of the King in 1791* (London, 1890), 430-56.
[8] Louis Blanc, *Organisation du Travail,* 9th rev. ed. (Paris, 1850), 67.

other but three times fought side by side, in the Crimean War and in the two World Wars—and that capitalistic Britain cannot exist without subjecting the whole world to its economic exploitation. "Aujourd'hui comme hier comme toujours, il faut que cette race indomptable dans sa cupidité cherche et trouve des consommateurs... L'Angleterre ... ne peut vivre, ainsi le veut sa constitution économique qu'à la condition d'asservir le monde par ses marchands." [9]

Michelet was convinced that France, which he identified with Europe and civilization, was threatened by two enemies from the outskirts of Europe, England and Russia. But the chief enemy was England. "The war of all wars, the struggle of all struggles, is that between Britain and France, the rest are episodes." England was to him "l'anti-France." [10] He denounced those who spoke of perpetual peace, while black smoke was rising over the arsenals in Kronstadt and Portsmouth. At that time Victor Hugo denounced the same enemies of Europe and disturbers of the peace: "Now as two hundred years ago, there are two powerful nations gazing at Europe with covetous eyes. A spirit of warfare, violence, and conquest is still rampant in the East; a spirit of greed and craftiness and adventure is still rampant in the West. The two giants seem to have moved a little further northward as if to seize the Continent a little higher up. Russia has taken the place of Turkey, England has succeeded Spain." [11] In that situation Hugo like Michelet and other French intellectuals looked for Franco-German cooperation to form a "third force" to save Europe and civilization from Atlantic commercialism and Eurasian barbarism. They had no apprehensions in regard to Germany, least of all of Prussia. Madame de Staël as a Protestant had sympathized with Prussia, the heir of Luther and Kant, and the younger generations followed her by seeing Prussia as the home of

---

[9] *Organisation du Travail*, 5th revised edition (Paris: Au Bureau de la Societé de l'Industrie Fraternelle, 1848), 97-101. Louis Blanc was no pacifist, no more so than Michelet. France should not fight England, Louis Blanc wrote, for reasons of economic competition—and to that end she should abandon competitive economy which not only leads to wars but to misery—however, "que la France tire l'épée pour la liberté des peuples, tous les hommes de coeur applaudiront" (101). Michelet too was convinced that France, except under the bourgeois rule of Louis Philippe, was not a mercantile country. "La France n'a pas l'âme marchande sauf ses moments anglais, comme celui de Law et celui-ci, qui sont des accès rares." *Oeuvres Complètes de Michelet, Histoire Sociale* (Paris: Calmann-Lévy, n.d.), VI, 145. Proudhon too believed that Cobden's free trade agitation was a hypocritical device for ruining France. On March 18, 1852 he wrote to Dr. Cretin "Mordez les libre-échangistes, les anglophiles, jusqu'au sang. Ne craignez pas, à cet égard, de réveiller le vieux chauvinisme français, anti-anglais."
[10] *Loc. cit.*, 307.
[11] Victor Hugo, *The Rhine* (Guernsey Edition, Boston, n.d.), II, 167.

the Enlightenment and not of militarism and regarding Austria as traditionally hostile to France and liberty. Prussia was *the* intellectual Germany, and this Germany was in Hugo's eyes France's "natural collaborator." No mean commercialism threatened from that quarter, as it did from England which, as Hugo wrote, waged a "sometimes secret, sometimes open, but never flagging warfare against France." No Frenchman could "help thinking of the old Punic spirit that struggled so long against civilization in ancient times. The Punic spirit is the spirit of commerce, . . . the spirit of greed, the spirit of selfishness. Eventually, England will either be crushed by the formidable opposition of the universe, or she will be brought to realize that the reign of Carthage is past." [12] But if a Frenchman turned his eyes from the neighbor beyond the channel to the neighbor east of the Rhine, how different and uplifting was the sight there. Germany was the home of the mind, of disinterested spirituality, fundamentally similar, as Hugo thought, to France—poetical, imaginative, and liberal. As if replying indirectly to the words and sentiments of Mlle Lespinasse, Hugo wrote in January 1842 that "Germany is one of the lands he loves and admires. He has a filial sentiment for this noble and holy fatherland of all thinkers. If he were not a Frenchman, he would wish to be a German." [13] Hugo wrote this after one visit to the Rhine. Six years before, when he entered Germany for the first time, Gérard de Nerval exclaimed "L'Allemagne! la terre de Goethe et de Schiller, le pays d' Hoffman, la vieille Allemagne, notre mère à tous, Teutonia!" He came there full of admiration for the German poets whom he loved and translated and full of the idyllic images which Madame de Staël had drawn of a good and peaceful Germany, where thinkers and poets dreamt of absolute poetry and philosophy and noble and dedicated youth fought for the realization of liberty.[14]

This view of Germany had litle to do with reality even at the time more than a quarter of a century before, when Madame de Staël traveled there. Nerval, in spite of his frequent visits to Germany, with his dreamy mind never understood the Germany of his time.

---

12 *Ibid.*, 229 f.
13 *Ibid.*, Introduction, xxiii.
14 *Souvenirs d'Allemagne, Loreley* (Paris, 1860), 16. On p. 12 he calls Germany "ma seconde mère." See also Julia Cartier, *Un Intermédiaire entre la France et l'Allemagne, Gérard de Nerval* (Geneva, 1904). In his drama "Leo Burckart" which he wrote in 1839 Nerval took the assassination of Kotzebue by the student Sand as the starting point to discuss the Burschenschaften as picturesque and mysterious societies of noble utopians who dreamt of justice and liberty.

Other Frenchmen noticed the new active dynamism, the aspirations for practical and political life, which animated Germany after 1830. But they were convinced that the Germans were enthusiastically following in the wake of France, adhering to the same liberal ideas as the French intellectuals, that they desired to cooperate "plus ardemment que jamais à la sainte alliance des peuples." Taillandier wrote this in 1848, in the very year when the unchained nationalisms in central Europe defeated the hopes of liberalism and of a peaceful cooperation among nationalities.[15]

Taillandier knew German literature well; yet he believed in the strength and future of the French liberal ideas in Germany, ideas represented by poets like Heinrich Heine and historians like Karl von Rotteck and Friedrich Schlosser, but whose impact on the German educated public was rapidly diminishing. The French intellectuals refused to see that Germany led by Prussia raised territorial claims—justified or not—against France which had not been realized in 1815; they disregarded Heine's prophetic warnings that the German intellectual classes bitterly opposed the very ideas which had triumphed in July 1830. These illusions held not only poets like Victor Hugo spell-bound, but scholars who knew the history and geography of Germany well like Philippe Le Bas. He clearly recognized the new, hard-driving Prussian dynamism: "La Prusse, jeune encore, est aussi pleine de sève, de force, d'espérances, et surtout d'ambition. De Berlin, des universités prussiennes, est parti en 1813 ce cri de guerre qui embrasa l'Allemagne. L'enthousiasme des Prussiens a réveillé de sa léthargie le reste de la nation, a fait naître ces rêves de grandeur auxquels elle a dû une vigueur nouvelle." [16] He admired Prussia like most progressive and enlightened Frenchmen of that day as a model of administration and instruction. He was convinced, like Victor Hugo, that this progressive Prussia was France's natural ally, destined to live in peace with her and to follow French (or as he thought: universal) civilization; therefore Prussia would gladly cede the left bank of the Rhine to France. For that reason, France should view with sympathy the progress and aggrandizement of Prussia: "Malgré toute la différence du génie des deux nations, l'Allemagne est destinée à vivre en paix avec nous; la Prusse

[15] Saint-René Taillandier, *Histoire de la Jeune Allemagne, Études Littéraires (Paris, 1848)*, xvi. See also 329, 385 f.
[16] Ph. Le Bas, *États de la Confédération Germanique, pour faire suite à l'historie générale de l'Allemagne* (Paris, 1842), section on Prussia, 74.

est notre alliée naturelle, comme elle est notre rivale en lumières, en vigueur, en nobilité, en bonne administration. Seulement, fortifiée par son protectorat sur l'Allemagne entière, elle devrait nous abandonner . . . ces provinces de la rive gauche du Rhin, si nécessaires à notre défense du côté de l'est et du nord-est . . . Nous pourrions alors entretenir avec l'Allemagne des rapports basés sur des besoins identiques et sur un gouvernement semblable, et cette union nouvelle ne serait point précaire comme celle que nos gouvernants avaient si chèrement achetée de ces insulaires toujours dominés par leurs intérêts mercantiles." [17]

If a sober scholar could arrive at this conclusion, there is little wonder that the romantic poet went much further. German romanticism was conservative, nationalist, and opposed to the ideas of 1789, French romanticism was liberal, cosmopolitan, and inspired by the faith in rational progress. Yet to the French romantic poet, France and Germany seemed almost twins. "France and Germany are really Europe. Germany is the heart; France is the head. Germany and France are essentially civilization: Germany feels, France thinks; the heart and brain composed a civilized man. . . . They were of the same origin; they struggled together against the Romans; they were brothers in days gone by, they are brothers now, they will be brothers in times to come. Their mode of formation, too, has been the same. They are not isolated nations; they did not acquire their possessions by conquest; they are true sons of European soil." [18] Hugo carried this identification of the essential character and the interests of the two countries so far that in the preface to his trilogy "Les Burgraves" he hoped for the resurrection of the "glorious military messiah of Germany," of the sleeping imperial hero. That the awakening of Barbarossa might evoke the *furor teutonicus* against France and bring military disaster to her, did not dawn upon the French poet.[19]

---

[17] *Ibid.*, 75 f. Le Bas saw Prussia's arrogance and aggressiveness, but was convinced that Prussia would conduct herself in the near future with greater wisdom and restraint. Her militarism was explained and excused by the geo-political situation of Prussia and was therefore regarded as a passing phenomenon. (77 f.)

[18] Hugo, *op. cit.*, 188.

[19] The preface is dated March 25, 1843. The passage reads: "Qu'il serait beau peut-être de réveiller pour un moment et de faire sortir des profondeurs mystérieuses où il est enseveli le glorieux messie militaire que l'Allemagne attend encore, le dormeur impérial de Kaiserslautern, et de jeter, terrible et foudroyant, au milieu des géants du Rhin, le Jupiter du douzième siècle, Frédéric Barberousse." *Oeuvres Complètes de Victor Hugo* (Paris, éd. Hetzel-Quantin, L. Hébert, n.d.), IV, 250. In the same preface Hugo proclaimed the existence of a European nationality, resembling the Greek nationality at the time of the independent city-states: "Partout où est la lumière, l'intelligence se

Under these conditions the French believed it easy to find a solution to the Rhine problem, not according to Arndt, who proclaimed the Rhine Germany's stream and not Germany's frontier, but by making the Rhine a river, common to both nations. E. Lerminier, a student of German literature and of international law, appealed to the Germans and the French to join hands across the Rhine: "Enfan[t]s de Charlemagne, Germains et Gallo-Francs, vous n'êtes pas voués à d'éternelles inimitiés; nous nous embrasserons un jour, et nous trinquerons ensemble sur les bords du Rhin, ce fleuve qui comme Charlemagne appartient à l'Allemagne et à la France!" [20] Hugo, too, saw the Rhine as the common link between the two nations, "both fertilized and closely united by that regenerating stream." In their union they would find strength, France to force England back into the ocean, Germany to expel Russia back into Asia. Thus Europe and civilization could be saved. But England and Russia were bent on dividing France and Germany. To that end they had insisted on taking the left bank of the Rhine from France and giving it to Germany, apparently—though Hugo doesn't say it expressly—against the true wishes of Germany. As a result of these British and Russian intrigues, France and Germany, "two nations which were by nature constituted to understand and love each other feel a mutual antipathy which really amounts to hatred." Under these circumstances there was only one way left to defeat British greed and Russian lust for conquest: "return to France what God gave her—the left bank of the Rhine." [21] Did any real threat to France come from Germany, Hugo was forced to ask himself a short while after the Franco-German tension of 1840. He emphatically denied it. These two generous nations, sisters by

---

sent chez elle et est chez elle . . . la civilisation tout entière est la patrie du poète. Cette patrie n'a d'autre frontière que la ligne sombre et fatale où commence la barbarie. Un jour, espérons-le, le globe entier sera civilisé, tous les points de la demeure humaine seront éclairés, et alors sera accompli le magnifique rêve de l'intelligence: avoir pour patrie le monde et pour nation l'humanité." *Ibid.*, 254 f.

[20] Lerminier, *De l'influence de la philosophie du XVIIIe siècle sur la Législation et la Sociabilité du XIXe* (Paris, n.d), 317.

[21] Hugo, *The Rhine, op. cit.* vol. II, pp. 189, 191, 194, 224. After 1815 Russia became in French eyes the second antagonist of France and of European civilization. During the French Revolution it had been Britain alone. A. Thiers, *Histoire de la Révolution Française* (Leipzig, 1846), II, 299-301, wrote about the rôle of England. ". . . enfin l'Angleterre laissant la France se déchirer elle-même, le continent s'épuiser, les colonies se devaster, et abandonnant ainsi le soin de sa vengeance aux désordres inevitables des révolutions . . . Pitt . . . voulait, en un mot, rendre sa patrie maîtresse du monde, . . . Tandis que, par cette logique machiavélique, il désenchantait les Anglais de la liberté française, il soulevait l'Europe contre nous, et ses envoyés disposaient toutes les puissances à la guerre . . . On livrait la France à Pitt, parce qu'elle avait voulu se donner la liberté qu'elle n'avait pas encore!"

blood as well as in thought, would certainly become reconciled. "Germany, who has proved herself so valiant in war, is sure to become reasonable and considerate in time of peace." Germany would even love Napoleon. He "was too truly great for Germany to be able to long withhold her admiration from him, too unfortunate for her not to love him again eventually; and to the French who never have, and who never will, forget St. Helena, any person who loves and admires the great emperor is a Frenchman." Hugo's pacifist reasonings were as unfounded in the case of Germany as they were in the case of France. He called both "disinterested and noble-hearted nations, formerly nations of warriors but now nations of thinkers." Yet in France and Germany, the military spirit was alive, in France as a heritage of Napoleon, in Germany as a heritage of the struggle against Napoleon.[22] Hugo's conviction about French pacifism was not then shared by Michelet. He proudly asserted that France was in 1846 the only nation "that has a genuine army" where the people still have "the sentiment of military honor always renewed by our heroic legend, the invisible spirit of the heroes of our wars, the wind of the old flag. . . . Sacred bayonets of France, take care that nothing will darken that light which shines over you and which no eye can bear."[23] Hugo on the other hand regarded France of that time as basing her world supremacy, "that never can be taken from her, no longer on arms but on her literature, on her language, and the always profound sympathies of her sister nations."[24] But the idea that the Germans might reject French cultural leadership and might go so far as to deny French intellectual and moral equality, was never even considered by Hugo.

One of the few Frenchmen who saw Germany in a different light was Edgar Quinet. Like his friend Michelet, he had been an ardent admirer of Germany, but his intimate knowledge of the country made

[22] Hugo, *op. cit.*, 194. Heine, who disliked the British thoroughly but loved both the Germans and the French with an ever lively and critical mind, wrote in his letter to the *Augsburger Allgemeine Zeitung* (May 20, 1840): "The French, apart from all republican peculiarities, are by nature fundamentally Bonapartist. They are wanting in simplicity . . . in inner and external repose; they love war for its own sake; even in peace their life is all battle and noise; old and young are gay and happy in the roll of drums and gunpowder smoke and explosions of every kind." *The Works of Heinrich Heine*, tr. by C. G. Leland (London, 1893), VIII, 71. On German militarism see the excellent article by Ludwig Dehio, "Um den deutschen Militarismus," *Historische Zeitschrift*, 180 (Aug. 1955), 43-64.

[23] Hans Kohn, *Prophets and Peoples, op. cit.*, 61 f.

[24] Hugo, *op. cit.*, 222. Hugo was convinced that French as the accepted universal language would create world unity through interchange of ideas and thereby perpetual peace (227).

him remark as early as 1831: "Il est un pays qui nous a toujours trompés dans nos jugements. Toujours nous l'avons cherché à un demisiècle de distance de la place où il était réellement, tant son génie est peu conforme au nôtre, et nous donne peu de prise pour le saisir." [25] Quinet pointed out that the weak and inefficient despotism of Austria was harmless compared with the intelligent and enterprising despotism of Prussia which exercised a great attraction on the national spirit of all Germans. As France suffered from the defeat of 1815, so Germany, Quinet pointed out, suffered from the treaties of 1648 and was intent upon undoing them. The recent idolization of German intellectual life by non-Germans was changing the former German humility into an arrogant susceptibility, which at the slightest criticism gave the Germans the feeling of being a misunderstood nation not appreciated according to its true worth.[26]

Quinet wrote in the 1830's in such a way about the Germans that during the First World War his articles could be republished as a "prophetic" voice. The former people of poets and thinkers, Quinet warned, has become since the creation of the Customs Union "the practical people par excellence" who believed they could seize world domination. Such an exaltation of national sentiment would be in itself praiseworthy, even in its fantastic triumphs, Quinet went on, if it were a nationalism carrying a generous message, a promise of liberty and higher life for the whole of Europe. But German nationalism, as it had developed by then, involved no universal embrace, no concern for the whole of mankind, no positive aspirations. Instead of opening and intensifying contacts with the world, German nationalism was trying to build a Chinese wall around Germany and expressed itself in haughty rejection of everything alien and especially everything French.[27]

But Quinet remained a lonely voice even after 1848. The situa-

[25] *Oeuvres Complètes de Edgar Quinet*, 23 vols. (Paris, n.d.), VI, 142.

[26] On March 3, 1831 Quinet wrote to his mother from Heidelberg: "Creutzer, et tous les autres ont été excellents pour moi. Seulement la faiblesse de notre gouvernement les a singulièrement enorgueillis et ils ne parlent que de tirer leur rapière contre la France à la première agression sur la rive gauche du Rhin." *Correspondances, Lettres à sa mère* (Paris, n.d.), II, 184.

[27] *Oeuvres Complètes, op. cit.*, VI, 253 f. part of Ch. XV, "La Teutomanie" of the essay on "Allemagne" in the book "Allemagne et Italie." There he discussed also with much wit the Handbook of Universal History by the then well-known German historian, Professor Heinrich Leo (1799-1878), in which the German scholar characterized the French as "ein Affenvolk" and Paris as "das alte Haus des Satans." Leo attacked the French Revolution with utmost vehemence as an expression of the Celtic race which is moved by bestial instinct (tierischer Trieb) whereas the Germans act under the impulse of saintly thoughts (heilige Gedanke).

tion did not change fundamentally under the Second Empire. In all this intellectual Germanophily of the nineteenth century there was, however, a fundamental difference from the Anglophily of the eighteenth century. As Professor Ottavio Barrié has indicated, while England was a model both intellectually and politically, love for Germany was confined entirely to intellectual matters and did not influence French legal and political development. The French government continued to cooperate with Britain and many French intellectuals instinctively felt the community of liberal attitudes linking the two countries. Men like Tocqueville knew Britain well and appreciated her political and social ways. During the Crimean War, Tocqueville wrote to an English correspondent that he welcomed the Anglo-French alliance. His point of view resembled that of Saint-Simon. "I have always believed it the most desirable event which could take place. It alone can assure not only the general liberties of Europe but the prospect of the individual liberties of the European peoples." In the middle of the nineteenth century, however, Tocqueville saw a new factor rising of which at the beginning of the century few had been conscious. "For Russia," he went on, "is the cornerstone of despotism in the world, and were this stone torn from the hand of the despots, it would sooner or later lead to the fall of all absolute governments. Hence, I hope with all my heart, both as a European and as a Frenchman, that the alliance will last and will be successful." [28] There was in the nineteenth century more intellectual cross-fertilization between France and Britain than between France and Germany, though French intellectuals thought much more about Germany than about England. Yet after 1848 they continued to know little about Germany and to understand less. The thesis of some French nationalist writers that German thought after 1815 much influenced French thought and literature turning it away from the pure French tradition is hardly borne out by the facts.[29]

[28] Letter to Wm. R. Greg (1809-1881) of April 26, 1854. Tocqueville, *Nouvelle Correspondance entièrement inédite* (Paris, 1866), 325 ff.

[29] See Louis Reynaud, *L'influence allemande en France au XVIII*e *et au XIX*e *siècle* (Paris, 1922) and *Le Romantisme: ses origines anglo-germaniques; influences étrangères et traditions nationales; le réveil du génie français* (Paris, 1926). Also Jean-Marie Carré, *Les écrivains français et le mirage allemand, 1800-1940* (Paris, 1947). Reynaud's views are reduced to much more reasonable proportions in André Monchoux, *L'Allemagne devant les Lettres Françaises, de 1814 à 1835* (Toulouse, 1953) and I. A. Henning, *L'Allemagne de Madame de Staël et la polémique romantique; première fortune de l'ouvrage en France et en Allemagne*, 1814-1830 (Paris, 1929). On Michelet, see Werner Kaegi, *Michelet und Deutschland* (Basel, 1936); on Quinet, Horst Neumann, *Das Deutschland-Erlebnis bei Edgar Quinet* (Hamburg: Seminar für Romanische Sprachen

In spite of Quinet's and Heine's warning, the French intellectuals in the 1850's and 1860's favored the unification of Germany under Prussian leadership. Napoleon III, in his general support of the principle of nationality and in his dislike of the continental order stemming from 1815, looked with favor upon Bismarckian Prussia as a progressive dynamic country rejecting the status quo of Metternich and of Nicholas I. Many French writers recognized that there were traits in the Prussian character and in German nationalism which were hardly reconcilable with liberal ideas and with Franco-German cooperation. But still captivated by the views of Madame de Staël, they generally found ways to discount or excuse the disturbing factors if they noticed them. Prussian unification of Germany, the French liberals thought, might endow the great neighbor east of the Rhine with French ideas, above all with universal suffrage, the gift which the French Revolution of 1848 had brought to France and to mankind.[30]

The events of 1870 caused a rude awakening. French intellectual Germanomania became now a thing of the past. But many did not lose their balance. In the *Revue des Deux Mondes* on September 18, 1870 Renan deplored the war between the two countries as the greatest misfortune which could have befallen civilization. He pleaded for the closest alliance between France, Germany, and Britain which alone would be able to integrate Russia into Europe, and to mitigate Prussia's aspirations in the interest of the Germans. Rarely has a great historian written such prophetic words. "In fact, if we leave aside the United States of America whose undoubtedly brilliant future is

---

und Kultur, 1933). On the German side there is the recent discriminating study by H. O. Sieburg, *Deutschland und Frankreich in der Geschichtsschreibung des neunzehnten Jahrhunderts* (Wiesbaden, 1954). There are few studies on Anglo French relations in the nineteenth century outside of the purely diplomatic field. Among them are Jean Duhamel, *Louis Philippe et la Première Entente Cordiale* (Paris, 1951) and Eric H. Partridge, *The French Romantics' Knowledge of English Literature (1820-1848) according to Contemporary French Memoirs, Letters, and Periodicals* (Paris, 1924).

[30] In 1860 the well-known French writer Edmond About (1828-1885) published a pamphlet *La Prusse en 1860* (Paris, 1860) which was translated into Italian (*La Prussia nel 1860, opuscolo politico*, Milan, 1860) and into German, (*Preussen und Louis Napoleon in Jahre 1860*, Berlin, 1860). He demanded that Napoleon should help Prussia to become Germany's Piedmont. Hans Rosenberg, *Die nationalpolitische Publizistik Deutschlands vom Eintritt der neuen Ära in Preussen bis zum Ausbruch des Deutschen Krieges*, 2 vols. (Munich, 1935) quotes several German pamphlets attacking About. One (Rosenberg, no. 374) threatened that if France did not remain peaceful, the Germans would incorporate France, for the German ancestors of the Franks were the Frankish conquerors of both. Another pamphlet by Julius Grosse, *Deutsche Pflichten* (Munich, 1861) proclaimed it as a German duty to reduce France to the frontiers of Louis XIII's time.

still obscure and which in any case occupies a secondary rank in the original labor of the human mind, the intellectual and moral greatness of Europe rests on the triple alliance of France, Germany, and England. Its rupture would be deeply grievous for progress. United, these three great forces would lead the world and lead it well. They would necessarily lead the other elements, each of considerable importance, which compose Europe. They would, above all, imperiously trace a road for another power which one should neither exaggerate nor depreciate—Russia. Russia is a danger only if the rest of Europe abandons her to the false idea of an originality which she perhaps does not possess, and allows her to unite the barbaric peoples of central Asia. . . . France is one of the conditions of Britain's prosperity. The alliance of France and Britain is well-established for centuries to come. Let Britain think of the United States, of Constantinople, of India; she will always find that she needs France and a strong France. . . ." And, let us add, French liberty needs Britain even more. We are back to the vision of Saint-Simon and Augustin Thierry in 1814. But Renan sets it into a broader context, whose pertinency only the twentieth century has made manifest.

Renan ended the article with a general warning to hegemonial powers, a warning as applicable to France in the recent past as to Germany in the near future. "All the great military hegemonies, that of Spain in the sixteenth century and those of France under Louis XIV and Napoleon, have ended in quick exhaustion. Let Prussia take heed. Her radical policy can engage her in a series of complications from which it will not be easy to disentangle herself. A penetrating eye could perhaps now perceive the formation of future coalitions. The wise friends of Prussia will tell her, not as a threat but as a warning: *vae victoribus,* woe to the victors." One year later Renan repeated the warning in his letter to David Friedrich Strauss. "By abandoning herself to the statesmen and warriors of Prussia, Germany has mounted a frisky horse which will lead her where she does not wish to go. You play for too high stakes. Your conduct exactly resembles that of France at a period with which one reproaches her most. In 1792 the European powers provoked France; France defeated the powers, which was her right; then she pushed her victory to excesses, in which she was wrong. Excess is bad; pride is the only vice which will be punished in this world." What the Germans were doing in 1871, in partial realization of their intentions of 1815—the annexation of territories on the strength of ancient history or of racial ties—Renan warned, might soon be turned against them. "Every affirmation of Germanism is an affirmation of Slavism. A glance at the affairs of Austria shows that to full evidence. There are twice as many Slavs as Germans. Like the Dragon of the Apocalypse the Slav will one day drag behind him the hordes of Central Asia, the ancient clientele of Genghis Khan and Tamerlane. How much better it would have been for you if you could have reserved for that day the right to appeal to reason, to morality, to friendships based on common principles." The common principles were those in the name of which Renan wished to unite liberal Britain, liberal France, and a liberal Germany.[31]

Renan's view was still confined to Europe. Forty years later Jean Jaurès, in his speech on December 20, 1911 before the French Chamber of Deputies for the ratification of the Franco-German agreement ending the second Morocco crisis, supported the Anglo-French entente but pleaded at the same time for a conciliatory policy towards Germany. He was hopeful about the preservation of peace. The most significant passage of his great speech was the one in which he pointed out that there were today three active forces working for peace: the international organization of the working class, the economic interdependence of modern capitalism, and "Anglo-Saxon America, reborn from the old Puritan ideals." "We do not know the great American people or the American conscience," Jaurès said. "We only see men obsessed by millions and by business, . . . [Yet] we find today in America a revival of idealism, beneath the dollar era, unearthing America's Puritan soul with its roots in the enthusiasm of the Biblical prophets, and which, in its manner, has dreamt of a free and just society. . . . Should Europe be foolish enough to divide and tear itself apart tomorrow, this great enlightened American idealism would shame it with its proposals."[32] France found herself after 1815 between west and east, between Britain and Germany: in her attitude toward both, there were strangely intermingled elements of recognition and resentment, of affinity and divergence, of attraction and repulsion. Necessity and common traditions turned France westward for support and survival; intellectual fascination and illusions directed many French eyes longingly eastward where the period of the Napoleonic wars had discovered a new intellectual message. Orig-

[31] Ernest Renan, *La Réforme Intellectuelle et Morale* (Cambridge University Press, 1950), 79-104, 119-127.
[32] *Oeuvres de Jean Jaurès, Pour la Paix, Europe Incertaine* (Paris, 1934), 423-34.

inally, Britain and Germany represented the east-west tension for France, politically and spiritually. After 1870 farsighted Frenchmen saw the United States appear behind Britain and Russia behind Germany. In this broadened context the twentieth century has carried on the debate which started in France after the Napoleonic wars in 1815. The events of the last forty years have clarified some of the fundamental issues involved; they have not yet settled them.

12

Dostoyevsky and Danilevsky: Nationalist Messianism*

The great Russian libertarians Herzen and Bakunin belonged to the same generation, they were born in 1812 and in 1814 respectively. The great event which inspired their boyhood was the Decembrist uprising, the axis of their life was formed by the Revolution of 1848. Their common concern was the liberation of the individual personality, in Europe and in Russia, two worlds which were equally near to their heart and which they tried to harmonize in a common effort of freedom. Both lived the greater part of their mature life in Europe. Fyodor Mikhailovich Dostoyevsky and Nikolai Yakovlevich Danilevsky belonged to the following generation: they were a decade younger, Dostoyevsky was born in 1821 and Danilevsky in 1822.[1] The decisive period through which they lived were the years between

---

* Reprinted by permission of the publishers from Ernest J. Simmons (ed.), *Continuity and Change in Russian and Soviet Thought* (Cambridge, Mass.: Harvard University Press, 1955).

[1] See on Dostoyevsky my *Prophets and Peoples* (New York: Macmillan, 1946), pp. 131-160, 198-206, and on Danilevsky my *Pan-Slavism, its History and Ideology* (new ed., Vintage Books, New York, 1960), pp. 152-166, 302-304. In *Prophets and Peoples*, p. 201, I remarked that unfortunately no English translation of Dostoyevsky's *Dnevnik Pisatela* existed. Now it exists: *The Diary of a Writer*, tr. by Boris Brasol, 2 vols. (New York: Scribner's, 1949).

the Crimean War and the Congress of Berlin, the conflict between Russia's imperial ambitions and European resistance, the two decades during which the nationalist movements in Italy, Germany and the Balkans found their initial fulfilment thanks to the combination of a semi-mystical nationalist ideology and a semi-Machiavellian political strategy. In this general atmosphere, Dostoyevsky and Danilevsky were less concerned with individual liberty than with Russian national power and destiny. They boundlessly loved and admired Russia, they harbored no such feelings toward Europe. During the years which Dostoyevsky lived in Europe, his letters were a continuous outcry of utter indignation and misery. The two decisive events for them in the Russia of their time were the emancipation of the serfs in 1861 and the Polish uprising in 1863. The one filled them with immeasurable pride and hope, the other was a dire warning of the evil West's intentions.

While the violent revolutions of 1848 had failed in Europe, while the freeing of the slaves in democratic America was achieved only at a terrific cost of blood and devastation, was a social revolution not consummated peacefully in Russia, thanks to the blessings of autocracy and the greater morality of the Russian people? The emancipation of the serfs in Russia proved the civic primacy of the Russian people and of their governmental system, it promised social harmony and the avoidance of revolutionary chaos and civil wars which were the fate of Europe and America. The West's understandable envy and hostility became manifest in 1863 when official France, Britain and Austria, and general public opinion everywhere outside Russia, sympathized with the Poles. Few Russians indeed took a stand opposed to Russian imperialism; among them Bakunin and Herzen unequivocally defended the Polish and Ukrainian right to independence. Other Russian liberals like Mikhail Nikiforovich Katkov turned, as a result of the Polish uprising, to a fervent Russian nationalism. "Russia," he wrote in 1867, "needs a unitarian state and a strong Russian national idea. We shall create such a national idea on the basis of a common language and a common faith for all the inhabitants (of the Russian Empire) and on the basis of the Slav *mir*. Whatever opposes us, will be overthrown by us." [2] Dostoyevsky and Danilevsky became the most famous exponents of this Russian national idea. In nineteenth-century Europe no other nationalism

---

[2] Th. G. Masaryk, *Russland und Europa. Studien über die geistigen Strömungen in Russland* (Jena: Eugen Diederichs, 1913), vol. II, p. 198.

approached the messianic fervor, the *Sendungsbewusstsein,* the expectation of a decisive apocalyptic struggle against the alien world, expressed by Dostoyevsky and Danilevsky. Even in the Russia of their time they represented a minority. Only seventy years later, though Dostoyevsky was the least popular Russian classic and Danilevsky was not reprinted in Stalin's Russia, the Russian nationalist messianism which flourished in the later years of Stalin's regime showed surprising similarities with the views put forward so decisively by the two nineteenth century Russian spokesmen.[3]

Nationalist messianism was in the nineteenth century in no way an exclusively Russian phenomenon. There were overtones of it in Johann Gottlieb Fichte's praise of the German *Urvolk,* in Michelet's glorification of France and above all in Mazzini's expectation of the Third Rome.[4] But by 1860 this mood had almost completely vanished in Europe. Cavour and Bismarck were as alien to all *Schwarmgeisterei* as were the representative political and imaginative writers of later nineteenth century Europe. In Dostoyevsky and Danilevsky nationalist messianism found its strongest expression anywhere in the nineteenth century; similarily Stalin's nationalist messianism went farther and was presented in a more extreme and authoritative form than any other nationalism in the middle of the twentieth century. Danilevsky's nationalism—in his nationalist messianism the emphasis was on nationalism—was stated in his *Russia and Europe, an Inquiry into the Cultural and Political Relations of the Slav and the Germano-Latin Worlds* which first appeared in 1869 in the monthly *Zarya,* before being published two years later in book form. Dostoyevsky who was then abroad and who had known Danilevsky as a fellow-member of the socialist Petrashevsky circle in St. Petersburg

---

[3] "The curious fact is if one substituted communism for (Dostoyevsky's) conception of the mission of the Orthodox faith, and world revolution for his notion of a Pan-Slavic war against Europe, the identity of his whole position with that of modern Soviet Russia would be striking." Ernest J. Simmons, *Dostoyevsky, The Making of a Novelist* (New York: Oxford University Press, 1940), p. 327. "Danilewski gibt darin eine klare und freimütige Darstellung der sich aus seiner allgemeinen Kulturtypenlehre für die russische Aussen und (in geringerem Grade) Innenpolitik ergebenden allgemeinen Grundsätze und konkreten Postulate, die eine auffallende Verwandtschaft mit der gegenwärtigen aussenpolitischen Praxis der Sowjetunion zeigen." Alexander von Schelting, *Russland und Europa im russischen Geschichtsdenken* (Berne: A. Francke, 1948), p. 392.

[4] Compare also Vincento Gioberti's "In the Italian Nationality are founded the interests of religion and the civil and universal hopes of mankind. Italy is the chosen people, the typical people, the creative people, the Israel of the modern age." *Prophets and Peoples,* p. 183. See also Guido de Ruggiero, *The History of European Liberalism* (London: Oxford University Press, 1927), p. 298 f.

twenty years before, wrote an enthusiastic letter to *Zarya*'s editor, his friend, Nikolai Nikolayevich Strakhov:

> Danilevsky's article . . . will assuredly be for many a day the "household companion" of every Russian. . . . The article is so in harmony with my own views and convictions that here and there I stand amazed at the identity of our conclusions; as long as two years ago, I began to jot down certain of my reflections, for I had proposed to write an article with a very similar title, and with the same tendency and the same conclusion. How great was my joy and amazement when I beheld this plan, which I had hoped to carry out in the future, already carried out, and that . . . with such knowledge as I, with the best will in the world, could never have brought to the task.[5]

In fact, Dostoyevsky was then expressing his messianism—in his nationalist messianism the emphasis was on messianism—in the two great novels *The Idiot* (1868) and *The Possessed* (1871-72); later, from 1873 to 1880, he expanded and applied his ideas to the intellectual and political problems of contemporary Russia in many articles of *The Diary of a Writer*. In the above quoted letter to Strakhov he mentioned the one great difference between him and Danilevsky, a difference of emphasis. Danilevsky thought primarily in historico-political terms and tried to approach the subject in a scientific spirit; for Dostoyevsky the core of the problem and of all problems, was Russia's own Christ. Like Tolstoy, Dostoyevsky was fundamentally a religious anarchist and a God-seeker, but Tolstoy was a humanitarian optimist who believed in a rationalist and universal Christ, Dostoyevsky was a Christian pessimist who proclaimed a Russian God and the world's salvation through Him.

Nationalist messianism has grown out of a twofold root, the one in Israel and its all-pervasive consciousness of being a chosen people, the other in the world-vision of Augustan Rome. In the Christian Roman Empire the two branches met. The religious element deepened national political hopes into the belief that their fulfilment was a pre-ordained action of divine justice and that the struggles for their realization must be carried on as God's commands: the nation, the chosen vehicle of God's designs, sees in its political triumph the

---

[5] Letter from Florence, March 18 (30), 1869. *Letters of Fyodor Michailovitch Dostoyevsky to his Family and Friends*, tr. by Ethel Colburn Mayne (New York: Macmillan, n.d.), p. 165 f.

[6] See the chapter on Messianism in my *Revolutions and Dictatorships*, 3rd ed. (Cambridge, Mass.: Harvard University Press, 1943), pp. 11-37.

march of God in history.⁶ It thus transcends the limits of a historical or social concept and becomes a holy body sanctified by God; nationalism is no longer a political loyalty but a religious duty, burdened with responsibility toward God and the redemption of mankind. In all these conceptions nationalist pride, often cloaked in humility and grounded in real or imaginary sufferings and offenses, claims to serve the cause of universal peace and justice. Narrow tribalism and lofty ideals, dominion and compassion are often inextricably mixed.

To Dostoyevsky and to Danilevsky Russia appeared as a new Israel. Israel was the religious people *kat exochen*. "The religious aspect of their life and activity was so exalted and so perfect," Danilevsky wrote in the last chapter of his book, "that this people is justly called: the people chosen by God." With the coming of Christ, the Christians became the true Israel; Danilevsky and Dostoyevsky had no doubt that the Russians were the truly Christian people, in the succession of the Orthodox Church, and thereby the new Israel, or, after the Hebrews and Byzantium, the Third Israel. "From an objective, factual viewpoint, the Russians and the majority of the Slavs became," Danilevsky wrote, "with the Greeks, chief guardians of the living traditions of religious truth—Orthodoxy, and in this way the continuators of the high calling, which was the destiny of Israel and of Byzantium, to be the chosen people." Russian nationalists were convinced that not only by historical succession but by its very character the Russian people with its deep humility and its willing suffering, was the true Servant of God, the bearer of the fulfillment of history, a fulfillment visualized as coming about in an apocalyptic struggle between the forces of Light and the forces of Darkness.

Neither Dostoyevsky nor Danilevsky had the slightest doubt who the forces of darkness were: middle class Western society, with its spirit of greed embodied in capitalism and its violent internal dissensions expressed in the multiparty system and in racial and class strife. They, especially Danilevsky, did not deny a certain greatness to modern Western civilization as Karl Marx likewise had recognized the progressive achievements of bourgeois society. But through its social injustices and the alienation of man from his true humanity, the West in spite of its apparent strength and proud achievements, was doomed to go down in the inevitable struggle with the new Israel—Russia in the case of Dostoyevsky and Danilevsky, the proletariat in the case of Marx, Russia and the proletariat in the case of Stalin. The God of History was on the side of righteousness.

Russia, however, was not only the new or Third Israel but also the new and Third Rome. From the fourth to the sixteenth century the thought of the Christian world acknowledged the Roman mission of world leadership; the question which divided it was that of Rome's succession. In the twelfth century Bishop Otto of Freising wrote his *Chronica sive historia de duabus civitatibus* to prove how the imperial power was transferred from the Romans to the Franks or Germans—quo modo ad Francos, qui occidentem inhabitant, translatum fuerit. The German humanists not only accepted the theory of the translatio imperii—Ulrich von Hutten addressed Maximilian as successor Augusti, aemule Trajani, dominator orbis, rector humani generis—they and the writers of the Reformation added the point that the Germans had not only conquered Rome but were entitled to it by moral superiority. Following Tacitus, they contrasted Roman depravity and German piety. Such a contrast was even more emphasized by the Russians, only that with them Roman depravity included the Germans and the true piety was reserved for the Russian people. To the Orthodox Greeks Papal Rome and the Western Empire were usurpers who had inherited the spirit of pagan Rome; the unparalleled horrors perpetrated by the Western crusaders in the conquest of Constantinople, the second Rome and the true Christian Rome, bore witness to this spirit. When Constantinople was conquered for the second time—by the Turks instead of the West—, Moscow which meanwhile had grown by God's guidance into a seat of power became the Third Rome, the successor of Byzantium and the guardian of the true faith. This translatio imperii to the Russians burdened them with the twofold task: the opposition to, and ultimate salvation of, the West and the reconquest of Constantinople. For Dostoyevsky and Danilevsky these two tasks fused into one, the reconquest of Constantinople for the true faith became the key to the defeat and conversion of the West. It presupposed a total and undeviating devotion of the Russians to their national idea; the rejection of all spiritual servility before the West; and the growing material power of Russia. The inevitable war was no war for conquest or power; it would usher in a new era for mankind.

Dostoyevsky and Danilevsky were convinced that the new Russian civilization which would emerge from this victory would be a pan-human civilization, the fulfillment of all historical trends, the first all-rounded universal civilization. "Russia," Dostoyevsky wrote in his *Diary* for January 1877, "in conjunction with Slavdom, and at its head, will utter to the whole world the greatest word ever heard, and that word will precisely be a covenant of universal human fellowship, and no longer in the spirit of personal egoism by means of which at present men and nations unnaturally, because of the struggle for existence, unite with each other in their civilization, . . . digging ditches for each other and spreading about each other lies, blasphemy and calumnies. . . . The Russian national idea, in the last analysis, is but the universal fellowship of men." [7] Thus the Third Rome and the Third Israel are at one in the preparation of the advent of the messianic order. To Dostoyevsky and Danilevsky the 1870's seemed the age of conflict immediately preceding the fulfillment; to Stalin perhaps the 1940's held a similar promise. They overrated the dynamic force of the Russian *Sendungsbewusstsein,* they underestimated the strength of the West.

Of them only Danilevsky was a systematic thinker, who tried to clothe his diagnosis of the present and his wishful expectations about the future with the scientific respectability of a theory of history of his own. To that end he adapted or invented a doctrine according to which history passes through a cycle of independent civilizations, or historico-cultural types, of which "Europe" was the latest but not the last one. Europeans liked to think of their civilization as the final and therefore universally valid stage of human development, the mature fruit and radiant crown of all history. The Russians had accepted this evaluation and willingly put themselves into a position of inferiority. In reality Europe was, like all preceding civilizations, only a passing stage in the march of history and by the nineteenth century in full decay without acknowledging it even to itself. Europe nevertheless felt that its end was fast approaching and that another historico-cultural type was to replace it: Russia was the bearer of the new civilization. For that reason Europe hated Russia and pretended to despise it. The heir of Europe's world position was envied and feared; not out of premeditation but instinctively Europe always united against Russia, whenever the latter tried to grow in strength.

For the realization of her world-historical mission Russia had to turn away from imitating Europe and to concentrate on the development of her own spiritual resources. But Russia alone was not strong enough for the task. She needed a broader basis to gain the feeling of

[7] *The Diary of a Writer,* tr. by Boris Brasol, p. 578.

security and destiny. She had to gather around her all the lands inhabited by kindred Slavs. "For every Slav: Russian, Czech, Serb, Croat, Slovene, Slovak, Bulgar (I wish to add also Pole)—after God and His Holy Church—the idea of Slavdom must be the highest idea, higher than any earthly good, for none of these is attainable to him without its existence, without an intellectually, nationally and politically independent Slavdom; on the other hand all these blessings will be the inescapable consequence of its independence and originality (*samobytnost*)." [8] Only if Russia succeeded in expanding her hold over all the Slavs, could she bring the original Slav civilization to fruition. A Pan-Slav union was the indispensable condition for the flowering of the new historico-cultural type and thereby for the fulfillment of history. In 1869 Danilevsky anticipated the composition and frontiers of the Pan-Slav union which the disintegration of the Austro-Hungarian empire made possible and which Stalin almost realized in 1945. It was to consist of eight parts:

> The Russian Empire in its frontiers of 1869, including Poland and with the addition of Austrian Galicia and northern Bukovina and of Hungarian Carpatho-Ukraine;
> The kingdom of Bohemia, Moravia and Slovakia (Czechoslovakia);
> The Kingdom of the Serbs, Croats and Slovenes (Yugoslavia) which would also include Montenegro, Bosnia-Herzegovina and northern Albania from Turkey, the Voivodina and the Banat from Hungary, Dalmatia, Istria, Carniola, two-thirds of Carinthia and one-fifth of Styria from Austria;
> The Kingdom of Bulgaria with the greater part of Macedonia;
> The Kingdom of Rumania with half of Austrian Bukovina and of Hungarian Transylvania;
> The Kingdom of Hungary shorn of the territories ceded to Russia, Bohemia, Serbia and Rumania;
> The Kingdom of Greece with Thessaly, Epirus, south-west Macedonia, Crete, Rhodes, Cyprus and the Anatolian coast of the Aegean Sea;
> Constantinople and its environment.[9]

Danilevsky did not wish to annex Constantinople to Russia but to establish it as a city common to the whole Orthodox and Slav world. Like Stalin's Russia eighty years later, Danilevsky's Russia was in his

---

[8] *Zarya*, 1869, no. 3, p. 38.
[9] *Zarya*, 1869, no. 9, p. 21. The quotation is in chapter 14 which is entitled "Tsargrad," the Russian name for Constantinople.

interpretation neither imperialist nor aggressive. Her function in international relations was diametrically opposed to that of the West, in spite of the misinterpretations of her intentions and actions by her enemies. The European powers, in order to grow in strength, had to subject or to enslave other peoples and to numb their cultural growth; Russia on the contrary had to liberate other peoples and to help them to realize their destiny. "In this divine and perhaps unique coincidence of moral motives and obligations with political advantage and necessity, we must see a guarantee for the fulfillment of Russia's great task. Otherwise our world will be only a miserable chain of accidents and not the reflection of supreme reason, right and goodness." But not only history was on the side of Russia and the Slavs; it was supported by their superior number and moral force. "It is as impossible to fight the historical course of events as it is impossible to fight superior violence. From these general considerations we gain the certitude that the Russian and Slav sacred cause, which is in truth the universal and panhuman cause, cannot be lost." Danilevsky sounded no less confident than Stalin's spokesmen were.

In order to fulfill her historical mission the Slavs had to be strong, united and above all freed from subservience to European mentality. The continuous politico-cultural struggle with Europe (which is called today "cold war") would separate the Slavs from Europe and unite them more closely with Russia. But to heal the deep wounds inflicted by the imitation of Europe and to restore the purity of the Slav historico-cultural type, a real war was needed which would inaugurate "a series of events the like of which the world has not seen since the fall of the western Roman Empire." The outcome of the war could be in no doubt, for the West lacked the burning devotion of the Slav world to the One all absorbing cause. "We must have the firm faith that our goal is sublime and sacred, that only that which leads to it should concern us, that we promote every good cause— humanity, freedom, civilization etc.—only if we serve our goal and in no other way." For that purpose the Russian leaders had to understand the immutable laws of historical development as shown by Danilevsky.

> Only a false concept of the general development of the relationship of the national to the pan-human, a concept incompatible with the real principles of the systematization of scientific natural phenomena as well as with so-called progress, could lead to the confusion of European civilization with universal civilization. Only such

concept could lead to such a pernicious delusion as Westernism which . . . assigns to us and our brothers the pitiful insignificant role of imitators of the West. Such a delusion deprives us of the hope for any cultural significance, i.e., for a great historical future.

I attempted to develop this theoretical approach and to supplement it with indications about the main differences between the Slav and the Germano-Roman cultural-historical types and about the fatal consequences of this Westernization or Europeanization, and how far it is the origin of the disease from which Russia's social body suffers, a disease which is the source of all our social ills. Only the healthy force of historical events can remedy this disease and can raise the spirit of our society, suffering precisely from spiritual decay and abasement. The cure is possible and probable because luckily the disease has so far penetrated only the surface of the social structure. We can see such an event, or rather a whole series of events, endowed with a healthy dynamism, in the latest phase of the struggle known as the Eastern Question, which . . . shortly must stamp its imprint upon an entire historical period. The importance of this inevitably approaching struggle forces us to try to understand the objections raised against the only decision useful to the Slav world—the full political liberation of all the Slav peoples and the formation of a Pan-Slav union under Russia's leadership—and the guarantee of our success in this struggle.[10]

All preceding great historico-cultural types have never realized the fullness of civilized existence, which embraces four different aspects, in which the creative abilities of a type can unfold: religion; humanities and science; political order; and social-economic organization. In antiquity Israel had excelled in the first of those aspects, Greece in the second, Rome in the third. Modern Europe developed the second and third of the four aspects to new heights. But only the coming Slav historico-cultural type will realize the total human civilization, as soon as it will have achieved complete independence and thereby "eradicated the cancer of imitativeness and the servile attitude towards the West, which through some unfavorable circumstances has eaten its way into the Slav body and soul." Because the Slavs were at the time when Danilevsky wrote not yet spiritually and politically independent, they had not yet had the opportunity of showing their full measure in the humanities and science.[11] He has

---

[10] From the beginning of the 17th and last chapter of Danilevsky's book.

[11] Against all historical evidence, Danilevsky insists on the nationalist contention that great cultural creations presuppose national independence and power. Italy during the Renaissance, German classicism from 1760 to 1830, the Polish *émigré* literature in the 1830's and Jewish intellectual life in the Diaspora contradict Danilevsky's assumption.

no difficulty to prove the exceptional religious gifts of the Slav type. More ingenious are his arguments for the unique qualifications of the Slavs to create a true political order; they anticipate some of the recent Soviet arguments.

> Russia does not have colonial possessions, like Rome or England. The Russian state from early Muscovite times on is Russia herself, gradually, irresistibly spreading on all sides, settling neighboring non-settled lands, and assimilating into herself . . . foreign populations. This basic character of Russian expansion was misunderstood by the distortion of the original Russian point of view through Europeanization, the origin of every evil in Russia. . . . Is the Russian people capable of freedom? . . . There hardly ever existed and exists a people as capable of enduring such a large share of freedom as the Russians and being less inclined to abuse it, due to its ability and habit to obey, its respect and trust in the authority, its lack of love for power and its loathing of interference in matters where it does not consider itself competent. If we look into the reasons of all political troubles, we shall find their root not in the striving for freedom but precisely in love for power and in the vain craving of people to interfere in affairs that are beyond their comprehension. . . . This nature of the Russian people is the true reason why Russia is really the only state which never had (and in all probability never will have) a political revolution, i.e., a revolution having as its aim the limitation of the power of the ruler.

But Russia is above all called upon to realize the perfect social economic organization, which Europe with its contradiction between political democracy and economic feudalism was unable to achieve.

> Russia is the only large state which has solid ground under its feet, in which there are no landless masses and in which, consequently, the social edifice does not rest on the misery and insecurity of the majority of the citizens; in Russia alone there cannot and does not exist any contradiction between political and economic ideals. . . . On this health of Russia's social-economic organization we found our hope for the great social-economic significance of the Slav historico-cultural type. It has been able for the first time to create a just and normal system of human activities, which embraces not only human relations in the moral and political sphere, but also man's mastery of nature, which is a method of satisfying human needs and requirements. Thus it establishes not only a formal equality in the relations between citizens, but a real and concrete one.

In his scientific approach Danilevsky stressed frequently that the new Slav type, following the European type in the course of history, would not be the last word of history. But at the end of his work he is overcome by the messianic finality of his vision.

> The main stream of universal history starts from two sources on the banks of the ancient Nile. From there the one, celestial and divine, has reached by way of Jerusalem and Constantinople, in perfect purity, Kiev and Moscow; the other, terrestrial and human, divided itself again into two rivers, that of culture and that of politics, and flowed through Athens, Alexandria and Rome into Europe, sometimes desiccated, then again enriched with new and ever fuller waters. On Russian soil a new and fourth river originates, a social-economic system which satisfies the masses in a just way. These four rivers will unite on the wide plains of Slavdom into a mighty sea.[12]

Dostoyevsky had not the scientific hesitations of Danilevsky. To him as to Shatov in *The Possessed,* the Russians were the only God-fearing people on earth, "destined to regenerate and save the world in the name of a new God, and to whom are given the keys of life and of the new world." [13] Shatov's further words

> If a great people does not believe that the truth is only to be found in itself alone (in itself alone and in it exclusively); if it does not believe that it alone is fit and destined to raise up and save all the rest by its truth, it would at once sink into being ethnographical material, and not a great people. . . . But there is only one truth, and therefore only a single one out of the nations can have the true God, even though other nations may have great Gods of their own.

were repeated by Dostoyevsky himself a few years later in his *Diary*:

> Every great people believes and must believe if it intends to live long, that in it alone resides the salvation of the world; that it lives in order to stand at the head of the nations, to affiliate and unite all of them, and to lead them in a concordant choir toward the final goal preordained for them.[14]

The law of history which Dostoyevsky here formulated has as little general validity as another "law" which he proclaimed: "There is a

---

[12] These are the final words of Danilevsky's 17th chapter from which also the two preceding quotations are taken.
[13] *The Possessed,* part II, chapter 1, VII, tr. by Constance Garnett, Modern Library ed., pp. 250-256.
[14] *The Diary of a Writer,* January 1877, tr. by Boris Brasol, p. 575.

political law, even a law of nature, according to which one of two strong and close neighbors, whatever their friendship may be, wishes to destroy the other and sooner or later will realize that wish." Dostoyevsky was not the only one who generalized his own theory and desires into general maxims. Dostoyevsky, as apparently the Stalinists today, could not conceive that other great nations were not driven by the same dynamic messianism which he believed characteristic of the Russians. That explains his conviction of the inevitability of the fast approaching decisive struggle between Russia and the West, which on the part of Russia was not a war but a crusade for a holy cause. In January 1877 he started his *Diary* by asking "In point of fact, what awaits the world not only in the last quarter of the century but even perhaps, this year? . . . Apparently the time has come for something eternal, millenarian, for that which has been moulding itself in the world ever since the beginning of its civilization. . . . (With the rise of the Russian or Slav idea) we have something universal and final, which, though by no means solving *all* human destinies, brings with it the beginning of the end of the whole former history of European mankind." In the May issue of the *Diary* he foresaw for Europe a gigantic, elemental and dreadful catastrophe and congratulated himself that Russia had separated herself from Europe and thus has become more than ever independent of the fatal problems besetting decrepit Europe. Never was Russia more powerful than at present, Dostoyevsky jubilated, and that at a time when the great world problems could no longer be settled by "appeasing diplomatic means."

Dostoyevsky's *Diary* is one of the most illuminating sources for an understanding of Dostoyevsky and of Russian anti-Westernism. In a letter to Vsevolod Sergeyevich Solovyov, Vladimir's brother, Dostoyevsky emphasized the importance of the June 1876 issue of the *Diary*:

> I have never yet permitted myself to follow my profoundest convictions to their ultimate consequences in my public writing—have never said my *very last word*. . . . So I decided that I *would* for once say the last word on one of my convictions—that of Russia's part and destiny among the nations—and I proclaimed that my various anticipations would not only be fulfilled in the immediate future, but were already partly realized. . . . One may set up any paradox one likes, and so long as one doesn't carry it to its ultimate conclusion, everyone will think it most subtle . . . , but once blurt out the last word, and quite frankly declare: "This is the Messiah!" why,

nobody will believe in you anymore—for it was so silly of you to push your idea to its ultimate conclusion.[15]

Dostoyevsky's paradox consisted in his classifying the most ardent Russian Westernizers, the advocates of radical reforms, as fervent champions of Russia and of the Russian spirit, to which European culture had been hateful. Did they not join the extreme left in Europe, the very group which rejected Western modern society and civilization and which was most critical of all the manifestations of European culture felt alien to the Russian soul? Was there not hope that the misunderstanding being dispelled these Westernizers would discover themselves full-blooded Russians? Will they not join the Slavophiles in believing in Russia's disinterested leadership towards the brotherhood of men, a union founded upon the principles of common service to mankind?

In the *Diary* Dostoyevsky returned again and again to his fundamental conviction that Europe was unalterably hostile to Russia and unable to understand her true intentions. Though Russia stands in Dostoyevsky's opinion for peace and love, his writings on her behalf are so full of detestation and invective that in their shrillness they recall the discrepancy between Stalin's gospel of peace and its wording of hatred. Two forces in Europe arouse Dostoyevsky's special animosity: money—plutocracy, big business, the stock exchange, the Jews—and the Catholic Church. He was deeply convinced that these two forces conspired against Russia. It is difficult to say which he abhorred more, but the "Roman conspiracy" appeared to him more dangerous. Many passages of the *Diary* read like restatements of Prince Myshkin's famous outburst against the Catholic Church which he called not only an un-Christian religion but worse than atheism.[16] The Russian intelligentsia, Prince Myshkin and Dostoyevsky maintained, having lost its root in the Russian people and idea, embraced atheism, the product of Catholic Europe, and by turning it into a new absolute religion proved thereby their truly Russian character. But let them discover the true humanity on the basis of the Russian idea, the Russian God and Savior, Prince Myshkin went on, and the world will be astonished and incredulous at the sight of Russia as a powerful, wise and benign giant, "for Europe

---

[15] *Letter from Bad Ems* in July 1876, *Letters, op. cit.*, p. 215 f.
[16] It is interesting that Dostoyevsky regards socialism and materialism as a product of Catholicism, while some Catholic thinkers believe socialism and materialism to be the result of anti-Catholic trends.

expects from us only the sword and violence, because it judges us after its own image and cannot imagine us without barbarism."

Against the corruption of man by the powers (or the lust for power) of money and of the Catholic Church Dostoyevsky put his hope of salvation in the true faith of the Russian people and its national messianic vocation.

> Isn't there in Orthodoxy alone both the truth and the salvation of the Russian people, and—in the forthcoming centuries—of mankind as a whole? Hasn't there been preserved in Orthodoxy alone, in all its purity, the Divine image of Christ? And, perhaps, the most momentous preordained destiny of the Russian people, within the destinies of mankind at large, consists in the preservation in their midst of the Divine image of Christ, in all its purity, and, when the time comes, in the revelation of this image into the world which has lost its way! [17]

Thus Dostoyevsky wrote in 1873. Four years later it was no longer Orthodoxy as such but the Russian national genius which was the hope of the world, or perhaps that inextricable fusion of the Russian national genius with the true universal faith which also characterizes the later stage of Stalinism.

> Our great Russia, at the head of the united Slavs, will utter to the world, to the whole of European mankind and to civilization, her new, sane and as yet unheard-of word. That word will be uttered for the good and genuine unification of mankind as a whole in a new, brotherly, universal union, which starts from the Slav genius, above all from the spirit of the great Russian people who have suffered so long, who during so many centuries have been doomed to silence, but who have always possessed great powers for clarifying and settling many bitter and fatal misunderstandings of Western European civilization.[18]

Europe, Dostoyevsky believed, did not fear so much Russian imperialism as the very fact that Russia brought salvation. For the Russian eagle

> seeks no conquest or acquisition, no expansion of his borders, but the liberation of the oppressed and the downtrodden, giving them new life for their benefit and that of mankind. . . . It is this that Europe refuses to believe. . . . Europe fears not so much the possible

[17] *The Diary of a Writer,* tr. by Boris Brasol, p. 63.
[18] *Ibid.,* p. 780.

growth of Russia's strength as she fears the fact that Russia is capable of undertaking such task. . . . To undertake something not for one's direct benefit seems to Europe so unusual, . . . that Russia's act is naturally regarded by Europe not only as the barbarity of "a backward, bestial and unenlightened nation" capable of *vileness* and *stupidity,* of embarking in our age upon something on the order of the crusades of the dark ages, but even as the most immoral fact fraught with danger to Europe and supposedly threatening her great civilization.[19]

The wars of Dostoyevsky's Russia like those of the Soviet Union were not wars of conquest, but wars for the liberation of the oppressed. Such wars are sacred, they fulfill the command of History. In September 1877 Dostoyevsky felt the inescapable fate knocking at the door. Dying papal Catholicism was preparing to fight the last battle for its existence against the whole world, and France was its instrument. The Russian-Turkish war, then waged for the solution of the Eastern Question, would inevitably be converted into an all-European war, which would end with the victory of the East. Though much precious human blood would be shed, Dostoyevsky comforted himself with the thought that this blood would save Europe from a ten times greater loss of blood should the war be postponed. Above all, the war would solve so many problems and would establish such new and progressive relationship between men and between nations, that one should not fear too much the last convulsions of Europe on the very eve of her great regeneration through Russia's victory.

Dostoyevsky relied not only upon the guardianship of the true faith for his claim of Russia's messianic leadership, but he adduced certain historical character traits of the people which qualified them for their sublime task. In 1873, apropos of a showing of Russian paintings to be sent to an international exhibition in Vienna, he maintained that the Europeans were incapable of understanding Russia while the Russians understand everything European and alien perfectly well, a theme to which he returned in the famous address on Pushkin which he delivered at the meeting of the Society of Lovers of Russian Literature on June 8, 1880. Russians had an intuitive understanding of everything human (or at least, as Dosto-

---

[19] *Ibid.,* p. 781. An article like "The Very Last Word of Civilization," which Dostoyevsky wrote in July 1876 (*ibid.,* pp. 376-378) could have appeared with minor changes in any Stalinist paper after 1945, if Stalinist scribes had the power of Dostoyevsky's pen. The same is true of his "The Metternichs and the Don Quixotes," which he wrote in February 1877 (*ibid.,* p. 607).

yevsky emphasized, of everything European and Aryan) and thus could rise to the height of universal man. In this disinterested service to Europe, Slavophiles and Westernizers could find common ground, for in uttering Russia's ultimate word of universal harmony, they would reconcile all the discords and controversies rending Europe and as genuine Russians embrace all in their brotherly love. Like the Stalinists, Dostoyevsky extolled Pushkin as the purest incarnation of Russian genius and as the miraculous, unique and most complete re-incarnation of the spirit of all foreign nations, thereby surpassing even the greatest poets of all other civilizations.

In addition to their pan-human national character, Dostoyevsky maintained that the Russians were the people most capable of real liberty, of firm unity and of social justice. In the last month of his life, in the very last piece published by him, he returned again to the virtues of Russian autocracy and Russian "socialism," to the fundamental difference between the West with its need of legal safeguards and formal constitutions and the freedom of the chosen people.

> Civil liberty may be established in Russia on an integral scale, more complete than anywhere in the world, whether in Europe or even in North America. It will be based not upon a written sheet of paper, but upon the children's affection of the people for the Tsar as their father, since children may be permitted many a thing which is inconceivable in the case of contractual nations; they may be entrusted with much that has nowhere been encountered, since children will not betray their father, and, being children, will lovingly accept from him any correction of their errors.[20]

Such a complete liberty under the loving care of a great father and teacher of his peoples was claimed for Russia by Stalinist writers who "knew" at the same time how limited the liberties were in actual life which the constitutional countries of the West enjoyed. That was due, in the imaginary Russia of Dostoyevsky and of the Stalinist writers, to the unbreakable monolithic unity of the Russian people. Europe was threatened, Dostoyevsky wrote in 1877, by the unrest of the oppressed and suffering classes. She was altogether dependent upon the stock exchanges of her bourgeoisie and purchased the momentary tranquillity of her proletarians with the last resorts of her governments. In Russia similar weaknesses could be observed, but only because she showed herself subservient to European ideas;

---

20 *The Diary of a Writer*, tr. by Boris Brasol, p. 1033.

once she will have returned to her original nature, all the millions of European gold and of the European armies cannot prevail against her. After his address on Pushkin, in a lengthy and violent reply to a liberal critic of his, Professor Alexander Dmitriyevich Gradowsky, who argued that Europe was far ahead of Russia in social justice and reforms, he exclaimed: "Why, Europe is on the eve of a general and dreadful collapse. . . . Our social and civic ideals are better, more solid and even more liberal than your European ideals! Yes, they are more liberal for they emanate directly from our people and are not a slavish transplantation from the West." For all these reasons Russia was "stronger than the rest," Dostoyevsky wrote in April 1877, and yet in spite of her ever growing strength she will not as the Europeans expect draw the sword against them. "Not only shall we not seize and take away anything from them, but the fact itself that we shall greatly strengthen ourselves—through the alliance of love and brotherhood, and not usurpation and violence—will, finally enable us not to draw the sword, but on the contrary in the tranquillity of our might, to reveal an example of sincere peace, international fellowship and disinterestedness."[21] In view of this ultimate goal, Russia's wars could not be judged with the same yardstick as other wars; they were "the first step toward the realization of perpetual peace, of *real* international fellowship and *true* human welfare."

While adhering in all his mature years firmly to these principles and ultimate end, Dostoyevsky showed a surprising flexibility in his "foreign policy." In April 1876 he was convinced that "the future of Europe belongs to Russia," and in November 1877 it was an axiom with him that "Constantinople must be *ours,* conquered by *us,* Russians, from the Turks and remain ours forever." On the conquest of Constantinople depended then the future of Russia, for it would give her the opportunity "of fostering the brotherhood of the peoples and of ardent motherly service to them as to dear children."[22] Apparently to Dostoyevsky Russia was to become the motherland of all truly peaceloving mankind. The need to conquer Constantinople was not an outcome of modern power politics. Dostoyevsky stressed repeatedly that it was a fundamental Russian idea, going back to the time of the rising Moscow Tsardom and that to leave it without solution, "would be equivalent to smashing Russia into pieces."

Yet only three years later, on the last pages of his *Diary,* he came

21 *Ibid.,* p. 667.
22 *Ibid.,* p. 906.

to the conclusion that at the present time nobody would consider it common sense that Constantinople must be ours, save in some remote unknown future. His restless mind had discovered new and greater spheres of conquest. He hoped to see Russia's domination established over all Asia. Russia was as much Asiatic as European, he maintained, "our hopes lie perhaps more in Asia than in Europe: in our future, Asia will be our salvation." In Asia the Russians would not appear as imitators but as civilizers. Yet Dostoyevsky thought of Russia's Asiatic mission as a means to the end which was always before his mind, Russia's messianic role in the world. Russia should for the time being turn away from Europe, as she should have done in 1812 after having driven Napoleon from her territory. If she then had divided the world with Napoleon, leaving to him the West and conquering the East, then Napoleon's dynasty would have been overthrown in the quarrels of Europe, but the Orient would have remained Russian, "and we would at present have controlled the oceans and could have opposed England at sea as well as on land." [23] Dostoyevsky visualized Asia becoming Russia's America, where the Russians would produce immense wealth and, with the help of science, exploit the resources and build mighty industries and thus acquire a new sense of power, dignity and creative joy. This new Russia in Asia would regenerate old Russia and make her masses understand her destiny. With the productive power and the population of her Asiatic empire, Russia would become materially and morally strong enough to fulfill her world mission. Meanwhile Europe, freed from the spectre of Russian aggressive desires, would start to quarrel among themselves, and as soon as their discord came to a crash, Russia would find an opportunity to solve the Eastern Question and to seize Constantinople. In the meanwhile Dostoyevsky advised patience and non-interference in Western affairs.

A Western reader of Dostoyevsky's *Diary* today will not only admire the depth of his convictions and the flight of his imagination, he will be comforted by the thought that—to conclude from Dostoyevsky's own violent vilifications of the Russian liberals and Westernizers—his opponents must have been very numerous and that probably the majority of the Russian educated classes of his day were truly European in their thought and aspirations. Nor was such abuse and hatred

---

[23] He proposed a similar partition of the world with Germany in November 1877. See *Prophets and Peoples*, p. 153. Such a division became possible in 1940; it foundered then on Russia's insistence on the control of Constantinople. See also *Prophets and Peoples*, p. 204.

of Western middle-class civilization confined to Russian writers. Danilevsky's *Russia and Europe* found its counterpart in Oswald Spengler's *Untergang des Abendlandes;* Dostoyevsky's *Diary* was matched by Thomas Mann's *Betrachtungen eines Unpolitischen.* Dostoyevsky wrote in a period of comparative liberty, when liberals could still freely object to national self-glorification and when Vladimir Solovyov could regard the idealization of the Russian people and Russia's isolation from the West as a misfortune for the nation and the greatest obstacle for its progress. Today in Russia all such objections have been silenced. Are we allowed to conclude from the violent vilifications of servility before the West, of cosmopolitanism and objectivity in the Stalinist press, that today too nationalist messianism does not hold an undisputed sway over the Russian mind and perhaps represents only a minority opinion? In any case, there is one fundamental difference between Dostoyevsky's age and the concluding years of Stalin's Russia: then nationalist messianism was voiced by individuals and small groups, among whom a spiritual giant and man of genius, who claimed to speak on behalf of the silent Russian peoples; under Stalin nationalist messianism was authoritatively proclaimed by the men in power who, though they seemed to descend from the *Possessed* whom Dostoyevsky abhorred, were the illegitimate heirs of some of Dostoyevsky's most cherished and characteristic visions.

13

Toynbee and Russia*

A student of history may disagree with Toynbee's fundamental view of the meaningful unfolding of history and take issue with the conceptual categories which the learned author applies to an under-

* An address before Loyola University, Chicago, November, 1955, and reprinted by permission from E. T. Gargan (ed.), *The Intent of Toynbee's History* (Chicago: Loyola University Press, 1961), pp. 113-131.

standing of its course. But there are few readers who do not recognize that Toynbee's work may rank, in spite of possible errors in detail and the doubtfulness of its general frame of reference, in the appreciation of later generations as the major achievement in the study of history in the middle of the twentieth century. Such a reader will admire not only the wealth of new insights offered in the ten [now twelve] volumes which were published over a period of more than twenty years, and the ecumenical sweep of Toynbee's vision expressed at a time when the *oecumene* had for the first time become a reality, but also the practical and sound common sense with which the classical scholar approaches many complex and vexing issues which form the substance of present-day political decisions. Not in vain did Toynbee work twice in critical periods of recent history as an official in the foreign and intelligence service of his country, and not in vain has he for many years analyzed contemporary events and collected and studied the relevant documents. Thus students in search of more light on one of the major problems in the world political arena of the twentieth century—the relationship between Russia and the West—may well turn to Toynbee for enlightenment. Naturally this problem does not occupy a central position in Toynbee's monumental survey which covers all civilizations and all the recorded past of mankind. Nevertheless, Toynbee's analysis of the Russian-Western relationship and also of the Russian-Asian relationship deserves the close attention not only of the student of history but of the student of contemporary affairs as well.[1] Toynbee's approach may help us to understand the underlying causes of the anti-Western attitude of Russia in terms of the historical background of civilizations.

It is true that Toynbee's emphasis shifts in the four last volumes of his work, which were published fifteen years after the preceding installment, from "civilizations" to "higher religions," yet throughout civilization remains the principal unit of history. The development and the clash of civilizations has not ceased to represent to him the main theme in history. More than thirty years ago, in studying the process of Westernization of the Near East, with which he was familiar as a Byzantine scholar and which attracted his attention during his official activity in the First World War, Toynbee

[1] The best criticism of Toynbee in English which I have encountered is Kenneth W. Thompson, "Toynbee's Approach to History Reviewed," *Ethics*, 65:287-303 (July 1955). See also Hans Kohn, "Toynbee Glaubensbekenntnis. Kritische Bemerkungen zu A Study of History," *Der Monat*, VII, 83:464-69 (August 1955).

insisted that the community of peoples sharing the traditions and attitudes of modern Western civilization is "a closer and more permanent unity than ... the independent states that form and dissolve within its boundaries." [2] A society and civilization related to that of the West in its origins but distinct in its character and development is the one which Toynbee first met in the Near East and which he calls the Orthodox Christian Society. Within its framework Russian society and civilization presents an "offshoot," which followed its own peculiar way from the beginning because it was established on "virgin soil on which no civilization had ever grown before" and was isolated from the main body of Orthodox Christianity by a double barrier of sea and steppe. Russian expansion succeeded in overcoming this barrier only in the eighteenth century,[3] at a time when Russia knew herself much stronger than, and superior to, the original main body of Orthodox Christianity.

In that society a "rabid Anti-Westernism became the master passion" after the twelfth century,[4] and this anti-Westernism was fully shared by Russian society. It abated with the beginning of Westernization of Orthodox Christianity; yet the feeling that the West was different and in some ways inferior continued to influence the Westernized Russian mind down to recent times. Crossing the border of the Russian Empire westwards, the Russian traveler as late as the end of the nineteenth century knew that he was entering an alien world, Europe, which included every Western country—Germany and Italy, France and England—and represented a way of life distinct from that of Russia. One of the central themes debated by the Russians throughout the nineteenth century was the relationship of Russia and Europe.[5] In that sense "Europe" is neither a geographic nor a racial concept—for Muscovy is geographically part of Europe and the Russians are members of the same race, many of them being taller and stronger than the typical Nordics—"Europe" here is a politico-cultural concept corresponding to that of Western society.

[2] Arnold J. Toynbee, *The Western Question in Greece and Turkey: A Study in the Contact of Civilisations* (London: Constable and Co. Ltd., 1923), p. 4.
[3] Toynbee, *Study*, I, p. 34; II, p. 80.
[4] *Ibid.*, IV, p. 618.
[5] See Hans Kohn, *The Mind of Modern Russia: Historical and Political Thought of Russia's Great Age* (New Brunswick: Rutgers University Press, 1955; paperback edition, Torchbooks, Harper and Brothers, 1961). When T. G. Masaryk published the most comprehensive study written by any Westerner "of the intellectual trends in Russia," he called it *Russia and Europe* (Jena: Diederichs, 1913). The English translation blurred this, in Masaryk's view, fundamental opposition of two civilizations by calling the book *The Spirit of Russia* (London: Allen and Unwin, 1919).

The use of the word "Europe" in this sense was not confined to Russians. To the great Greek patriot, Adhamándios Koraïs, the word "Europe" carried the same meaning when on November 8, 1810, he wrote from Paris to Smyrna: "Europe used to despise us as an uneducated nation unworthy of our splendid forefathers." Koraïs was a thorough Westernizer—anti-Byzantine and inspired by the form which modern Western civilization had taken in England and Anglo-America. He was convinced that only the introduction of enlightened education from the West could make the Greeks part of "Europe," though they were geographically and perhaps racially the heirs of the oldest and in many respects most glorious stage of European civilization.

In this process of Westernization the Russian branch of Orthodox Christianity preceded by 100 years the older branch settled in the Balkans, the original homeland of Orthodox Christianity. In the early part of the nineteenth century many Orthodox Christians from the Balkans came into contact with the West through semi-Westernized Russia. In their longing for a regeneration of their life they went to Russia. There, as one of them wrote, they gained a new understanding of liberty and humanity; they experienced the exhilaration of breathing a new life-giving air, but, as Toynbee rightly remarks, its source was neither Russia nor Orthodoxy.

> ... the distant source of this spiritual elixir [was] in Holland and Britain and America. The atmosphere in early nineteenth century Russia that inspired the Ottoman Greeks was a Western atmosphere to which Russia was merely giving passage; and in succumbing to this atmosphere they were opting, even if unconsciously, not for Russia, but for the West.[6]

Soon the Balkan peoples, however, turned directly to the West; after the middle of the nineteenth century they looked to Paris and not to Moscow or Odessa; nor did they preserve the anti-Western resentment which continued to characterize so much of Russian thinking.

Russia's leadership within Orthodox Christianity was not only due to her size; the earlier Westernization of Russia established her superiority over the heirs of the Byzantine Empire, the Ottoman Turks, who had subjected the main body of Orthodox Christianity. Toynbee regards the founding of St. Petersburg by Peter the Great in 1703 as the symbolic act with which the real Westernization of Rus-

---

[6] Toynbee, *Study*, VIII, p. 198.

sia began, and compares its significance with the founding of Constantinople by Constantine the Great. There is a certain parallel in their motives. Both rulers wished to inaugurate a new age in their realm. In 333 the Roman emperor intended to convert the Hellenic world to Christianity. Thirteen hundred and seventy years later the Russian emperor decided to convert Muscovy to the Western outlook. Undoubtedly post-Petrinian Russia represented something new beyond the imagination of pre-Petrinian Russians: " . . . a first infusion of Western Civilization was inspiring an Orthodox-Christian body politic with fresh energy and arming it with newfangled weapons." [7]

But the Westernization of Russia was not only a turning point in the history of Russia and of Orthodox Christianity; in the course of the following two centuries its importance proved world wide. Through Westernization the Russians were able, in the second part of the eighteenth century, to defeat the Turks who ruled the cradle and heartland of Orthodox Christianity. The Russian victory of 1774, coming from Orthodox Christians whom they knew as their subjects, surprised and humiliated the Turks and resulted in the "first essay in the 'Westernization' of the Ottoman military establishment . . . the thin end of a wedge which has since penetrated to the heart of Ottoman life." [8] But the Westernization of Russia set the example not only for Balkan Orthodox Christianity and its Ottoman lords. Russia's pains in the process of Westernization prefigured the pattern followed in other non-Western lands when they underwent the travail of Westernization. This affinity may explain the fact that, although the Russians are a "white" people and have conquered much vaster parts of Asia than any other European power, Asians often have not regarded them as "aliens" to the same degree that they did other "white" people. U Nu, Prime Minister of the Burmese Republic, followed this pattern of Russian-Asian relations when, during his visit to Moscow on November 1, 1955, he invited the Soviet Union to participate in the future Asian-African conferences to be held in the wake of the one which met in Bandung in April 1955. "To my surprise," the Burmese Buddhist declared, "I have found the Soviet Union is an Asian country. There are many things in common in our way of life." [9]

[7] *Ibid.*, III, p. 19. See also VI, p. 343; and II, p. 158.
[8] *Ibid.*, III, p. 48.
[9] *New York Times,* November 2, 1955.

Having followed Toynbee so far, let us note here one point of fundamental disagreement. Toynbee seems often to identify modern Western civilization with the marvels of technology. He regards Peter the Great not only as a Westernizer, but as an anticipation of the *Homo Occidentalis Mechanicus Neobarbarus* of the late nineteenth and early twentieth century, to be placed in the same portrait gallery as Edison and Ford, Rhodes and Northcliffe.[10] But modern Western civilization is infinitely more than science and technology, which are by-products of the Western freedom of inquiry and the Western sense of personal initiative. It is unthinkable without respect for individual liberty and tolerance of diversity, an attitude unfamiliar to, and not understood by, Peter the Great. The shortcomings of the Westernization of Russia and Asia were due not only to the West's failure in self-understanding, which Toynbee points out in his perhaps oversimplified brief broadcasts published as *The World and the West,* but also to non-Westerners' deliberate emphasis on the West's technological and material achievements without a true appreciation of the underlying ethos. Recent Communist emphasis on economic progress in Russia and in Asia has powerfully increased the trend.[11]

Westernization was often only the attempt to gain a new technological armor to protect a non-Western civilization against the West and its liberal outlook, while haughtily rejecting the West's individual-liberal ethos. From the sixteenth century on, a strong self-assurance grew up in Moscow, which regarded itself as a society and civilization pregnant with the future hopes of mankind. A similar conviction with roots even more deeply embedded in the past was to be found in Peking and to a lesser degree in Tokyo. But the Far Eastern societies came into contact with the West only two centuries after Russia and 100 years after the Near East. Thus Russia, as Toyn-

---

[10] Toynbee, *Study,* III, p. 279. "The most 'American' of all Peter's traits was the combination of this manual ability with the lynx eye of the prospector and the entrepreneur." See also p. 280.

[11] Many of the later Russian Westernizers, however, understood and accepted the full meaning and implications of modern Western civilization with its message of liberty and tolerance. The two outstanding examples are perhaps Vladimir Solovëv and Georgii Fedotov (see Kohn, *Mind of Modern Russia,* pp. 212 ff.; 257 ff.). Examples of this true Westernization were to be found also throughout Asia, especially in the British colonies. The great difference of the effect of Russian and of British influence in Asia was pointed out half a century ago by a Hungarian scholar and explorer, Ármin Vámbéry, *Western Culture in Eastern Lands* (London: Murray, 1906). See also on the Westernization process in India the important analysis in Nirad C. Chaudhuri, *The Autobiography of an Unknown Indian* (New York: Macmillan, 1951).

bee points out,[12] was the first society to enter into competition with the modern West for "the spiritual allegiance of all the living societies that were neither Western nor Russian in their native cultural tradition, and—not content even with that—she must have the supreme audacity to carry the war into the enemy's camp by preaching the Russian faith in the West's own homeland." Russia did it in the name of a Westerner, of Marx, who, to quote Toynbee, in putting his finger on one point in Western practice in which there was in the middle of the nineteenth century a crying need for reform and which the West had largely remedied by the middle of the twentieth century, "had lost sight of all other considerations and therefore has produced a remedy that is worse than the disease." [13] But more important than preaching the Russian faith in the West was preaching it in non-Western lands. Obviously it was impractical to preach this faith in the form of traditional Orthodox Christianity. Communism offered infinitely greater chances not only because it was a product of an age of faith in science and technology, but also because it represented an anti-Western critique of Western origin, which could easily be turned against the West.

In this process of Westernization, technology can become "demoniac," and the contact with modern Western civilization can become "corrosive" because it is eagerly taken over without the underlying modern Western ethos. Without a foundation on the ethos of individual liberty, even the most imposing and efficient economic and technological superstructure may prove weak. Technological Westernization had centered on the modernization of the armed force, of the administrative machine, and of the educational system. Peter the Great tried to do this, but failed. Full realization in Russia was only attempted under Lenin and Stalin. But Russia was not the only country to carry through such a thorough technological Westernization. The Prussian reformers after their country's collapse in 1806 set perhaps the first example. They wished to strengthen Prussia in her struggle against modern Western ideas by improving the army, the administration, and the general level of education in their country to a degree even beyond the achievements of the contemporary West. But they left the foundations of their society authoritarian and rejected the civilian middle-class spirit of Western

[12] *Study*, VIII, p. 134.
[13] Arnold J. Toynbee, *The World and the West* (New York: Oxford University Press, 1953), p. 16.

society. The Prussian example was followed with equal success and under much more difficult conditions by Japan after 1868. Within a few decades Japan not only far surpassed every non-Western society, including that of Russia, in the organization of its armed forces, in administrative skill and efficiency, in its educational system, but equaled the West. Nevertheless, Prussia and Japan, after initial success, broke down in the crises which they themselves had provoked out of their feeling of superiority because they had not sufficiently Westernized, and that means liberalized their society and civilization. The authoritarian and "collectivist" character which Prussia and Japan regarded as a mark of superiority and source of strength revealed itself in a serious test as a fundamental weakness.

The similarity between Prussia and Russia, both European and Christian powers, is, as far as I could find, nowhere stressed by Toynbee, though Lord Acton clearly recognized it,[14] perhaps because he had a better understanding of the nature of modern Western civilization than Toynbee, who sees the rise of the modern West in the seventeenth century as simply a substitution of technology for theology. Therefore Toynbee can regard liberalism, fascism, and communism as secular ideologies on an equal footing that have arisen in the modern West as substitutes for Christianity which the West had discarded. Toynbee does not distinguish between secular liberalism as a legitimate manifestation of Western civilization, in which the

[14] Lord Acton wrote about the Prussian and the Russian governments that "government so understood is the intellectual guide of the nation, the promoter of wealth, the teacher of knowledge, the guardian of morality, the mainspring of the ascending movement of man." This characterization, so antithetically opposed to the role of government in modern Western civilization, applied as well to the German government under Bismarck as, at least in theory, to the government of St. Petersburg. To a high degree, of course, it applies to the governments of Lenin and Hitler, which Acton could not foresee. But long before the rise of Hitler, Acton, who knew more of Germany than any other British historian, warned, speaking of the Prussian government erected on the foundations which he described, "That is the tremendous power supported by millions of bayonets, which . . . was developed, . . . chiefly at Berlin; and it is the greatest danger that remains to be encountered by the Anglo-Saxon race." Lord John E. Acton, *Lectures on Modern History* (London: Macmillan, 1906), p. 289. Thomas Mann equally insists on the close affinity of Germany and Russia and on their fundamental opposition to modern Western civilization. In his *Betrachtungen eines Unpolitischen* (Berlin: Fischer, 1920), he wrote during the First World War, in which Germany and Russia fought on opposite sides: "Are the Russian and the German attitudes toward Europe, the West, civilization, politics, and democracy, not closely akin? Have not we Germans also our Slavophils and our Westernizers? . . . If spiritual affinity can form the foundation and justification of political alliances, then Russians and Germans belong together: their agreement now, their union for the future, has been since the beginning of this war the desire and dream of my heart. It is more than a desirability: it is a political and spiritual necessity in case that the Anglo-American alliance should endure."

ideals of classical humanism and of Christian piety live on, and fascism and communism, which reject modern Western civilization and Christian piety.

Toynbee identifies liberalism not with the spirit of tolerance and of individual liberty, which came to fruition in northwestern Europe in the seventeenth century, but with capitalism or free enterprise.[15] This interpretation of modern Western civilization leads Toynbee to call the German invaders of Russia in 1941 "abominable Western invaders." Abominable they certainly were, but though to the Russians they clearly came from the West they were men who were—and proudly professed to be—anti-Western. The fascist German invaders of Russia hated and despised liberal civilization as much as the Communists did. As the Communists were the product of an insufficient Westernization of their native society and civilization, so were the Fascists. As communism presented a crude exaggeration and vulgar generalization of certain Slavophile trends in nineteenth-century Russian history, so National Socialism was a crude and vulgar intensification of German anti-Western attitudes which went back to the struggle against Napoleon I.[16] In both countries, in Russia and in Germany, the triumph of communism and of National Socialism eliminated, at least for the duration of this triumph, certain truly Western forces which of course were much deeper rooted in Germany, especially in Germany west of the Elbe, than in Russia. These forces can legitimately be called liberal, not in the sense of capitalism, but in the sense of the humanism of a Goethe or Kant or of the Christian piety and tolerance of a Vladimir Solovëv.

Toynbee's overevaluation of the technological and material aspects of modern civilization makes it possible for him to assume that industrialization and modern armament may in their wake bring about a true Westernization. He quotes with approval the optimistic outlook of Gibbon at the end of the thirty-eighth chapter of *The History of the Decline and Fall of the Roman Empire*:

> Europe is secure from any future irruption of barbarians; since, before they can conquer, they must cease to be barbarous. Their gradual advances in the sciences of war would always be accompanied, as we may learn from the example of Russia, with a proportionable

---

[15] Toynbee speaks of the "Modern Western way of life which was called 'Capitalism' by its critics and 'Free Enterprise' by its advocates." Toynbee, *Study*, VIII, p. 112, note.
[16] See Hans Kohn, *The Mind of Germany: The Education of a Nation* (New York: Charles Scribner's Sons), 1960.

improvement in the arts of peace and civil policy; and they themselves must deserve a place among the polished nations whom they subdue.[17]

Gibbon was a rationalist liberal of the eighteenth century. He could not foresee twentieth-century Fascists and Communists who, with all the advances in the science of war, could very well remain barbarous or even proudly unlearn the arts of parliamentary liberty and civil policy.

Sharing Gibbon's optimism, Toynbee in the first part of his work, published in 1934, before the Fascist and Communist offensive against the West openly manifested itself, wrote that "even if one day the Communist dispensation were to fulfill the Russian Communists' hopes by spreading from Russia over the whole face of the planet, a world-wide triumph of Communism over Capitalism would not mean the overthrow" of Western civilization. Toynbee saw even then the Janus-like face of Russian communism. On the one hand, he called Lenin "a prophet of Holy Russia who has been great enough to gather up into his own career and personality the whole reaction of the Russian soul against the Western Civilization." On the other hand, Toynbee believed that Lenin's mechanization and industrialization would insure the triumph in Russia of the very civilization which the Communists were even more bitterly denouncing than the extreme Slavophiles had ever done.[18]

Toynbee's work, spread over many years, reflects the changes not only of his views but of much of informed Western opinion on Russia. When the second part of his work was published in 1939, many observers noted the increasingly Russian nationalist aspect of Stalinism. Such a change did not come unexpected. When Lenin started his revolution it claimed to mark a complete break with the Russian past and the beginning of an entirely new chapter in the history of mankind. Similar claims had been voiced in the year I of the French Republic. The French Revolution, which originally tried to reform France in the spirit of Locke and Montesquieu, soon regarded itself

[17] Edward Gibbon, *The History of the Decline and Fall of the Roman Empire*, Vol. 4 (Boston: Little, Brown and Company, 1854), pp. 408-09.
[18] Toynbee, *Study*, III, pp. 200-202, 364 ff. "The curious fact is that if one substituted communism for [Dostoevski's] conception of the mission of the Orthodox faith, and world revolution for his notion of a Pan-Slavic war against Europe, the identity of his whole position with that of modern Soviet Russia would be striking." Ernest J. Simmons, *Dostoevski, the Making of a Novelist* (New York: Columbia University Press, 1940), pp. 327 ff.

as the inauguration of a new era of liberty for the human race. But its policy of centralization and expansion followed, with much greater efficiency and popular backing, the work of Richelieu and Louis XIV, and the revolutionists and republicans far from understanding the true meaning of liberty succumbed to the spirit of dogmatism and absolutism characteristic of the *ancien régime*.

Similarly after 1934 the Russian national tradition and character manifested themselves more and more in the Russian Revolution. Thus Toynbee could find in the Soviet Union

> a strongly pronounced tendency to withdraw allegiance from Humanity at large in order to concentrate it upon that fraction of the living generation of Mankind that is at present penned within the frontiers of the U.S.S.R. In other words, Soviet Communism seems at this moment to be changing under our eyes from a worship of Humanity into the worship of a tribal divinity of the type of Athene Polias or the Lion of Saint Mark or Kathleen na Hoolihan or Britannia.[19]

But though communism may accept elements of the worship of a tribal divinity, and we should remember what Toynbee tends to overlook—that tribal divinities can be very different in the kind of worship they demand and in the spirit and morality with which they inspire their worshipers—the relationship of the Russian traditional sense of mission and the international faith animating communism is of much greater complexity than Toynbee, and with him many others, in 1939 apparently believed.[20] The events after 1945 quickly disillusioned those observers who believed in a nationalist normalization of Stalinism. The global threat of communism revealed itself only after Hitlerism had sharpened man's understanding for the new "civilized" barbarism with its world-encompassing pretensions, and after Stalin had begun fully to exploit the opportunities created by German and Japanese aggression.

In the middle of the twentieth century, then, the West found itself faced with an unexpected situation. For from the time of Gibbon to the beginning of the twentieth century modern Western civilization regarded itself as free from any external threat. Such freedom from

[19] Toynbee, *Study*, IV, p. 302. Toynbee goes even so far as to seriously compare Russian communism with British positivism, because both reject transcendental religion. See also VIII, p. 146.

[20] Ernest J. Simmons (ed.), *Continuity and Change in Russian and Soviet Thought* (Cambridge, Mass.: Harvard University Press, 1955).

external aggression was a new experience for the West. As late as 1683 Turkish armies had camped at the gates of Vienna. Throughout its preceding history the West had to fight repeatedly for its very existence against non-Western aggressors and empire builders. Although the eighteenth and nineteenth centuries were not a period of peace, the wars fought by the West then were internal wars. Even the Russia of St. Petersburg participated in these wars as one of the European powers. But already in the nineteenth century some Russian thinkers like Danilevsky refused to accept this position. They pointed out that Russia was too great to be merely one of the European powers, that she was a society and a world by herself.[21] Yet Danilevsky's apocalyptic visions of mankind did not materialize then. On the contrary, Russia made at the beginning of the twentieth century fast progress in the fullness of a true Westernization. She became more and more an integral part of Europe and entered the war of 1914 as a European power, an ally of Britain and France. The war in 1914 was neither a war for world control nor a war for the souls of man. Only in 1917 did the character of the war change. Lenin withdrew Russia from her alliance with the West, turned her toward Asia, in which he saw the ally in the coming and, according to him, inevitable struggle with the West, and reversed Peter's symbolic transfer of Russia's capital from Moscow to St. Petersburg.[22]

Communistic control of Russia's destinies inspired the rise of anti-Western movements in central Europe and Asia and set the framework for the Second World War, which differed fundamentally from the war of 1914. It was no longer a war within the European society. It was a war for the control of the world and for the soul of man. Germany and Japan fought against the spirit and the traditions of modern Western civilization. After the defeat of Germany and Japan, the struggle against the West was continued by Russia. But it should not be forgotten that only the preceding German-Japanese aggression made possible the expansion of Russian control into central Europe and into the Far East. This destroyed the Western position there and produced chaos and a spiritual vacuum, enabling Russia to stretch out her hand for the prize of world domination to which the

[21] In his very summary treatment of post-Petrinian intellectual Russia, Toynbee nowhere mentions Danilevsky. See more on him in Hans Kohn, *Mind of Modern Russia* (New York: Harper Torchbooks, 1962), pp. 195-210; and Hans Kohn, *Pan-Slavism: Its History and Ideology* (New York: Vintage Books, 1960), pp. 190-208.

[22] See Kohn, *Mind of Modern Russia*, pp. 236, 246. Lenin expected a Russian-Asian alliance against the West as the vehicle of world revolution as early as 1913.

Germans and Japanese had aspired with insufficient strength and with an insufficient ideology.

In 1939 the West, under Britain's leadership, opposed Germany's bid for world domination. In 1947 the United States assumed the leadership of the West in opposition to Russia's bid for world domination. In the 1930's the Fascist leaders boasted that fascism represented the way of the future and that the West was doomed by its moral and social inferiority. Likewise, the Communist leaders in the 1950's were convinced that the twentieth century would end with a world-wide victory of communism over the socially and morally decaying West. Fascists and Communists made open claim to world domination. But the government and the people of the United States shrunk back even from the leadership of the Western world until there was no choice left. Whatever limited leadership the United States came to exercise, it was thrust upon her, much against her hope and will. It is impossible to call the post-1945 period as Toynbee does, "a competition for the same prize [of world domination] between the United States and the Soviet Union." [23] Only communism has, after the defeat of fascism, the *hubris* of claiming world leadership.

When Toynbee wrote the last part of his work, his thought was understandably dominated by the growing conflict between Russia and the West. Fortunately Toynbee's mind, very different therein from Danilevsky's and Spengler's, is not obsessed by the irrational fears and triumphs of an apocalyptic war vision. Toynbee rightly refuses to act as a prophet. In his humility he knows too well the limitations of man and of the historian. "In circumstances that were so plainly precarious but in other respects so enigmatically obscure," he wrote in 1952, "a dogmatic optimism was as unwarrantable as a dogmatic pessimism, and the living generation of Mankind had no choice but to reconcile itself as best it could to the disturbing knowledge that it was facing issues in which its very existence might be at stake, and that it was at the same time impossible at this stage to guess what the event would be." [24] Nor was Toynbee fascinated by the spectacle of totalitarian power and of vast multitudes; he clearly recognized the weaknesses inherent in the Soviet, as in every totalitarian, system. The Soviet Union put forward the claim of having saved a primitive peasantry from economic disaster and thus ap-

---

[23] Toynbee, *Study*, VIII, p. 111. See also IX, pp. 544-46.
[24] *Ibid.*, IX, p. 535.

parently held out a promise to the peasantry in other backward lands, but as far as it had improved the peasants' lot at all, it had done so at the terrifying price of forfeiting both liberty and happiness.

Communist society which likes to call itself the proletarian homeland and paradise was in that very respect one century behind Western society. "If a proletariat may be defined as a class whose members have no personal stake in the society in which they find themselves, and no say in the ordering of their own lives," Toynbee writes, "the twentieth-century workers in the factories and collective farms of the Soviet Union would pass this test as well as the factory workers and agricultural labourers of a nineteenth-century Great Britain." [25] Nor has Toynbee any doubt about the unpopularity of Russia in the East European countries. It is remarkable, however, that he apparently underrates the centrifugal tendencies presented in the Soviet Union itself by its many non-Russian nationalities, especially by the most numerous of them, the Ukrainians and the Mohammedans, though he is well aware of the fundamental tension between the ideologies of Marxism and nationalism.[26] Nor does he stress the Western orientation of the Ukrainians and of the Baltic peoples who often regard themselves rather as Western marches against Moscow than as Moscow's [Eastern] marches against the West.

It must be considered to Toynbee's credit as an analyst of contemporary events that he believed in 1952 that "the twentieth-century tension between the Soviet Union and the United States was not bound to result in war in the nineteen-fifties, but might alternatively relax without catastrophe, as the nineteenth-century tension between the Russian Empire and the British Empire had relaxed in the eighteen-eighties." [27] But the parallel which Toynbee draws does not entirely fit the circumstances. In the nineteenth century the British and the Russian empires faced each other as rivals for limited goals. Neither of them claimed the totality of mankind, neither of them raised any messianic pretensions. In the twentieth century there exists no tension between the Soviet Union and the United States similar to the nineteenth-century tension between Russia and Britain. There exists something different: a tension between the Soviet Union and the non-communist rest of mankind among which at the moment by accidents of geography and history the United States is

[25] *Ibid.*, VIII, p. 689, note.
[26] See Toynbee on the satellite countries, *ibid.*, IX, p. 533; on the Ukrainians, IV, pp. 189 f.; on nationalism in the Soviet Union, VI, p. 110.
[27] *Ibid.*, VIII, p. 146.

the strongest single power. For the Soviet Union does not aim, as the Russian Empire of St. Petersburg did, at the control of limited territories but at the guidance of mankind as such; thus the Soviet Union does not conflict with a rival empire or with several rival empires, but with every non-communist part of mankind whether it be Britain, the United States, Norway, Switzerland, Iran, or Japan.

Nevertheless Toynbee's hope that the Soviet Union may be reluctant to go to war in order to achieve its goals may well be justified. The reason for it, however, lies not so much in any parallel with the past but in the unprecedented fact that the nations of the West have created a firm union even before Soviet aggression openly materializes on a large scale. Toynbee himself recognizes this factor as the main hope for the maintenance of peace. In a situation in which, to quote him, "Lands outside the frontiers of the Soviet Union herself and her involuntary satellites, have found security against their fear of Soviet attack and Communist penetration by voluntarily entering into a free political association with the United States and with one another to the extent required for effective common defence and common pursuit of material and spiritual welfare," the Soviet Union may be expected to desist from aggression, if the union of the Western nations will prove sufficiently firm and enduring, in spite of the threat offered by excessive nationalism, today above all in France, to Western unity and Western civilization. But when Toynbee expects an easy stabilization of the world with the Soviet Union playing "something like the role which the Parthian and Kushan Powers have played in the Transeuphratean continental hinterland of a Hellenizing World," he overplays by far the much abused parallel between the situation today and that at the end of the ancient world. Neither can the modern West be compared to the Roman Empire nor is it appropriate to underestimate the driving power of Russian imperial ambitions and the revolutionary dynamism of Communist messianism to which hardly a parallel can be found in the Parthian and Kushan Powers.

It would not do justice, however, to Toynbee's approach to history in general if we ended the discussion of Russia on a predominantly political plane. Many of Toynbee's most penetrating and illuminating insights are contained in footnotes, and in such a footnote he points out that the Russians have always been at their worst in the role of rulers. There has, however, been another role in which the Russians were at their best, and that was the role of martyrs:

The noble army of Russian martyrs, whose ranks had been perpetually recruited by one generation after another of intrepid volunteers from the eleventh century to the twentieth, bore witness to the historical fact that the tyrannical vein in the Russian ethos had always been under challenge from an antithetical Russian spirit of self-sacrificing love that had known no fear of "them which kill the Body but are not able to kill the Soul."[28]

Perhaps the Russian tragedy of our time—a tragedy involving a great and noble part of mankind and through it mankind itself—consists in the very fact that the Soviet rulers not only show Russian rule at its worst but that they have silenced the protest of martyrdom in Russia so that the spirit and the intrepid testimony to truth and human dignity no longer shine forth in Russian life and letters as they did even in the worst periods of czarist oppression.

14

The Impact of Pan-Slavism on Central Europe*

Pan-Slavism is one of the elusive idea-concepts which can be easily defined. But the historian can hardly say how far it corresponds to a political reality which exercises a decisive impact on the course of history. A similar contemporary idea-concept is Pan-Africanism, propagated and commended by most Africans. So far it has failed to create a political or economic union. The only example of that kind, and that on a very minor scale, the Mali Federation, dissolved after a short existence. The same holds true of another similar concept,

[28] *Ibid.*, IX, p. 546, note 2.

* A paper read before the Annual convention of the American Historical Association in New York on December 30, 1960, and first published in *The Review of Politics*, Vol. 23 (July 1961), pp. 323-333. Reprinted with permission.

Pan-Scandinavianism, which is approximately as old as Pan-Slavism but better based on a much closer cultural and religious affinity.

Pan-Slavism originated in Central Europe and not among the Eastern Slavs. After some medieval beginnings among the Poles and Czechs there was an interesting Pan-Slav movement among the Croats during the Renaissance. Of its representatives Juraj Križanić (Georgius Crisanius, 1618-1683) is the best known, and Professor Halecki and Angelo Tamborra have revealed to us several of his precursors.[1] But they had no impact whatsoever and their works and lives were only rediscovered by scholars in the nineteenth century when Pan-Slavism for the first time became a movement much discussed by journalists, diplomats, and scholars, and, even then, less in Russia than in Central and Western Europe. Around 1830 Pan-Slavism began to haunt many European minds as the form in which they expressed their fear of Russian domination over the continent. But, as Professor Petrovich has noted, Pan-Slavism in Russia itself did not emerge as a public movement before 1856.[2]

Even the program of later Russian Pan-Slavism which might be better called Pan-Russianism was developed by a Western Slav, L'udevit Stúr (1815-1856). In the last years before his death he wrote a book on "The Slavs and the World of the Future." He himself was a Slovak Lutheran and he wrote the book in German. For over a decade it remained in manuscript. It was published in 1867 in a Russian translation and became popular among the Russian Pan-Slavs because it demanded not only the union of all Slavs under Russian leadership but also the adoption of the Eastern Orthodox faith, of the Russian language, and of the Russian alphabet by all Slavs.[3]

Stúr is a good illustration of S. Harrison Thomson's assertion that "there was always an element of the unreal and the naive in Pan-Slavism." [4] Characteristically Stúr had never visited Russia and his

---

[1] See Oscar Halecki, "The Renaissance Origin of Panslavism," *The Polish Review*, III (1958), 7-19 and Angelo Tamborra, "Panslavismo e solidarità slava," *Questioni di Storia Contemporanea* (Milan, 1955), II, 1777-1872.

[2] "Panslavism as a public movement did not assert itself in Russia until the Crimean War and the beginning of Alexander II's regin in 1855." Michael Boro Petrovich, *The Emergence of Russian Panslavism 1856-1870* (New York, 1956), p. 3. But even Prince Alexander Gorchakov (1798-1883) who during the whole period (from 1856 to 1882) was Russian Foreign Minister and later Chancellor, the first "Russian" in this post, "had always been contemptuous of the Panslavic program." *Ibid.*, p. 121. See also Hans Kohn, *Pan-Slavism, Its History and Ideology*, 2nd ed. (New York, 1960), p. 126.

[3] See Michael B. Petrovich, "L'udovit Stur and Russian Panslavism," *Journal of Central European Affairs*, XII (1952), 1-19 and Hans Kohn, *op. cit.*, pp. 15-18.

[4] S. Harrison Thomson, *Czechoslovakia in European History* (Princeton, 1943), p. 230.

description of Russian conditions revealed utter ignorance. That was equally true of Stúr's older fellow-Slovak, Jan Kollár (1793-1852) who, like Stúr, was a Lutheran and wrote his chief Pan-Slav prose work in German. The Russian Pan-Slavist Vladimir Lamansky (1833-1914), who translated Stúr into Russian, spoke of the "well-known brochure of that progenitor of modern Pan-Slavism Kollár, which created such a stir in its own time in Central Europe."

Kollár and Stúr were awakened to their Pan-Slavism by similar experiences when they studied in German universities, the former in Jena, the latter in Halle. There, they both came under the influence of German romantic nationalism and became conscious of the extinction of the Slavic tribes who centuries ago had lived between the Saale and Elbe rivers. Thus, Central Europe even in its non-Slavic parts had a decisive influence on the origins of Pan-Slavism. Though Kollár's program was more moderate than that of Stúr—he demanded neither political unification nor Russification but only a closer cultural contact among the Slav peoples—it remained unreal too. Until around 1940 the cultural ties of Czechs, Croats, and Poles were much stronger with France and even with Germany than with Russia or with each other. In many ways one can perhaps speak of the impact of Central Europe on Pan-Slavism with greater validity than one can speak of the impact of Pan-Slavism on Central Europe.

It is well known that three Central European movements or events which in their origin had nothing to do with the Slavs stimulated the rise of Pan-Slavism—German romantic nationalism, the movement for German unification, and the Austro-Hungarian compromise. Of minor importance was the influence of the Italian Risorgimento on Pan-Slavism. Some of the Italian leaders, above all Mazzini, dreamed of an alliance of the awakening Italian people with the awakening Slav nationalities of the Habsburg monarchy against the common enemy. Like most Western liberals Mazzini dreaded the expansion of Russian power and Russia's possible use of the Western and Southern Slavs in its service. Again like most Western liberals, Mazzini looked to the Poles for his hopes of organizing a Central European Pan-Slavism as a barrier against Russian despotism.

Only a Western Pan-Slavism, so Mazzini thought, in an alliance with Mazzinian Italy could preserve European peace. "We who have ourselves arisen in the name of our national right," Mazzini addressed the small Slav nations in 1871, believe in your right, and offer to help you win it. But the purpose of our mision is a permanent and peaceful organization of Europe. We cannot allow Russian Tzarism — a perennial menace to Europe — to step into the place now occupied by your masters, and no partial movement executed by a single element amongst you can be victorious; nor, even were victory possible, could it constitute a strong barrier against the avidity of the Tzar: it would simply further his plans of aggrandizement. Unite, therefore; forget past rancour, and unite in one confederation.[5]

Mazzini's plan of a confederation of the Western Slavs as a bulwark against Russian and German expansionism and for the preservation of peace in Europe had much in common with Palacký's famous letter to the German National Assembly in March, 1848. But there were two fundamental differences between them. First, while Mazzini was bent on the destruction of the Habsburg monarchy, Palacky's Austro-Slavism demanded the preservation of the monarchy as a protective roof for the various Slav peoples who would form the majority of its population. Second, Mazzini and other Italian Philoslavs, especially in 1848, hoped for a close friendship of Magyars and Western Slavs. Palacký's Austro-Slavism was as much a safeguard against Magyar as against German and Russian hegemonial aspiration. In reality, Mazzini's as well as Palacký's program remained without consequences. In the Austrian Littoral, in Dalmatia and in Fiume Italian nationalism clashed with Slav nationalism and this clash survived the Habsburg monarchy and became even more bitter in the decades following the First World War.

We can speak, then, not of a Pan-Slav movement, but, as in contemporary Africa, of local pan-movements, a Pan-Russian, a Pan-Serbian or a Pan-Polish movement, each one at times using Pan-Slav slogans to win the sympathy of other Slav peoples or to establish its control over them. The word Pan-Slavism was probably more used by non-Slav publicists after 1830 than by the Slavs themselves. These non-Slav publicists were sometimes moved by sympathy for the Central European Slavs, more often by fear of Russia which was identified by them with Pan-Slavism.[6] Differing therein from Mazzini, some suggested a strong Austria as a bulwark against Russian Pan-Slavism. Pre-eminent among them, before 1870, were German

[5] See Hans Kohn, *Prophets and Peoples. Studies in Nineteenth Century Nationalism* (New York, 1946), pp. 94, 185, 188, and Angelo Tamborra, *op. cit.*, pp. 1822-1827.
[6] See Hans Kohn, *Pan-Slavism,* pp. 102-122.

Catholics who hoped for a united Central Europe under the leadership of a German Austria, which would be organized on a federal basis and respect all historical national individualities.

The most prominent spokesman of this school of thought was Dr. Joseph Edmund Jörg (1819-1901) who in 1854 published in the *Historisch-Politische Blätter,* the ultra-montane Munich review which he edited, an article in which he foresaw Europe's decline caused on the one hand by the rise of the United States with its economic liberalism and Protestant humanitarianism and on the other by the expansion of Orthodox Russia. He feared Russia not only for its alleged attraction to, and propaganda among, the other Slav peoples, but also because he regarded Russia as the home of the revolution. "Who knows," he wrote, "whether the place where the communists will gather will not one day be Russia? Perhaps not we but certainly our children will see the unfolding of an astonishing tragedy in Europe's East." Jörg was one of the foremost opponents of Bismarck and of Prussia's domination of Germany because he believed that an Austria excluded from German leadership would become a Slav and Magyar state.

A similar attitude toward Central Europe and the Pan-Slav danger was taken by another German arch-conservative, Konstantin Frantz (1817-1891), who though not a Bavarian Catholic but a Protestant Prussian, rejected Bismarck's Greater Prussia as fervently as Jörg did. Like him he regarded the United States and Russia as the two decisive great powers of the future, whose imperialism could be checked only by a federated Central Europe under German cultural and Habsburg political leadership, a revival of the supranational Holy Roman Empire. He demanded a friendly relationship between the Germans and the Western and Southern Slavs, especially the Poles. Frantz attacked Bismarck not only for the immorality of his militaristic power policy but also for his friendship with Russia, to which he sacrificed Poland. In his last work, in the three volumes of *Die Weltpolitik unter besonderer Bezugnahme auf Deutschland,* which appeared in 1882-83, he called upon the Germans to stop all this talk about Holy Russia and to end once for all the friendship with Russia. He characterized the friendship with the Muscovite state the shame of Prussian history.[7]

Bismarck followed the tradition of the Prussian court in basing his

[7] For the various federal ideas of that period, see Jacques Droz, *L'Europe Centrale. Évolution historique de l'idée de Mitteleuropa* (Paris, 1960).

policy on cooperation with Russia. He neither approved nor understood the appeals of Pan-Slavism or Pan-Germanism. He was ready to incite Czech nationalism against Austria in 1866 as he was ready to use Italian or Magyar nationalism for the same purpose. But once his goal of a Greater Prussia was reached, he was quite prepared to help preserve the Habsburg monarchy against Pan-Germanism and to cultivate good relations with the Russian monarchy in spite of the danger of Pan-Slavism. His revolutionary role in upsetting the Holy Alliance and the principle of legitimacy was over. It had served its purpose and so it was discarded in favor of a triumphant conservatism which, in an altered form with Prussia now in the lead, restored the Holy Alliance as a firm bulwark for monarchical principles and against the danger of the penetration of liberal and democratic ideas from the West.

The court of St. Petersburg followed a similar policy guided by a purely Russian raison d'état and by conservative monarchical principles until the vacillating and slightly megalomaniac policy of William II forced the Romanovs to abandon the "natural" and historical friendship with the Hohenzollerns for the much less natural or historic one, with the radical and agnostic French Republic. Russia's drive towards Constantinople was not dictated by Pan-Slav aspirations or principles. It predated them. It was based on purely Russian strategic and commercial interests and on a purely Russian historical mystique. Alexander III is reported to have said in 1885: "We ought to have one principal aim: the occupation of Constantinople so that we may once for all maintain ourselves at the Straits and know that they will remain in our hands . . . everything else that takes place in the Balkan Peninsula is secondary to us. . . . The [Balkan] Slavs must now serve Russia and not we them." [8] This mystique of Constantinople did not run counter to a German or Austrian mystique but to that of the Slav Bulgarians and the Orthodox Greeks.

Insofar as Pan-Slavism became identified in many Western European minds with Pan-Russianism, it played a role only among a very small number of the Central European Slavs, the Old Ruthenians in eastern Galicia and in the Carpathian Ukraine. This trend represented a minority among the Ukrainians in the Habsburg monarchy. These Old Ruthenians regarded themselves as, and wished to become, Russians. From Russia they expected liberation from the

[8] Quoted in Arthur J. May, *The Hapsburg Monarchy 1867-1914* (Cambridge, Mass., 1951), p. 275.

Poles and from Catholic pressure which aimed to introduce the Latin liturgy among them. The Ukrainians in eastern Galicia and in the Carpathian Ukraine were the least favored of the Slavs in the Habsburg monarchy. Their depressed position was due not so much to the Habsburgs but in the one case to the Slav Poles, in the other to the Magyars.[9] The Young Ruthenians who predominated among the growing class of Ukrainian intellectuals were neither pro-Russian nor Pan-Slavs. They regarded the Ukrainian part of Galicia as the Piedmont or the Serbia for the future reunion of all Ukrainians, of whom the majority lived in the Russian Empire. They were Pan-Ukrainians and found their national evolution threatened by two other Slav peoples, the Russians and the Poles.

Modern Pan-Slavism originated and found its foremost spokesmen among the Czechs and Slovaks. Prague was its first home. This remained true throughout the history of Pan-Slavism, though the most realistic Czech thinkers, Karel Havlíček (1821-1856) at the beginning of the period and Tomáš G. Masaryk (1850-1937) towards its end persistently raised their warning voices against it. As a young man Havlíček, like the educated Czech youth of that time generally, fell under the spell of a vague and romantic Pan-Slavism, but in his well-known article "Slav and Czech" in 1846 he expressed the most clear-headed rejection of Pan-Slavism and Russophilism.[10] The Neo-Slavism of the beginning of the twentieth century was again inspired from Prague; under the leadership of Dr. Karel Kramář (1860-1937) it was based upon the hope of the emergence of a liberal or democratic Russia and of a Polish-Russian reconciliation which a democratization of Russia would make possible. These hopes were quickly disappointed by Russian reality.

Masaryk knew Russia well and had little hope in a democratization of Russia or in any sincere interest of the Russians in the other Slavs. In 1914, according to Masaryk's testimony, Czech public opinion "was uncritically Russophile in the expectation of liberation by the Russians and their Cossacks." Against the apparently general demand for a Russian prince as Czech king, Masaryk expressed his fears "of the Russian dynasty and even of a Russian governor, since Russian ignorance of [Czech] things and men, their absolutism and their indolence would soon demolish our Russophilism." [11]

[9] See Robert A. Kann, *The Multinational Empire* (New York, 1950), I, 327.
[10] See Hans Kohn, *Pan-Slavism*, pp. 23-26.
[11] T. G. Masaryk, *Světová revoluce za války a ve válce 1914-1918* (rev. ed., Prague, 1933), p. 15.

In October, 1914, Masaryk told R. W. Seton-Watson that "all Czech parties without exception have the Slav program and Slav sentiments. The nation is Russophile and Serbophile, and this fact cannot be changed." In the same interview Masaryk insisted on the union of Czechs and Slovaks, but excluded the Ruthenians of Hungary. The Carpatho-Ukraine, he proposed, should be incorporated in the Russian Empire, a step which would establish direct borders between Russia and the new Czechoslovakia, a proposal forecasting the situation of 1945. Masaryk did not share the Russophile sentiments of his fellow-Czechs. His long study of the Russian mind and political thought had convinced him that Russia would be unable to bring liberty to the western Slav nations. He remained faithful, during the war and after it, to his conviction that the fate of his nation was bound up with that of the Western democracies and the United States.[12]

Czech Russophile Pan-Slavism had no parallel among the Austrian Poles or Slovenes, and the Russian Pan-Slavs did not care very much about these Western and Catholic Slavs. Of the Catholic and Protestant or Hussite Czechs and Slovaks the Orthodox Russian people knew very little and had hardly any interest in them. The situation with regard to the Orthodox Balkan Slavs was different. There the community of faith coincided with common hostility to the infidel Turks. Nevertheless, Pan-Slavism was much weaker as a living force among the Southern Slavs than among the Czechs. The Serbs or Bulgars expected and accepted in the hour of need Russian help against Turkey and later against the Habsburg monarchy, where and when their national interests coincided, but Serbs and Bulgars followed on the whole a self-centered, not a Pan-Slav or Russophile policy. For the last eighty years Serbs and Bulgars have been absorbed by a bitter struggle against each other. It is also noteworthy that in 1914 the Croats who hoped for independence in case of the defeat of the Central powers wished to create a Croatian kingdom under an English, not a Russian, prince.[13]

The situation which prevailed in Central Europe after the First World War was quite unique. Pan-Slavism seemed even more dead than Pan-Germanism. For the first time since the late eighteenth century Russia played no large role in Central Europe or in European

[12] R. W. Seton-Watson, *Masaryk in England* (New York, 1943), pp. 40, 44 f., 54 f.
[13] Masaryk, *Světová revoluce*, p. 26. On the "abysmal ignorance" of Russian statesmen regarding the Southern Slavs, see Seton-Watson, *op. cit.*, p. 67.

international diplomacy. Also for the first time, three Western Slav states played such a role. Socially, culturally, and politically they were as much separated from Russia as any other Western state. They took full part in all aspects of Western life; they were important in the councils of the League of Nations; their alliances with France, in the Little Entente and in the Balkan pact, were at least partly directed against Russia. Moreover, there was no Western Pan-Slavism. The Western Slavs followed their own self-centered policy as much as did the other nation-states which after World War I separated Russians and Germans. No sharper denial of Pan-Slav ideals can be imagined than the reality of independent Slav life after 1918. Even after the official revival of Pan-Germanism and after the German aggression against Slav states and the Slavs generally had started in earnest—an aggression supported by other Slavs, by the Poles in the case of Czechoslovakia, by the Russians in the case of Poland—some Slav peoples—Slovaks, Croatians and Bulgarians, Catholic Slavs as well as Orthodox Slavs—sought fulfillment of their nationalist aspirations in close collaboration with the German-led Axis powers. German aggression reawakened the old Russophilism only among the Czechs.

At the beginning of 1941 some attempts were made to realize a Western Slav cooperation and to extend it to other nations in Central Europe. In February, 1941, the Polish and the Czechoslovak governments in exile appointed representatives to coordinate all political, legal, economic, financial, defense, and cultural activities. In a joint declaration of January 23, 1942, the two governments agreed to form a confederation, its membership open to other states who would have a common policy regarding all basic matters. This attempt came to nothing when the Soviet Union, rekindling the embers of Great Russian nationalism, resumed a Pan-Slav policy. In March, 1943, a "Union of Polish Patriots" was formed in Moscow to express "the genuine opinion of the Polish people." On December 11 of the same year Dr. Edvard Beneš arrived in Moscow to sign a treaty of friendship between Czechoslovakia and the Soviet Union. Both countries promised non-interference in the internal affairs of the other state. There is no doubt that Czechoslovakia meant this promise sincerely.

Czechoslovak policy during the later stages of World War II and after its end was guided by Dr. Beneš' illusions about the democratic nature of communism and the sincerity of the new Soviet Slavism. It is true that Dr. Beneš ended his *Reflections on Slav Problems* which he wrote in London during the War and which were republished in

Prague in 1947 with an emphatic statement that any Slav policy resembling a protectorate over other Slav peoples or involving a Pan-Russian element—even a democratic populist or communist Russianism or one trying to introduce a common dominant ideology among all the Slavs—would make future Slav cooperation impossible.[14] But the Russians did not heed Dr. Beneš' pious warnings. This time they had the power which the Pan-Russians of 1867 did not possess.

Thus in 1945 all Slavs found themselves united, for the first time in history, under the Pan-Slav banner with Russian leadership and a Russian ideology imposed upon all of them. Moscow was the unchallengeable center of the whole Slav world. An odd fact was that at that moment Belgrade and not Prague was the center of this new Pan-Russism. The fact that non-Slav states like Hungary and Rumania formed part of the Russian-Slav community had been foreseen by the Pan-Russians of 1867. Nikolai Danilevsky's (1822-1885) *Russia and Europe, an Inquiry into the Cultural and Political Relations of the Slav to the Germano-Latin World,* which in 1869 was hailed as the bible of Pan-Slavism, stipulated frontiers for his Russian Pan-Slav union which remarkably coincided with those reached by Russian influence in 1945.[15] By 1948, however, the Slav situation returned to its more familiar configuration. Belgrade asserted its independence from Moscow and followed its own self-centered policy, whereas Prague became the most cooperative and Moscowphile Slav center and has remained so.

Yet it should not be overlooked that Moscow's control of Central Europe is not based on a Slav or Russian ideology but on Marxism, an ideology which owes its original foundation to three Germans—Hegel, Marx, and Engels. Twice in history German thought has achieved a world-wide influence, through Luther and through Marx. With all his pride in the achievement of the Russian proletariat, Lenin looked to Germany as the home and center of Marxism. Before and after World War I the organized Marxist movement was stronger in Germany than elsewhere. In the last free elections before Hitler came to power, on November 6, 1932, the German Communist Party received 5,980,200 votes and together with the then officially Marxist Social-Democratic Party the "Marxists" achieved

[14] Edvard Beneš, *Uvahy o slovanstvi. Hlavní problém solvanské politiky* (Prague 1947), p. 300.
[15] See Hans Kohn, *Pan-Slavism,* pp. 190-208.

13,228,200 votes against 11,737,000 for the National Socialists. German ideological impact on Russian Pan-Slavism is, of course, nothing new. German romantic thought deeply influenced the early Russian Pan-Slavs. It is an equally curious fact that after 1945 the Soviet Union, the heir to the Russian Empire, established its hold on Central Europe and its Western Slav peoples on behalf of an originally German ideology. Marx himself who was hostile to Pan-Slavism might be rather surprised if he could find out that due to an unexpected turn in history Slav solidarity was realized in, and after, 1945 under the banner of a Marxism reinterpreted by Moscow.

15

The Heritage of Masaryk[*]

The great wars of the twentieth century have not only been wars for power; they have also been struggles for men's souls. The issues at stake were not so much a matter of economic gains as a determination of the shape and course of civilization. The war is still going on. In it, through its geographic and cultural position, Czechoslovakia has repeatedly played a symbolic part. As is well known, the prelude to World War II was enacted in Bohemia.

By prelude, I do not mean the pact of Munich in September 1938; though objectionable for many reasons, it could nevertheless be justified. What Germany demanded then was after all only the cession of the Sudetenland, a part of Czechoslovakia that was German in feeling, language, and descent. Hitler could invoke the right of self-determination, the principle of Woodrow Wilson, in support of his claims.

There was justification also in the weakness of those who should have been the guardians of the victory of 1918. The United States

[*] An address delivered before the American Academy of Political and Social Science, Philadelphia, April 2, 1948.

and Britain had completely and fatally demobilized their armies after World War I; their people, as much as those of France, were psychologically unprepared to understand totalitarianism and the German challenge, and much too peace-loving to take it up. It was only Hitler's march into Prague, in violation of the pact of Munich that aroused the British people—too late to avert war, but still in time for Britain to save the liberty of mankind from Hitler.

Hitler's march on Prague was, with important variations, repeated in February 1948. The new "Munich," for which, as for the original Munich, some justifications could be found, occurred in 1945, when President Beneš concluded an agreement with Communists. The Czech liberals trusted, as Chamberlain had done in 1938 in the case of Hitler, that Stalin would keep the agreement, and that a collaboration with the Communists was possible for liberals. The Communists tore up the agreement in February 1948, as Hitler had done in March 1939. This time their deed awakened the Western world—in all probability in time to prevent a third world war by concerted and powerful action to save the liberty of the West without paying the heroic price of war. But in each case, Czechoslovakia became a totalitarian state in which the Western way of life—democracy based on respect for the individual and on tolerance and free discussion—was replaced by an anti-Western absolutism ruling bodies and souls alike. In each case, the heritage of Masaryk was destroyed, at least temporarily. For all of Masaryk's lifework was devoted to one task: in the spiritual battle between East and West to align his people irrevocably with the West, morally, culturally, and politically. "In the history of Slav thought, Masaryk's philosophy represented a definite, decisive and triumphant turn toward the West." [1]

The Czechs are a Slav people. Throughout history, they have found themselves surrounded and endangered by Germans. Naturally, they turned with sympathy and expectation to the greatest Slavic people, the Russians. Sympathy and expectation were increased by distance and ignorance. The few Czech liberals who studied Russia closely warned against illusions about the colossus of the East. They regarded the Czechs as an integral part of Western civilization. No one spoke more sharply against the dangers of Pan-

[1] See the important essay by Masaryk's friend and collaborator, Emanuel Rádl, the late Professor of Biology at the University of Prague, "Masaryk et la philosophie occidentale," in *Festschrift* in honor of Masaryk's eightieth birthday (Bonn: Friedrich Cohen, 1930), Vol. II.

Slavism than Karel Havlíček, the first and greatest journalist of Czech democracy. The leading Czech historian, František Palacký, proudly pointed out that the Reformation which never touched Russia originated in Hussite Bohemia, and linked it with the Western struggle for freedom of conscience and individual liberty. In 1848 a Pan-Slav congress was called in Prague, but it did not look to Russia for guidance or help; it looked to Western liberalism. The struggle between East and West always meant to the Czechs a struggle between Europe and Russia. It had the same meaning in Russia, where the Westerners throughout the nineteenth century strove to bring to their land the Western concept of liberty under law. Masaryk's sympathies were entirely with the Russian Westerners. Among all the Slavs he might be regarded as the foremost Westernizer. He opposed Pan-Slavism as he opposed Pan-Germanism, that twin curse which has distorted nationalism in Central and Eastern Europe.

Masaryk was a professor of philosophy until the unexpected turn in his life, when, nearing the age of retirement, he assumed the political leadership of his people and became the first President of the new republic. This was an office which he filled for more than sixteen years, when old age forced him to abandon it. Though he wrote no systematic treatise on politics and culture, he laid down his thought in three main works, more critical than positive: *Socialní Otázka* (a philosophical and sociological critique of Marxism, published in 1898), *Russland und Europa* (a study of the spirit of Russia, published in 1913), and *Světová Revoluce* (memoirs of the World War, which he published in 1925 under the title "World Revolution" and which were translated into English as *The Making of a State* in 1927).

In the center of Masaryk's philosophy stood the Western concept of the dignity of the individual and of the objectivity of truth. His teachers were Descartes and Locke, Hume and Mill. In his study on Russia, he regarded Dostoevsky as a true representative of the Russian spirit and the Russian Revolution. He rejected him as being too Asiatic or Oriental, and regretted that the Russians had never come under the influence of Kant and his critical spirit. "The philosophical criticism we expect from the Russians will have to return to Hume and to Kant . . . it will have to discard uncritical revolutionism." [2] When he left on his long pilgrimage of exile, he took only two books with him—the Bible in its classical Czech translation

---

[2] *The Spirit of Russia* (London: Allen & Unwin, 1919), Vol. II, p. 562.

The Heritage of Masaryk

and "The Testament" of Comenius, the famous Czech educator and admirer of Bacon, who of all the early Czech thinkers stressed most strongly an affinity to the West.

In opposition to the Slavophiles, Masaryk declared: "Through my education I am consciously European; by that I mean that the civilization of Europe and America suffices intellectually for me." Though he never wrote a system of ethics, his whole world outlook was fundamentally ethical. From that point of view he fought the famous battle of the historical manuscripts in which he proved that two famous medieval poems on which the Czechs based their claims to early cultural prominence were forgeries. It took great courage—the courage to stand alone against the nationalist passion and pride of the vast majority—to wage this battle for truth and intellectual honesty in disregard of supposed national interests.

The same ethical yardstick that Masaryk applied to nationalism he applied also to socialism. Though he subjected Marxism to extremely sharp criticism in his *Socialní Otázka*,[3] he was in no way hostile to socialism as long as it respected the dignity of the individual and the objectivity of truth. He might be regarded as a moderate evolutionary socialist, akin to English Christian socialists in his emphasis on the ethical component of socialism. He was akin to them also in his pacifism. He summed up his position in the antithesis "Jesus or Caesar," and put himself unreservedly on the side of Jesus. But he was no absolute pacifist. He recognized that in extreme cases war was necessary and preparedness indispensable, and he believed that revolutions might be justified under exceptional circumstances when oppression became really unbearable. Thus the March Revolution of 1917 in Russia was justifiable; the November Revolution of 1917 was not.

Masaryk's philosophy explains his absolute rejection of Lenin's revolution and of Bolshevism. Many Western intellectuals, who have long since lost their sympathy for Lenin's work, at first hailed the November Revolution and its promise. Masaryk, who knew Russia better than probably any other Occidental, never shared this illusion. He was in Russia during the revolution. In the Christmas issue of the *Lidové Noviny* for 1920 he pointed out that Lenin's revolution was

[3] A new edition of this work was published in Prague by Čin in the fall of 1946 in two volumes. Despite the fact that the book is not easy reading and, as a work of more than 900 pages, was naturally expensive, 9,000 copies of it were sold within one year. Though written half a century ago, it is still of topical interest, and an English translation would be well worth while.

not undertaken in defense against an oppressive regime, since Russia was by then on her way to liberty, but that it sprang from a lust for power. "I saw with my own eyes the horrible acts of the Bolshevik revolution. They revealed an almost barbarian cruelty, something almost bestial, but I felt the greatest moral horror for the apparently superfluous sacrifices of human lives." He repeated the same fundamental criticism in his *Making of a State*. The Bolsheviks, he wrote, "were guilty of much superfluous destruction. Particularly do I blame them for having reveled, after a truly Czarist fashion, in the destruction of human life. Degrees of barbarism are always expressed in the way men deal with their own lives and those of others." [4]

As Masaryk refused to see in backward Czarist Russia a model for the Czechs, so did he refuse to see one in backward Bolshevist Russia. He regarded bolshevism as determined by Russian traditions, and Lenin's theory of revolution as primitive and barbaric. He found in Leninism more of Bakunin than of Marx. For Masaryk, individual initiative and the right to think for oneself were the indispensable foundations of political and intellectual life. "Uncritical, wholly unscientific infallibility is the basis for the Bolshevik dictatorship, and a regime that quails before criticism and fears to recognize thinking men stands self-condemned." [5] Masaryk the European and Masaryk the democrat had as little use for Bolshevik theory and practice as Masaryk the ethical philosopher and teacher of his people. He wished to strengthen European democracy among the Czechs and he desired the Europeanization of Russia.

What is happening in Russia and in Czechoslovakia today is the very opposite of what Masaryk struggled for. Lenin's revolution destroyed Masaryk's hopes for Russia. After 1945 some expected Czechoslovakia to prove that Masaryk's spirit could live on in accommodation with Leninism, or, as it was said, that Czechoslovakia could be a bridge between the East and the West. The *coup d'état* of February 1948 destroyed this illusion. Like Hitler's march on Prague in March 1939, it taught a salutary lesson. This time, however, the blow was dealt not by an enemy without, but by an enemy within.

Europe was on the way toward unity at the beginning of the twentieth century. Masaryk could then hope for the integration of

---

[4] *The Making of a State: Memories and Observations, 1914-1918* (New York, Frederick A. Stokes, 1927), p. 181.

[5] *Ibid.*, p. 180. The early opinions of Masaryk are accessible in French translation in his *Sur le Bolchévisme* (Geneva: Société anonyme des éditions Sonor, 1921).

Russia with Europe—for the cross-fertilization of the two worlds, each opening up to the other. Since then, Lenin's revolution has split Europe and the world into two opposed camps, and Russia has become a more closed society than she was before. As Masaryk clearly saw, in this separation of two worlds it is not economic issues that are involved, on which a compromise could easily be reached with good will; but there are fundamental differences on the nature of man and the meaning of history. On these issues, at least for the time being, a silenced Czech people has decided against Masaryk. His heritage, however, has become part of that Western civilization for which he stood and to which, let us hope, his people will return.

16

Zion and the Jewish National Idea[*]

From the very beginning of its history two national concepts have dominated Jewish life—the concepts of the Chosen People and the Promised Land. From the ancient Hebrews nationalism everywhere took over these two concepts: the first of a unique and exclusive relationship, God or History having selected one people as pre-eminently called upon to serve a Cause, often the greatest and ultimate Cause; and, secondly, the concept of a part of this earth being singled out by destiny and mystery to be owned forever by the one people. Though most Jews lived in Palestine only the shorter part of the last three thousand years, and though a Jewish state or states existed there only precariously for a few centuries, nevertheless the Jews felt tied to the Land throughout the three thousand years by a close and unique link. Separated from the Land for many generations, they longed to return. But the Zion to which they longed to return was, until recently, the place where the Temple of the Lord stood, where

[*] First published in *The Menorah Journal*, issue of Autumn-Winter 1958. Reprinted with permission.

the faithful could sacrifice to God as the Bible prescribed, and could live their lives in fulfilment of all His ancient commands. Nothing else would have been Zion nor a return to the Land.

"Zion" meant to live according to the word of the Lord. Such a life was a heavy burden. The Bible tells the story of the ever-repeated attempts of the Hebrews to escape the burden, to liberate themselves from the yoke, to live a "normal" life. The unending procession of rejections started at the very beginning, with the dance around the Golden Calf. It is still going on. It has been one of the unifying threads of Jewish history. It took various forms at various times. Seen in a secular light, it can be interpreted as a search for the meaning of the Jewish national idea, for the realization or rejection of the message of Zion.

Of its ancient history only three high points need be mentioned here. At the very outset of a Jewish state-existence the Bible tells us of the Hebrew elders approaching the prophet Samuel with the request to set a king over them, such as all the other peoples have. What they asked for was something "natural"—to be a people like all the other peoples, to have a government like other governments, a state with all its paraphernalia. Yet Samuel refused their request. God, however, as the Bible narrates, told him to do according to the people's wishes; for, the Lord continued, in their desire to be like all other nations they have not rejected thee, but Me. Samuel warned the people once more, pointing out the consequences: they would become the state's servants instead of God's servants. But the people insisted on forming a state and having a king of their own, "so that we too may become as all the Gentiles are." Then Samuel, against his better judgment, yielded.

After the state had endured for some time amid the vicissitudes and injustices that were normal in the very existence of states, the long line of major prophets from Amos to Jeremiah arose, solitary voices, to challenge the state. Amos, a shepherd from the poor South, shocked his hearers who had gathered to celebrate the victory and prosperity of Israel. In the name of the Lord he proclaimed a new and daring interpretation of the familiar "Chosen People" idea. Recalling the deed by which the Lord had first shown His concern with the children of Israel—leading them out of Egypt into the Promised Land, from bondage to liberty—the Lord declared through Amos: "From all the families of the earth I have chosen you alone; for that very reason I will punish you for all your iniquities." Swollen with confidence and pride, the Israelites were made to hear that to be "chosen" does not imply the assurance of victory or prosperity; being "chosen" brings only the burden of more severe punishment for "normal" unrighteousness.

Amos was even more radical in reinterpreting the "Promised Land" idea. Through his mouth the Lord proclaimed that the children of Israel were unto Him no better than the children of the Ethiopians. True, God had brought up Israel out of the Land of Egypt; but equally He brought the Philistines (then Israel's hereditary enemies) from Caphtor, and the Syrians from Kir, guiding each one into its land. Isaiah cherished a similar vision when he saw Egypt and Assyria, the valley of the Nile and Mesopotamia, united, with Israel a link between them, and the Lord of Hosts blessing them, saying: "Blessed be Egypt My people, and Assyria the work of My hands, and Israel My inheritance."

The third high point was reached when the statehood which began with Samuel was for a second time coming to its end. In the besieged city of Jerusalem the zealots fought heroically against the Roman might. But the leading representative of the Judaism of the day, Jochanan ben Zakkai, the disciple of Hillel, abandoned the cause of the Jewish state. Escaping from the city by a ruse, he founded outside its walls, with the agreement of the Roman commander, the academy at Jabne. The state perished. Judaism survived.

The state had been a passing phenomenon, buffeted by all the storms of history, like the states of all other peoples. Judaism lived, developed, grew, a unique phenomenon, strongly rooted in the spiritual instead of the political realm.

* * *

The dispersion of the Jews throughout the Graeco-Roman world started long before the final end of the Jewish state and the destruction of the Temple. Even after that event many Jews continued to live in Palestine. Wherever they lived, they longed for the rebuilding of the Temple. But also, wherever they lived, they adapted themselves to the environment. For almost two thousand five hundred years Judaism unfolded, in the diaspora, a life of spiritual fertility and variety. Periods of greater productivity alternated with periods of relative sterility. The Jews lived among other "peoples of the Book," Christians and Mohammedans, both of whom derived much of their own thought and spiritual life from the Jewish tradition. In the Age of Religion the Jews formed a distinct group, often persecuted and often tolerated like other religious groups. But though they lived on the peripheries of the Christian and Islamic worlds, they were nevertheless in close contact with them. Though they kept themselves separate, the Jews underwent common influences and participated in the great intellectual movements of the times.

When the Age of Emancipation dawned for Europe in the eighteenth century, it dawned for the European Jew too. The renovation of life through individualism, through a new intensity of personal feeling, through a new concept of the dignity of man and the oneness of mankind, penetrated into the Jewish communities of the various countries to the same degree it permeated those countries—in the West much more strongly than in Central Europe and hardly at all in Eastern Europe. Thus the intellectual movements of the eighteenth century—the Enlightenment and Pietism—made their influence felt among the Jews. Religious Pietism received the Hebrew name of *Hassidism,* the *hassid* being "the pious," and the rational Enlightenment was called *Haskalah,* again a literal translation of the European term "Enlightenment."

The fate of the Jewish communities in the nineteenth century coincided with the strength of the general forces of intellectual Enlightenment and political Emancipation in the various countries. These two forces were most powerful in the West, especially in the United States which built its national life on them in the eighteenth century. In the Western world the Jews, like other newly emancipated groups, were becoming integrated into the national societies, stable political and social organisms in which they could fully participate. In Central Europe the situation was different. In the early nineteenth century neither a firm political and social form nor a strong liberal intellectual foundation existed there. The modern political form was found in Germany only in the latter part of the century, but at the price of the withering of the weak shoots of liberalism. The Habsburg Monarchy in Central Europe did not succeed at all in forming a modern national society within which Jewish emancipation and integration could have easily proceeded. That was true throughout the multi-ethnic empire with its burning nationality struggles. The Jew in Prague did not know whether to integrate with the Czechs or the Germans; in Czernowitz (Bukovina) the German, Roumanian, and Ukrainian incipient national societies competed with each other.

The situation of the Jews in Central Europe was as fundamentally different from that in the English-speaking countries as the general political life differed in these two regions. Thus for the Jews living there, Central Europe held, as in all its political and social life, an intermediate position between the West and the East.

In nineteenth-century Eastern Europe the Enlightenment and Emancipation never took firm hold—in fact, political and cultural emancipation for all classes and groups of the population began only half-heartedly with the year 1905. Under these conditions Eastern European Jews continued their life of former times, a distinct and compact group, with its own culture, its own social structure, its own hopes and desires, without much contact with the surrounding world to which they did not and, in many cases, did not wish to belong. Yet among them, too, the desire and hope for emancipation was strong in the third quarter of the century, as it was among most of the people in Russia. The year 1881 marked a cruel setback for them, as for all the hopes of emancipation in Russia. It is understandable that the Eastern European Jews reacted to this shock of disillusionment, which made their present even more unbearable, in two ways: by starting a mass emigration to the liberal countries of the West, where they could find emancipation and where their children could be integrated in the life of modern nations; and by a renewed longing for the Promised Land, a hope for the restoration of a past seen in historical transfiguration. Looking to this past in the Age of Nationalism, which had meanwhile come to Eastern Europe too, they no longer envisaged it primarily as the restoration of the Temple, the resumption of the sacrifices, a life in the ways of the Lord, but as a state like the other modern nation-states, similar in nature to that which then enticed the hopes and imaginations of all the other unemancipated peoples in Eastern and Central Europe.

Thus from the eighteenth century onward the Jews shared fully in the life of their respective countries, different as they were. In their political and social ideals they reflected the aspirations of their fellow-citizens. In 1830 they regarded themselves in Central Europe, with Gabriel Riesser, as "the sons of a century whose breath is freedom." As the century progressed, freedom grew in the West; but the hopes of a similar growth in Central and Eastern Europe were often blighted. Many Jews felt in the Enlightenment, or thought they felt, a profound kinship to Judaism, at least to its prophetic tradition. Were not the foundations of the Age of Enlightenment laid in seventeenth-century Holland and England, to a large extent in the covenants and bills of rights of Anglo-American Puritans who were deeply influenced by the Hebrew Bible? The growth of capitalism and urbanization which facilitated, and was in its turn stimulated by, Enlightenment and Emancipation accelerated in the West the social and economic integration of the Jews. From the early nineteenth century on, the hostility to Jewish emancipation in Central and Eastern Europe was based on the rejection not only of the Enlightenment but also of capitalism.

Wherever nineteenth-century Emancipation succeeded, it enhanced—like all spiritually liberating movements—Jewish creative productiveness in all fields. The Jews participated prominently in all cultural activities, many of which were open to them now for the first time, in science and philosophy, in secular music and literature, in painting and sculpture. For obvious though opposite reasons Jewish life in the West and in the East was less fraught with complex intellectual tensions than Jewish life in the German-speaking lands. In the West the Jews were fully integrated in the life of their homelands; in the East they continued to live on its margin. In Central Europe the very tensions of an uncertain and questionable relationship became at the same time the soil for great dangers and great achievements.

In Germany the *Wissenschaft des Judentums,* putting Jewish scholarship on entirely new foundations, bore fruit in rejuvenating Jewish learning and thought throughout the world. In Heinrich Heine Jewish Germany contributed one of the greatest German poets, the landmark of German poetry between the death of Goethe and its new flowering at the turn of the century. Marx, Freud, Einstein were among the creative thinkers of the age who influenced it as strongly as Hegel, Darwin, or Nietzsche. An astonishing burst of creativeness rapidly threw the Jews, after centuries of relative sterility in the pre-Emancipation ghetto, into the ranks of all the cultural and social movements of the late nineteenth century.

Thus it was only natural that with the progress of the Age of Nationalism, in the countries where Emancipation was partly stultified by the survival of pre-emancipatory social structures or political ideologies, a Jewish nationalism should develop, though a late-comer among the national movements of Eastern and Central Europe. It was born out of the historical and ideological conditions in those countries; and, like all other national movements here, it looked for its historical foundations, its justification and its promise for the future, to the distant past which it reinterpreted in the light of the desires and aspirations of the modern movement.

* * *

The Jewish national movement as it arose in Eastern and Central Europe presented an amalgam of the traditional longing for Zion and an urge, an emotional attitude, which originated in the conditions of the late nineteenth-century environment. The latter had nothing to do with Jewish traditions; it was in many ways opposed to them. The rising tide and the specific temper of Eastern and Central European nationalism, and the socio-political trends of the time, provided the framework within which Jewish nationalism interpreted the past and viewed the future.

Those Jews in Eastern Europe who were willing to abandon the exclusive structure of Jewish traditional life had hoped for political and social emancipation by the tide of liberalism which was to transform Eastern Europe to accord with Western ways. The dark years Russia lived through from 1881 to 1904 seemed to extinguish the hope. It was under these conditions that Dr. Leo Pinsker, a physician in Odessa, published his pamphlet "Auto-Emancipation."

Like other nationalists of the nineteenth century, Pinsker called upon his people to liberate themselves by their own effort. This effort would make the Jews a nation "like all other nations, a people with a common language, common customs, and a common land." Pinsker's call to action was coupled with the nineteenth-century belief in the redeeming force of productive manual labor and contact with the soil. Jews had been going to Palestine and had lived there throughout the centuries to pray and to study, to fulfil the commands of God, and to await the coming of the Messiah and the rebuilding of the Temple. Now they were to go and settle there as farmers and artisans in the hope of building a "normal" state where Jews would live what late nineteenth-century Europe regarded a "normal" life, in which the rebuilding of the Temple and even the fulfilment of all the commandments had no place, or at least no central place. In that sense Pinsker's "Auto-Emancipation" marked a break with Zion and with the Jewish tradition.

Pinsker's words moved only a very small circle of East-European Jews. An insignificant number of pioneers went forth to Palestine; the vast majority of emigrants preferred the West. The first Jewish agricultural settlements in Palestine, nurtured with great love by the society of "Lovers of Zion" founded by Dr. Pinsker, were saved from collapse by Baron Edmond Rothschild.

A decade later, however, a new start was made. This time a much more powerful personality than Pinsker, without knowing anything of Pinsker, of the East-European movement or of the Jewish tradition, assumed leadership. Its call came not from far-off Odessa but from Vienna. Theodor Herzl was a young successful journalist who represented the leading liberal Viennese newspaper in Paris at the time of the Dreyfus Affair. During those years antisemitism was becoming a vital force in Vienna under the leadership of men like Georg von Schönerer and Dr. Karl Lueger. Under the pressure of the rising nationalist movements liberalism was retreating throughout the Austrian Empire. The experience of the Dreyfus Affair created in Herzl an impression of the ubiquity and inevitability of antisemitism. In a sudden inspiration he wrote his pamphlet *Der Judenstaat* ("The State of Jews"). From that moment (1896) he dedicated himself for the rest of his short life to the cause of creating an internationally recognized Jewish state, which would by its very existence end antisemitism. Through the power of his personality and through indefatigable labor he succeeded in creating the first world-wide international political Jewish movement. He gave it a representative tribune in the Zionist Congress. In its name he negotiated with statesmen and diplomats and tried to impress his faith upon the consciousness of the world. Characteristically he named the official organ of the movement *Die Welt* ("The World").

On the fiftieth anniversay of *Der Judenstaat* Dr. Hannah Arendt pointed out, in a profound analysis in *Commentary*, that Herzl regarded antisemitism as a perpetual immutable force which the Jews must learn to use to their own advantage. He pictured the Jewish people everywhere and at all times "surrounded and forced together by a world of enemies." In his oversimplified picture of history and reality, "any segment of reality that could not be defined by antisemitism was not taken into account and any group that could not definitely be classed as antisemitic was not taken seriously as a political force." Regarding the situation of his own time and place as an eternally durable one, Herzl proposed a solution based upon the premises of his time and place, namely, to constitute the Jews, whom he considered a biological group, as a nation like all other nations in their own state. At the beginning he was interested neither in the history and character of the Jews and Judaism nor in the land where they were to settle. At first he did not think of Palestine as the needed homeland, nor of a Jewish cultural life expressed in its own language. His solution was a simple one—to give to the people without land a land without people. What kind of people this was, or whether such a land existed, were not his primary considerations.

His contact with the East-European Zionist movement made him determine on the land, Palestine, though not on Hebrew. But Palestine was not a land without people. Herzl, under the influence of the liberal ideas that still prevailed when he was brought up, took this fact into consideration. In his Diaries (which Marvin Lowenthal has handsomely edited in English), Herzl wrote: "My testament for the Jewish people: so build your state that a stranger will feel contented among you." He visited Palestine only once and very briefly, not to get in touch with the Jewish population nor with the Arabs of the land, but to present a request to the German Emperor who was then visiting Turkey. Yet he perceived more clearly than many others what was going on in the Middle East. On his visit to Egypt he was struck by the intelligence of the young Egyptians, and he recorded in his Diary: "They are the coming rulers of the country; and it is a wonder that the British don't see this." Others understood the rising force of Arab nationalism even less than the British. Yet for none outside the Middle East was the new force of Asian nationalism of so great and vital a significance as for Jewish nationalism in its territorial Zionist form. This latecomer among the nationalisms of Central and Eastern Europe threatened by its transfer to the Middle East to come into conflict with the new nationalisms of Asia.

Herzl wished to avoid this conflict, perhaps because it ran counter to his liberal background, perhaps because he understood that such a conflict might ruin Zionism. In the last book he wrote, *Altneuland* ("Oldnewland"), which he left as a testament to the movement he had founded and inspired, he drew a picture of the future Jewish state, envisaging it as a New Society.[1] In its basic traits it reflected the

[1] Lewis Mumford in his analysis of *Altneuland* ("Herzl's Utopia") in *The Menorah Journal* of August 1923, wrote: "To have arrived at such a clear and definite conception of a new organic polity was a singular achievement. Perhaps Herzl did not realize its importance; perhaps he did not see how thoroughly his plans for a scientifically designed polity in *Altneuland* were at odds with the notions outlined in *The Jewish State*. If Herzl himself did not see this great disparity, and did not follow out its implications—a fact partly accounted for, perhaps, by his early death—it is not altogether surprising that those who were immersed in the Zionist movement did not observe it either. At any rate, the piece of original thinking which makes *Altneuland* a distinctive

liberal views of the Viennese Jews at the beginning of the twentieth century. Life in the Jewish state was not based on Jewish traditions, nor was Hebrew spoken there. It was not a new ghetto, living in seclusion from the world and animated by a feeling of hostility to its environment. "It is founded on the ideas which are a common product of all civilized nations," Herzl summed up his vision of his open society. "It would be immoral if we would exclude anyone, whatever his origin, his descent, or his religion, from participating in our achievements. For we stand on the shoulders of other civilized peoples. . . . What we own we owe to the preparatory work of other peoples. Therefore, we have to repay our debt. There is only one way to do it, the highest tolerance. Our motto must therefore be, now and ever: Man, you are my brother."

Picturing an electoral campaign in the new state, Herzl directed his wrath against the nationalist or chauvinist party which wished to make the Jews a privileged element in the land. Herzl regarded that as a betrayal of Zion, for Zion was identical to him with humanitarianism and tolerance. That was as true in politics as in religion. "Matters of faith were once and for all excluded from public influence," he wrote. "Whether anyone sought religious devotion in the synagogue, in the church, in the mosque, in the art museum, or in a philharmonic concert, did not concern society. That was his private affair."

One of the central passages of *Altneuland* deals with the situation of the Mohammedan Arabs in this new Zion. Their spokesman, Reshid Bey, explained to a Christian nobleman, Mr. Kingscourt, that the Arab inhabitants had lost nothing but gained very much from the new order. "You are strange people, you Mohammedans!" Mr. Kingscourt exclaimed. "Don't you look upon these Jews as intruders?" "Christian, how strange your speech sounds," the Mohammedan replied. "Would you regard those as intruders and robbers who don't take anything away from you but give you something? The Jews have enriched us, why should we be angry at them? They live with us like brothers, why should we not love them?"

Fifty years after Herzl wrote his testament to the movement, the reality turned out to be the opposite of the hope he had expressed.

---

contribution to politics, by suggesting the expedience of forms of political co-operation and government outside the framework of the national state, has remained unnoticed; with the result that the classic modern discussion of the *Genossenschaft* and *Genossenschaftsrecht* is currently supposed to be solely that of Gierke in his *Political Theories of the Middle Ages*."

Nowhere in the world was a Jewish community regarded with the hostility, distrust, and fear directed at the Jews in Palestine by their neighbors. Nowhere have Jews felt so exposed as in Palestine. Whereas Herzl erred in his generous prediction of Zionist humanitarianism, his oversimplification of antisemitism which formed the premise to the conclusions in *Der Judenstaat* seemed to be borne out, for a brief time at least, by the new and fearful reality of Hitlerism. Herzl had regarded antisemitic governments as Zionism's best allies, because they would help the transfer of Jews from their homelands to the Jewish state. In an indirect way, foreseen by neither Herzl nor Hitler, Hitlerism did make the Jewish state possible.

Herzl's great liberal vision of Zion as a common home of happy Jews, Mohammedans, and Christians was never accepted by the large majority of his followers. But his oversimplified analysis of the Jewish situation did win him, after 1933, many millions of new adherents. Yet this analysis of the Jews everywhere and at all times, actually or potentially, living among enemies, could not make the realization of Zionism easier. "The universality with which Herzl applied his concept of antisemitism to all non-Jewish peoples made it impossible from the very beginning for the Zionists to seek truly loyal allies," writes Dr. Hannah Arendt. "His notion of reality as an eternal, unchanging hostile structure—all *goyim* everlastingly against all Jews—made the identification of hard-boiledness with realism plausible because it rendered any empirical analysis of actual political factors seemingly superfluous. All one had to do was to use the 'propelling force of antisemitism,' which, like 'the wave of the future,' would bring the Jews into the promised land. . . . If we actually are faced with open or concealed enemies on every side, if the whole world is ultimately against us, then we are lost."

* * *

As Hannah Arendt has said, "Herzl thought in terms of nationalism inspired from German sources."[2] According to the German theory, people of common descent or speaking a common language should form one common state. Pan-Germanism was based on the idea that all persons who were of German race, blood, or descent, wherever they lived or to whatever state they belonged, owed their primary loyalty to Germany and should become citizens of the Ger-

---

[2] See her article "Zionism Reconsidered" in *The Menorah Journal* of Autumn 1945 (Vol. XXXIII, No. 2), page 188.

man state, their true homeland. They, and even their fathers and forefathers, might have grown up under "foreign" skies or in "alien" environments, but their fundamental inner "reality" remained German.

Such ideas of nationalism run counter to those held by the Western peoples, among whom it is not common descent nor even a common language that determines the national character and personal loyalty. The great nations of the West, above all the United States, are products not of "immutable laws of race," but of an intermingling of peoples and individuals of varied and often unknown descent. Herzl himself never carried his concept of Zionism as a pan-movement to an extreme. The Jewish state in Palestine, as he conceived it, was not to gather all Jews into their "true" homeland. It was to be a refuge for those who could not or did not wish to remain in their old homelands. Their emigration, Herzl believed, would diminish anti-semitism everywhere and thus make the assimilation of the remaining Jews easier.

Far more important was the fact that Herzl's concept of "political" Zionism broke with two thousand years of Jewish history, during which the Jews were "a people of thinkers and poets." They called themselves *am hasepher*, "the People of the Book," or *am haruach*, "the People of the Spirit." Herzl's appeal to Central and East-European young men was so powerful because it seemed to conform to a general trend of the time—from religion to secularism, from contemplation to activity, from the ivory tower to politics. Herzl himself never drew the ultimate conclusions inherent in his point of view. For he was too much a child of the mid-nineteenth century, an age when traditional ethical and humanitarian values survived in secularized form as a living force. That situation changed in Central and Eastern Europe with the approach of the twentieth century.

Under the influence of an oft misunderstood Nietzsche, a young Hebrew writer who had come from the strictest Jewish orthodoxy of Russia to the intellectual fermentation of Berlin, Micha Joseph Berdychewski, rejected the Jewish tradition in an attempt to re-evaluate all values. To him Nietzsche was the prophet of will-to-power and of the master-man, who proclaimed the need of a new vitality, of overflowing joy of life, of an ecstatic affirmation of primitive nature. Under his influence a reinterpretation of Jewish history became fashionable. The Hebrew prophets and the long line of rabbis and scholars of the last two thousand years appeared as the grave-diggers, the corruptors and defamers of the true Jewish life which was represented by the "sinful" kings, and the men of the soil, and the nationalist zealots of ancient Israel and Judah whose statesmanlike wisdom and heroic deeds equaled those of other peoples. Berdychewski turned to the Bible, to the documents of ancient Jewish tradition, in an entirely new spirit, to find remnants there of the natural polytheism, of colorful myth and barbaric strength, which the ancient Hebrew tribes had possessed and which prophets and priests later expurgated. The ancient Hebrews, Berdychewski believed, must have more resembled full-blooded pagans than the later "anemic" spiritualized and intellectualized Jews who lost all their natural vitality under the yoke of God's law.

Similarly, one of the notable modern Hebrew poets, Saul Tchernichowsky, celebrated the primitive Hebraism of those tribes which, emerging from the desert under Joshua's leadership, overran and conquered Canaan. To Tchernichowsky they were virile and beautiful like the ancient Greeks and to their tribal god Tchernichowsky paid homage in his poem "Before the Statue of Apollo," in which he turned his back upon Judaism.

> I have left the ancient paths,
> And far behind me in the dark wander the sons of death.
> See me here, the first who turns to thee.
> My living earthly soul,
> Which hates the eternal rigidity of dying,
> Will now break the fetters of the spirit.
> Living sentiment, degenerated in the course of time,
> Breaks out of the prison built by one hundred generations . . .
>
> Thine image is a symbol of light in life.
>
> I bow before thee, life's strength and beauty,
> Bow before youth which like a whirlwind
> Frights and chases away those withered dried-up people
> Who have tried to take my God's life,
> And who fetter with their prayer-straps
> *El shaddai,* the lord of the deserts,
> Who led Canaan's daring conquerors.

Thus Tchernichowsky turned away from the God of Israel to the tribal idol of the desert, glorifying its survival in the nature-cults of Baal and Astarte. Such pagan revolts have been known throughout ancient Jewish history; those "festivals of life" burst forth frequently, but always they were rejected as apostasy. Judaism did not arise in the gods of nature, of soil and blood, which the primitive Hebrew tribes may have adored as did their contemporaries. It was as a religious ethical insight that Judaism began. Without this there may be Hebrew tribes as good or as bad as other primitive peoples, but no Judaism.

Divested of their philosophical aura, the attitudes of Berdychewski and Tchernichowsky influenced the gifted Russian journalist Vladimir Jabotinsky. Jabotinsky called upon the Jewish youth to remember the heroic battles of the ancient zealots and to fill themselves with a soldiering spirit. He revived the names of Bethar and Massada, those small fortified positions where the last defenders of the Jewish state held out in a desperate struggle. He strove to reawaken pride in military deeds, in combat and arms. He held up those who died fighting the Arabs in Palestine as models to be ever present in the minds of the youth. Immediately following World War I he demanded the establishment in Palestine—a country where the Arabs then formed 90 per cent of the population—of a regime which would make possible such a mass immigration of Jews that they would rapidly become the majority. Such a "colonial" regime could be maintained only by strong armed forces against the bitter resistance of the Palestinian population and in complete disregard of their rights. The frontiers of Jewish Palestine were to be extended as far as they had ever reached in any period of history.

Naturally, Jabotinsky rejected Herzl's concept of the coming Jewish state as outlined in *Altneuland*. Jabotinsky was convinced that the Arabs could not be reconciled to Jewish domination of Palestine. Rather, he believed that the same methods must be applied there as in other schemes of European colonization in backward lands. Like so many of the young men in Eastern and Central Europe after World War I and after the rise of fascism, Jabotinsky was deeply impressed by the "realism" of toughness. The old liberal world of the West seemed doomed. New forces, which scornfully rejected humanitarianism or concern for the rights of others, claimed to represent the wave of the future. National egoism alone seemed to guarantee survival in a world which gloried more in biological vitality than in ethical rationality.

The early triumph of Hitler convinced many that Jabotinsky was right. They overlooked the fact that Hitler like Mussolini went down in defeat, and that neither of them contributed to the strength or betterment of their peoples. What appeared supreme realism later revealed itself as a cynical illusion.

* * *

Until World War II Jabotinsky and his followers represented only a small minority in the Zionist movement. Its official leader, Chaim Weizmann, was a steady target of Jabotinsky's violent attacks. Weizmann, though a fervent Zionist, was at the same time a true realist and a liberal. He was born in Eastern Europe, but lived his mature life in Britain, acquiring there the liberal outlook of the West. He knew the assumption that Zionism wanted to build a state at the expense of the national claims of the native population was, to liberal world opinion, especially in the English-speaking countries, the strongest argument against it.

In a penetrating study (in *Jewish Social Studies* of July 1, 1951), Robert Weltsch analyzed the tragedy of Weizmann's leadership. Weizmann had to mediate between liberal world opinion and the often disparate wishes of his followers. Officially the Zionists emphasized "that the Jews did not come to Palestine in order to dominate the Arabs, and they also declared most solemnly on many occasions that no Arab shall be expelled from the country." At the meeting of the Zionist General Council in Berlin in August 1930, Weizmann declared that a transformation of Palestine into a Jewish state was impossible, "because we could not and would not expel the Arabs. . . . Moreover, the Arabs, he said, were as good Zionists as we are; they also loved their country and they could not be persuaded to hand it over to someone else. Their national awakening had made considerable progress. These were facts which Zionism couldn't afford to ignore." To speak of a Jewish state would make people believe the "calumnies" which were steadily being spread that Zionism aimed at the expulsion of the Arab population.

On the eve of the seventeenth Zionist Congress which met in Basle in 1931, Weizmann opposed proclaiming a Jewish state as the aim of Zionism. "The world will construe this demand only in one sense, that we want to acquire a majority in order to drive out the Arabs." In a speech before the Congress Weizmann rejected this interpretation as unfounded. "We Zionists know that this [to dominate the Arabs or to drive them out] is not our aim and we have always emphasized it. . . . A numerical majority alone would not be a sufficient guarantee of the security of our National Home. The security has to be created by reliable political guarantees and by friendly relations to the non-Jewish world surrounding us in Palestine. . . . It is our desire to eliminate all fear and to avoid everything that could cause fear, however erroneously, and in this way to create an atmosphere of quiet and confidence, which according to my view will be the best foundation for our work and for the growth of the National Home."

Robert Weltsch calls Weizmann one of the last representatives of humanist Zionism, a Zionism based on the assumption "that the reborn Jewish nation would avoid all those national excesses from which Jews had so much to suffer among other nations. Intolerant, brutal, egotistical nationalism would be unacceptable to Jews who had learned to know what it means. The Jewish people which has recovered its national self-consciousness and pride would be sympathetic to other peoples in similar conditions who are striving to recover their national freedom, and from this attitude a mutual understanding could arise which would enable different nationalities to live together and to co-operate for the sake of the well-being of all."

Such an attitude alone could mean "Zion." It had inspired also Herzl's vision of *Altneuland*.

The climate of strident nationalism and fascism after World War I changed the outlook of many Zionists. Weizmann lost his influence over the movement to the "activism" of David Ben-Gurion. During World War II Jabotinsky's program was accepted as the official Zionist goal in the so-called Biltmore Program. In his autobiography Weizmann described the atmosphere which he found in Palestine in 1944 with a curious air of understatement. "Here and there a relaxation of the old traditional Zionist puritan ethics, a touch of militarization, and a weakness for its trappings; here and there something worse—the tragic, futile, un-Jewish resort to terrorism . . . and worst of all, in certain circles, a readiness to compound with the evil, to play politics with it, to condemn and not to condemn it, to treat it not as the thing it was, namely an unmitigated curse to the National Home, but as a phenomenon which might have its advantages."

The "evil" was not only here and there; it was rapidly taking root and growing. Military victory created the new state; and, like Sparta or Prussia, on military virtue it remained based. The militarization of life and mind represented not only a break with humanist Zionism, but with the long history of Judaism. The *Zeitgeist*, or at least the *Zeitgeist* of twentieth-century Central and Eastern Europe, had won out over the Jewish tradition.

* * *

Yet this development did not go unchallenged within the ranks of Zionism. The first to foresee it, and to combat it, was a fervent lover of Zion, a Russian Jew, who could not imagine a Zionism that would not be a fulfilment of Judaism. Ahad Ha-am (in Hebrew, "One of the People") was the pen-name of Asher Ginzberg. He assumed it when at the age of 33 (in 1889) he published his first article and became "accidentally" a writer, "a thing I had never thought of till then." He became the foremost Hebrew writer of his time, the creator of the modern Hebrew essay and the teacher of a whole generation; but he never got to be a professional writer. He wrote only when he felt impelled by his deep sense of responsibility for the Jewish heritage and for the Jewish future. The pen-name is not without some irony. He considered himself as not more than "one of the people," with every fiber of his being devoted to the people's revival. Yet, in his emphasis on the spiritual and moral aspects of the national revival, Ahad Ha-am found himself increasingly opposed to the popular political nationalism which the people embraced.

He grew up in "one of the most benighted spots" in the Jewish districts of Russia, where the segregation from the surrounding world was complete to a degree incomprehensible to citizens of the West. His whole education was steeped in traditional Judaism. He was not allowed to look at the letters of the Russian alphabet, let alone to learn Russian. "The reason was," he wrote in his reminiscences, "that my mother's father had with his own ears heard one of the great religious leaders say that the sight of a foreign letter made the eyes unclean." Only at the age of twenty, and almost surreptitiously, he began to learn Russian and German. At thirty he escaped from the "isolation and fanaticism" of his small home town to Odessa, then the center of the Zionist movement. There he edited a famous Hebrew magazine, *Hashiloah*. The name was chosen from a passage in the prophet Isaiah, in which God threatened to punish Israel because it despised "the waters of Shiloah which flows softly" and instead trusted in strength and might. The monthly was not to be a party organ, but an open forum that would seek for a deeper understanding of the Jewish problem, and an unprejudiced approach to it.

The first essay that Ahad Ha-am published was called "This Is Not the Way." It contained the warning, which all his future writings continued, that the revival of Zion was desirable and practicable only if the Jews did not become like other peoples. He opposed a settlement in the Holy Land based upon over-valuation of numbers and power and speed. He knew that the means determine the end, and the way in which the foundations are laid defines the strength of the structure. Like all ethicists, he was modest as regards the goal and exacting about the means. "The main point, upon which everything depends, is not how much we do but how we do it," he wrote in his report, "The Truth from Palestine," after his visit there in 1891.

There for the first time Ahad Ha-am laid his finger on the problem which, for practical and ethical reasons alike, was the fundamental though neglected problem of Zionism in Palestine—the Arab problem. To the eyes of most Zionists the land of their forefathers appeared empty, waiting for the return of the dispersed descendents, as if history had stood still for two thousand years. From 1891 on Ahad Ha-am stressed that Palestine was not only a small land but not an empty one. It could never gather, as the prayer-book demands, all the scattered Jews from the four corners of the earth. The Bible foresaw this ingathering for the days of the Messiah, when all problems would be solved in a regenerated mankind. To confound Messianic hopes with political potentialities must lead of necessity to moral and ultimately physical disaster.

Ahad Ha-am pointed out that there was little untilled soil in Palestine, except for stony hills or sand dunes. He warned that the Jewish settlers must under no circumstances arouse the wrath of the natives by ugly actions: must meet them rather in the friendly spirit of respect. "Yet what do our brethren do in Palestine? Just the very opposite! Serfs they were in the lands of the diaspora and suddenly they find themselves in freedom, and this change has awakened in them an inclination to despotism. They treat the Arabs with hostility and cruelty, deprive them of their rights, offend them without cause, and even boast of these deeds; and nobody among us opposes this despicable and dangerous inclination." That was written in 1891 when the Zionist settlers formed a tiny minority in Palestine. "We think," Ahad Ha-am warned, "that the Arabs are all savages who live like animals and do not understand what is happening around. This is, however, a great error."

This error unfortunately has persisted ever since. Ahad Ha-am did not cease to warn against it, not only for the sake of the Arabs but for the sake of Judaism and of Zion. He remained faithful to his ethical standard to the end. Twenty years later, on July 9, 1911, he wrote to a friend in Jaffa: "As to the war against the Jews in Palestine, I am a spectator from afar with an aching heart, particularly because of the want of insight and understanding shown on our side to an extreme degree. As a matter of fact, it was evident twenty years ago that the day would come when the Arabs would stand up against us." He complained bitterly that the Zionists were unwilling to understand the people of the land to which they came and had learned neither its language nor its spirit.

Ahad Ha-am was a dedicated Jewish nationalist. But this Jew from the most secluded mid-nineteenth century Russian ghetto was akin in spirit to the English liberalism of Mill and Gladstone. So little does race or even early upbringing and environment count as compared with the spirit. In this spirit Ahad Ha-am who loved Hebrew, who never wrote in any other language, who mastered Hebrew as did no other writer of his generation, opposed the boycott which the Hebrew teachers in Palestine proclaimed against the Jewish Institute of Technology in Haifa, when for practical reasons it decided to employ an "alien" language of instruction. In a letter of May 19, 1914, he wrote: "I am in general absolutely opposed to all forms of boycott. Even in childhood I detested the Jerusalem *herem* [religious boycott proclaimed by orthodox rabbis], and this feeling has remained in my heart to this day, even if the boycott emanates from the Hebrew Teachers' Union. Call it *herem* or call it boycott, I loathe it. If I were in Palestine, I would fight this loathsome practice with all my might. I do not care if they call me a reactionary, or even traitor; what was ugly in my eyes thirty years ago remains ugly now."

In a letter of November 18, 1913, to Moshe Smilansky, a pioneer settler in Palestine, Ahad Ha-am had protested against another form of nationalist boycott, proclaimed by the Zionist labor movement in Palestine against the employment of Arab labor, a racial boycott: "Apart from the political danger, I can't put up with the idea that our brethren are morally capable of behaving in such a way to men of another people; and unwittingly the thought comes to my mind: if it is so now, what will be our relation to the others if in truth we shall achieve 'at the end of time' power in *Eretz Israel?* If this be the 'Messiah,' I do not wish to see his coming."

Ahad Ha-am was in the prophetic tradition not only because he subjected the doings of his own people to ethical standards. He also foresaw, when very few realized it, the ethical dangers threatening Zion.

Ahad Ha-am returned to the Arab problem in another letter to Smilansky written in February, 1914. Smilansky had been bitterly attacked by Palestinian Zionists because he had drawn attention to the Arab problem. Ahad Ha-am tried to comfort him by pointing out that the Zionists had not yet awakened to reality. "Therefore, they wax angry towards those who remind them that there is still another people in *Eretz Israel* that has been living there and does not intend at all to leave its place. In the future, when this illusion will have been torn from their hearts and they will look with open eyes upon the reality as it is, they will certainly understand how important this question is and how great is our duty to work for its solution."

In his confidence in the strength of the ethical tradition among his fellow Zionists, Ahad Ha-am erred. Nearly half a century later the illusion of which he wrote in 1914 still persisted, and the reliance upon power and diplomacy had grown to an extent none could foresee in 1914.

In 1902 Ahad Ha-am subjected Herzl's *Altneuland* to a devastating criticism. Herzl's Zionism was to Ahad Ha-am too political, too devoid of Jewish traditional concepts, too mechanical, relying far too much on antisemitism as its driving force and not on the rebirth of the Jewish heart. Yet, despite their fundamental differences, the Hebraist steeped in the tradition of his people and the assimilated Central European Jew met on one decisive point. *Altneuland* was full of thriving Arab cities and villages with a highly contented population that had profited and increased as a result of the coming of Zionist settlers, with whom they lived in mutual respect and harmony. Neither Ahad Ha-am nor Herzl, neither the moralist nor the political leader, could envisage the dispossession of the Arab Palestinian people. Such an eventuality seemed to them not only ethically repugnant but realistically most unwise, because it would hinder the growth of an atmosphere of peace between Israel and its neighbors. Without such an atmosphere Zion could not be built, and the existence of Israel would be ever threatened, not only morally but practically. Such an atmosphere of peace could be built only upon deeds and not upon words, upon compromise and not upon conquest.

* * *

When after World War I Ahad Ha-am settled in Palestine the situation had deteriorated. Throughout Eastern and Central Europe the War had destroyed the forms of Jewish life. A violent wave of sanguinary pogroms swept the Ukraine and Poland. Under its impact the hopes of political Zionism were rekindled. Should not, in this hour of an apparent birth of a new world-order, the Jewish nation also be restored to its historic homeland? This hope was fanned by the Balfour Declaration of 1917 in which the British Government promised "to view with favor the establishment in Palestine of a national home for the Jewish people . . . it being clearly understood that nothing shall be done which may prejudice the civil and religious rights of existing non-Jewish communities in Palestine. . . ." When this formula was originally submitted to the Zionist Organization it wanted to substitute the words "the reconstitution of Palestine as the national home" for "the establishment in Palestine of a national home"; but the British Government rejected that demand.

Nevertheless, the Zionists interpreted the Balfour Declaration as a promise to restore the Jewish state in Palestine. They even demanded the inclusion of Trans-Jordan, Hauran, Hermon and the southern part of Lebanon in the area of the promised Jewish national home. Their hopes and expectations were high. After two thousand years of migration they at last stood at the gates of a country which they regarded theirs by divine as well as historical right. Their indignation was great when they found the land occupied by a people who disputed their right to it.

By a tragic historical coincidence the Arabs were then, like all Asian peoples, awakening to national consciousness and undergoing a process of profound psychological change. World War I had stirred them to the depths; to them, as to the Zionists, the promises of the great Powers had offered the vision of a new glorious life, the breath of a new freedom, the revival of their national culture. Few then understood the reality. In a speech in London on August 20, 1919 Weizmann pointed to the universal unrest then sweeping the East. Palestine's economic and ethnic conditions, he said, linked it with Syria and to some extent with Egypt, and all events in those two countries found their echo in Palestine where the pan-Arab movement had by then penetrated.

The consequences of the Balfour Declaration became quickly visible. The Arabs, not only in Palestine, opposed it violently. They saw in it an attempt to occupy an Arab land and to drive a wedge against Arab unity at its most vulnerable junction. J. Ramsay MacDonald, then the leader of the British Labor Party, visited Palestine in 1922 and in a pamphlet published by the Zionist Labor Party he wrote: "We encouraged an Arab revolt against Turkey by promising to create an Arab kingdom including Palestine. At the same time we were encouraging the Jews to help us, by promising them that Palestine could be placed at their disposal for settlement and government; and also, at the same time, we were secretly making with France the Sykes-Picot Agreement partitioning the territory which we had instructed our governor-general of Egypt to promise to the Arabs. No one who has felt the undercurrents of Eastern movements can console himself with the belief that the Arab has forgotten or forgiven, or that the moral evil we committed will speedily cease to have political influence. Our treatment of the Moslems has been a madness."

From 1919 on the Arabs had felt all their hopes dashed by the imperial policies of the West; and their bitter disappointment and resentment have in no way been diminished by the events that followed after 1945. From the Arab point of view, the policy followed by the West after both World War I and World War II seemed to have the purpose of weakening, dividing, and humiliating the Arabs and driving them, against their will, into an attitude of hostility towards the West.

Nor did Western policy fulfill Zionist aspirations. The British tried to safeguard the minimum of Arab rights and interests in Palestine. The first British High Commissioner, Sir Herbert Samuel, who was appointed because of his active sympathy with Zionism, declared on June 3, 1921: "I hear it said in many quarters that the Arab population of Palestine will never agree to their country, their holy places, and their lands being taken from them and given to strangers. . . . People say that they cannot understand how it is that the British Government, which is famous throughout the world for its justice, could ever have consented to such a policy. I answer that the British Government . . . has never consented and will never consent to such a policy . . . [The Balfour Declaration] means that the Jews, a people who are scattered throughout the world, but whose hearts are always turned to Palestine, should be enabled to find their home, and that some among them, within the limits that are fixed by the numbers and interests of the present population, should come to Palestine in order to help by their resources and efforts develop the country to the advantage of all its inhabitants. If any measures are needed to convince the Moslem and Christian population . . . that their rights are really safe, such measures will be taken. For the British Government, the trustee under the Mandate for the happiness of the people of Palestine, would never impose upon them a policy which that people had reason to think was contrary to their religious, their political and their economic interests."

This statement was confirmed in the House of Commons on June 14, 1921 by Winston Churchill, at that time Colonial Secretary. Its spirit animated the declaration of British policy on Palestine of June 3, 1922.

But this British attitude satisfied neither the Zionists nor the Arabs. To the majority of Zionists the Balfour Declaration appeared meaningless unless it was to lead to a Jewish state in Palestine. Only in Palestine, they believed, could Jews form the ruling majority; whereas the Arab nation possessed in Syria, Iraq, and elsewhere, vast countries of its own. And only in a state of their own, the Zionists declared, could the Jews develop their capacities unhampered. The Arabs, on the other hand, resisted, as would every people, being turned into a minority in their own country by immigration from without. The Arabs accused Britain of promising something to the Zionists that did not belong to her. In the name of self-determination and democracy they demanded the right to determine the future of their country. Zionism, they predicted, would introduce an upsetting element of bitter strife into the whole Middle East, for the Arabs could not consent to being deprived of Palestine.

Thus, immediately after World War I, two apparently irreconcilable claims were staked out, and the blood-soaked and fear-ridden future of the "Holy Land" began to unfold.

Yet for many years after the Balfour Declaration funds provided by world Jewry for "building the Jewish homeland" were small, and Jewish immigration to Palestine was so slight that there seemed no prospect of establishing a Jewish majority. Before the victorious sweep of Hitlerism neither Zionist hopes nor Arab fears were borne out by reality. From 1920 to 1929 the average yearly net Jewish immigration to Palestine amounted to 7700, the excess of Jewish births over deaths to 3500, so that the Jewish population in Palestine gained by about 11,000 a year. In the same period the settled Arab population, not counting the nomadic tribes, grew by natural increase alone at the rate of 16,000 yearly. Even after 1933, when anybody with a "capital" of $5,000 could freely immigrate into Palestine, and when the American quota was wide open, relatively few Jews were willing to leave their European and American fatherlands. Everything pointed to the possibility of a realistic compromise which would make a peaceful co-existence probable. The events seemed to bear out Ahad Ha-am's analysis and vision.

But though it then appeared unlikely that a Jewish majority could be attained in Palestine, the Zionists strove for it and the Arabs feared it. The Arabs believed that the Zionists had not only the world-wide support of Jewish wealth and power but also the support of the League of Nations and the British Empire; and though Britain did not fulfil all the wishes of the Jews she maintained them in Palestine by her power, and allowed them to gain steadily in strength at the expense of the Arabs. To the Zionists a Jewish state in Palestine appeared the only hope of survival. This conviction gave them a buoyant vigor which strengthened their power far beyond their numbers. In the Balfour Declaration they saw the beginning of the fulfilment of the Bible's messianic promise, which, however, they divested of its religious meaning.

* * *

In 1920 Ahad Ha-am opposed the Zionist interpretation of the Balfour Declaration. Introducing a new edition of his collected essays, *At the Crossroads,* he warned against exaggerated Zionist hopes. "The Arab people," he wrote, "regarded by us as non-existent ever since the beginning of the colonization of Palestine, heard [of the Zionist expectations and plans] and believed that the Jews were coming to drive them from their soil and deal with them at their own will." Such an attitude on the part of his own people seemed to Ahad Ha-am unthinkable. In his interpretation of the Balfour Declaration he stressed that the historical right of the Jews in Palestine "does not affect the right of the other inhabitants who are entitled to invoke the right of actual dwelling and their work in the country for many generations. For them, too, the country is a national home, and they have a right to develop national forces to the extent of their ability. This situation makes Palestine the common land of several peoples, each of whom wishes to build its national home there. In such circumstances it is no longer possible that the national home of one of them could be total. . . . If you build your house not in an empty space, but in a place where there are also other houses and inhabitants, you are unrestricted master only inside your own house. Outside the door all the inhabitants are partners, and the management of the whole has to be directed in agreement with the interests of them all."

Years before World War I Ahad Ha-am had written a short essay which he called "In the Footsteps of the Messiah, Impudence Will Grow." In it he rejected the new dogmatic activists and enthusiasts—nationalists or socialists—who were convinced they could lead the people to "redemption." He feared their success, their arrogant self-assurance that they were acting as the spokesmen of destiny and the fulfillers of historical missions. He knew his own loneliness among them. "How hard is life in such an age," he had written in 1907, "for one who is not of them and who cannot go with closed eyes in the footsteps of this or that messiah; for one who does not hear the voice announcing redemption [*geulah*], neither for the immediate nor for the more distant future, neither for his own generation nor for the time when his grandchildren will be buried; one for whom truth and knowledge and reason remain mighty gods standing above all the camps and judging them all impartially, not as servants of the Messiah to herald him as his standard-bearers and trumpeters."

Many Eastern and Central European peoples have followed the will-o'-the-wisp of such messiahs in the half-century since Ahad Ha-am wrote these words. To his greatest sorrow some of his own people were among them. Ahad Ha-am died, a lonely man, in a Zion which he did not recognize.

The concluding passage of one of Ahad Ha-am's last letters speaks of his loneliness and despair. The old man had heard rumors of acts of Jewish terrorism and primitive vengeance against Arabs. He whose whole life was dedicated to the love of Zion wrote a pathetic and prophetic protest: "What should we say if this rumor is really true? My God! is *this* the end? Is *this* the goal for which our fathers have striven and for whose sake all generations have suffered? Is *this* the dream of a return to Zion which our people have dreamt for centuries: that we now come to Zion to stain its soil with innocent blood? Many years ago I wrote an essay in which I stated that our people will willingly give their money to build up their state, but they will never sacrifice their prophets for it. This was to me an axiomatic truth. And now God has afflicted me to have to live and to see with my own eyes that I apparently erred. The people do not part with their money to rebuild their national home but, instead, their inclination grows to sacrifice their prophets on the altar of their 'renaissance': the great ethical principles for the sake of which they have suffered, and for the sake of which alone it is worth while to return and become a people in the land of our fathers. For without these principles, my God, what are we and what can our future life in this country be, that we should bring all the endless sacrifices without which this land cannot be rebuilt? Are we really doing it only to add in an Oriental corner a small people of new Levantines who vie with other Levantines in shedding blood, in desire for vengeance, and in angry violence? If this be the 'Messiah,' then I do not wish to see his coming."

* * *

Ahad Ha-am's interpretation of the Balfour Declaration was not accepted. The Zionists expected much more, long before Hitler. A well-known liberal Protestant clergyman of New York, a trusted friend of the Jews and one filled with deep sympathy for Zionism, John Haynes Holmes, wrote after his visit to Palestine in 1929: "Even the moderate Zionists show a disquieting tendency to take for granted Jewish ascendancy. They do not think at all in terms of violence or oppression. Yet they were silent when England and her allies tore to tatters the nationalistic aspiration of the Moslem world. They have refused the request of the Palestinian Arabs, presented in not immoderate terms, for co-operation in securing some form of popular government, and thus have conspired, as an obstructive minority backed by alien power, to deny to the majority their public rights. . . . However temperate the spirit of the Jews in Palestine, however idealistic their expectations of the future, the logic of the policy which they are tempted to follow is repression of a native population, interference with its rights, frustration of its ambitions, with all the inevitable consequences of sporadic rebellion and ultimate civil war. In such a policy of force, the whole destiny of Zionism is at stake. It is the one policy, of course, best calculated to precipitate those very chances of destruction which it was instituted to appease."

The events twenty years later bore out these predictions. Pseudo-messianism and modern nationalism had gained the upper hand over the realism and the ethos of Ahad Ha-am's Zion.

In 1919 a philosopher in Prague, Hugo Bergmann, who was soon thereafter to settle in Palestine, wrote in a book called *Yavne and Jerusalem* that Palestine might become a Jewish state and yet be an entirely un-Jewish land—un-Jewish to such a degree that the smallest traditional Jewish school in a far-off Polish village would mean more for Judaism than all the new national institutions. "The trial by fire of the truly Jewish character of our settlement in Palestine will be our relationship to the Arabs," he went on. "An agreement with the inhabitants of the land is much more important for us than declarations of all the Governments in the world could be. Unfortunately, Zionist public opinion has not yet become conscious of it. What happened in Palestine before the [First World] War was almost totally of a kind to turn the Arabs into our enemies. A peaceful confrontation and understanding with them, however, is for us the question of life."

In the same year Martin Buber demanded that the Zionists should abstain from all political activities "except those measures which are necessary to create and to maintain an enduring and solid agreement with the Arabs in all fields of public life, an encompassing brotherly solidarity."

Ahad Ha-am's insistence on quality rather than numbers, and on regard for the rights and human dignity of the Arab people, was indeed accepted by some Zionists. There were among them names well known outside Palestine, like the American rabbi Judah L. Magnes and the German philosopher Martin Buber. There were many more unknown men among them. Gratitude and piety demand the mention of at least two of them, who both came from orthodox Russian Jewish homes and preserved their faith, who both lived in *Eretz Israel* for well over fifty years and dedicated all their life and thought to Zion. They may not have influenced the events in their lifetime; but they unflinchingly bore witness to the prophetic and spiritual tradition of Judaism under the most difficult circumstances.

The first was Moshe Smilansky, one of the pilgrim fathers of Zionism. When he died in 1953 Robert Weltsch, in a deeply felt and beautiful article of commemoration, wrote about his "independence of mind and the sacred fire of his moral conviction which made him a spiritual leader of the kind who, alas, is very rarely listened to by his own people. He never lost sight of supreme human values, which he regarded as overriding any guiding principles of collective as well as personal action. A nationalism which was merely founded on *sacro egoismo* and not rooted in humanity appeared to him utterly repulsive."

For many years Smilansky corresponded with his friend and mentor Ahad Ha-am over the steady deterioration of Jewish-Arab relations. His growing despair did not prevent him from raising his voice in the wilderness whenever the occasion warranted. In his last article, published when the Israeli parliament passed the "Land Requisition Law of 1953" that legalized the expropriation of Arab lands, Smilansky wrote: "When we came back to our country after having been evicted two thousand years ago, we called ourselves 'daring' and we rightly complained before the whole world that the gates of the country were shut. And now when they [Arab refugees] dared to return to their country where they lived for one thousand years before they were evicted or fled, they are called 'infiltrees' and shot in cold blood. Where are you, Jews? Why do we not at least, with a generous hand, pay compensation to these miserable people? Where to take the money from? But we build palaces . . . instead of paying a debt that cries unto us from earth and heaven. . . . And do we sin only against the refugees? Do we not treat the Arabs who remain with us as second-class citizens? . . . Did a single Jewish farmer raise his hand in the parliament in opposition to a law that deprived Arab peasants of their land? . . . How does sit solitary, in the city of Jerusalem, the Jewish conscience!"

Smilansky hated nothing more than the "double bookkeeping" which is so widely accepted in modern nationalism everywhere—a two-fold scale of moral judgment, defining the same action as right for one's self but wrong in the neighbor.

The second of these men was best known under the pen-name of Reb Binyomin. He too wrote an article in 1953, "For the Sake of the Survival," in which he drew the conclusions of over half a century of intimate knowledge and connection with life in the Holy Land.

"After the State of Israel was established I began receiving news about the terrible things perpetrated both during and after the Israeli-Arab war. I did not recognize my own people for the changes which had occurred in their spirit. The acts of brutality were not the worst because those might have been explained somehow or other as accidental, or an expression of hysteria, or the sadism of individuals. Far more terrible was the benevolent attitude toward these acts on the part of public opinion. I had never imagined that such could be the spiritual and moral countenance of Israel. . . .

"What separates us from the mass of our people? It is our attitude toward the Arabs. They consider the Arab as an enemy, some even say an eternal enemy. So speak the candid among them. The less candid speak supposedly about peace, but these are only words. They want a peace of submission, which the Arabs cannot possibly accept. ... We, however, do not see the Arab as an enemy, not in the past and not today. It is a mistake to think that we are dreamers and do not understand reality. No ... we are realists with the Ten Commandments, and they are the wise men, the realists without the Ten Commandments. ...

"War gave us a state, and war gave the Arabs, besides military defeat and the loss of territory, the problem of refugees. At the same time it also gave them the concern that, when the State of Israel feels strengthened economically and population-wise through immigration, it will attempt sooner or later to invade the neighboring Arab countries. Theirs is a very simple calculation: if the small army of Israel, which had to be developed underground and which hardly possessed any arms, was able to defeat all the Arab armies, then a large organized and disciplined Israeli army, which has now taken women too into its ranks, will surely be able to do it in the future.

"The Jewish state is dear to us because it could turn into a treasure for its inhabitants and for Jews all over the world. ... But the first condition for its continued existence is a true peace with the Arab states. What we failed to do before the war we must do now. ... Such a solution is not easy, but it is a guarantee for the very existence of the State of Israel. ... The Arabs were once a warlike people. But the Turks who vanquished them suppressed their warring spirit. When the Arabs were freed from the Turkish yoke, they were least prepared to develop a military spirit. They had no stimulus. Their wars of the past were carried out with the power of Moslem religious fervor. This fervor still lives among them, but it has no warlike character whatsoever. They know that the period of religious military conquest is gone, and they do not want to see it revived. The national idea was still alien to them. ... They had neither a national hymn nor a national flag. ... In the years after their liberation the Arabs were dilettantes in questions of politics, armies and war. ...

"That was true until the war with Israel. ... The outcome of the war has created for the Arabs that 'enemy' which serves as a stimulus for a new military spirit. None of the European Powers, not even Turkey, can become that kind of enemy. Israel presents almost an ideal opportunity. It prepared, and carried through, a war which brought humiliating defeat on the Arabs. Israel is proud as a peacock over its victory and boasts of it. Israel is not prepared to give in on any issue for the sake of peace. Israel is in the very midst of the Arabs.

Truly, an 'ideal enemy' that can serve as a factor in the military education of the Arabs in this generation and in generations to come, if Israel will not discover the way to assure a real peace in the near future. The Arab peoples have plenty of time. . . .

"I have written all this not for the sake of propaganda," the old man concluded. "I am not so foolish as to believe that these words would have any influence on today's rulers of Israel. I have not written this for the sake of polemics either. I wrote it because I believe that it is my duty to say what I think."

He was right. The large majority of Zionists did not heed his or his friends' anguished words. For the youth in the new state the old hopes and dreams of the early Zionists have meant little. Yet it should never be forgotten that there were men in Israel who raised their warning voices for Zion.

Many of the young Israeli generation in Palestine not only look down on the native Arabs; they have turned also, with pride in their own valor and in bitter disgust, from the two thousand years of the diaspora, from the life of their fathers and grandfathers, which they reject. They have cut themselves off from the "ghetto" and they try to restore a link with a far-off primitive past. Over thousands of years they stretch out their hands to reach the zealots who died defending Bethar, Massada, and Jerusalem; the Maccabees who threw off the foreign yoke; the proud kings who conquered neighboring lands and against whom the prophets rose; and the desert tribes who subjugated and exterminated the native population of Canaan. Out of opposition to the spiritual foundations of prophetic Judaism and Jewish life in the diaspora, the youth wishes to be the more "valiant," the more tough-minded. From one extreme they have gone to the other.

The events of the year 1948 appeared to them a miracle that initiated a new epoch of history. But the "miracle" was performed by the toughness and all-out dedication of the Jewish army which in 1948 won "the war of liberation." The question, from whom was the land "liberated," is difficult to answer. From the British, whose administration after 1920 had alone made possible the growth of the Jewish settlement against the will of the great majority of Palestinians? From its native inhabitants who, though ruled by foreign empires, had tilled and owned the soil for many centuries?

Few people realized that the victory of 1948 was due not only to the superior quality of Zionist military training, equipment and dedication, and the exaltation of nationalism among the youth. The victory was due also to the disunity and backwardness of the Arab regimes and the still underdeveloped nationalism of the Arab people. These, however, were temporary conditions which the coming years were to change. Indeed, the victory of 1948 and its territorial exploitation created the very conditions some early Zionists had feared: the stimulation of the Arab national revival, unity, and strength.

In the long run the foundation of a nation-state on military victory and its continuing temper usually defeats its own purpose. Militarism rapidly changes the whole character of the nation which succumbs to its temptation, and establishes in firm control those trends which Ahad Ha-am in "The Truth from Palestine" and Herzl in *Altneuland* saw, for both ethical and realistic reasons, as a threat to Zion.

* * *

For Ahad Ha-am hoped and believed that the return to Zion would rekindle the spiritual heritage and ethical tradition of Judaism. Like so many Central and East-European nationalists, he believed in the biological-spiritual continuity of generations over hundreds and even thousands of years. He saw in the Jews of his own day the heirs of the prophets—as the Greeks, when they achieved their independence in 1821, were convinced they were the heirs of the poets and philosophers and artists of ancient Greece and independence would revive their spirit and deeds.

But does such a continuity exist? Are biological endurance, national independence, and national language the sources of creative insight and imagination? Did not Spinoza and Marx, Freud and Bergson contribute to man's patrimony, though they lived in "exile" as seen by the Zionists, and though they did not write in Hebrew? Would they have contributed more if they had lived in a Jewish state and written in Hebrew? Can two thousand years of existence be simply effaced or regarded as sterile?

Might not perhaps the "abnormal" existence of the Jews represent a higher form of historical development than territorial nationalism? Has not the diaspora been an essential part of Jewish existence? Did it not secure Jewish survival better than the state could do?

Such questions were affirmatively answered by the historian Simon Dubnow, whose theories Professor Koppel S. Pinson has recently presented to the American public;[3] and also by a lonely God-seeker, Nathan Birnbaum, who is almost forgotten today.

In his youth Birnbaum started as a Zionist in Vienna more than a decade before Herzl wrote *Der Judenstaat;* he ended as a deeply pious orthodox Jew. Love of Zion, of a quiet unostentatious life on its soil, always remained a source of hope and inspiration to him. But he could not regard the diaspora as either an evil or as an historical accident. To him it was the specific form of latter-day Jewish existence, the existence of a people which is not like the nations of this earth and yet lives amidst this world.

It is of interest to recall that at the beginning of the nineteenth century the poet Goethe willingly foresaw a similar fate for the Germans. He was convinced that they could best fulfill their real task in history without creating a nation-state. With little hesitation he accepted and predicted for them a future like that of the Jews, surviving as a people, preserving their character, and accomplishing great things without a common fatherland. Goethe judged that the Germans, like the Jews, were most valuable as individuals but rather "miserable" as a people. In his conversations throughout the years he returned to this analogy several times. "The German nation is nothing," he told his friend Friedrich von Müller on December 14, 1808, "but the individual German is something, and yet they imagine the opposite to be true. The Germans should be dispersed throughout the world, like the Jews, in order fully to develop all the good that is in them for the benefit of mankind."

Dubnow and Birnbaum, whatever the validity of their theories, testify to the variety and breadth of Jewish life throughout all the ages and in its many homelands. Its unifying link has been a spiritual conception which, fundamentally ethical, has found expression in changing forms. The "miracle" and "uniqueness" of Jewish life is based not on political structures. Through three thousand years, whether there was a Jewish state or not, whether Jerusalem formed part of it or not, the Jewish people and Judaism have lived—and in all probability will continue to live.

As long as they live, there will be a "Jewish problem." It is an oversimplification to believe that there exists one "solution" to the Jewish problem. The Jewish problem is not the same in various ages,

---

[3] In a book of selected writings by Dubnow, *Nationalism and History,* edited with an Introductory Essay by Professor Pinson (The Jewish Publication Society of America, Philadelphia 1958).

in various countries, nay, even in various individuals. The form of modern Jewish life in the context of East-European society with its theories of ethnic nationalism and national minorities was and will be different from Jewish life in the West, above all in the United States where people of many ethnic origins are integrated into one open society and one dynamic civilization. The life of the Jews everywhere depends on the historical and social conditions and the political ideas prevailing in their environment.

Ultimately the Jewish problem is but part of the human problem. In 1854, when he had found his way back to the God of Judaism, Heinrich Heine added to his memorial for Ludwig Marcus that "Jews will achieve their true emancipation only when the Christians do." The cause of the German Jew was to him identical with that of the German people. "The Jews must not demand as Jews what has long been due to them as Germans."

Modern Jewish life with its great promise of creativeness in freedom is based on Enlightenment and Emancipation everywhere. Enlightenment and Emancipation are nowhere secure against the resurgence of atavistic forces. Enlightenment and Emancipation have to be defended and revitalized everywhere and at all times. This is the difficult task of modern life of which the Jews form part. As a result of their history they are, wherever they live, in an exposed position. For wherever Enlightenment and Emancipation are rejected or scorned, they will be endangered, morally or physically, more than others.

In that sense, even in a secular age, the Jews continue, willingly or not, to bear witness to the verities which their prophetic tradition first established so many centuries ago.

17

The Totalitarian Philosophy of War[*]

Characteristic of our time is the progressive disintegration of language as an instrument of universally accepted rational concepts. The same words cover different and sometimes opposite meanings, and much confusion is due to the indiscriminate and ambiguous use of words. One of the words which has lately changed its meaning is "war." Until very recently war was regarded, even by Clausewitz or Bismarck, as a strictly circumscribed and exceptional state of affairs. War was an instrument of politics, to be used only as the ultima ratio, as a case in extremis. Politics was the art of avoiding war which was considered an anormality. The effort of statesmen concentrated upon maintaining the normal life, and the occurrence of war was frequently regarded as a proof of faulty statesmanship, as a bankruptcy of policy. Even Mussolini ended the article which he contributed under the title *Audacity* to the first issue of his *Il Popolo d'Italia* on November 15, 1914 with the words: "This cry is a word which I would have never used in normal times . . . : a frightening and fascinating word: war!"[1] In the last years, however, Fascism has proclaimed war the normal state of life, not an aberration, caused by an intellectual or moral insufficiency, but the culmination in which the vital and ethical energies of man reveal themselves at their best. Politics now becomes a preparation for war, receives its direction and meaning from this extreme "Ernstfall." War ceases to be anything strictly circumscribed and limited; the border lines between war and peace grow more and more fluid, everything becomes part of warfare, actual or potential, and everything may therefore be called peace. Where the whole way of life is dominated by the norm of war, the words war and peace themselves lose their meaning.

A similar society is known to us from the descriptions of Spartan life in antiquity. This Peloponnesian state, with its economic foundations in the serf labor of the helots and in the exploitation of con-

---

[*] A paper read before the American Philosophical Society in Philadelphia on November 17, 1939, and first published in the *Proceedings* of the American Philosophical Society, Vol. 28, No. 1, 1940. Reprinted with permission.

[1] Benito Mussolini, *Scritti e Discorsi. Edizione Definitiva* (Milan, Ulrico Hoepli), vol. I, p. 10.

quests, was nothing but immense barracks where the spirit of the army shaped and permeated all expressions of civic and individual activity. In contrast to the Athenian democracy, no interest in arts or letters was evinced, no political life with party tensions and dissensions was allowed, the luxuries of civilized life were despised. Physical education predominated, the pedagogic effort was entirely concentrated upon building up bodies and characters hard as steel; even the teaching of ethics as far as any existed was entirely subordinated to the goal of rearing a warrior race.[2] Disobedience of even the most arbitrary commands was regarded as the greatest offense. Trade, commerce, and the arts of peace were haughtily scorned, justice and moderation derided as sentimentalism. From the cradle to the grave, men and women were regarded solely as means for strengthening the military machine.

This first example of the totalitarian state disappeared under the influence of stoic humanism, of Christianity, and later of that rational ethicism which Grotius developed from Stoic and Christian sources. Only the Prussia of Frederick William I revived consciously the Spartan ideal as a model for the state and a conduct of life for the citizen. "Concern for arts or for science appeared to him in no way better than one of the seven deadly sins. Nach seinem Willen sollte alle Welt nur eine Sache im Kopfe haben, die Männer das Kriegswesen, die Weiber den Haushalt."[3] As is well known Frederick II stated that under Frederick I Berlin had been the Athens of the north—an opinion greatly overstating the case—and that under Frederick William I it became Sparta—an opinion this time much nearer the fact. And Johann Wilhelm Gleim started his "Preussische Kriegslieder in den Feldzügen 1756 und 1757 von einem Grenadier" with the exclamation: "Berlin sei Sparta!"

But although Prussia foreshadowed the totalitarian philosophy of war, its application was limited by the acceptance of the moral standards of Christianity and of common western civilization. Bismarck's statesmanship employed war as a means for definite ends. Cynically and brutally he was ready to use this means, but it was

---

[2] Spartan children were instructed in stealing, robbing and deceiving. They were severely punished when caught, not because they were stealing, but because they were stealing badly. In the drabness of their life "the only relief found by the Spartans was spying on each other" (Leo Strauss in *Social Research*, November 1939, p. 517).

[3] Carl Biedermann, *Deutschland im achtzehnten Jahrhundert*, vol. II, Part I (Leipzig, J. J. Weber, 1858), p. 167 f. Frederick William I would have abolished the Prussian Academy founded by his father if the Academy had not proposed to help in training surgeons for the army by the study of anatomy.

never allowed to become dominant; it was always limited to its subservient function, and at a given moment stability and security were preferred to risk and expansion. The totalitarian philosophy of war derides stability and security with its accompanying preference for a quiet and comfortable life. War becomes the highest and normative state of life; what is called peace is only a pause between the "real" manifestations of life, preparing for them, subservient to them.

This totalitarian philosophy of war grew up under the influence of two intellectual movements, the roots of which we can trace back to the second half of the nineteenth century.[4] One of them is the belief that the substance of life and history is struggle and conflict. The application of Darwinism to the social sciences made war and strife appear as the normal manifestations of all nature of which man was only part. Soon the accepted moral values were revealed as ill-suited to this new conception. The fundamental basis of Chancellor Hitler's *Mein Kampf* is an interpretation of man according to which he is purely a natural being, biologically determined, and inescapably subject to the "iron logic of nature" which he has to obey as animals do, if he wishes to preserve or increase his strength and to be true to his "nature." In such a world strength and success alone count: the "idle dreams" of universal truth and justice disappear in the dust heap of bookishness before the triumphant march of full-blooded man. In the face of this nihilism, this twilight of all moral values, Life is exalted as the only and inexorable arbiter of all action and conduct. "World history is the world tribunal: it has always justified the stronger, the fuller, the more self-assured life, has given it the right to existence, whether or not it was regarded as good. It has always sacrificed truth and justice to might and vitality, and doomed those peoples to death who considered truth more important than deeds, and justice more essential than might."[5]

[4] I tried to trace the genesis of totalitarian "Weltanschauung" in my two recent books, *Force or Reason* (Harvard University Press, 1938) and especially *Revolutions and Dictatorships* (Harvard University Press, 1939).

[5] Oswald Spengler, *Der Untergang des Abendlandes*, Vol. II (Munich, C. H. Beck, 1922), p. 635. See also on p. 542: "Die Mächte des Blutes, die urwüchsigen Triebe alles Lebens, die ungebrochene, körperliche Kraft treten in ihrer alten Herrschaft wieder an. Die Rasse bricht rein und unwiderstehlich hervor: der Erfolg der Stärksten und der Rest als Beute. Sie ergreift das Weltregiment, und das Reich der Bücher und Probleme erstarrt oder versinkt in Vergessenheit." And eleven years later, in the first year of National Socialist domination, Spengler proclaimed in his *Jahre der Entscheidung*, Part I (Munich, C. H. Beck, 1933), p. 14: "Der Kampf ist die Urtatsache des Lebens, ist das Leben selbst. Der triste Zug der Weltverbesserer, der als einziges Denkmal seines Daseins Berge bedruckten Papiers auf dem Wege zurückliess, ist zu Ende," and on p. 24: "Menschliche Geschichte im Zeitalter der hohen Kulturen ist die Geschichte poli-

The other movement of ideas, closely connected with the first, is the denial of universal values and truth, their relativization and "nationalization." Thus two enemies facing each other are not united any more by a moral or intellectual community above the battle fields. This lack of common moral or intellectual attitudes is always noticeable, as war in reality is a permanent phenomenon. Even in so-called peace times each nation, according to the National Socialists, has its own peculiar thought processes, develops its own science, lives according to its own standards of national ethics and honor. All bridges of understanding and communication are destroyed. Nationalism reaches here its extreme manifestation: sovereignty is not only political, it is also economic and cultural as well. Not only all hope of world cooperation becomes futile, also the republic of letters, the oneness of mankind and civilization, do not exist any longer or are "unmasked" as idle cerebral fancies. Under these circumstances the word enemy gains a new meaning. Everybody is a potential enemy, and every enemy becomes a total enemy. The whole existence is always overshadowed by war. The army becomes the model of life, and its collectivism, as in Sparta, spreads to all fields of human endeavor, and is mistaken for socialism. This new "socialism," which is nothing but the collectivism of an army, is again proof for the strangely ambiguous use of words in our times. It was first Oswald Spengler in his *Preussentum und Sozialismus* which he published immediately after the First World War who identified Prussianism and socialism. This socialism is, according to Spengler, "will to power, struggle for the well-being, not of the individual, but of the whole." This whole, however, is never humanity; it is a fictitious whole, called organic, of a part of mankind, a state, nation or race, which acts as if it were the whole. Spengler carries even his prussification of socialism to the paradox of calling Frederick William I, and not Marx, the "first conscious socialist." [6]

A similar conception of "socialism" was propagated at about the

---

tischer Mächte. Die Form dieser Geschichte is der Krieg. Auch der Friede gehört dazu. Er ist die Fortsetzung des Krieges mit anderen Mitteln. . . . Ein Staat ist das 'in Form sein' einer durch ihn gebildeten und dargestellten völkischen Einheit für wirkliche und mögliche Kriege."

[6] *Politische Schriften* (Munich, C. H. Beck), p. 43. *Ibidem*, p. VII: "Socialism, as I understand it, presupposes private enterprise with its old Germanic delight in power and plunder," and about Prussia he says on p. 63: "In Preussen war ein wirklicher Staat vorhanden. Hier gab es streng genommen keinen Privatmann. Jeder, der innerhalb des mit der Exaktheit einer guten Maschine arbeitenden Systems lebte, gehörte ihmirgendwie als Glied an."

same time by Moeller van den Bruck. For him Prussia meant a nationalistic communism or collectivism on a hierarchical and aristocratic basis. In his *Das Dritte Reich,* in which he demands the complete separation of Germany from the West (for "am Liberalismus gehen die Völker zu Grunde"), and the fulfilment of a German mission by a new Germany of which the frontiers will be those of her mission, he states that each people has its own socialism. Socialism is for him definitely opposed to any international community. German socialism means "Verwurzelung, Staffelung, Gliederung." "Where Marxism ends, there begins socialism: a German socialism, whose mission it is to supplant in the intellectual history of mankind all liberalism. This German socialism is not the task of a Third Reich. It is rather its foundation." [7] This new militaristic collectivism differs, however, in one fundamental respect from its Spartan model, in its emphasis upon productive work and upon the importance of the industrial worker. The achievements of modern industrial society with its stress upon mechanization, standardization and disciplined team work, are not only fully accepted by the totalitarian régimes (in spite of some romantic impulses to toy with soil and primitive agrarianism), but regimented into a system of a military super-industrialism. The worker becomes a soldier, the border lines between industrial society and army become more and more fluid until they disappear, the factories become barracks, and the same discipline and devotion are demanded in both. Work becomes an obligation towards the state. The state fixes the compensations and conditions of labor, the freedom of exchange or contract is abolished, and property becomes a fidei-commissum. Ernst Jünger created in his *Der Arbeiter, Herrschaft und Gestalt* the apotheosis of a thoroughly mechanized and militarized worker, a modern machine-man, a member in a group closely knit together in hierarchical order and pervaded by one spirit, united for higher efficiency and external action.[8] In a similar way

[7] *Das Dritte Reich,* 3rd ed. (Hamburg, Hanseatische Verlagsanstalt, 1931), p. 67 f.
[8] Ernst Jünger, *Der Arbeiter* (Hamburg, Hanseatische Verlagsanstalt, 1932). In a former book *Das abenteuerliche Herz* (Berlin, Frundsberg Verlag, 1929) Jünger had expressed the underlying nihilism of the fascist attitude, its despair of any values in life, its glorification of vitality in itself: "To what purpose one exists, that may never be learned; all so-called goals can only be pretexts of destiny. But that one exists, that is the essential. . . . For that reason this time demands one virtue above all others: that of resolution. It is essential, to find will and faith, quite apart from and irrespective of any contents of this will and faith. . . . All the fight today about flags and symbols, laws and dogmas, order and systems, is humbug. Your very horror of these quarrels reveals that you are not in need of answers, but of sharp questions, not of flags but of combats, not of order but of rebellion, not of systems but of men."

Mussolini stressed the unity of soldiers and workers, he called his *Popolo d'Italia* the "newspaper of combatants and producers." His cooperative state is the expression of an "Italian socialism," based upon presuppositions hardly different from those of "German socialism."

This worker and soldier is being trained in the totalitarian states to accept hardness of life and risk as the normal life, tragic heroism as human destiny, and to reject contemptuously any desire for a sheltered and a comfortable life, for the amenities of the ridiculed bourgeois or western civilization. In intentionally terse and striking sentences Mussolini has tried to formulate this new way of life: "Tutta la nazione deve essere militarizzata . . . Nella vita la felicità non esiste . . . Io considero la Nazione Italiana in stato permanente di guerra . . . Vivere per me è la lotta, il rischio, la tenacia . . . Il Fascista disdegna la vita comoda . . . Il credo del Fascismo è l'eroismo." [9] Whereas it is characteristic that Lenin and Stalin had no need to boast of their humble origin, and certainly never emphasized that they had been common soldiers in the war or had wished to do their duty and regarded their soldierly duty and experiences as the zenith of their lives, Hitler and Mussolini both stress their humble origins and above all their experiences as common soldiers in the World War.[10] Asked by Emil Ludwig, of what Mussolini is proudest in his career, the head of the Italian government answered without hesitation, of having been a good soldier. The answer was probably sincere; it would have sounded improbable in the mouth of Bismarck or Crispi, of Lloyd George or Clemenceau, of Bethmann Hollweg or Neville Chamberlain.

In this new philosophy of life strategic considerations of soldiery take precedence over economic well-being. Walther Rathenau, the famous German industrialist and statesman, had pronounced economics to determine our fate. "Wirtschaft ist Schicksal." In this attitude the two great currents of the later nineteenth century, liberal capitalism and socialism, had agreed. Now they are confronted with the proclamation of the precedence of politics over economics. "Poli-

---

[9] *Op. cit.*, vol. I, p. 283; vol. II, p. 230; vol. V, p. 238 f.; vol VIII, p. 69; vol. IX, p. 43. These are only a very few examples taken at random.

[10] On Hitler see *Revolutions and Dictatorships*, p. 181 and 343. From Mussolini: "I am proud to be a son of laborers. I am proud to have worked with my own hands." And again: "Considero il momento più bello della mia vita quello in cui fui lacerato dalle ferite." And again: "I am and I remain on the ramparts (sulla breccia); I am bound, not to my caprice, but to my soldier's post." *Op. cit.*, III, p. 49; IV, p. 18, p. 248.

tik ist Schicksal," affirms Carl Schmitt. Politics is life and life is politics, as Oswald Spengler says; but with the discarding of economic man, the meaning of political man has been changed fundamentally. Now arises a concept of politics which receives its meaning, not from what has been considered the normal life of society, but from the border-line case. The normal does not try any more to dominate and limit the anormal; it is the anormal, the exceptional, the ultima ratio, which determines and directs the normal. A German political scientist has best expressed this new attitude. "One can say that here, as elsewhere, precisely the exceptional case has a particularly decisive meaning and reveals the heart of the matter. . . . It is from this most extreme possibility that the life of men gains its specific political tension." [11] In his theory about the origins and legitimacy of right, a theory which he calls decisionism, Carl Schmitt lets right be determined by the legislator who has the power to realize and enforce the decision. Ideal justice or positive law are discarded as norms of lawmaking. Starting from the extraordinary situation, the "Staatsnotstand" ("Not kennt kein Gebot"), where the necessities of existence seem to demand the disregard of abstract justice or of the existing positive law, Schmitt applies this "anormal" case to the "normal" course of existence. "Right" is thus always dependent upon the concrete situation and has its source in the decision with which the supreme power-authority meets the situation. "Jegliches Recht ist Situationsrecht." As each situation is unique and concrete, there cannot be any general and abstract norm. Each decision is valid only for its own situation. "Justice" becomes the function of the power which makes the essentially political decision; political and judicial functions are no longer separated, although political decisions continue to be made to appear as judicial ones. But in practice, and frequently in theory, the judicial function is subordinated to the political. In his address to the Deutsche Juristentag in 1936 Rudolf Hess repeated Treitschke's words: "Alle Rechtspflege ist eine politische Tätigkeit."

This exaltation of life over law—in Spengler's terminology of Dasein over Wachsein—produces a dangerous existence on the rim of an abyss. Carl Schmitt bases his concept of politics on the inescapable antagonism between friend and enemy, an antagonism as fundamental as that between good and bad, or between the beautiful and the

[11] Carl Schmitt, *Der Begriff des Politischen* (Hamburg, Hanseatische Verlagsanstalt, 1933), p. 18.

ugly. Political conflicts are therefore for Schmitt not rationally or ethically determined or solvable; they are "existential" conflicts,[12] in which existence itself is at stake. For this political theory war is the culmination, the zenith of political life and that means of life in general: the inescapable friend-enemy relation dominates all life. This political philosophy corresponds to the supposed primitive combative instinct of man, who tends to regard anyone who stands in the way of the realization of his desires as a foe who has to be done away with. This concept clearly marks all the policies, internal and foreign, of Chancellor Hitler's government. Civilized statesmanship, on the other hand, consists in finding the ways and means to overcome the primitive instincts by compromise, by patient negotiations, by an effort at reciprocity, and above all by the acknowledgment of universally binding law.[13]

Thus from all sides war is acclaimed as the supreme moment of life. Whereas in the western nations after the World War, the war itself was recognized as a great calamity and tragedy; a very large part of the German people did not regard the war as a tragedy or calamity, but the defeat. They blamed all the ills, which the western nations blamed on the war, on the peace treaties. Whereas the western nations blamed themselves for having got into the war and having made the peace, the large majority of the Germans never blamed themselves, but blamed only the enemy for having devised the peace. National Socialist propaganda increased this growing estrangement from the West by glorifying the war and the German army, and by strengthening the already too strong German tendencies of seeing the source of all their maladjustments, not in their own faults or shortcomings, but in the machinations of their "enemies." "We National Socialists know that the Great War from 1914 to 1918 will once live in the memory of later generations as a mythical great deed without

[12] Existential is one of the new expressions corresponding to attitudes in Germany produced by the post-war nihilism. The "existential" political theory of Schmitt corresponds to the existential philosophy of Heidegger. In his *Der Begriff des Politischen*, p. 8, Carl Schmitt says: "Der Feind ist in einem besonders intensiven Sinne existenziell ein Anderer und Fremder, mit dem im extremen Fall existenzielle Konflikte möglich sind. Derartige Konflikte können weder durch eine im voraus getroffene generelle Normierung, noch durch den Spruch eines 'unbeteiligten' und deshalb 'unparteiischen' Dritten entschieden werden." And on p. 15: "Der Krieg folgt aus der Feindschaft, denn diese ist seinsmässige Negierung eines anderen Seins."

[13] See my *Force or Reason*, p. 19 f. Schmitt says *op. cit.*, p. 48: "Die Höhepunkte der grossen Politik sind zugleich die Augenblicke, in denen der Feind in konkreter Deutlichkeit als Feind erblickt wird."

equal."[14] Hitler's racial theory had the effect of destroying the remaining sense of reciprocity and responsibility in the German people and of convincing them that on account of their superior qualities they are always right and that the heroic warrior ideal which they have cultivated justified their world domination. "The struggle for a German rebirth is a struggle for the assertion of the German hero ideal against the democratic shop-keeper ideal," says Rosenberg, and Hitler praises Germany because she was "a most magnificent example of a nation, created on the foundations of pure power-politics. Prussia, the germ cell of the Reich, arose through radiant heroism ('durch strahlendes Heldentum') and not through financial manœuvres or commercial transactions; and the Reich itself was only the most glorious reward for power-political leadership and warrior's courage in the face of death." [15]

Thus the pacifism which became predominant in the western democracies after the World War was stamped out by the new philosophy in Fascist countries. "War is to man what maternity is to the woman. I do not believe in perpetual peace; not only do I not believe in it, but I find it depressing and a negation of all the fundamental virtues of man." [16] The preamble to the statute of the Italian Fascist party of December 20, 1929, prides itself that "from its beginnings until now, the Party has always thought of itself as in a state of war. Fascism is above all a faith under the impulse of which the Italians work as soldiers, pledged to achieve victory in the struggle between the nation and its enemies." This attitude had already been foreseen by Mussolini during the years of the World War, and by Oswald Spengler in his *Decline of the Occident* where he characterized the new time: "Life is harsh. It leaves only one choice, that between vic-

---

[14] Alfred Rosenberg, *Das Wesensgefüge des National Sozialismus*, 4th ed. (Munich, Eher, 1933), p. 9.

[15] Alfred Rosenberg, *Der Mythus des 20. Jahrhunderts*, 37th ed. (Munich, Hoheneichen Verlag, 1934), p. 639. Adolf Hitler, *Mein Kampf* (Munich, Eher, 1933), Vol. I, p. 169.

[16] Mussolini, *op. cit.*, vol. IX, p. 98. Well known are the anti-pacifist passages in the often translated article by Mussolini on the doctrine of Fascism in the *Enciclopedia Italiana*. Translations can be found in Alfred Zimmern, *Modern Political Doctrines* (London, Oxford University Press, 1939), p. 31 ff. and in Michael Oakeshott, *The Social and Political Doctrines of Contemporary Europe* (Cambridge University Press, 1939), p. 164 ff. See there too on p. 180 f. the two Fascist Decalogues. The most characteristic passages are: "Above all, Fascism believes neither in the possibility nor in the utility of perpetual peace. . . . War alone brings up to their highest tension all human energies and puts the stamp of nobility upon the peoples who have the courage to meet it. . . . Fascism carries over this anti-pacifist spirit even into the lives of individuals. It is education for combat. . . . The Fascist looks on life as duty, ascent, conquest."

tory and defeat, not between war and peace. . . . Pacifism implies the personal renunciation of war on the part of the great majority, but with that also the unadmitted readiness to become the prey of others who make no such renunciation. It begins with the desire of a general reconciliation, and it ends with no one stirring a hand as long as the misfortune befalls only the neighbor." [17]

For outside consumption and for purposes of diplomatic war the spokesmen and advocates of the new philosophy of totalitarian war may speak sometimes of their desire for peace and may indulge themselves in some kind of pacifist propaganda, strictly forbidden under heaviest penalties to their own subjects. But even a cursory perusal of the fundamental sources of the new philosophy, be it the writings and speeches of Mussolini or Hitler, be it the vast literary output of their enthusiastic followers, reveals the unbridgeable gulf between their own profession of faith and their pragmatic toying with the pleasantness of peace. On August 25, 1934, Mussolini declared: "We are becoming and we shall become ever more, because we will it, a military nation. Because we are not afraid of words, I shall add: a militarist one. To say it fully: a warrior nation (guerriera), which will be endowed to an ever higher degree with the virtue of obedience, of sacrifice, of dedication to the fatherland. That means that the whole life of the nation, the political as well as the economic and spiritual life, must be directed towards our military necessities. . . . I recall to you that the military forces represent the essential element of the hierarchy among the nations. Nothing has yet been found which could substitute that which is the clearest, most tangible and most determining expression of the complex force of a whole people: that is the size, the prestige, the power of its arms on land, on sea and in the air." [18]

In the totalitarian régimes society is entirely subordinated to the state and even destroyed by it. There is no individual or social sphere outside the state. But even the state is not a true state; it is not more than the apparatus of one party which entirely identifies itself with the state and society, absorbing all their functions. The great differ-

---

[17] *Op. cit.*, p. 538, 545 f. See also in his *Politische Schriften*, p. 55: "War is always the higher form of human existence, and states exist for the sake of war. . . . Even were a weary and lifeless humanity desirous of renouncing wars, it would become instead of the subject of war, the object for whom and with whom others would wage wars."

[18] *Op. cit.*, vol. IX, p. 113-115. Se also p. 197 f.; vol. III, p. 60; vol. IV, p. 294; vol. V, p. 29, 118, 181; and passim.

ence even between Bismarcko-Wilhelminian Germany and the state created by National Socialism was clearly indicated by the declarations of the respective leaders at the outbreak of the great wars. In 1914 Emperor William II declared that he no longer recognized any parties among the Germans and that he stretched out his hands to all his internal opponents for cooperation and internal peace. At the outbreak of the war in 1939 Chancellor Hitler did not invite the cooperation of any internal opponents, but on the contrary, threatened them in terms unusually violent, even for him. The famous Protestant theologian, Karl Barth, rightly pointed out that the National Socialist state consists in the disintegration of the just or right state, that it is a state only, insofar as it is not yet National Socialist in certain remnants carried over from the old state, but that otherwise it is an anarchy tempered by tyranny, or a tyranny tempered by anarchy.[19] The disappearing social order is replaced by an extension and imitation of the order of the army. The terminology of war, warriors and struggle is applied to every phase of life, even the most civilian. All differences between the military and other walks of life are gradually abolished until the totality of life is subordinated to the set of values of the army, and farmers and teachers, industrialists and scholars are turned into soldiers of the regime.[20] As in an army, discipline and hierarchy, appeal to comradeship, and readiness to sacrifice are stressed. The personality of the leader gets full scope and is elevated by the amorphism of the masses beneath it. The fate of the individual in a nation which has become an army has been masterly formulated in Mussolini's famous words: "In the Fascist state the individual is not suppressed, but rather multiplied, just as in a regiment a soldier is not weakened but multiplied by the number of his comrades." The National Socialist youth exalted as its educational and social ideal the Männerbund, a soldiery order after the model

[19] *Die Kirche und die politische Frage von Heute* (Zollikon, Evangelische Buchhandlung, 1939), p. 35. This remarkable book has been published in an English translation, *The Church and the Political Question of Our Day* (New York, Scribner, 1939).

[20] The editor of the *Historische Zeitschrift*, Professor Karl Alexander von Müller, ends an editorial postscript about the war in the issue published September 15, 1939 (160, 3, p. 680): "It is in this battle of souls that we find the section of the trenches which is also entrusted to the German science of history. It will mount on guard. The watch word has been given by Hegel: The spirit of the universe gave the command to advance; such command will find itself blindly obeyed."

At the same time the lack of that chivalry which is so characteristic of non-totalitarian or real armies is astonishing in the totalitarian regimes. This lack expresses itself in the ostentatious feeling of superiority against weaker armies, in the undignified persecution of and brutality against defenceless groups, in the scorn heaped upon defeated foes, in the complete absence of any sense or feeling of reciprocity.

of the Teutonic knights or the Prussian officers' corps. "The principle," wrote Hitler, "which in its time made the Prussian army the most wonderful instrument of the German people, must in the future become the principle of the structure of our whole conception of the state: authority of every leader downwards and responsibility upwards." [21] The totalitarian philosophy of war has been aptly summed up by Carl Schmitt: "War is the essence of everything. The nature of the total war determines the nature and form of the totalitarian state." [22]

This philosophy of war gains even greater importance by the fact that in a war, in which a totalitarian nation is involved, we do not find one nation fighting against another as equal partners within a common humanity. The totalitarian nation fights inspired by its consciousness of a unique mission, the Sendungsbewusstsein, which is fulfilled in the war and invests its fight and victory with an almost sacral character. The racial theory, as evolved by the National Socialists, amounts to a new naturalistic religion for which the German people are the corpus mysticum and the army the priesthood. The new faith of biological determinism, fundamentally opposed to all transcendent and to all humanist religion, bestows upon the people an immense strength in their permanent total war against every other conception of man, be it Christian or rational. The people now represent the Reich, the realm of salvation; the enemy represents the Gegenreich; it becomes as much of a mystical and mythical fiction as the Reich itself; only that the one is invested with all imaginable virtues, and the other with all imaginable, and sometimes even unimaginable, vices. One of the weaknesses of this position consists in the fact that, whereas the Reich is a constant factor, the Gegenreich is a variable factor, according to circumstances, the political exigencies of one moment putting up another adversary than those of another moment. Here Chancellor Hitler made a master-move by pointing out the Jews as the Gegenreich,[23] and by identifying all his enemies

---

[21] *Mein Kampf*, p. 501. See also p. 734.

[22] "Totaler Feind, Totaler Krieg, Totaler Staat" in *Völkerbund und Völkerrecht*, Jg. 4, p. 139 ff. (June 1937). "Im Kriege steckt der Kern der Dinge. Von der Art des totalen Krieges her, bestimmen sich Art und Gestalt der Totalität des Staates." On the efforts of National Socialist science to arrive at a theory of international law, see the excellent book by Eduard Bristler, *Die Völkerrechtslehre des Nationalsozialismus* (Zürich, Europa Verlag, 1938), and more generally Edmond Vermeil, *Doctrinaires de la Révolution Allemande* (Paris, Fernand Sorlot, 1938).

[23] *Mein Kampf*, p. 355. "Among our people the personification of the devil, as the symbol of everything evil, takes on the actual appearance and figure of the Jew." On the mystical character of the race see Alfred Rosenberg, *Der Mythus des 20. Jahr-*

with Judaism. Thus he could "unmask" the accidental enemy of the hour, Russia and Communism, Great Britain and Democracy, France and the United States, President Roosevelt and capitalism, in short, whoever seemed to stand in a concrete situation in the way of the fulfilment of Germany's wishes, as an instrument of the devil, opposing the march towards salvation of the Reich. This attitude gives to the totalitarian politics at the same time an immense flexibility and, to its own followers, the appearance of a great persistency. Spengler had foreseen this attitude when he defined the new imperialist Caesarism which he saw coming as "that type of government which, in spite of all constitutional and philosophical formulation is by its inherent nature lacking utterly in defined form." [24] This flexibility allows the substitution of one enemy for the other most abruptly and enables the leader to direct the almost mystical totalitarian hatred of his followers against the most diverse objects. That explains the startling change in the attitude of the leader of the anti-comintern pact towards communism and the Soviet Union after August 1939. Only a very short while ago the "destruction of Bolshevism was regarded as a fundamental right of the law of the nations and to this extent an elementary duty." It was proclaimed that "the Soviet Union must be expelled from the juridical community of nations" and that the League of Nations was "no community based on law any more, because it had recognized the total enemy of right and law as de jure equal." [25]

---

hunderts, p. 114: "Heute erwacht aber ein neuer Glaube: der Mythus des Blutes, der Glaube, mit dem Blute auch das göttliche Wesen des Menschen überhaupt zu verteidigen. Der mit hellstem Wissen verkörperte Glaube, dass das nordische Blut jenes Mysterium darstellt, welches die alten Sakramente ersetzt und überwunden hat." See also p. 119 and 529.

[24] *Der Untergang des Abendlandes*, vol. II, p. 541. In reality the Gegenreich for National Socialism and Fascism is everything universal, everything that believes in the oneness of mankind, in common human aspirations, in a final harmony: Christianity in all its forms, liberalism, humanism, rationalism, capitalism, communism, freemasonry, the ideas of 1789, democracy, etc., even down to the Rotarian International or any of the most innocuous forms of human cooperation or civilized intercourse.

[25] E. H. Bockhoff, *Völker-Recht gegen Bolschewismus* (Berlin, Institut zur wissenschaftlichen Erforschung der Soviet Union, 1937), p. 238, 228, 99. This book had the honor of an introduction by the Reichsminister of Justice, Dr. Frank, who welcomed it as a contribution to the "struggle for the immortality and strength of the idea of right generally." In an article "Das Lebensrecht des deutschen Volkes" (*Deutsche Juristenzeitung*, 1936, p. 342) Karl Lohmann said: "As France allowed herself to conclude a pact of guarantee even with the devil himself (the author meant the Franco-Soviet pact), she created such a situation of menace that the measure of injustice necessarily came to overflow."

Mussolini also changed his attitude, this time with regard to Prussian militarism. On April 8, 1918, he said: "No man of good will, even not the last befuddled brain, could any longer believe that it is not Germany which did wish the war, and that it is not

The totalitarian army gains its strength not only from the concentration of the whole national and all individual life upon war. It draws its main inspiration from the totalitarian vision according to which each individual war is nothing but a step towards imposing the new way of life upon the whole of mankind. The totalitarian army knows itself as the instrument of a national will, aspiring to the highest goal, to make the nation not only a powerful nation in the Bismarckian sense, but a world nation for which its world-day has arrived with the adoption of the new philosophy which is destined to become the new faith of mankind. Spengler defines as the duty of the German youth "to work out a new mode of political will and action from the newly formed conditions of the twentieth century, to bring to light new forms, methods and ideas, which like the ideas of the French Revolution and the customs of the English House of Commons will spread as models from one land to the other, until the history of the coming time progresses in forms whose beginnings will in the future be found in Germany." [26] The German master-race feels the mission of bringing the new world order. The same vision enlivens the grandiose picture which Mussolini unfolds before the eyes of Italian youth. In 1932 he proclaimed proudly: ". . . L'appello alle forze giovani risuona dovunque: la Nazione che ha precorso i tempi, anticipando di un decennio l'azione degli altri Paesi, è l'Italia," and two years later, reviewing the astonishing developments of the preceding luster, he boasted: "From 1929 until today Fascism has become out of an Italian phenomenon a world phenomenon." The essence of Fascism he defines in the same way as Spengler and the National Socialists do: as an absolute revolution against western civilization, against Anglo-Saxon liberalism and against the achievements and consequences of the French Revolution. "We represent a

---

Germany which wishes to continue the war in order to reduce the whole world into a horrible Prussian barracks." *Op. cit.*, vol. I, p. 306. Six years later he proclaimed as the aim of Fascism "non la caserma Prussiana, ma la nostra caserma." *Op. cit.*, vol. IV, p. 321. Fourteen years later he introduced the Prussian goose-step into the Italian army and entirely Prussianized Italian life.

[26] *Politische Schriften*, p. 146. Spengler foresaw two revolutions, the revolution of the lower classes and the revolution of the colored races, class war and racial war. He regarded Prussian Germany as the savior of the "white" world against these two revolutions. But he did not foresee that National Socialist Germany which vulgarized and materialized his teaching, as they did with that of his master Nietzsche, would become itself the centre of race war and would ally herself against western civilization at one time with Japan, at another time with Soviet Russia, the representative of class war. Spengler regarded it as the hour of greatest danger for western civilization should race war and class war combine. "This possibility lies in the nature of things, and neither of the two revolutions will scorn the help of the other only because it is contemptuous of the other's bearer. Common hatred extinguishes mutual contempt." *Ibidem*, p. 164.

new principle in the world, we represent the clear-cut, categorical, definitive antithesis of the whole democratic world . . . , of the whole world, to say it in one word, of the immortal principles of 1789." From this starting point, he assured the people of Milan in a speech on October 25, 1932, of the coming world leadership of Fascist Italy. "Today, with a fully tranquil conscience I say to you, immense multitude, that the twentieth century will be the century of Fascism, the century of Italian power, the century during which Italy will become for the third time the leader of mankind (la direttrice della civiltà humana), because outside of our principles there is no salvation, neither for the individuals, nor even less for the peoples." [27]

The totalitarian philosophy of war makes wars at present fought by the totalitarian states fundamentally different from the wars of the nineteenth century and even from the first World War. It is for this reason that all analogies drawn from the first World War remain on the surface and do not touch the real problems involved in the war which started in 1939. As the Fascist imperialism of the thirties of our century is fundamentally different in its methods and aims from the liberal imperialism at the turn of the century, in spite of certain similarities and in spite of the confusing use of the same word for both—so the word war has acquired an entirely different meaning in the totalitarian states. For the liberal state war is a hateful necessity at some given moment, something anormal and even monstrous. Recognizing the interdependence and common interests of all men and the equality of all peoples, liberal statesmen strive for the creation of an international order which would eliminate war altogether. Wars exist, for the liberal conception, only as a result of the shortcomings of the political and social order which in a not too distant future may be overcome by the rational efforts of man. In the totalitarian philosophy war is the normal and welcome concomitant of all life, the supreme manifestation of vitality and virtue, an unalterable and dominating part of the whole system. Ultimately these two different and even opposite concepts of war rest upon two different concepts of the nature and destiny of man.

[27] *Op. cit.*, vol. VIII, p. 232; vol. IX, p. 32; vol. V, p. 311; vol. VIII, p. 131. The world leadership of Fascist Rome resounds in many other messages of Mussolini. "In questo mondo oscuro, tormentato e già vacillante, la salvezza non puo venire che della verità di Roma e da Roma verrà"; or "La Rivoluzione fascista non è soltanto il privilegio e lo sforzo dell'Italia, ma la parola d'ordine e la speranza del mondo," vol. VIII, pp. 140, and 254. On National Socialism in this respect see: *Revolutions and Dictatorships*, pp. 352 ff., 370 f.

18

The Soviet-Yugoslav Controversy: Nationalism and Communism*

The documentary record of the first decade of the Soviet-Yugoslav dispute broadens our factual knowledge and enhances our understanding of the position of communism in the contemporary world. It reveals some fundamental tensions in Communist doctrine and practice which often are hidden from the outside observer. Among those tensions the one caused by the prevailing strength of nationalism has played a prominent role in the dispute between the motherland of communism and the second most important Communist country in Europe. Soviet Russia under the leadership of Stalin and Khrushchev, and Yugoslavia under Tito's leadership, were in 1948, when the dispute started, and are today nations entirely subject to, and governed by, the Marxist-Leninist doctrine of history and society. Both were, and are, equally dedicated to it. What has separated them are not minor doctrinal differences but nationalist considerations.

The first Soviet document of the record presented here, a letter from Moscow to Belgrade dated March 20, 1948, speaks of the fact that the Yugoslav Communists had accused their fellow-Communists in the Soviet Union of "great-power chauvinism." In its reply the Yugoslav Communist Party stressed its love of its own country and complained that the economic position and the behavior of Soviet Russian experts in Yugoslavia exactly followed the pattern set, or supposedly set, by Western colonial administrators or "advisors" in dependent or semidependent territories. Naturally, the Yugoslav Communists did not formulate their complaint in these words, but the leaders in the Kremlin clearly understood the implication and answered accordingly. They termed the Yugoslav statement essentially anti-Soviet, because it identified the Russian Communist ambassador with an ordinary bourgeois ambassador, and put the foreign

* From the Introduction to Robert Bass (ed.), *The Soviet-Yugoslav Controversy* (New York: The East Europe Institute, 1959).

policy of the motherland of communism on a par with the foreign policy of capitalist imperialist nations.

The fundamental conflict between aspirations to national independence or self-determination, and a supranational imperial and ideological order based on the leadership of an "older brother" among the various participating nations, continues without letup. Khrushchev, who in 1955 sincerely tried to end the dispute, could not find ways of accommodation. The spirit of Yugoslav nationalism threatened to encourage nationalism throughout the Communist empire. In this situation Peiping, in May 1958, took up the cudgels for Moscow. Within the Communist realm, both Russia and China represent "great power chauvinism" in relation to the smaller nations. "Regarding the mistake of the Yugoslav Communist Party in departing from the principles of Marxism-Leninism and sinking into bourgeois nationalism," the Chinese Communists proclaimed, "we consider the criticism made in June 1948 by the Information Bureau of Communist Parties basically correct."

It is irrelevant to an understanding of the issues involved whether one calls the position taken by the Yugoslav Communists "bourgeois nationalism" or "national communism." Naturally the Yugoslavs themselves declare that they are free from, and opposed to, such a "heresy," whatever its name. Nor does it make much difference in the world of reality whether in the case of Soviet Russia one speaks of "great power chauvinism" or of the need for "the subordination of the interests of the proletarian struggle in one country to the interests of the struggle on a world-wide scale" with "the invincible camp of Socialist states headed by the Soviet Union." This is the way it was stated in the declaration of the Communist Parties at the fortieth anniversary of Lenin's seizure of power—a declaration which the Yugoslav Communists refused to sign.

Tension between nationalism and communism did not originate in 1948 with the dispute between Soviet Russia and Yugoslavia. Rather, it goes back to the time of Lenin's seizure of power. It is inherent in the attempt to establish a strictly unified world order in the age of nationalism. That tension has increased since 1945 when communism, until then confined to one country, became the official doctrine in a number of European and Asian nations outside the Soviet Union. But the one country controlled by communism after 1917 was itself a country inhabited by many nationalities. It was an empire holding against their will peoples of very different origins and backgrounds and subjecting them to the leadership of by far the most numerous among those nationalities—the Great Russians, who effectively occupied all positions of power. Lenin understood the potentialities of such tension within a multinational Eurasian empire from the beginning. Marx lived in western Europe in the middle of the nineteenth century at a time when the peoples of eastern Europe, of Asia, and of Africa were not yet stirred by nationalism. He had neither understanding of nor sympathy for the "awakening" of "dormant" nationalities. He recognized nationalism only for the highly developed "historical" nations of the West. Lenin, who grew up in eastern Russia, was one of the first to understand the growing impact of nationalism, not only among the peoples of eastern Europe but also among those of Asia and Africa. Marx foresaw in the Communist Manifesto that the twentieth century would become the age of pan-industrialization. What he did not foresee was the fact that the twentieth century is with much greater rapidity and intensity becoming the age of pan-nationalism. For tactical reasons, for the sake of communism and not of nationalism, Lenin tried to take the new nationalism into account.

He did it primarily within the confines of the old Russian Empire. The relationship between Great Russian or Soviet Russian nationalism on the one hand and that of peoples outside the Russian Empire on the other hand was for obvious reasons of no practical importance to Lenin. The Communist regimes of Hungary and of Munich were too shortlived to demand any tactical decisions about their relationship to the then as yet unconsolidated power of the Communists in Russia. For Lenin, therefore, nationalism was not a problem per se, nor did he accord to it any independent existence or rights. It was a subsidiary problem of the social revolution. It was subordinated to the question of establishing, maintaining, and expanding the dictatorship of the proletariat, or rather, of the international Communist Party which Lenin, consciously and theoretically at least, did not identify with Great Russian communism. Fundamentally, Lenin like Marx was an internationalist, hoping for the amalgamation of all peoples. In his ultimate world picture there was no room for small nationalities or for a multiplicity of tongues. His goal was the fusion of peoples into units of maximum dimensions as a step toward fusion on a global scale. For that reason he was, like Marx, partial to great nations, and in his case to the Great Russian nation and its absorption of all the small nationalities.

But as the master tactician that he was, he resisted every attempt to belittle the national question from an "international" point of view in the "transitional" period. His theory of nationalism was a weapon in his revolutionary struggle. "From the point of view of Socialism," he wrote, "it is absolutely a mistake to ignore the tasks of national liberation in a situation of national oppression." According to him the Socialists among the ruling or privileged nations were to stand, before the victory of communism, for the abrogation of all national privileges and for the right of the "oppressed" peoples to establish their independence. In every step they took they were to have regard for the sensitivities of oppressed peoples on national issues. Socialists among the oppressed peoples were, on the other hand, to proclaim the identity of the interests of their proletariat with those of the proletariat of the "oppressing" people. Thus, on the nationality question, the Socialists, under capitalism, had to "swim against the stream." Lenin was convinced that the nationality question would retain its significance for a long time even under the dictatorship of the proletariat, until Communist policy had succeeded in extirpating national hatred and mistrust. In his concluding speech at the Eighth Congress of the Russian Communist Party on March 19, 1919, Lenin declared: "The Bashkirs distrust the Russians, because the Russians are at a higher level of civilization and have used their civilization to rob the Bashkirs. Consequently in these remote districts the name Russian means 'oppressor' to the Bashkirs. . . . We must take that into account, we must combat it. But that takes a long time. We must go to work on this very cautiously. Above all such a nation as the Russians, who have aroused a wild hatred in all other nations, must be particularly cautious. We have only now learned to manage better, and even that only some of us as yet. Thus there are Communists among us who say that there should be 'uniform schools,' and that accordingly all instruction should be given in Russian. In my view a Communist who thinks in this way is a pan-Russian chauvinist. This tendency still exists in many of us, and we must fight it."

Thus Lenin devised a Communist nationality policy which for the time being, "as a transitional stage to the full unity of the workers of all peoples," proclaimed the principle of federation of equal nationalities. But in view of the strictly centralizing tendencies of Communist doctrine and the Soviet Party the question remained, "Who would set the tone and determine the language within the 'full unity of the workers of all peoples?' " There could not be genuine equality. During his last year of activity, 1922, Lenin himself became painfully aware of the degree to which Great Russian chauvinism asserted itself among the Party members. It would be better, he warned, "to stretch too far in the direction of complaisance and softness toward the national minorities than too little." He realized the importance of the issues at stake for the expansion of communism outside the Soviet Union. "It would be unforgivable if, on the eve of the emergence of the East, we should undermine our prestige there with even the slightest rudeness or injustice to our own minorities." In April 1923, the Twelfth Party Congress, under Stalin's leadership, rejected Lenin's warnings against Great Russian chauvinism. But at the Sixteenth Party Congress, in July 1930, Stalin himself complained of "the existing deviations in the Party in the field of the nationality question. I have in view in the first place the deviation of pan-Russian chauvinism and secondly the deviation of local nationalism. . . . These deviations exist, and the important thing is that they are growing. There can be no doubt about that." [1]

Only four years later, in 1934, Great Russian chauvinism ceased to be a deviation. The Soviet government itself directed the rewriting of the history of the Russian Empire and of the Soviet Union in a new, or rather in the old, nationalist tradition. For almost twenty years, until the death of Stalin, in 1953, the preponderance and leadership of the Great Russians among the peoples of the Soviet Union (and after 1945 the preponderance and leadership of the USSR represented by the Great Russian Communists among all the peoples living under Communist regimes), became official Moscow policy. Stalinist national communism went to great lengths in its chauvinistic fixation on Great Russian originality and priority. It outdid the nineteenth-century Czarist regime which had never accepted such an extremist nationalism as an official policy. In a similar way, when Stalin's efforts at friendship with National-Socialist Germany had failed, after 1941, communism under Stalin outdid previous Russian regimes in the official adaptation of pan-Slavism. Until

[1] The best introduction to the theory and practice of the national problem in communism will be found in Samad Shaheen, *The Communist (Bolshevik) Theory of National Self-Determination. Its Historical Evolution up to the October Revolution.* (The Hague: Lounz, 1956); Alfred D. Low, *Lenin on the Question of Nationality* (New York: Twayne, 1958); Richard Pipes, *The Formation of the Soviet Union, Communism and Nationalism, 1917-1923* (Cambridge, Mass.: Harvard University Press, 1954); and Frederick C. Barghoorn, *Soviet Russian Nationalism* (New York: Oxford University Press, 1956).

June 1941 Stalin had, of course, done everything possible to maintain good relations with Hitler in spite of German aggression against Czechs, Poles, and Serbs. In his report to the Moscow Soviet on November 6, 1941, however, he accused Hitler of the wish to "exterminate the Slav peoples, the Russians, Poles, Czechs, Slovaks, Bulgarians, Ukrainians, and Byelo-Russians."

The next day in his address during the Red Army parade he called upon Soviet soldiers to let themselves be inspired in the war by "the manly images of our great ancestors—Alexander Nevsky, Dmitri Donskoi, Kuzma Minin, Dmitri Pozharsky, Alexander Suvorov, Mikhail Kutuzov." By no dialectic could these feudal Orthodox saints and these Czarist Russian generals be regarded as the ancestors either of an army supposedly representing the many equal nationalities of the USSR or of an army which had its origin in a Marxist proletarian revolution. The principle of collective racial "guilt" was applied by the Moscow Communist government during the war against the Volga Germans, the Kalmyks, and several Mohammedan peoples in the northern Caucasus and in the Crimea. The Great Russian people, Moscow proclaimed, were the decisive factor in the victory of the Soviet Union in the Great Patriotic War against Germany. "For this reason the peoples of the USSR feel toward the Great Russians boundless confidence, tremendous love and gratitude." The same love and gratitude were expected from the Slav peoples, who, like the non-Russian peoples of the Soviet Union, were regarded as "younger brothers" of the Great Russians, since the Great Russians had not only won the war against Germany on behalf of the whole Soviet Union, but also had liberated the Czechs and the Poles, the Yugoslavs and the Bulgarians.

What the Moscow pan-Slavists had hoped for in vain in 1867—the union of all Slav peoples under the undisputed political and cultural leadership of the Great Russians—was almost realized by the Moscow pan-Slavists of 1945, thanks to official government support which had been refused in 1867. In his *Russia and Europe,* Danilevsky had demanded in 1869 the creation of a pan-Slav union under Russian leadership including all the lands east of a line drawn from Stettin on the Baltic to Trieste in the Adriatic. In 1945 this imperial dream seemed realized. On December 8, 1946, a pan-Slav congress met in Belgrade. It witnessed the triumphant affirmation of Moscow's hold over the Slav world. The Yugoslavs were regarded as the second-ranking Slav nation and Tito as the most trusted fighter for

Communist pan-Slavism, second only to Stalin himself. In his opening address Tito asked: "What would have happened if the glorious Red Army had not existed . . . with Stalin, the man of genius, at its head . . . which with innumerable sacrifices also liberated the Slav nations in other countries? For this great sacrifice which our brothers in the great Soviet Union made, we other Slavs thank them." A Pan-Slav committee was elected and Belgrade became its seat. A little more than a year later, Communist pan-Slavism came to an end. The Yugoslav "defection" created in the Slav "family of nations" a situation similar to that which existed in the nineteenth century as a result of the nationalist enmity of Poles and Russians. Like Poland then, Yugoslavia became the "Judas" and the "traitor," and a tool of "Western scheming" against the Slav cause which the Russians identified with Moscow and with their communism. The Yugoslavs rejected the "great brother" as the universal leader on the road to progress and liberty and as the protector of all Slavs and all Communists, to whom gratitude and veneration were therefore due. Though Moscow had to abandon its pan-Slavism, Communist dialectics continued to face the task of harmonizing the emphasis on Russia's nationalist uniqueness and the glorification of Russia's past with condemnation of even the slightest emphasis on the national originality of other peoples.[2]

The situation became so intolerable in the last years of Stalin's regime, and increased tensions so strongly within the Communist camp, that Khrushchev, as part of his de-Stalinization policy, tried to return to Leninist nationality policy. In his famous special report to the Twentieth Congress of the Communist Party of the Soviet Union, delivered in the closed session of February 24-25, 1956, Khrushchev referred to Stalin's "monstrous acts which were rude violations of the basic Leninist principles of the nationality policy of the Soviet state." Stalin, Khrushchev continued, followed a chauvinistic policy not only within the Soviet Union but also in its international relations. He played "a shameful role" in the development of the conflict with Yugoslavia. This conflict, Khrushchev insisted, "contained no problems which could not have been solved through Party discussions among comrades." But he underestimated the power of nationalism.

[2] See on this period, Hans Kohn, *Pan-Slavism, Its History and Ideology* (2nd ed.) (New York: Vintage Books, 1960); and, in a related field, Charles W. Hostler, *Turkism and the Soviets* (New York: Praeger, 1957).

Initially, Khrushchev succeeded in reducing the excesses of Great Russian chauvinism which had disfigured the Stalinist era. Through his visits to Jugoslavia, to India, and to other countries Khrushchev tried to break the circle of nationalist isolationism and egocentrism which Stalin had built around the Communist Great Russian Empire. But the relationship between communism and nationalism in the twentieth century represents a fundamental contradiction between Communist theory and practice, which no dialectic juggling with definitions, nor even diplomatic niceties, can solve.

The Soviet-Yugoslav dispute offers a perfect illustration of this contradiction. It is no accident that Yugoslavia's two Balkan neighbors, Communist Bulgaria and Communist Albania, have until now most faithfully adhered to the Stalinist line of anti-Yugoslavism. Yugoslavia and Bulgaria, fellow-Communists and fellow-Slavs, have for over seventy-five years, under all kinds of regimes, fought each other over the control of Macedonia. Tito's communism was unable to solve Yugoslavia's Albanian problem. Since the first Balkan war the Yugoslavs have claimed the northern part of Albania, and the Albanians have wished to "liberate" their racial brethren in Serbia, which is contiguous with northeastern Albania. These Albanians form the largest non-Slav minority in Yugoslavia. Following the principles and practice of Leninist nationality policy, Tito created the autonomous province of Kosovo-Metohija for the Serb Albanians, as he created the "republic" of Macedonia as a federal unit of the Federal People's Republic of Yugoslavia. How far he succeeded in solving the nationality problem in his Communist order can be as little ascertained or answered today as can the question of whether and to what degree Khrushchev has solved the nationality problem in his Communist order. It is significant, however, that the present leader of Soviet Russia delivered a sharp anti-Yugoslav attack on June 3, 1958, in a speech before the Bulgarian Communist Party in Sofia. In this speech he called the Yugoslav Communists a Trojan horse of imperialism. Today, as ten years ago, what separates the Yugoslav Communists from most of their fellow-Communists is not so much doctrinal differences as nationalist considerations.

19

The Problem of German Nationalism After 1945*

German nationalism has been characterized by the fact that of the two interwoven strains—an emphasis upon liberal constitutional rights after the Western pattern and a struggle for national power strengthened by authoritarianism and militarism—the second unfortunately carried the day in three decisive moments. The "war of liberation" of 1813 was directed primarily against the "alien" tyrant who embodied the spirit of the French Revolution; but the "liberation" helped the survival of domestic and largely unreformed tyrants. In the Revolution of 1848 the liberal elements were not strong enough to change the constitutional and social order in Germany. Their weakness was caused by their burning concern for "national" interests, for territorial expansion at the expense of Germany's neighbors. After 1866 the Liberal party in Germany was the very opposite of what is understood by liberal in the West. It was "the proudest standard bearer of Germany's imperialistic drives and the unquestioning defender of the Second Empire's policies and institutions. Indeed, the Liberal party was the prototype of a feudalist bourgeoisie, which acquiesced in the political dictates of an experienced ruling class and accepted its set of values and images." [1] It was Germany's misfortune that she had a Bismarck and not a Gladstone, even not a Cavour.

Bismarck's German Empire was the product of a victorious war. Probably it was the only modern state which was created and proclaimed in front of the besieged enemy's capital. There were Germans who in 1866 and in 1871 rejected Bismarck's ethos, doubted his wisdom and strenuously objected to the way in which he founded the German state. But their number was small. The majority of the Germans welcomed the proud edifice without scrutinizing its foundation. They attributed their military victory not to fortunate circum-

* From *Contemporary Review* (London), No. 1085, May 1956, pp. 261-266.
[1] Sigmund Neumann, *Modern Political Parties* (University of Chicago Press, 1956), p. 356.

stances and the diplomatic inferiority of Francis Joseph and Napoleon III but to an innate and permanent superiority of the German national system over the ways of Western liberalism. Yet less than half a century later—only twenty years after its founder's death —Bismarck's work built upon the Prussian monarchy collapsed. The German republic, which was proclaimed as a result of this collapse, was a republic with only few republicans, a democracy with only few democrats. It proudly carried the name Deutsches Reich and despised the less pretentious name Deutsche Republik. Thus it was no accident that in 1925, at a time when prosperity began to return to Germany and the war damage disappeared, the imperial Field Marshal Paul von Hindenburg became Germany's first popularly elected Reichspräsident. One year before, the old man had addressed a graduating high school class in the Republic. He told the young men that they "will revive the old Reich," and told the teachers to "educate the youth in this sense." Turning again to the graduating class he promised them that "you, my dear graduating class (meine lieben Primaner), will enter Paris as victors as your fathers did." [2]

It is true that Hindenburg did not foresee that it would be under Hitler's leadership that the young Germans would enter Paris, but he rightly sensed the general wish animating the Germans. They had after 1918 in their large majority learned nothing from the catastrophe of the Bismarckian Reich. The Third Reich was to revive, expand, popularize and vulgarize the glories of the Second Reich. National power and greatness took again, as they had in 1813, in 1848 and in 1870, precedence over human liberty and individual rights. In January 1935 the population of the Saar voted in full knowledge of the character of the Third Reich for nationalism against liberty, though the large majority of the voters were socialist workers and Roman Catholic. The Third Reich, too, as Bismarck's Reich, enjoyed great initial successes which seemed to prove to the enthusiastic Germans the superiority of their national system over that of the West. Yet Hitler's Reich which was to last for one thousand years and which even some people in the West regarded as the wave of the future, collapsed after only twelve years. The defeat of 1945 surpassed by far that of 1918.

The situation as it developed after 1945 was much more favorable to the growth of a liberal and pro-Western Germany than the situa-

[2] Adolf Grote, "Die beschönigte Katastrophe," *Deutsche Rundschau* (Stuttgart, January, 1956), p. 21.

tion in 1871 or in 1918. Two fundamental changes have occurred. There is no German Reich anymore, and though the Reich-mysticism still survives in small circles and in some oratory, a more sober view has on the whole accepted the transformation of the Reich into a republic. The old Reich tradition in Germany before the nineteenth century was non-nationalist and Christian. It was perverted in the nineteenth century into nationalist channels. One of its ancient good elements has however been revived in the post-1945 Germany, its federal character. The federal structure can provide a protection against the dangerous modern German trend towards the overevaluation of centralization, efficiency and bigness. The other change is the disappearance of Prussia. Königsberg in Eastern Prussia, where Frederick I was crowned the first Prussian king on January 18th, 1701, is today a Russian city, called Kaliningrad. The lands east of the Elbe which formed in their social-economic and psycho-political backwardness the backbone of the Prussian ruling class, are today partly under Polish administration and have been subjected to a social-economic revolution, which, whatever its final outcome may be, will not allow the restoration of the agrarian conditions which made Bismarck's regime possible. The center of gravity in Germany has shifted from east of the Elbe to western and south-western Germany, to lands of a social structure and political climate closer to Western attitudes. Both President Heuss and Chancellor Adenauer represent the traditions of western Germany where they were born.

The first decade of the existence of the German Reich under the Weimar constitution was full of storm and stress. Violent putsches and terrorist acts darkened the period. Bitter resentments and utopian expectations disfigured the vision of large circles, especially of the youth, who refused to see reality and were thus willing to follow any leader who promised to undo what they regarded as the unmerited defeat of 1918 and to realize the daring dream of that world leadership to which many Germans believed themselves entitled. In comparison with the first decade after 1918 the ten years which have elapsed since the breakdown of National Socialist Germany in 1945 have been quiet and orderly. The young men who were in their early twenties in 1945 had been hardly ten years old when Hitler assumed power. Their mental and moral formation had taken place in the Third Reich. The teenagers in the 1940's were born into the Reich. One could have expected to find among them fanatical resistance to the occupation and to the new Western political order established in the German Federal Republic. No terrorist acts were committed, however. The young German generation, perhaps for the first time in 150 years since the rise of the Burschenschaften in the "War of Liberation," showed itself sober and realistic. It may not be actively pro-Western; it certainly is not enthusiastically anti-Western. Anti-Western sentiments seem today much stronger in Germany among the generations in their fifties and sixties, who were born in the Kaiserreich and who have abandoned their faith in Hitler for a revived and re-interpreted faith in Bismarck than among the German youth. That too is one of the hopeful signs in the Germany of today.

It is more among the older than among the young Germans that one hears it said that the Western powers were stupidly mistaken by not joining Germany in her aggression against the Soviet Union. The Germans who speak in this way overlook the fact that National Socialist Germany was as anti-Western, anti-humanitarian and barbaric as the Soviet Union. The West did not select the Soviet Union as its ally nor was it Western policy which brought it into the heart of Europe. It was Germany which by dividing Poland with the Soviet Union and by abandoning the Baltic states to Moscow in 1939 destroyed those barriers which protected not only Europe but even anti-European Germany from the growth of the Soviet power. After having made common cause with Moscow against the West in 1939, Germany turned in her insatiable demand for conquest against Russia and thus unwittingly but by her own deeds brought the Soviet army into Central Europe. The West succeeded, in a war imposed upon it by Germany, to liberate large parts of Germany from the frightful tyranny of National Socialism. Unfortunately eastern Germany has not been liberated. It continues under a tyranny equally frightful and repulsive to that under which it has suffered and largely by free choice from January 1933. For Hitler's tyranny was to put it mildly no less brutal than the tyranny of the present rulers of eastern Germany.

The other argument advanced today by German nationalists of the older generation, unfortunately also among university circles, is the contention that National Socialism was not deeply rooted in some of the ideological and social traditions of Germany, especially of the Germany which developed in the nineteenth century, but was an importation from the West, a product of mass democracy and industrialization. It is true that National Socialism could not have risen in a purely aristocratic and pre-industrial society, but the fact is that it did not rise in the democratic industrial societies of the United States or of Great Britain, in spite of mass unemployment there. It rose in Germany because Bismarckian Germany became a highly industrialized country without fundamentally changing the authoritarian foundations of its society. National Socialism was not only the product of specifically German—or perhaps Central and Eastern European—conditions but above all the product of the insufficient Westernization and liberalization of modern Germany. The German Federal Republic is the first real attempt to create a Westernized and liberal modern Germany.

The West, and with it the German liberals, can on the whole be satisfied with the progress achieved by the Germans in the last ten years. Naturally the old trends are still there and are still strong, and it could not be otherwise. These last five years Germany has been extremely successful, and in modern times Germans were rarely capable to bear success without becoming overbearing.

Yet one should not overlook the great positive factors promoting the development of a liberal and Western, rational and moderate nationalism in the German Federal Republic. The youth is distrustful of the formerly so popular nationalist slogans and emotions. In the newspapers the reader will find a much greater sense of international responsibility than in the Weimar Republic. The sharp anti-French and anti-Western assertive nationalism coupled with a self-pitying sentimentalism which characterized much of the German press after the defeat of 1918 is very rare today. Even among the historians there has been a decided change for the better. After 1918 they organized a comprehensive campaign to vindicate Germany's innocence before and during the war and to convict the Allies as the cause of all evil. Such trends are of course not missing today, but they do not dominate as they did after 1918. The *Vierteljahrshefte für Zeitgeschichte,* edited by Hans Rothfels and Theodor Eschenburg, is a quarterly which tries to give an objective picture of the recent past and represents an important contribution to the political education of the Germans. In the famous *Historische Zeitschrift,* the oldest and representative organ of German historical scholarship, its editor Ludwig Dehio subjects Gerhard Ritter's defense of the German pre-Hitlerian militarism to a respectful but sharp criticism, which would have been unthinkable in the Bismarckian Reich or in the Weimar

Republic.[3] In an essay of unusual brilliancy Dehio shows the connection existing between Frederick the Great, Bismarck and Hitler, in spite of the great differences in the climate of the periods—the powerful and uniquely Prussian dynamism which has caused the catastrophies of the twentieth century. "The two hundred year old policy of militarism, which has transformed an unknown small country into the mightiest continental power, has inoculated the newly formed nation with the faith in armaments, discipline and authoritarian leadership, and finally led Germany from the continental soil, in which Prussian policy developed, into the alien oceanic spaces. The deepest roots of the catastrophe which befell Germany was the German imperialism with its tremendous navy, the outgrowth of the old militaristic Prussian policy in the midst of a new and different society," the nature of which the Germans did not comprehend.

Dehio's article is only one contribution to the discussion about the wrong turns which Germany policy—and even more the German mind—took in the last two hundred years; this discussion started in Germany after 1945 with an insight and a courage which has been unknown since 1870. In a recent short book Ludwig Dehio warns against the revival of old illusions, against the widespread German tendency to forget that the most terrible World War, a *German* world war, had cost mankind unprecedented sufferings.[4] Twice, Dehio says, the Germans erred in putting national unity and power before individual and constitutional liberty. He warns against a third attempt of this kind, the case for which is strongly put by many "neutralists." There is good reason for hope that the German Federal Republic will heed this warning. The chances for a free Germany in the Western sense of the word, a Germany co-operating with the West in the interests of human liberty and humanitarian civilization, seem better today, in spite of the recrudescence of manifestations of the older forms of German nationalism, than at any time in the last one hundred years.

[3] Ludwig Dehio, "Um den deutschen Militarismus," *Historische Zeitschrift*, vol. 180 (August 1955), pp. 43-64.
[4] Ludwig Dehio, *Deutschland und die Weltpolitik im 20. Jahrhundert* (Munich: Oldenbourg, 1955).

PART FOUR

*The World
In Which We Live*

20

One World?*

The Second World War raised many hopes for a decline of nationalism, for an accommodation of conflicting group ideologies, and for the growth of international society. Yet the end of the war saw everywhere national, class, and ideological conflicts exacerbated to a degree hardly known before. In the struggle against the German and Italian invasions, national sentiment, and thereby national ideologies, myths, and customs, were mobilized. These helped more in the "struggle for liberation" than any appeal of an ideal future world or general considerations of freedom. At the same time conflicts of various origins and backgrounds have become interlocked. The two most powerful emotional appeals of the late nineteenth century—nationalist and class ideologies—have been fused in our day by all the totalitarian movements. This fusion has increased the fervor and the antagonistic character of the nationalist, as well as of the class (socialist) attitudes. This phenomenon has been in no way confined to German National Socialism or to the various Fascist movements which united the appeal of social revolution with nationalist emotion. To the surprise of many, communism, originally a decidedly antipatriotic, purely class ideology, underwent a similar development.

These fusions of nationalist and class ideologies have strengthened the barriers against the growth of a world society and of a world consciousness. The process of the "nationalization" of communism in Russia during the years from 1934 to 1944 is well known and has often been described. Perhaps a historian may point out as one of its outstanding features the "liquidation" of the school of Pokrovsky, the foremost Marxist historian. Entirely absorbed in the schematism

* From *International Journal* (Toronto), Vol. II, No. 4, Autumn 1947, pp. 308-315. Reprinted with permission.

of economic class causation, he taught that Russia was following the same course all other countries had taken, only retarded, and that the development of all mankind was one. He sharply ridiculed all patriotic legends and national sentiments. He turned his critical objections especially against Russia. "In the past," he declared, speaking of imperialism, "we Russians were the biggest robbers imaginable." [1] He explained the war of 1914 as caused mainly by Russia and the Triple Entente. Pokrovsky's interpretation of history, which was one-sided and fanatical, was highly praised by Lenin. Until the historian's death in 1932, his word represented dogmatic truth in all historical questions. But a few years after his death the Bolshevik leaders called his history "essentially liquidationist," a cover for the "Trotskyite-Bukharinist retainers of Fascism."

Meanwhile the Bolsheviks had rediscovered the originality of the Russian national past and the glories of old Russia, of czars and saints, of generals and patriots. Even the Bolshevik October Revolution was now interpreted as a patriotic deed which had saved Russia from defeat in 1917 and had laid the ground for the national regeneration and thereby for the revenge of Russia. The high point in this revaluation of history was perhaps reached by Stalin himself in his brief address after the Russian victory over Japan. The defeat of 1905, which for forty years had been welcomed by all Communists as a just outcome of the worst imperialist aggression on the part of Russia, was now interpreted as a stain on Russia's history. Stalin expressed the joy of the men of his generation who had allegedly waited forty long years for this moment of history to undo the alleged ignominy of the 1905 defeat. That the 1945 victory was in any way due to the efforts of Russia's allies was not even mentioned in Stalin's triumphant address extolling the glorious deeds of Russia's armies.[2]

A similar fusion of national and class ideologies has taken place among the Communists outside Russia. In Paris the Communist organ, *L'Humanité,* is advertised as the organ "de la renaissance française." The poet Aragon to whom "mon parti m'a rendu les couleurs de la France," wrote a book entitled *Servitude et grandeur des Français* (Paris 1945). Communists who have discovered "true

[1] See Max M. Laserson, *Russia and the Western World* (New York: Macmillan, 1945), p. 152 ff.
[2] Address over the Soviet radio, September 2, 1945. See *New York Times,* September 3, 1945.

democracy," have become "truly French." "Français (voir bien français) est à la mode," Etiemble wrote. "Non pas, comme vous le croiriez, chez les disciples de Barrès. Chez les fidèles de Staline." In 1945 a book *Une Politique de grandeur française* appeared written not by de Gaulle but by Maurice Thorez, with a preface by Jacques Duclos.

The German Communist Party publishes today the *Deutsche Volkszeitung,* a title reserved fifteen years ago for German nationalists. Communist propaganda in Germany leads the most extreme nationalist demands for national unity and greatness. Anton Ackermann of the party's Central Committee said on February 5, 1946, before the first Central Cultural Congress of the German Communists, that only "the working people—by that we understand the proletarian and the peasant, the engineer and the artist, the scientist and the teacher—are the carriers of national concerns (Träger der nationalen Belange) and the champions of the interests of the fatherland." He demanded an indivisible and united Germany and violently opposed all demands for the separation of German territory (outside those eastern lands annexed by Russia or Russian satellites). Separatism was proclaimed the "moral enemy of German culture." [3] In Czechoslovakia a Communist prime minister officially proposed in 1946 to limit full political rights to Czechs and Slovaks; race, not class or party, decided; a conservative capitalist of Czech descent is privileged as against the Communist proletarian of non-Slav stock.

This mutual strengthening of class and national antagonisms is heightened by the new religious fervor which, in the modern age of masses and totalitarianism, invests all emotions and ideas with a new absoluteness and thus deepens the stresses and cleavages dividing mankind into unbridgeable abysses across which an understanding no longer seems possible. This development sharply reverses the trend toward universal understanding and international society which had been growing up since the eighteenth century. From the early Middle Ages to the seventeenth century mankind had been rent by conflicts in which group consciousness had been deepened to a degree of absolute exclusiveness by the identification of group and religion, of consciousness and salvation. Byzantium and Rome, Christianity and Islam, Protestantism and Catholicism faced each other with the claim that those outside the group were infidels and damned

[3] *Deutsche Volkszeitung: Centralorgan der Kommunistischen Partei Deutschlands,* February 6, 1946, p. 3.

souls. All manifestations of life—the family and festivals, the working day and economics, science, learning, and the arts—were encompassed by the faith.

The world was divided into war-tight compartments, into conflicting civilizations between which friendship and collaboration seemed unthinkable. The eighteenth century changed all that in the process of secularization. The various fields of human endeavour became autonomous. Faith lost its totalitarian character. It was replaced by a new attitude of tolerance. In the liberal age various nationalities, classes, religions, and ideologies could collaborate. This attitude spread in the nineteenth century from its point of origin in Western Europe all over Europe and penetrated even into Russia and Asia. In that century intercourse all over the globe became freer than ever before. Europe broadened into the world. The most remote corners of the earth were opened up—men, goods, and ideas travelled with few hindrances; peace seemed assured; the language of constitutional liberty promised to become a universal language; long-lasting wars among civilized nations were thought absurd; and more and more nations were drawn into the compass of the fast-growing one world and one civilization. For the first time in history mankind was on the way to becoming an open society.

Today ideological—religious or pseudoreligious—stresses and cleavages rend the world apart as never before. It has become full of closed societies again. Travel is restricted, free exchange of communications is hampered, liberty is under the control of secret police. The absoluteness of faith of the Middle Ages has returned to many men and lands: this time intensified by the dynamism of national emotionalism, of social revolution, and of technological progress. Nothing impressed me more strongly during my visit to Russia in 1931 than this new Middle Ages, to use an apt expression proposed by the Russian philosopher Nicholas Berdyaev. I wrote then that Russia

> is turning back past the age of Enlightenment and even the Renaissance, past which we cannot retrace our steps and by which her masses have scarcely been touched, to the beliefs of mediæval mankind. Communism asserts the same claim to absoluteness as mediæval faith. The outlook on life of those who adopted it has nothing in common with Europe. For the Western way of thought is the product of the Renaissance, and above all of the Enlightenment. These have built up humanism on the basis of which scepticism has been ac-

cepted as a legitimate intellectual attitude, and critical consideration as an indefeasible right of the individual. Only such a scepticism, prepared to admit that alongside one's own path to truth there may be others, can permit liberty of thought and can practice tolerance and form as basis for the growth of individualism. What Europe has won thus in breadth and freedom, it has lost in certainty. The fanaticism of the Communist springs from the mediaeval absoluteness of his type of faith. The consciousness of the saving truth gives him his assurance: the opponent is always wrong, for he supports the enemy of the true ordering of things: the Communist is always right, for he is contending for God's world. There can be no compromise: objectivity or a cautious weighing of issues under the promptings of conscience or of the knowledge of the processes of life and of history, are not admitted. In this secularized gospel the hardness that shrinks from nothing is the true service to the attainment of the goal. The Communist's certainty of victory is based on an eschatological confidence free from all moral contexts.[4]

What I wrote in 1933 is even truer today. For, as a result of Russian survival and victory in the Second World War, the Communist faith has hardened in its certainty.

A similar attitude animates all other totalitarian creeds. Tolerance and compromise which alone can make the growth of one world society possible are not only scorned; from the point of view of totalitarian faith they represent a sin against mankind's salvation. Men who do not share the faith and movements which run counter to its aims are regarded as representations of the evil which has to be eradicated and with which no communion is possible.

At the same time these new faiths, carried on with the impulsion of great and self-confident mass movements and fusing nationalist and socialist emotions, naturally develop aggressive tendencies. They wish to create the one world of their own, a monolithic world without the latitude and plurality of the liberal age. Such a one world alone assures, or seems to assure, to the new nationalistic and socialist totalitarian religions the certainty of salvation for the whole of mankind and of security for themselves. Only if the enemies of the true faith are liquidated or at least rendered harmless can there be complete security. For the coming period of history is regarded as an inescapable struggle between the forces of absolute good and the forces of absolute evil. Of the inevitability and decisiveness of this conflict

[4] Hans Kohn, *Nationalism in the Soviet Union* (London: Routledge, 1933), p. ix.

on a world-wide scale all totalitarian faiths are deeply convinced.

These modern totalitarian movements which undermine the growth of a world community and of an international society gain their weighty armor by combining the universal appeal of their faith with their identification with one powerful nation which becomes its standard bearer. There is no accidental choice involved: the chosen nation, heir to the chosen people idea of the Old Testament, is one that is prepared for its task by its historical development and its national traditions. Thus Germany became the standard bearer of fascism, Russia of communism. Such an identification of a universal movement with a national tradition and a national destiny is not entirely new. Salvador de Madariaga in a recent book has described Spain in her golden century in such a way that with few changes of names it could apply to Russia or Germany of our days:

> Philip II was a Spanish king, but of a Spain which he had identified with the interests of the Church. He did not discriminate between the interests of Spain and those of the Church, because for him they were the same. All over the world, and in particular in England, in France and in the Netherlands, the Catholic party worked for him, whether subsidized by him or not; for Catholics everywhere knew that if Philip of Spain lost a battle they lost it also. The Catholic party was thus both the Spanish party and a universal party knowing no frontiers. It was a party which everywhere with vociferous insistence demanded to be allowed freedom of worship and propaganda; but which at home tolerated no other faith. Strong, unified, solidly united under the King, Catholic Spain was ever ready to subsidize or even organize armed risings and revolutions in other lands in order to put the Catholic party in office. It kept a close watch on the few Spaniards it allowed out and an even closer watch on the still fewer foreigners it allowed in. Books were welcome but on condition that they conformed to a strict orthodoxy.[5]

It is in recollection of this golden century that the Spanish Falange has rekindled today the dream of a total faith with Spain as its center. But present-day Spain is much too poor in material and human resources to advance beyond the stage of a dream to that of a real threat. Totalitarian faiths become a serious danger to an international society only if, backed by one of the greatest military powers

---

[5] Salvador de Madariaga, *Victors Beware* (London, 1946), pp. 191 ff.

of the period, they can hope to establish an international society according to their own idea and image.

This disruption of the basis of international society is also promoted by various pan-movements. Those most fashionable today are not so much movements of true unity as threats to international society. In recent years pan-Germanism and pan-Slavism have, on a basis of racial unity, of the call of the blood, tried to undo the history of 1,000 years and to wipe out all profound differences of civilization which separate the German-speaking Prussians from the German-speaking Alsatians or Swiss, and the Slav-speaking Muscovites from the Slav-speaking Czechs. While the Germans dreamt a short while ago of pushing the German borders to include thirteenth-century Hanseatic settlements and eighteenth-century centers of emigration, the Slavs have now carried their frontier to where it was in the thirteenth century, on the Oder and the Neisse. While the Germans planned to expel and move whole populations to fulfill their aspirations of uniformity, Slavs are now expelling Germans from the soil where they had been rooted for many centuries, in order to abolish that diversity which according to Mill nourishes liberty best.

A few years ago many hoped for the United States of Europe, or at least for Danubian and Balkan federations which would replace the Austrian and Ottoman empires in their important functions as guardians of the peace. This movement of European unity can be based upon many centuries of a common civilization, the legacy of Rome and of the Middle Ages, of Renaissance and Reformation, a community of traditions which includes all the nations from England to Poland, from Italy to Norway. While this pan-European movement is rapidly losing ground, a fictitious unity of pan-Asia is being loudly proclaimed, a solidarity of the colored races who have little in common but a passing negative situation in their relations with the highly industrialized nations. Otherwise there is no link connecting the Bantu and the Hindu, the Malay and the Berber, the Arab and the Chinese. In fact the deep racial, religious, and class antagonisms within Asia are only momentarily covered up by a common antagonism towards the white man. The tension between Mohammedan and Hindu, the treatment of the darker races in India, the competition of Chinese and Indian imperialisms in the Himalaya region, in Burma and Malaya and the conflicts with the native nationalisms—these are only symptoms of the stresses and cleavages in Asia that will develop as soon as the control of the white man is removed, which for the last century has maintained peace over wide areas and assured a growing equality of races, castes, and classes before the law.

At a period, therefore, when means of technology seem to bind the various parts of the globe more closely together than ever, and when the objective conditions for the development of international society seem propitious to an unprecedented degree, the beliefs and loyalties of peoples over vast parts of this globe have taken on forms which aggravate conflicting ideologies and deepen antagonistic class and national consciousness. It is impossible to predict whether we are facing a purely transitional situation which may give way to a new age of enlightenment, of growing tolerance and therefore of an easier mutual accommodation of the various groups of mankind, or whether we have entered, as many German and Russian thinkers have proclaimed, a period of conflict—the outcome of which will decide the fate of the globe and the type of man. As far as we can judge from historical experience, however, no single totalitarian faith will be able to impose itself upon or to undo the plurality and diversity of mankind. As soon as this hard fact will be accepted—and it will be the task of statesmanship to bring about this realization at as low a cost of suffering and sacrifice as possible—the fervent faiths of today will lose some of their absoluteness and aggressiveness. International society can only grow when fanatical ideologies will lose their hold upon the mind and spirit of so many millions and will give way to a broader spirit of tolerance and compromise, of self-criticism and fair-minded objectivity. Then only will men of different convictions and religions and people of different nationalities and races be able to live together in an international society with emphasis on common human values and individual personal independence, and not on national rights or exclusive schemes of world salvation.

21

Germany and Russia: Old Dreams and New Realities*

In the Second World War as in the First World War, Germany and Russia confronted each other in a life-and-death struggle which was to determine, for a long time to come, the old rivalry between Germans and Slavs for the control of central eastern Europe. Both resumed the struggle in a new revolutionary garb, but below this garb the old aspirations and trends live on. National Socialist Germany continued, in spite of all the bitter scorn which its spokesmen poured on the Wilhelminian and the Weimar periods of the Reich, all the decisive dreams and errors of the past, exaggerating them in every instance to such a degree that the quantitative change almost became qualitative. Yet from Bismarck to Hitler the forces of history have shown their tremendous staying power.

Viewed superficially, the case of Russia has been different. There the Revolution seemed to mark a complete break, a really new beginning. Yet very soon men who knew Russia could point out that the so-called dictatorship of the proletariat was in many of its measures and forms only a continuation, and an exaggeration, of traits of Russian life familiar from pre-Revolutionary times. And as time went on, the conscious and even emphasized continuity of Russian historical trends began to transform all aspects of Soviet society and Soviet cultural life, until at present the deep-rooted Russian traditional imperial aims have become manifest to every observer.

The Second World War entered the decisive stage with the tremendous battles on the eastern front, in which Russia and Germany found themselves at grips after the fateful June day in 1941 when Hitler attacked the Soviet Union. The conflict came, in spite of the fact that the Kremlin showed itself most anxious to avoid it, and had in every way tried to prevent or at least postpone it by compliance with the demands of the German dictator, for whom Stalin probably felt more sympathy and respect than for the unfamiliar

* From *International Journal* (Toronto), Vol. I, No. 2, 1946. Reprinted with permission.

forms of political life and liberties in the Western democracies. Hitler himself originally had wished to avoid the war on two fronts of which Bismarck had been so afraid and which his masterly diplomacy had so successfully avoided. Hitler had bitterly blamed Wilhelm II for having fought simultaneously Germany's enemies on both fronts. And now Hitler was to repeat the mistake of Wilhelminian diplomacy.

Both world wars arose, at least partially, from Slavo-Germanic tensions in the lands between the Baltic and the Adriatic. The First World War had its immediate cause in the conflict of German and Russian imperial expansion in the Balkans, and the Second World War in a struggle between Germans and Slavs for the Baltic Sea. The acute tension between Russia and Germany in the Second World War began at the moment that their conflicting ambitions again openly clashed in the Balkans, with Germany's march into Bulgaria and Yugoslavia in the early spring of 1941. That Hitler turned this tension into war, very much against the Kremlin's ardent hopes, resulted largely from his faulty interpretation of history. Hitler became a victim of his own racial theories. As a result, the Baltic and the Balkan regions have become exclusively Russian spheres of influence.

In his *Mein Kampf* Hitler had directed Germany's expansionist aims against Russia:

> Here Fate itself seems desirous of beckoning us. By handing over Russia to Bolshevism, it deprived the Russian people of that intellectual leadership which so far had brought about and guaranteed its existence as a state. For the organization of the Russian State was not the result of the political abilities of the Russian Slavs but only a wonderful example of the state-forming efficacy of the German element in an inferior race.

Like many other Germans, Hitler saw Russia as a product of the imposition of the positive state-building efforts of the German race, from Rurik's days to the Germanized courts of the czars, upon the anarchistic tendencies of the Slav race. Hitler interpreted the Russian Revolution as a godsend for Germany, for it de-Germanized Russia's leading class and in Hitler's imagination Judaized it:

> For centuries Russia lived from this Germanic core of its upper leading classes. Today this core can be regarded as almost totally

exterminated and extinguished. In its place the Jew stepped in. Impossible as it is for the Russians to shake off the yoke of the Jews by their own strength, it is equally impossible for the Jew to preserve the mighty empire for a long time. He himself is no element of organization but a ferment of decomposition. The giant empire in the east is ripe for collapse. And the end of Jewish rule in Russia will also be the end of Russia as a state. We have been chosen by fate to become witnesses of a catastrophe which will be the mightiest confirmation for the soundness of the racial theory.

Hitler's vision guided German foreign policy. It was to prove his racial theories. The fight against Soviet Russia was to be the fight against the Jewish world danger. To Hitler, who had considered the Jew the real cause for the German debacle in 1918, Russia ruled by Jews seemed ripe for debacle. And this catastrophe would be a turning point in world history, a *Weltwende,* which would not only establish forever a Germanic age, but end also the Jewish era of history with all that it comprises—Christianity, liberalism, and bolshevism. While Russia, according to this view, disintegrated under Jewish influence, Germany was built up by Hitler into an even more strictly unified and centralized power. But the history to which Hitler appealed showed that his premises had been wrong. The racial theory proved unsound. The Slavs were not unable to form a state, the Jewish element did not disintegrate Russia; on the contrary, Russia emerged from the Revolution a stronger and more integrated nation than she had ever been before. But the visionary Hitler could not perceive the discrepancy between reality and his racial theory. Even in 1941 he lived in a dream world in which he saw Russia, as "entirely out of the picture as a technical factor, Russia which even today [1926] cannot claim possession of a single factory capable of producing a motor vehicle that really runs." His reading of history led Hitler to a racial or national enterprise, a *Germanenzug,* which ended with a definite victory of the Slavonic world over the Germanic. The catastrophe prophesied by Hitler came, but it took a very different course from that he had so confidently expected in 1926 and in 1941. Thanks to the regime which he had instituted in Germany, nobody could raise a voice of reason against the tumult of passions which out of the depths of his heart Hitler had kindled in the whole German nation.

Hitler with his contempt for reason and for the rational eighteenth century forgot the wise words which Frederick the Great, whose militarism and Machiavellianism he so often imitated, wrote in the preface to his *History of My Own Time*:

> Whoever wisely and with a feeling heart considers these matters must be touched by the many misfortunes which rulers bring over the peoples by lack of thought or by passion. . . . The most profound thought is needed; for not only must the true nature of things be fully considered, but also all consequences of an enterprise must be foreseen. If it is not reason alone which decides, but if passion interferes, such an enterprise cannot possibly have a happy result. Statesmanship demands patience; and mastery of an able man shows itself in his doing everything in its right time.

Swayed by prejudice and passion, Hitler launched his country into an adventure which brought about an unprecedented integration and strengthening of the Russian state and the complete disintegration of the German state as created by Bismarck and carried on by Hitler.

In setting out triumphantly eastward in September 1939, Hitler dreamt of fulfilling German destiny. The Germans followed him willingly, dazzled by the vision of German world power, a prospect which seemed to them attainable since Bismarck had formed the German Empire as the strongest military power on earth. They even regarded the realization as due them by Providence, for had not the Germans the best army, the best order, the highest efficiency, the finest morality? Hitler represented and formulated the deep-seated conviction of their superiority which has animated the German masses since Bismarck. In 1937-1938 the older people regarded the coming war with some misgivings, because they remembered the privations suffered during the First World War. But Douglas Miller, the capable commercial attaché at the American embassy in Berlin, reported in 1937 that the "youth of the country, with its career to make, is talking and thinking about war continually. The public has heard so much about it that practically everyone has come to accept the inevitability of war. It is upon this basis that the boys of today are planning their own lives." [1] In 1938 and again after the German-Russian pact in 1939 even the older Germans felt happy. They became confident that Hitler would achieve their goal of world hegemony without war or at least without any dangerous war. This joyful

---
[1] Douglas Miller, *Via Diplomatic Pouch* (New York: Didier, 1944), p. 244.

expectation which united almost all Germans behind Hitler and his inspired strategy received its first shock when the German armies had to live through the first Russian winter, and later a much ruder shock after Stalingrad.

Few if any Germans in the eighteenth century dreamt of anything like German world hegemony. The educated classes were liberal humanitarians; the masses were entirely uninterested in any political or national aspirations. With the beginning of the nineteenth century, German intellectuals, professors, writers, and poets began to dream of the German world mission (pan-Germanism is not the product of industrialists or Junkers, but of intellectuals). However, only after Bismarck had through blood and iron put the greater part of Germany under Prussia's domination, pride in the power of their arms and faith in the superiority of their morale imbued the German masses with a mirage of German world leadership, pursued with an unparalleled, methodical seriousness. The Weimar Republic in no way represented a break with the Bismarckian Reich; it was its continuation, the Deutsches Reich under a republican guise.

With Hitler's fall the Bismarckian Reich had disintegrated. Following the interval of Allied occupation, during which there is no central German government, no spokesman for the Reich, a fresh beginning may be made, characterized not necessarily by a breakup of a unified Germany, but in any case by the creation of a different Germany on an entirely new foundation.[2] The catastrophe, the *Weltwende* foreseen by Hitler, will end the dream of the German millennium and the German Reich.

Thus this war may liberate the Germans "from the terrible dream of being a great power—a dream which is terrible for them even more than for others."[3]

* * *

[2] The foremost Protestant theologian of the German tongue, Karl Barth, has pointed that out in his *The Church and the War* (New York: Macmillan, 1944): "I venture to voice a general thought with a view to Germans, which I have especially at heart, and which I suppose will have to be taken up seriously, namely: when the German menace is somehow completely ended, if at the same time a real service is to be rendered to the constituent German nations and people, then we shall have to dare to understand the Germans better than they understand themselves and thus nullify the unfortunate work of Bismarck—the worst of the nationalistic errors of the nineteenth century. We shall have to restore their local sovereignty to the different German states to a degree and in a sense still to be determined. The German Reich rests on a misapprehension which has worked out ill not only for other peoples and nations but above all for Germany itself."

[3] Karl Barth, *op. cit.*, p. 44.

Out of the Second World War Russia emerges as a great world power, much greater than that which emerged from the victorious wars of Peter I against the West and from the victorious wars of Alexander I which helped to destroy the power of Napoleon and carried the Russian armies into the heart of Europe. This vast empire, which since the sixteenth century has expanded east and west as no other empire in history, now for the first time resumes its advance march simultaneously east and west, through Europe and Asia and even into Africa. For Russia has weathered successfully a crisis which shook her foundations more dangerously than the invasion of the Poles at the beginning of the seventeenth century or that of Napoleon at the beginning of the nineteenth. In this crisis Russia found her salvation by appealing to the strength of her millenary tradition. In 1917 the world was startled by the conquest of Russia by bolshevism; today traditional Russia has absorbed bolshevism. The "International" has been replaced by a new anthem emphasizing the role of *Velikaya Rus,* of Great Russia. While the "International" in the ferocious individualism of its French author proclaimed that "nobody will bring us liberation, neither a Czar nor a God nor a hero," the new anthem glorifies Stalin in the way in which the greatest Czars of the past wished themselves acknowledged as the real and only source of all Russian greatness.[4]

It is as wrong to regard National Socialism as an international doctrine—fascism—which had taken hold of Germany, as it would be to regard bolshevism as a local and almost accidental manifestation of an international ideology—communism. Though there are certain similarities with movements in other lands, National Socialism has its roots deep in German history and carries on some of the most fundamental traditions of German civilization. The same is true about bolshevism in Russia. Bolshevism has deepened and strengthened Russian nationalism; it has made the names of the great Russian writers of the nineteenth century known and beloved to the hundred million inhabitants of the Russian empire, Russians and non-Russians, to whom the names formerly were entirely unknown. It has made of dim heroes of the past like St. Alexander Nevsky, St. Dmitri

---

[4] Walter Kolarz, *Stalin and Eternal Russia* (London: Lindsay Drummond, 1944), p. 25: "In the eyes of the masses, the absolute power and glory of the person at the head of the state are the best possible evidence of continuity with the Russia of old, in which the highest representative of authority was not only a sanctified person but was also one whose right it was to effect the most abrupt and brutal changes in the personnel of the State apparatus."

Donskoi, or Alexander Suvorov—the man who smashed the social rebellion of Pugachev and the national revolution of the Poles and almost defeated the French Revolution on behalf of autocracy—shining examples inspiring the imagination and the loyalty of countless soldiers and workers. It has replaced the passive, aimless Russian of the nineteenth century, the Oblomov type, by the "hero of socialist labor" who creates with immense pride a new Russia, transforms a vast land, and finds full scope for his energies in directed empire-building, without demanding political rights or activities.

It has been the subject of frequent comment that Russian literature of the last five years has glorified all the "counterrevolutionary" heroes of Russia's religious and Czarist past and scorned the revolutionary heroes of Russia or of mankind whose names twenty years ago filled the pages of Soviet writings. The Stalin prizes for literature have been awarded to these patriotic glorifications of the past. Probably no nation at war produced such a typically "patriotic" literature as Stalinist Russia did; even patriotism there has been fanatical, uniform, and standardized. Sergey Borodin received the prize in 1941 for his novel extolling Dmitri Donskoi; Vladimir Kostylev and Alexey Tolstoy have made Ivan the Terrible the hero of a novel and a play; Vladimir Solovyev has brought Field Marshal Kutuzov to the stage, as Bakhterev and Razumovsky did with Field Marshal Suvorov; while Sergey Sergeyev-Tsensky, one of the most respected older writers of Russia, has gained new fame by two historical novels, *Sevastopolskaya strada* (Sevastopol's ordeal during the Crimean War), and *Brusilovsky proryv* (the story of Brusilov's offensive of 1916). The approach to the past has been thoroughly revised, from feudal saints to the officers of the First World War. Lenin's generation would hardly recognize the present mind and face of Russia.

Two familiar sights characterize the face of Russia today as they have of old: the army, with its discipline and etiquette, its gold-braided and epauletted officers with their orderlies and special clubs, and its decorations (among them the order of Alexander Nevsky, created by Peter I in 1725, abolished by the Russian Revolution, and reintroduced by Stalin in 1942); and the Church, which, though there is as little religious liberty as there are other liberties, has been revived in its ancient and hallowed splendor and become again a willing instrument of state policy and imperial expansion.

The Russian mind expresses itself in literature and in the interpretation of history. Alexander Nevsky was regarded in 1930 in the

Soviet Encyclopaedia as a man who had "performed valuable services to Novgorod mercantile capitalism"; his present title to fame, his victory over the Teutonic Knights, was not even mentioned. Pugachev, regarded only a very few years ago as a forerunner of bolshevism, leading the great rising of peasants and peoples of the Volga and the Urals, has been discarded for Suvorov, who defeated the people's leader in the eighteenth century. Stalin in his speech of November 7, 1941, called out to the Russian people: "Let the manly images of our great ancestors—Alexander Nevsky, Dmitri Donskoi, Kusma Minin, Dmitri Pozharsky, Alexander Suvorov, Mikhail Kutuzov—inspire you in this war." [5] National ancestors, not socialist fighters; Russian aristocrats, saints of the Church, generals of the Czar —one only a patriotic commoner—not leaders of the revolutionary movement in Russia or among the proletarians of the world: that is the source of inspiration in the great patriotic war out of which the Russian Empire—with its ancient pride of Moscow as the Third Rome, the seat of the true empire and the true faith—is emerging, rejuvenated and firmly anchored in the proud consciousness of the masses.

For Lenin in 1917 the Russian Revolution was only the starting point of a world-wide movement, in which not backward Russia but the advanced Western countries would take the lead; for Russian youth today, as for the Slavophiles in the nineteenth century, Russia, as a result of her peculiar character, is the center which through its religion (formerly Orthodox, now Communist) will save the world which is disintegrating under false doctrines and heretic errors. In this new and yet old light, Russian history becomes one, from Ivan the Terrible to Stalin the Great.

Present Russian historiography even fosters the legend that in 1917 the regiments under Bolshevist influence fought better against the Germans than the others. Mikhail Glinka's opera, *A Life for the Czar,* which in 1836 marked the birth of Russian national music and was the official apotheosis of czarist Russia, (its peasant hero Ivan Susanin saved the life of the czar at the time of the Polish invasion of Russia in the seventeenth century), has been re-adapted one hundred years later by shifting peasant loyalty from the czar to the nation. Into the great song of praise for the dynasty, such words as the following were interpolated:

[5] Joseph Stalin, *The War of National Liberation* (New York: International Publishers, 1942), p. 38.

Glorify thyself, native soil. Glorify thyself, my native land.
May for ever and for eternity be strong our beloved native land.

Stalin's foreign policy at present everywhere follows faithfully but infinitely more efficiently and ruthlessly the line of the former policy of the Russian empire. The old Russian imperial patriotism drove Moscow, as soon as the opportunity was favorable, even in 1921, to reincorporate Georgia and other trans-Caucasian lands into the empire; it now restores and expands the western borders of the empire. Like in 1795 and 1861, it organizes and finds a pro-Russian party among the Poles, and it pushes now the imperial policy in the Middle and Far East. Even under the official coloring of bolshevism, the Russian patriotism, the old Russian distrust of the West, of liberal and capitalistic society with its individual rights, the unbounded faith of the Russians in themselves and their mission, persisted. "Throughout their whole history, during centuries of oppression and tyranny, Russians have always fought well against an invader, and they have always deeply loved Russia. They loved her when the words Mother Russia were jeered at because a proletarian is supposed to have no fatherland." [6] Now this Russian patriotism has come openly to the fore.

Russia emerges from the war as the strongest military land power in Europe and Asia, following her own path so different from that of Western liberalism, and assuming the defense of all the former Russian Pan-Slav and Pan-Asiatic aspirations in their most advanced form. Russian power and German folly have created a new situation in Europe: Germany, since Bismarck the strongest power in Europe through numbers, industrial equipment, and efficiency, will find itself in all these three fields dwarfed by Russia, even should Germany revive as a power. In Russia the growing contact with the freedom of the West, if not artificially suppressed by the government, may start again that fermentation and that revolutionary cycle which began when her victorious troops under Alexander I came into contact with and learned about Europe. As the result of this meeting of

---

[6] Markoosha Fischer, *My Lives in Russia* (New York: Harper, 1944), p. 266. Mrs. Fischer gives a most informative and intimate picture of the real life of Russia after the revolution and down to 1939. Mrs. Fischer is much too faithful to the ideals of liberal humanitarianism to feel at home in the autocracy and the nationalism which Stalin's Russia inherited from old Russia and made more efficient and all-pervading. She tells how one day her boys came home from school all flushed with excitement. In both schools they had been told about the wonderful heroes of Russia's past, and old czarist generals had been presented as anti-Fascist fighters.

Russia and Europe, that astonishing flowering of the Russian intelligentsia began, which not only gave the world one of its greatest literatures, but also forced Russian autocracy to abandon traditional Russian lawlessness and gradually to introduce the rule of law and of individual rights. There is no reason why we should not hope for a similar process of transformation in post-war Russia. But the necessary condition for a true liberalization of Russia is the example and faith of the West in its civilization and values of liberty under law, not an admiration for Russian power and ideals like that it has shown for German power. The hope of the future lies in the full integration of Russia—a process which began in the eighteenth century and ended abruptly in November 1917—and the reintegration of Germany, into Western civilization.

22

Germany Between East and West*

Germany likes to call herself the heartland of Europe. That is geographically true. But culturally and spiritually Germany since Roman times throughout most of European history has been a frontier land of Western civilization. In the Middle Ages and in the eighteenth century Germany was an integral and important part of the West. During those periods Germany was the mediator through whose good offices Western civilization flowed eastward. Yet there were times, from Arminius to Hitler, when Germany spearheaded the war against the West. From German Romanticism on, Germany also influenced the anti-Western ideas and movements among the peoples further east. Romanticism in other lands was an individualist trend of poetry and art, in Germany it was a political and social

* From *Current History*, April, 1955. Copyright by *Current History*. Reprinted with permission.

philosophy, an all-encompassing *Weltanschauung*.[1] German Romanticism played a great role in the awakening of nationalism in Central and Eastern Europe. A similar role was played by German historicism. To the Germans who looked for inspiration westwards, Ranke pointed out that everything of value in Germany had been developed in contrast to the West. Ranke asserted the right of any state to follow its own logic in politics, to be different from Western liberalism. The German break with Western liberal thought in the first half of the nineteenth century "was carried forward in a destructive but inevitable chain reaction into Slavophilism, Sinophilism, Indophilism, etc." Wherever the standards of the most advanced Western nations clashed with local traditions, "an ideological revolt against the West was the consequence of local nationalism." [2]

In the First German Reich the center of gravity had been in the west and south. The multiform German states there, not the borderlands of Austria and Prussia, represented Germany. Bismarck's Second Reich, which arose out of a revolution against many German spiritual and political traditions, shifted the center of gravity eastward. Berlin became for the first time the capital of Germany and was to hold this position for seventy-five years. More important, Prussia's easy victories carried the conviction of German moral superiority and might over the West from a limited circle of intellectuals into the broad masses. Treitschke who now occupied Ranke's chair in Berlin became the representative spokesman of the widespread contempt of the West and Western ideas.[3] Bismarck's system of alliances was not only formed to help maintain Germany's position but also to act as a bulwark against the penetration of Western ideas. Bismarck felt an intense contempt for British statesmen. "For ten years he played on their convictions and aversions, their ignorance and their false assumptions, with uniform success. Each time his trickery became obvious he relied on English military weakness to prevent hostile action, and on the gullibility of the London government for the possibility of renewed deception; each time England acted as he had foretold. He did not even attempt to hide his contempt. . . . By exposing the weakness of liberal England, he was

---

[1] See Hans Kohn, "Romanticism and the Rise of German Nationalism," *The Review of Politics*, XII, (Oct. 1950), pp. 443-472.
[2] See Theodore H. von Laue, *Leopold Ranke, The Formative Years* (Princeton University Press, 1950), pp. 73 f., 99 ff.
[3] See Hans Kohn, *Prophets and Peoples* (New York: Macmillan, 1946) ch. IV.

making more difficult the revival of German liberalism."[4] In that respect Hitler followed in Bismarck's footsteps.

The War of 1914 was widely regarded in Germany as the war against the West. The most literate expression of this view can be found in the *Betrachtungen eines Unpolitischen* which Thomas Mann wrote toward the end of the war. "An almost unanimous opinion has held from the very beginning that the spiritual roots of this war, which has been called rightfully the German war, lay in a new and perhaps the most magnificent eruption of the ancient German struggle against the spirit of the West." Mann had no doubt that the German and the Russian mentality were united in a similar concept of humanism and that both were opposed to the West. "Are the Russian and German attitudes toward Europe, the West, civilization, politics and democracy, not closely akin? Haven't we Germans also our Slavophils and Westernizers? . . . If spiritual affinity can form the foundation and justification of political alliances, then Russia and Germany belong together: their agreement now, their union for the future, has been since the beginning of this war [the war of 1914] the desire and dream of my heart. It is more than a desirability: it is a political and spiritual necessity should the Anglo-American alliance endure."[5] Few books are as important for an understanding of Germany, and of Thomas Mann today, as these Reflections of a Non-Political Man.

The defeat in this First German War of the twentieth century did not lead to a re-consideration of the German spiritual and political attitudes with which Germany had entered the war. Germany prepared, spiritually, her revenge against the West. Many Germans sought therein the cooperation of Russia where Lenin had succeeded to overthrow the short revolutionary government with its Western ideas and had turned Russia resolutely against the West. The election of the aged Fieldmarshal Paul von Hindenburg as "republican" President of the German Reich (for the German republic of 1919 considered itself as the German Reich with its center in Berlin) marked a visible turning point.

In the lectures which Lord Acton delivered at the University of Cambridge in 1900, he pointed to the similarity and simultaneity of

---

[4] See Raymond James Sontag, *Germany and England, Background of Conflict 1848-1898* (New York: Appleton, 1938), pp. 45-90, 233 f., 313-341.

[5] Thomas Mann, *Betrachtungen eines Unpolitischen* (Berlin: S. Fischer, 1920), pp. 7, 443 ff. See also pp. 16, 150, 186 f., 328, 332, 346, and his *Rede und Antwort* (Berlin: S. Fischer, 1922), pp. 273 f., 168 ff., 208.

the Prussian and Russian monarchies which rose in the eighteenth century and which he regarded as a new type of government. "Government so understood is the intellectual guide of the nation, the promoter of wealth, the teacher of knowledge, the guardian of morality, the mainspring of the ascending movement of man. That is the tremendous power, supported by millions of bayonets, which grew up in the days of which I have been speaking at Petersburg, and was developed, by much abler minds, chiefly at Berlin; and it is the greatest danger that remains to be encountered by the Anglo-Saxon race." [6] After 1918 the fact of a diplomatic and military cooperation between Germany and Russia was less remarkable (after all, both nations had lost the war and were eager to restore and expand their former imperial frontiers) than Germany's spiritual openness toward the east. The inclination to radical extremism, to utopianism and to the contempt of the West was thereby enhanced to a dangerous degree. With uncanny insight D. H. Lawrence wrote in 1928, before the onset of the economic crisis, from Germany to a friend: "Immediately you are over the Rhine, the spirit of the place has changed. It is as if the life had retreated eastwards. As if the Germanic life were slowly ebbing away from contact with Western Europe, ebbing to the deserts of the east. Something has happened which has not yet eventuated. The old spell of the old world has broken, and the old bristling savage spirit has set in. . . . Back, back, to the savage polarity of Tartary, and away from the polarity of civilized Christian Europe. This, it seems to me, has already happened. And it is a happening of far more profound import than any actual event. It is the father of the next phase of events."

That Germany was attracted by the east and could think of preparing for the Second German War was partly the fault of the West. Germany had almost won the first war, especially after Lenin's Russia had turned against the Allies. Only the very late (and imperfect) cooperation of the Western democracies defeated Germany. Clemenceau pleaded in vain for the maintenance of this unity. Its dissolution almost immediately after victory offered to the Germans a mighty temptation. The isolationism of the democracies disorganized Europe and undermined the peace structure. A strong and united West might have attracted Germany: instead, the West offered also spiritually the spectacle of a society doubting its own values and steeped

---

[6] Acton, *Lectures on Modern History*, ed. by J. N. Figgis and R. V. Lawrence, published as *Renaissance to Revolution* (New York: Schocken Books, 1961), p. 289.

in cynicism and illusionism. A book like Oswald Spengler's *Decline of the West* exercized an immense influence upon the German mind. The conviction became general among German intellectuals that the West was exhausted, that there were no longer any regenerative forces at work, that Germany was called upon to fill the political and spiritual vacuum created by the self-abandonment of the West. The apparent weakness of Western liberal society seemed to support the predictions of German romanticists and historians, of Russian Slavophils and Communists, the thesis of the West's decrepitude. In a new "age of longing" many Western intellectuals looked eastward for the wave of the future.

The Second World War reunited the Western democracies, this time much more effectively than in the First War. It dispelled also some of the current clichés about democracy—the inefficiency of an economic order based upon private initiative and the relative freedom of labor and capital, and the weakening or disappearance of the democratic spirit and institutions under the strain of a major war. On the contrary, democracy emerged from the war stronger in Britain and the United States. This time Germany was defeated far beyond the scope of 1918. The Bismarckian Reich which essentially had survived in the Weimar Republic was destroyed. Prussia ceased to exist. The center of gravity in Germany shifted again westward. At the same time, however, Germany became the center of the new conflict between East and West. Again she became a frontier land of Western civilization.

The new conflict between East and West was directly Hitler's work. Communism had been contained in Europe by the barrier of intermediary states from Finland to Romania. Hitler destroyed this barrier and brought Stalin's rule into Central Europe, first by his accord with Stalin in 1939 and then by his attack upon Stalin in 1941. It is one of the most disturbing factors in present-day Germany that some Germans reproach the Western powers of not having sided with Germany against Russia, and even add that it should have been done in defense of Western civilization. The Germans, and not the West, destroyed Poland and paved Stalin's road westward. The Germans were then as much opposed to the West and Western civilization as the Russians were. Through German fault, the whole of continental Europe, with the exception of the two small enclaves of Sweden and Switzerland, was early in 1941 under the control of totalitarian powers, hostile to the individual liberalism, the freedom of thought and the spirit of tolerance of the West: Stalin and Hitler, Mussolini and Franco, shared proudly and confidently the European continent, all of them equally convinced of the aproaching fall of Britain and of the end of liberal democracy.

Hitler's attack on Russia forced the democracies and the Soviet Union into an unwilled cooperation which given the nature of Russian Communism could not last in spite of some wide-spread illusions of the West. Though in the long run Russian communism is the more formidable foe of Western civilization—on account of the size and the resources of the Russian empire and on account of the potential universal appeal of Marxism and Leninism, which the racial arrogance and the power emphasis of German nationalism lacked— German nationalism has been in the nineteenth and twentieth centuries the spearhead of the war against Western civilization; the high intellectual qualities and achievements of the Germans, their great past as a member of the Western community in the Middle Ages and in the eighteenth century, made this spearhead even more dangerous.

The defeat of Germany in 1945 had two unavoidable consequences. The "strange alliance" came to an end, though public opinion in the United States was unprepared for it and received Mr. Churchill's great speech at Westminster College in Fulton, Mo., and the late Ernest Bevin's courageous policy in Greece as proofs of British "warmongering." Mr. Churchill called for an Anglo-American "fraternal association" to hold the "expansive and proselytizing tendencies" of Soviet Russia. These tendencies were directed above all against Germany. For the second unavoidable consequence of the German defeat was the effort on the part of Eastern totalitarianism and Western democracy to win Germany for its side. Thanks to her geographic position, her great industrial resources, her scientific standing and the work-habits of her large population, Germany was the pivot for the control of continental Europe. Soviet Russia understood it long before the United States knew it. For that reason the Soviet Union annexed Königsberg and half of eastern Prussia and encouraged the procommunist regimes in Poland and Czechoslovakia to expel Germans living in territories settled by them about seven centuries ago. This action of a ruthless Slav nationalism, which had been preceded by similar measures of a ruthless German nationalism, tied Slav Poland and Czechoslovakia for their own protection against a resurgent German nationalism indissolubly to Russia. It is understandable that the expelled Germans long for a return to their ancient homes. It is hardly conducive however to the lessening of Slav fears when some German scholars hark again upon the theme of the civilizing and Europeanizing mission of the Germans in eastern Europe and go even so far as to claim that the Sudetenland or Poland were parts of Europe immediately before 1945, that means under Hitler.

Many German and European-continental intellectuals saw in fascism an effort to unite Europe against the danger of Atlantica and Eurasia, of the United States and Russia. Some German intellectuals even today propagate a unification of Europe under German leadership—some even wish to include the other "young" peoples, Spaniards and Italians, as junior partners—against the threat by West and East. Was not Hitler right? they ask. Did the Americans and the Russians not meet at the Elbe and divide Europe and Germany, its heartland, between them? It is forgotten that Hitler alone brought America and Russia to the Elbe. The Americans never had the slightest desire to go there. The Russians might have wanted it but they had not the slightest opportunity or chance to do it. What fascism foresaw as a possibility and what it allegedly wished to prevent, the destruction of Europe, it alone brought about.

The crime of fascism of having destroyed Europe cannot be undone by good intentions or wishful thinking. For a long time to come, Europe will be divided and Germany with it, not between America and Russia but into a part freely belonging to the West and into a part where the war against the West is continued, not on military battlefields but in every realm of the mind and in every branch of social life. As a result of the war, started by Germany, this country will be for the foreseeable future divided as Europe will be divided. There seems no reasonable prospect for Russia allowing eastern Germany to become soon again a land of Western civilization. Any concession there would dangerously weaken the Russian control of her other satellites. Free elections in a Soviet land are unthinkable, for if conceded in one land they could be claimed in other lands. They are so contrary not only to communist practice but to communist doctrine that they would undermine the whole communist structure. Communism is only thinkable as the total rejection of everything which the West calls freedom; even in Russia Lenin came to power by disregarding the will of the revolutionary Russian people and its expression in the one freely elected Russian parliament, the Constituent Assembly.

Yet compared with the situation of 1941 many European lands have been restored to Western civilization. The boundaries of free society have been widely expanded in Europe during the last ten years. One of the great achievements was the restoration of freedom to the majority of the German people. Freedom does not mean national independence; the Germans under Hitler, the Russians under Stalin, certainly had national independence. What they entirely lacked was freedom. By regaining freedom, they are rejoining the West. American and British policy in Germany may have committed many mistakes but that could not have been otherwise. The Western people had fought a bitter war against an enemy professing openly atrocious doctrines and frequently fully living up to them. They were faced by an unprecedented situation, not only in Germany but in the world. Soon however a promising policy emerged, though it was never fully clarified, which was the policy of integrating Germany as far as she was not under Russian occupation into the West. This policy presupposed, though it was again not clearly recognized, the very unity and strength of the Western democracies which after 1918 was sorely missing. The closest Atlantic union is not only necessary to contain Russian communism: it is equally indispensable for winning the Germans to the West and for removing the temptation of the revival of a German aggressive nationalism and of European hegemonial aspirations.

It is understandable that a deep distrust of Germany still prevails in many European countries. It is now almost one hundred years that German liberalism suffered in the constitutional crisis in Prussia (1859-1866), a crushing defeat from which it never recovered. The defeat was due not to the lack of the appeal of liberalism to the educated classes in Prussia and Germany at that time but to the fact that they preferred national unity and power—there was no question of independence because Germany was independent—to individual liberty and respect for constitutional rights. Is there a chance for German liberalism now? The prospects are better than they were at any previous time. Free Germany—and it should not be overlooked that this Germany is in population and economic power still the strongest state west of Russia proper and east of the Atlantic Ocean—is no longer a Reich, as the Weimar Republic was, it is a Federal Republic; its capital is in the West; with the complete breakdown of the German state in 1945 new foundations could be laid for national life. Above all—and that was the most astonshing fact after twelve years of Nazi indoctrination—the German youth was sobered and had lost the spirit of the nationalist radicalism and the socialist utopianism which characterized the Weimar period. The quick economic recovery of Germany, due partly to American help, partly to German industriousness and the free enterprise system, has restored some of the old and undesirable traits of the old Germany. This should not surprise us; in an age of excessive nationalism in so many parts of the world it could hardly be otherwise. This situation demands the very thing which was lacking after the First World War: on the part of the Western democracies unity and vigilance; on the part of the German liberals (the word liberals taken in its broadest context) resolute courage not to succumb to the lures of German nationalism as they succumbed in 1866 and after 1918. Both these demands are equally difficult of fulfillment. Natural inclinations fight in the democracies against unity and vigilance and among German liberals for nationalism. Yet on their fulfillment depends the future of Germany and, to a large extent, of the West.

The integration of the German Federal Republic into the Western World has too much been discussed lately under the aspect of Germany's contribution to the military defense of the West. It is gratifying that for the first time since 1866 there has been no demand for German rearmament by the Germans themselves. The German youth does not welcome the reappearance of German uniforms. One hears frequently people in the West saying that one could not hinder Germany to rearm. That is an obsolete point of view. There was an eagerness in Germany to rearm after 1918: then only the unity of the democracies could have either prevented it or kept it within reasonable bounds. Today this desire does not exist. This is rather a good augury for the future. As things stand at present, Germany's contribution to a reasonable and united Atlantic defense force cannot be dispensed with. Properly directed in Germany and balanced by the unity of the Western Allies the new German military forces need not weaken German democracy. It is even not impossible that the army of the Bonn Federal Republic, slowly and systematically built up on new foundations, will fundamentally differ from the armies of the German Reich which marched in 1871 and again in 1918 through the Brandenburg Gate in Berlin. One much discussed danger seems to me non-existent: it is out of the question that this new army could become under any foreseeable conditions a threat to the Soviet empire. A much smaller and weaker Soviet empire resisted successfully Hitler's grandiose armies.

But there is a danger in the overemphasis put upon the military integration of the German Federal Republic. It is a secondary issue, for Germany and for the West. The main issue is the spiritual and political integration of Germany into the West. Without it, the rearmament of Germany might become ultimately a danger, not so much to Russia as to Germany and the West. American policy today concentrates, not only in Germany but also in Spain, too much on military issues. There is already some foolish talk in Germany of a German-Spanish axis supported by America. Neither a nationalist Germany nor a fascist Spain can strengthen the free world, though under certain circumstances the free world could enter into a "strange alliance" with them against an over-powering Russian communist threat as it entered into a similar alliance with Russian communism against the then overweening force of fascism. But in a long-range view the West can gain only through a Germany which has made Western ways its own—in its own fashion, for there is much room in the West for great diversity, as it exists between Americans and Britishers, Frenchmen and Norwegians. Such a Germany would no longer be a spearhead of the struggle against the West but add greatly to its intellectual strength and its democratic security.

23

Germany in the New Europe*

Europe ten years ago, in 1946, was in the throes of the aftermath of the intellectually, socially, and economically most devastating war engulfing the whole of the continent. Out of this chaos a new order and a new prosperity have emerged in the astonishingly brief space

* From *Current History*, November 1956. Copyright by *Current History*. Reprinted with permission.

of a decade. Order and prosperity are today to be found everywhere in the free countries of Europe.

None of the countries of free Europe has made a more dramatic recovery than the German Federal Republic. Ten years ago there was no German state, no German administration or government existed, and the rubble and ruin of the German cities offered examples of ghastly poverty and hopelessness. Today the German Federal Republic represents the most modern state the German people have ever achieved, and the German population has one of the highest standards of living in contemporary Europe.

This turn of events is partly due to the innate efficiency and discipline of the Germans, but it is also largely due to American foreign and economic policy, exemplified in NATO and in the Marshall Plan, which gave to free Europe military and economic security for the most difficult transitional period of the last decade.

Yet the Germans of the German Federal Republic are presented with an issue of a national importance and of a gravity unknown after 1918. In 1918, Germany lost some territories which were largely inhabited by non-Germans, and the German minorities living there were of course allowed to stay and enjoy, in most cases actually, in a few cases perhaps only theoretically, civic and political equality.

In 1945 millions of Germans were driven out of homes where their ancestors had been settled, worked and died, for many centuries, and these territories were resettled by non-Germanic populations. Of the remainder of Germany, about one-fourth was turned into a Communist state and shared the fate of the Eastern European lands.

The issue of a reunion of the two Germanies—the German Federal Republic and the German Democratic Republic—and the resettlement of the expelled Germans in their homes are very serious issues, infinitely more serious than the two issues plaguing Germany after 1918, the wrongs of the Treaty of Versailles and the "abnormality" of what was called by the Germans the Polish Corridor. These were largely fictitious, yet deeply felt issues which inflamed German nationalism. And the flames, not extinguished by energetic action from the West or by German liberals, caused the conflagration of the 1930's. The present issue is a legitimate and serious one, yet it is not deeply felt, it does not feed the flames of German nationalism, and as far as the future can be foreseen, it will not by itself cause a conflagration.

The elections of September, 1953, turned into a vote of confidence for the leadership of Dr. Konrad Adenauer, the most pro-Western chancellor Germany had for a very long time. He became the head of a coalition which seemed firmly entrenched and commanded a secure majority. In the last months this majority has been shaken, there appear deep cleavages in the coalition, and the firm grip of the chancellor, who is now an octogenarian, is visibly slipping.

Under these circumstances, the coming elections of September, 1957, seem to leave the field wide open for a new leadership. As in other European states, the older generation, the generation of the men who grew up in the nineteenth century, and who determined Europe's future in the years immediately following 1945—the generation of Churchill, Attlee, de Gasperi, Adenauer—is fast receding from the stage of history. The question of succession is everywhere posed, not only in Germany. In Germany proper the question can be formulated thus: after Adenauer, what?

Adenauer was not an easy taskmaster. A man of autocratic temper and by training an administrator and not a parliamentarian, he has nevertheless accomplished much: the Germans, a people without a strong or highly esteemed parliamentary tradition, have become accustomed to the game of parliamentary life; and Bonn, a most improbable site for a capital, is slowly affirming its position. More important, under Adenauer's leadership, the Germans have for the first time in their modern history associated themselves unquestioningly with the West. They have renounced, at least for the time being, the game which they played under the Weimar Republic, of regarding themselves either as a spiritual bastion against the West or playing a self-centered policy of balance between East and West.

These are Adenauer's lasting achievements, whatever his many shortcomings may be; these are his great services to Germany and to the West; these perhaps will make him appear one day a more constructive statesman (though certainly not so great a personality) than Bismarck. Many critics will, not without some justification, object to Dr. Adenauer for his having excluded one of the two great Western-oriented parties in Germany, the Social Democrats, from participation in his administration, and for having relied exclusively on his own Christian Democratic Union.

Until very recently this attitude seemed to relegate the Social Democratic Party to a permanent minority position, a very regrettable fact for democracy and the West. But perhaps it was good that in the first years of the new Germany, a Western-oriented party formed the opposition. Had both Western-oriented parties, the Christian Democratic Union and the Social Democrats, formed a coalition government from the beginning, the role of the opposition would have fallen upon non-Western-oriented, democratically unreliable parties, and a dangerous situation could have arisen.

In no democracy, as is well known from the case of the United States, is it desirable that any one party should too long and too exclusively be entrusted with the task of administration. The Christian Democratic Union in Germany seemed as firmly entrenched as the Democratic Party in the United States at the height of the popularity of the late President Franklin D. Roosevelt. It is certainly in the interest of the development of German democracy that the struggle for leadership in the German Federal Republic become much more open. The German parliamentary system will then more closely approximate that of the Anglo-American countries. Then politics will consist of a struggle between the "ins" and the "outs," and no longer of bitter hostility between irreconcilable ideologies.

For it is one of the great achievements of the German Federal Republic, which Adenauer probably did not intend, that the Germans today are far less addicted to metaphysics, to *Weltanschauung*, than they formerly were and boasted to be; that they have become sober and practical; that they think—though they do naturally not always talk—in the framework of political and social realities instead of daring nationalist desirabilities.

It was one of the greatest mistakes of the Social Democrats under the Weimar Republic that they did not actively participate in the building of the Weimar army for doctrinaire reasons, and that they thus left this indispensable instrument of power in the hands of the enemies not only of social democracy, but of democracy and of the West.

Today the situation is different. After 1918, most Germans desired the restoration of Germany's armed power; and their love of the uniform and of the paraphernalia of militarism had survived the non-accepted and non-believed defeat of 1918 and perhaps even gained in ardor. Today this love has gone. German youth, including the veterans of the last war, men now in their thirties, reject the former adoration of the army. The new German armed forces will play the role which armed forces play in the English-speaking countries.

The danger of a renewed halo over the army is at present negligible. A more realistic attitude on the part of the German Social Democrats, their active participation in building up the spirit and the body of the new German armed forces will completely remove the danger. On July 7, the parliament of the German Federal Republic accepted the military service bill with 270 against 166 votes after a long and heated discussion. Nobody can read the speeches without being impressed by the high level of the discussion, and of German parliamentary life in general. In his concluding words, the Speaker of the House tried to express what both parties, those who had accepted and those who had rejected the bill, had in common:

> It must never happen again that the world fears or distrust us. If the world does not love us, it should at least respect us and it should trust the new Germany.

For the future of Europe, of the West, and above all, of Germany, the development of NATO is of utmost importance. NATO has started as a military alliance in an emergency. As such it has fulfilled its task remarkably well. It has acted as a shield behind which free Europe and free Germany could consolidate themselves. But NATO is potentially much more than a military alliance, and it can continue to secure the peace and prosperity of free Europe and of free Germany in the years ahead only if it becomes more than a military alliance, a firm union of peoples who share similar fundamental attitudes toward individual liberty and parliamentary representation and who wish to cooperate for the strengthening of their free institutions and their economic life.

Such a closer and more integrated North Atlantic community is perhaps for no other nation as important as for Germany. For it is the safest guarantee against the revival of that anti-Western or self-centered spirit which in the last 100 years has wreaked so much havoc, politically, and above all, spiritually, in Germany, and through Germany in the free world.

24

Germany and Russia*

German-Russian relations belong to modern history. For most of the past, Germany's center and German interests were in the West. Only the rise of Prussia to ascendancy in the eighteenth century and the simultaneous westward expansion of Russia started the process of German-Russian relations. It was not without significance that Prussia became a kingdom in 1701 by a ceremony held in Königsberg, Prussia's easternmost city. In the Seven Years War (1756-1763) the Russians originally fought as Austria's allies against Prussia. They invaded eastern Prussia and in October, 1760, even entered Berlin. The position of Frederick II, Prussia's famous king, became desperate. He was saved unexpectedly by the death, in January, 1762, of Empress Elizabeth of Russia, whose successor Peter III, Frederick's fervent admirer, defected from the alliance, made peace with Prussia and thereby saved Frederick and his realm.

From that time on, Prussia and Russia were on the whole on friendly terms. Frederick II and the Russian Empress Catherine II were the main movers in the partition of Poland. A long common frontier of the two countries was thereby established. After the defeat of Prussia by the French in 1806, it was the intervention of the Russian czar which saved Prussia from extinction. At the beginning of 1813 the Prussian army was the first to join the Russian armies which advanced into Europe, in the pursuit of the French. During the ensuing period of the Holy Alliance the court of Berlin relied generally on the court of St. Petersburg. Both were determined to stop the penetration of Western liberal ideas into central and eastern Europe. It was at that time that the Prussian monarchy rose to leadership in Germany. The Prussianization of Germany in the nineteenth century—a process which none could have predicted in the early eighteenth century—put German-Russian relations into the forefront of German policy.

The Prussian statesman who was mainly responsible for this development, Otto von Bismarck, worked for the preservation of

* From *Current History*, January, 1960. Copyright by *Current History*. Reprinted with permission.

German-Russian friendship. His attitude was based on two considerations: Russia's and Prussia's common interests in keeping Poland partitioned and subjected, and their common hostility to Western liberalism and democracy. This hostility was one of the motivating forces behind Bismarck's policy of alliances. The treaty which he concluded with Austria-Hungary and Italy on May 20, 1882, declared that one of its aims was "to fortify the monarchical principle and thereby to assure the unimpaired maintenance of the [existing] social and political order." As long as Bismarck directed German foreign policy he succeeded, in spite of his alliance with Austria-Hungary, in keeping Russia in close friendship with Prussia in pursuit of their common anti-liberal ideas.

The picture changed with the adventurous new foreign policy of Bismarck's successors. This policy drove autocratic Russia and republican France into a defensive agreement against the vague threats of the new German policy. Theories of race and national destiny, alien to Bismarck's thought, now found expression among German and Russian intellectuals. Pan Germanism looked to the east and southeast for the fulfillment of the historical mission of the German people; Pan Slavism looked to the west and southwest as a field in which the manifest destiny of the Russian nation would be realized. The war of 1914 found Germany and Russia in opposite camps. In fact, the war started in a struggle between Slavism supported by Russia and Germanism supported by Germany. Whereas German conservatives saw England and English liberalism as the chief enemy in the war of 1914, German socialists justified the war as a conflict with Russian autocracy.

The war ended in 1918 with an unexpected result, the defeat of both antagonists, Russia and Germany. Both lost, for the time being, in power and territory. The many nationalities which lived between Germany and Russia from the Arctic Sea in the north to the Aegean Sea in the south and which were subject before 1914 to Russian or German control or influence, gained their independence and established their territorial borders, to a large extent, at the expense of Russia and Germany.

The fact that Germany and Russia emerged as defeated nations from the war of 1914, that they were treated as outcasts by the victors, and that the victors represented Western democracy which the Russian and the Prussian regimes had always scornfully rejected, created a common bond between the two nations. They found themselves united in their violent opposition to the peace treaties of 1919. The ideologies which became dominant in Russia and Germany after 1918 had one fundamental common trait—they regarded Western democracy as decadent and doomed. "The great gamble on the disintegration of the Western bourgeois world" was facilitated by Western disunity and disarmament, by widespread intellectual cynicism and indifference, and a few years later, by the economic depression. The Germans were determined to undo the defeat of 1918. Two roads seemed open to them, to achieve future greatness, either in cooperation with, or in a life and death struggle against, Russia, which had emerged from the war under Communist domination. The final German answer to the question which road to take in the war against the West was given only on June 22, 1941.

The Reichswehr under General Hans von Seeckt supported after 1918 close cooperation with Russia. In a memorandum of July, 1922, to the then German Chancellor Joseph Wirth, Seeckt declared that Poland's very existence was "incompatible with the vital needs of Germany." Three months before, Germany had signed the Treaty of Rapallo with Soviet Russia. Though the text of the treaty was innocuous, it marked a decided success for Soviet policy. It ended Russia's isolation and it bore out Lenin's prediction that Soviet Russia would be able to exploit the antagonisms among the "capitalist" nations. Similarly, the Germans greeted the treaty as a beginning of a new independent power policy which broke through the circle of "enslavement" imposed by Versailles. Germany started to defy the disarmament clauses of the Treaty of Versailles; the Reichswehr produced the forbidden weapons—military aircraft, poison gas, tanks and heavy artillery—in Soviet Russia. This cooperation brought Russia the benefits of the most modern technology in armaments.

Many German intellectuals went much farther than the German government. In the 1920's Germany had the strongest Communist party outside Russia. In the elections of November, 1932, it received almost six million votes. Even among the Rightist intellectuals, sympathy for "socialist and revolutionary" Russia as against the despised "bourgeois" West was not unknown.

Less than two decades after the peace treaty of Versailles, which as the Germans and some Westerners claimed had crippled Germany for any foreseeable future, Germany was strong enough to try to undo the defeat of 1918 and to impose her will upon Europe. Meanwhile, Russia too had made great progress from the state of devastation, into which the defeat in World War I, the Communist revolution and the civil war had plunged her. In view of the weakness and disunity of the West the time was fast approaching when the new independent nations in central-eastern Europe, situated between Germany and Russia, were again to face an attempt by Germany and Russia to impose their control upon these lands. Were Germany and Russia to cooperate, as they did in the nineteenth century, or were they to fight about central-eastern Europe? The answer did not lie with the Russians but with the Germans.

In 1939, German leadership decided to cooperate with Russia. The two countries again partitioned Poland as they had done in the eighteenth century. In agreement with Germany Russia pushed her frontier westward and regained not only eastern Poland but the Baltic republics, Bessarabia and northern Bukovina. Meanwhile, Germany expanded far into central-eastern Europe. The events of June 22, 1941, reversed the official German policy. By her aggression against Russia Germany not only gained full control of all central-eastern European lands but expanded this control deep into Russia. This time, however, the outcome was different from that of the war of 1914. Benefiting from the help of the West, Russia turned the invading German armies back and pursued them into the heart of Germany. As they had done in the middle of the eighteenth century, Russian troops again entered Berlin. Königsberg became a Russian city and was renamed Kaliningrad. The whole of central-eastern Europe, including the eastern part of Germany, was in 1945 under Russian control.

The defeat of 1945 produced fundamental changes in the political structure of Germany and in German attitudes toward democracy. Prussia has ceased to exist. The Junker class has lost its economic hold on, and its political influence in, the lands east of the Elbe. The center of gravity in Germany has shifted again to the west and southwest where it had been in the many centuries before Prussia rose to ascendance in Germany. Berlin, which became Germany's capital only in 1871 as a result of Prussia's victories over the German Confederation in 1866 and over France in 1870, has been replaced by Bonn, a city on the western bank of the Rhine. The German Federal Republic, in the larger part of Germany, bears no resemblance to the German Reich of 1871, of 1919 or of 1933. Its orientation is definitely towards the West. It is in closer relationship—politically, spiritually and economically—with the West than Germany has ever been in modern times.

Nevertheless, some people in the West, remembering the past and the policies of Bismarck, of Rapallo and of the August, 1939, treaty, ask the anxious question: whether Germany will not again turn toward collaboration with Russia in an easy or uneasy, in a holy or unholy alliance? Or will Germany resume her policies of 1914 and 1941 and go to war against Soviet Russia to re-establish her control over at least some of the central-eastern European lands? To this writer the answer is an unhesitating "no." For since 1945, not only Germany herself, but the European and world framework within which German policy has to work has fundamentally changed.

The situation of the 1920's offered Germany a tempting chance to resume her drive toward European or world hegemony. Spengler and Hitler regarded Russia and the United States as feeble and unstable countries, the one disintegrating through Bolshevism, the other through capitalism. The years since 1942 have revealed the error of this assumption. Even a "united" and highly armed Germany could not entertain today the hope of defeating the Soviet Union. The weakness and isolation of Germany's eastern and southernmost neighbors which after 1918 tempted even German liberals and Socialists to a campaign against Poland no longer exist. Today, these nations are undergoing a process of rapid industrialization and are protected by the power of the Soviet Union.

Even more important for a limitation of German desires for a new power policy is the close unity of the Western democracies, above all of Britain and the United States. If such a unity had existed in the 1920's, it could have prevented the rise of Hitler and the outbreak of World War II. The economic depression which hit the West eleven years after the end of World War I has, contrary to popular expectations, not reappeared after World War II. The two main weapons of post-1918 Germany in preparing her new war—the successful agitation against Western unity and democratic confidence, and the "independent power game" between Russia and the West—have become blunted, perhaps irreparably so.

A revival of a militant German chauvinism comparable to the situation in the Weimar Reich, which would turn against Russia for the reconquest of central-eastern Europe, is, to say the least, most improbable in the Federal Republic of Germany. It is equally improbable that the Federal Republic will pursue the unification of the two Germanies that emerged as a result of German aggression against Russia in 1941 through accommodation with Soviet Russia. Such an accommodation could be had only at a price—not only the abandonment of the ties with the West, but the abandonment of the free society which has so auspiciously developed in the Federal Republic. For this free society can be maintained in Germany only in closest cooperation with the free West.

One of the leading German historians of today, Professor Ludwig Dehio, in a brilliant and penetrating analysis, published in his *Germany and World Politics in the Twentieth Century*, has summed up the present situation in the following courageous words:

> For today liberty—that is the liberty of the individual, not of the state—can only be preserved as the common property of a consolidated group of nations, and any nation which draws aside to save its own unity will lose it. A hundred years ago the most pressing goal was national unity; for the preservation of freedom offered no problem in the sense in which it does today, whereas unity was the natural demand within that system of nation states which is lying in ruins today. Now, however, after the Third Reich has abused and thrown away our unity by denying freedom, unity must be subordinated to the superior and wider aim of freedom, for today a demand for unity surely has an anachronistic flavor about it. No political watchword can be transplanted into a new situation without carrying with it traces of the soil in which it grew previously.[1]

The question of German unity is closely connected with two other problems. One is the question of the eastern frontiers of Germany. Throughout the history of German nationalism this problem has played an unfortunate role. It weakened the position of German liberals in 1848, when the assertion of the principle that national power and greatness take precedence over individual liberties and the rights of the citizen took hold of the German mind in connection with the problem of the eastern frontiers. After 1918, the question of the eastern frontiers of Germany was again one of the most powerful factors undermining German democracy. Public opinion in the Weimar Reich almost unanimously (even among Socialists) regarded

[1] Professor Dehio's article first appeared in *Aussenpolitik* of June 1953. It is reprinted in an English translation in his *Germany and World Politics in the Twentieth Century* (New York, Alfred A. Knopf, 1959), p. 138; a book which has so far not received the attention that it deserves as the most original interpretation of the German-European siutation of the present century.

Germany's eastern frontiers as "unbearable." To which frontiers should Germany "return," in the case of unification? Those of 1919 aroused utmost indignation in Germany. Certainly a return to the frontiers of 1914, perhaps enlarged by the addition of Austria and the Sudetenland, is unthinkable.

This brings us to a second consideration connected with the problem of German unification. The present division of Germany is not the result of Western mistakes but of the German *Drang nach Osten,* of German aggression and miscalculation. By imposing their system on part of Germany the Communists did not replace there liberty or a civilized regime by terror. They replaced one heinous tyranny with another. It was the fault of the Germans that Communist tyranny was imposed on many non-German lands east of Germany. In the general misery, brought about by National Socialism, the German territory still under tyranny can hardly expect preferential treatment. Nor as long as the present world tension lasts—and that means for any foreseeable future—can the Communists be expected to abandon such economically and industrially valuable territories as eastern Germany and Czechoslovakia. Until recently some Germans harbored the illusion that they could induce the Soviet Union to abandon its advanced Communist positions in Central Europe by offering the neutralization of Germany. But the Soviet Union does not want the neutralization of Germany but the integration of Germany into the Soviet system. This is unacceptable to the large majority of the citizens of the Federal Republic.

The question of unity and eastern frontiers does not exercise that obsessive power over the German mind today which undermined democracy in the Weimar Republic. The Weimar Republic perished because many of its citizens thought of it and its frontiers as a temporary makeshift enforced by Allied victory. Today most Germans accept, at least tacitly, the Federal Republic. They know, as Professor Dehio pointed out, that under today's conditions a free society can only be preserved by close cooperation with other free societies and that freedom must take precedence over unity.

25

The United States and a United West*

The recent crisis over the Suez Canal has for the time being strained the relations not between the United States and NATO but between the United States and two of its NATO partners, Great Britain and France. The suspicion that by opposing the invasion of Egypt, the United States wished to abandon NATO, is of course, unfounded. NATO after all owes its existence as much to the initiative of the United States as does the Marshall Plan. Both were destined to strengthen Western Europe and to preserve it from the extension of Soviet influence. Both these goals have been achieved. It was the United States, too, which insisted on the unification of Western Europe, so much so that the Europeans resented this American attitude as an interference. Now some British and French propose a closer European integration as an act of "independence" from the United States, as if the United States had not always welcomed such a step.

Marshall aid and NATO were originally envisaged as emergency measures to counter Soviet aggression. With the imminence of the Russian military threat receding, it became most desirable, especially in the minds of many Americans, Canadians, and representatives of the smaller European nations, to transform NATO into something more enduring than a military alliance. A committee of three ministers—representatives from Canada, Italy and Norway—was appointed to study ways and means of broadening the NATO program to include closer political and economic cooperation and to create instruments for political consultation among all the member nations.

During the preparation of this report, the French and British acted in support of Israeli aggression against Egypt without consultation with any other NATO member. Their action not only endangered NATO but also the United Nations and world peace. Israeli aggression could have been stopped easily if the French and British had not interposed their veto in the Security Council. Britain and France were stalwarts of the principles of international

* From *Current History*, March 1957. Copyright by *Current History*. Reprinted with permission.

morality embodied in the United Nations; Israel was a creation of the United Nations and of the diplomatic and economic support of the United States. Yet these three nations acted in complete disregard of the United Nations. The world was brought nearer to the brink of a great war than at any time since 1945, and not by the Americans who have often been called "trigger-happy" by their European friends.

The Israeli-Franco-British aggression provided also a much-needed alibi for Khrushchev. Following the latter's famous speech of February, 1956, the Communist empire was subjected to serious internal tensions, and an even more serious crisis made itself felt among the Communist intellectuals. The revolutions in Poland and Hungary started among intellectuals and students. This fact is the more remarkable because the Communist regimes concentrated their indoctrination on these very groups. University youth in the satellites was carefully selected by the authorities and ideologically scrutinized and supervised.

Yet recent events have shown that Communist education—like all totalitarian education—has turned out to be a failure. Boredom engendered by the prohibition of independent thought and by the insistence on non-problematic conformism led to revolt as soon as the window to the West was slightly opened, even though this youth was so young in years that it had no personal experience of Western freedom. Moscow felt for the first time that it could no longer rely on the satellites and perhaps not even on its own youth. The revolutions in Poland and Hungary put a momentous decision before the Kremlin. It had to choose between allowing the relaxation of its grip over the satellites or facing the loss of all the great gains of Khrushchev's diplomacy in the last two years—the rapprochement with India and Yugoslavia and the fulfillment of Lenin's original hope of creating an anti-Western alliance between the new Asian-African nationalism, the "colored world" on the move, and Russian communism.

In that dilemma, tragic from the Russian point of view, the Israeli-Franco-British aggression disarmed the West morally. It gave the Russians an "alibi" to act in Hungary and to pose at the same time as the defenders of the Arabs, and of Asia and Africa in general, against imperial aggression. Israeli, French and British decision to chase after unattainable goals in the Middle East made it impossible to concentrate United Nations pressure upon Russia which would have prepared the relaxation (though not the abandonment) of the Russian hold on central-eastern Europe.

It was quite clear from the onset of Israeli aggression that even the fall of President Gamal Abdel Nasser of Egypt would not mean the weakening of Arab nationalism. On the contrary, it could be easily foreseen that the action against Nasser would strengthen his prestige. Thus the Iraqi representative, who can in no way be regarded as friendly to Nasser, told the General Assembly of the United Nations on December 6 that on the Israeli issue "all the Arab world is Egypt and all Arab statesmen are Nassers."

The time when Arab nationalism—or any other Asian nationalism —could in the long run be cowed by a show of superior force is long gone, in Egypt as well as in Algeria or in Palestine. Israeli-Franco-British aggression against Egypt would have strengthened Soviet influence throughout Asia and Africa, if the Russians had not acted with ruthless brutality in Hungary and if the United States had not restored, by its disassociation from the invasion of Egypt, the moral position and influence of the West in Asia and Africa and thereby strengthened the United Nations and ultimately NATO.

The Russian repression in Hungary aroused the active sympathy of Western Europe. But the West could not do much. The situation was not greatly different from that which prevailed throughout Europe in 1831 and in 1863 when the Russians crushed the insurrections in Poland, and in 1849 when they did the same in Hungary. Everywhere great demonstrations of sympathy for the Poles and Hungarians were then held; the Western governments tried to intervene on their behalf but none of them were willing to accept the risk of a war. Palmerston, then British Foreign Secretary, thought of Austria and Russia, as the historian A. J. P. Taylor writes, in 1849 exclusively in terms of the Near East.

But the days of Palmerston are long gone in the middle of the twentieth century. A United Nations, not preoccupied with Middle Eastern aggression, could have become much more effective in Hungary. Even so today it is likely that, thanks to the world forum of the United Nations, Russian repression in 1957 will not be so uninhibited as it was in 1849 or 1863, and that some degree of liberty, a very relative degree which can be called liberty only in comparison with the situation which existed before 1956, will survive in Hungary and Poland.

Therein the increase of the prestige of the United Nations as a result of its Middle East action will be helpful too. This action was not the result of United States initiative alone. Some commentators have demagogically presented the case as if the United States had ganged up with Russia against Britain and France. In reality, the Israeli-Franco-British aggression was viewed with greatest alarm by the overwhelming majority of public opinion throughout the free world, by Scandinavia as well as by Canada, and above all, by a very considerable section of the three British parties and of the most highly regarded British publications.

In fact, some of the most incisive analyses of the Middle Eastern aggression, which appeared in the United States press, were supplied by prominent British observers—Professor D. W. Brogan in *The New Republic* of December 17, 1956, Mr. Woodrow Wyatt in *The New York Times Magazine* of December 16, 1956, and Mr. Geoffrey Crowther in *Foreign Affairs* of January, 1957. The many voices raised in Britain against the invasion of Egypt testified to the undiminished moral vigor and sense for political practicability which still prevailed there. These qualities have made Britain not only the motherland of modern liberty but also the example of how to guide dependencies on their road to independence.

No similar voices of protest were heard from Israel or France. The French apparently hoped that the defeat of Nasser would help them to repress Arab nationalism in Algeria, a feat which two years of extreme exertion on the part of almost the whole French army were unable to achieve. In Israel the small Ihud group founded by the late Dr. J. L. Magnus raised its warning voice.

The Israeli-Franco-British aggression produced the very condition which it was designed to prevent: a strengthening of Asian-African nationalism. "Nationalism is mounting," Professor Brogan wrote, "it is a dangerously heady novelty in Asia and Africa. . . . By not opposing openly this wave (of the future), the Americans have avoided the follies and crimes of the Eden-Mollet policy. . . . That future has been brought rapidly nearer by the folly of Franco-British policy."

It should be stressed, however, that until this recent mistake, the British were foremost in trying to find a reasonable adjustment between the West, whose power has waned relative to its position in the nineteenth century, and the mounting tide of a frequently emotional anti-Western nationalism, full of resentment and devoid of historical perspective. Future historians may view the third quarter of the twentieth century not so much as a power-conflict between the Soviet

Union and the United States but as "the post-imperial age"—to use Mr. Brogan's title for his article—which witnessed the unexpectedly rapid rise of non-Western peoples to an ever-growing voice in world affairs. "The struggle for the world," Vice-President Richard M. Nixon reminded us in his remarkable speech of December 6, 1956, "will be finally determined by what happens to the millions of people now neutral who are trying to decide whether they will align themselves with the communist nations or with the free nations."

The Western world which for three centuries was in undisputed control of the globe and of civilization is now facing a terrible and fundamental reassessment of its relationship to the rest of the world. The Western nations—above all the United States and Britain—have to face this reassessment together. As long as they exert the Western virtues of political restraint and public morality, they can hope to turn the destructive and inflammatory passions of twentieth century nationalism and socialism—provided they are not totalitarian—into more constructive and civilized channels. Nothing would have been more disastrous for the United States and for its Western European friends and allies than American support for what most Americans and many Britishers regarded as an act of doubtful morality and undoubted impracticability.

The unity of the West does not preclude difference of opinion about immediate political and economic ends and means. Such dissension is inherent in any democratic system, which demands the free airing in a responsible mood, yet with candor, of any disagreements. The American objection to the Middle Eastern aggression did not spring from any unwillingness to support British or French objectives in themselves. On the contrary, the United States is deeply conscious of its absolute need for a viable and strong England and, to a lesser degree, of a healthy and stable France. After all, England was the great bulwark of free Western civilization which held forth undaunted throughout both world wars, and England, through Ernest Bevin and Winston Churchill, was the first to draw the attention of the United States to the totalitarian danger of communism.

Americans did not forget that President Nasser often acted in a provocative way and did not show the restraint of true statesmanship. But provocations are not rare in the twentieth century. Communist China and the Chinese government now on Formosa and the Republic of Korea and North Korea have accused each other, and not without justification, of many provocative acts and intentions in the last years. It was important for the sake of world peace to prevent them from being "provoked" into taking what they might claim to be protective police action.

There is certainly on the American side no desire to diminish in the slightest America's close friendship, or fraternal association, with Britain, and its cooperation with NATO. NATO has been and remains a cornerstone of American policy. Western unity is for many Americans not a negative or a temporary goal directed against other civilizations, but a positive long-range vision for the strengthening of Western civilization in a rapidly changing world. In his speech, Mr. Nixon stressed that "history may show that neither we nor our allies were without fault in our handling of the events which led to the crisis in which we now find ourselves. . . . Now is the time for us all to recognize that recriminations and fault-finding will serve no purpose whatever. The cause of freedom could suffer no greater disaster than to allow this or any other incident to drive a wedge between us and our allies." The French and some Britishers have lost sight of this fundamental fact more than most Americans. A Soviet policy has at present two goals: to weaken NATO and to convince the Asian, Arab and African peoples that they have nothing to hope for from the West. A wise Western policy will allow neither of these two goals to materialize.

The full and graceful acceptance by Britain—and *only* by Britain—of world public opinion represented by the United Nations, in contrast to the defiance of the United Nations by Communist Russia, may enlighten many who are skeptical about Western values but open to reflection on the fundamental difference between Western and Communist morality. In isolation the Western nations, even the United States, are weak and can easily underrate their real strength; a united West, on the other hand, can, with a patient urbanity, represent before the world the ways of rational moderation and individual freedom, which since the Glorious Revolution have formed the true strength of the English-speaking peoples and of the modern West.

Nor has the West any reason to regard the world situation in too pessimistic a light. President Eisenhower's decision to support the security of the Middle East against Communist aggression may make this area as secure as Greece and Turkey were made by President Truman's declaration of March, 1947, ten years ago. The reports emanating from interested sources in the last months of 1956 about

Syria lost to the Communists or turned into a Soviet military base have been proven unsubstantiated. Nasser turned to the Soviet Union only when he could not acquire arms from the United States and when, in an inexcusably abrupt way, the United States refused the already promised help for building the Aswan dam.

The West can draw on the whole some encouragement from recent developments. At the end of 1955, Khrushchev and Bulganin had returned from a triumphant tour through India and Burma, having apparently achieved their main goal of cementing the closest friendship possible with the Bandung nations. At the end of 1956 this friendship had somewhat paled and Jawaharlal Nehru, the organizer of the delirious manifestations which greeted the two Communist leaders, was visiting Washington and Ottawa. At the end of 1956, the Communist empire was in a state of disintegration. This may be stopped but no one would have predicted its start at the end of 1955, nor could anyone have foreseen Khrushchev's speech of February, 1956.

There are also minor successes strengthening the West which nevertheless are considerable and seemed improbable a year ago. I refer to the Franco-German agreement concerning the Saar and the independence which the French were wise enough to grant Tunisia and Morocco. Above all, for one who remembering the League and knowing the nature of communism, had no great expectations regarding the United Nations, this world body meeting on the shore of New York's East River has shown a surprising vitality in these last months. Its Secretary General, Dag Hammarskjöld, has proven himself not only an international official but an international statesman. The creation of the United Nations emergency force was the first step ever undertaken in the almost 40 years since Woodrow Wilson launched the idea of collective security to bring his ideal nearer to realization.

This United Nations force is still at its very beginning, a loose and haphazard organization which has a long way to go before becoming an effective force. But for an observer who thinks back over these 40 years, this first step is a milestone on a road which may lead to some world order. That this force consists of contingents of smaller nations from all over the world and not of forces supplied by the great powers is a most hopeful and unexpected development. The *Atlantic Monthly* of January, 1957, in its Report on the Middle East, expressed the opinion that the United Nations emergency force presented the best chance for Israel's survival.

The action of the United States has strengthened the United Nations and at the same time the Western alliance. The United States knows that it will have to help Western Europe over the economic difficulties created by the invasion of Egypt. The flow of oil from the United States to relieve the oil shortage in Western Europe started practically immediately after the disruption of the normal supply. Throughout 1955 continuing through the first week of November, 1956, the average daily shipment from Gulf ports to Western Europe was 44 thousand barrels. But, as Arthur Krock reported in *The New York Times,* the daily average rose in the second week of November to 212 thousand barrels, in the third week to 521 thousand barrels and in the last week of November, long before the complete withdrawal of the Anglo-French forces (from Port Said) to the mighty total of 944,000 barrels. From December on a daily average of 550,000 barrels was to be maintained as an over-all target.

But more will be needed than ample American help to Western Europe and the mere continuation of NATO. The dangerous implications of the invasion of Egypt should persuade the West of the need for growing political consultation and cooperation. The dialogue between the United States and Western Europe, a dialogue in which Canada and Scandinavia, Germany and Italy have to participate as much as the United States and Britain and France, must go on, unhampered by recriminations. It must seek constructive solutions for the urgent problems confronting the West, solutions in harmony with the realities of the twentieth century and with the ideals of the United Nations, which after all, are only the application of principles of modern Western civilization to an international community in which the West no longer plays the dominant role.

26

The French Rightist Revolution[*]

The revolution of May 13, 1958, which started with the cooperation of the French army among the French settlers in Algeria, has been approved by the French general elections held on November 30, 1958. The new French chamber has been compared by Raymond Aron, the Walter Lippmann of French journalism, with the *"chambre introuvable"* elected in 1815. The Chamber of 1815 was an ultra-royalist chamber, going far beyond the expectations and wishes of the then King Louis XVIII. The new deputies elected in the name of royalism tried to reduce the more moderate king to a subordinate position. Soon Louis XVIII was to doubt his luck in facing an overwhelmingly royalist chamber elected on the strength of a new electoral law and of a sudden switch of the French electorate to an extreme Rightist nationalist temper. Today's situation is perhaps similar.

As the royalist elections of 1815 were only outwardly a triumph for the king, so the de Gaullist elections of November, 1958, were only outwardly a triumph for de Gaulle. In reality, they were an acceptance of the May 13 revolution by the majority of the French people. They were more than a personal vote of confidence for the lonely and enigmatic figure of General Charles de Gaulle. They went beyond de Gaulle. Even today the support for de Gaulle in France may well be larger than the support for the new chamber. This support for de Gaulle is not a new phenomenon in French history. A similar overwhelming support was given in December, 1848, to Prince Louis Napoleon and in June, 1940, to Marshal Henri Pétain. The three men—Louis Napoleon, Pétain and de Gaulle—are very different in their personality and of the three de Gaulle is by far the most impressive. Nevertheless, all three appealed to the military tradition in France, and the vote for them was an expression of the shift to a Rightist and nationalist position. All three were a vote against democracy. All three were an appeal to French traditions of

[*] From *Current History*, May 1959. Copyright by *Current History*. Reprinted with permission.

grandeur, though each one interpreted the French past somewhat differently.

World public opinion has not been entirely just toward the Fourth French Republic. It emerged from the military and moral collapse of France in World War II. It was based on the unfortunate fiction that France had been one of the victor nations of World War II and a great military power. Burdened with the double legacy of collapse and victory—a legacy never digested intellectually or morally—the Fourth Republic was born under unfortunate circumstances.

Nevertheless, it achieved much. It brought to the French people, and above all to the French workers, an unprecedented degree of individual prosperity. It started to modernize the French economic structure. France enregistered for the first time an increase in its birth rate. In its foreign policy the Fourth Republic accepted, and even started, the first steps toward European and North Atlantic integration. Hesitantly it even started a liberal and enlightened policy in its African colonies south of the Sahara. It had the courage to recognize the independence of its former protectorates of Morocco and Tunisia. All this is in no way a mean record for a democratic regime built upon such psychologically unstable foundations as the Fourth Republic.

In the elections of January, 1956, a majority of the French voters voted for a coalition of Socialists and Radicals led by Guy Mollet and Pierre Mendès-France. Before the elections Guy Mollet declared the Algerian war an absurdity and demanded negotiations and a reconciliation with the Algerians fighting for their independence. When he went to Algeria on February 6, 1956, immediately after the elections, to realize his program, he was frightened by the opposition of the French army and the French settlers. He accepted their policy and after his return to Paris tried to carry it through. He and his friend Robert Lacoste, both members of the Socialist party, covered up the campaign of ruthless terrorism pursued by the French army in its effort to stamp out the Algerian demand for independence, probably the blackest spot in the otherwise rapidly brightening contemporary record of European colonialism in Asia and Africa. The French army and the French settlers in Algeria succeeded on April 6, 1956, in imposing their policy on the French Republic. From this cancer the Fourth Republic perished. With the revolution of May 13, 1958, the army and the settlers consummated their success of February, 1956.

In the elections of November, 1958, the anti-democratic forces in France achieved an overwhelming victory. This was partly due to the new electoral law. The new chamber offers an aspect rarely seen in French parliamentary history. It is a chamber without an opposition. The democratic parties are represented by about 50 deputies, the Communists by 10 deputies. Yet democrats and Communists received about 40 per cent of the popular vote. As against them there is arraigned a massive majority of 188 deputies of the *Union pour la Nouvelle République,* 132 Independents and 71 deputies from Algeria elected under the patronage of the French army and representing none but the extreme wing of the French settlers in Algeria. Even Guy Mollet who was one of the staunchest supporters of General de Gaulle last fall has been forced into opposition to the Fifth Republic as it emerged from the elections.

But the victory of the extreme nationalist groups in the recent elections was not only the result of the new electoral law. It reflected also the mood of a large number of the French people, a mood made up, as in December, 1848, and in June, 1940, of indifference to politics in general and disgust with democracy. Equally important was the wave of xenophobic nationalism which swept large parts of the French electorate. Whenever the voters had a choice between a moderate de Gaullist and an extreme nationalist, they voted for the candidate who was for the most ruthless prosecution of the war against Algerian self-determination and who stressed French military greatness and great power position, as expressed in the maintenance of the French colonial empire.

The difference between original de Gaullism and the Fifth Republic as it emerged can be best seen by a comparison of the attitude of André Malraux, who was de Gaulle's first minister of information, and the present official Algerian policy. In a famous pre-referendum press conference Malraux promised the release of Rahmani, a Muslim Algerian officer of the French army who had been imprisoned. In a letter to the President of the Republic Rahmani had described the anguish the Algerian war was causing him and had asked for the end of torture of Algerian suspects, and the dispatch of three leading French writers to Algeria to investigate the tortures. Rahmani is still in prison; the writers never left for Algeria; and on February 17, 1959, a non-political group of highly respected French jurists under the presidency of René-William Thorp, formerly head of the Paris bar, denounced the persistent recourse in Algeria to certain inhumane methods of extra-penal repression, under the form of tortures, their progressive extension in Metropolitan France, and the existence of unexplained disappearances in detention centers.

Liberal publications like the weekly *Express,* which follows the political line of Mendès-France, continue to be seized by the government. No solution is in sight for Algeria; instead the Algerian cancer is still growing and eating the substance of French democracy. As Guy Mollet did, de Gaulle shuns political solutions, promises economic improvement without being able to start it, and allows the army to continue its war of repression. Malraux has stepped into the background.

Jacques Soustelle and the French settlers in Algeria have emerged as the real victors. The Algerian problem is farther from solution than it was before the establishment of the Fifth Republic. The new French Premier, Michel Debré, appointed by President de Gaulle, repeated on February 9, 1959, in Algiers his unshakable determination to maintain French sovereignty and authority in Algeria. *"Algérie Française,"* the battle cry of the French extremists of May 13, 1958, seemed confirmed as French official policy.

What is de Gaulle's personal position in this rapid evolution of an extremist French nationalism? Nobody knows. In October, 1958, he had the opportunity to take the courageous step of negotiations with the Algerian nationalists. Instead, he demanded their surrender. He was responsible for holding "elections" in Algeria, for having exclusively "integrationists" elected and thus confirming the official demand of the May 13, 1958, revolution for the "integration" of Algeria into France. President Habib Bourguiba of Tunisia, a devoted friend of France, of de Gaulle and of the West, asked to be allowed to meet de Gaulle and to offer his mediation in the Algerian war. President de Gaulle did not answer him. On February 17, 1959, President Bourguiba drew attention to a recent "grave deterioration" in French-Tunisian relations. Yet with all that, many friends of France abroad and many liberals in France still look to President de Gaulle as a possible brake on the rapid shift of France to a Rightist nationalism. Their hope may be justified. But General de Gaulle is, of course, subject to all the accidents of human nature; he may also follow the example of withdrawal which he has set before. The hope that de Gaulle will be able to reverse the decline of democracy in France may or may not be in vain.

French experience of the last 150 years has been one of many shifts and turns. France has found herself repeatedly at the crossroads between a liberal democracy and an authoritarian militarist nationalism. In spite of crises and counter-revolutions French liberal democracy has reasserted itself again and again. In the long run French democracy can put more reliance upon men of the type of Vincent Auriol than on de Gaulle. On February 12, 1959, it was announced that Auriol, the first President of the Fourth Republic, had resigned, after 54 years, from membership in the Socialist party. Like Mollet, he had supported Charles de Gaulle in May, 1958. But for years he had opposed Mollet's "desiccating opportunism" and his Algerian war policy. "Today," Auriol wrote in his letter of resignation from the Socialist party, "I see everything collapsing at a time when it is necessary to regroup, in a single great truly socialist organization with a high ideal and a clear doctrine adapted to the modern world, all the workers divided between the communist and the socialist parties." Men like Auriol uphold the tradition of French democracy. He is not alone. There is no doubt that the forces of French democracy and the opposition to the ruthless war in Algeria are still strong in France.

The *gloire* which many Frenchmen apparently seek today in maintaining their empire and thus in compensating for their collapse in 1940 is an outdated *gloire*. It does not conform to the rapidly changing world of the mid-twentieth century. The glory of the French nation does not rest on imperial domination or military power but on literary and artistic genius and on an ability to find new, more liberal and more humane ways of individual life and social cooperation.

In the midst of all the many political changes of the last two centuries the French system of government has shown little aptitude for adjustment. Concessions were made in phraseology rather than in reality. In December, 1946, the newly-created *Union Française* officially rejected the colonial regime and the subjection of the African and Asian peoples to French domination. But it remained a piece of paper. Some French writers compared it with the British Commonwealth. They forgot that the members of the Commonwealth are independent nations with their own foreign policy, cooperating on a basis of strict equality. Nothing of that sort existed in the *Union*

Française, nor does it exist in the *Communauté Française* which took its place in 1958.

Nevertheless, the *Communauté* marks a definite progress which was, however, started by the *loi cadre* of June 23, 1956, one of the liberal steps taken by the Fourth Republic. General de Gaulle's plebiscite of September 28, 1958, went a step further. It gave the French colonies [with the exception of Algeria, juridically and administratively considered a part of the Metropole] four choices: to continue the status quo; to join the centralist administration of metropolitan France; to attain autonomy, though in a strictly limited way, within the French community; or to gain independence.

Practically all important territories decided for autonomy; one alone, Guinea, under the leadership of Sekou Touré, chose independence. But even those who chose autonomy did it as a step towards independence. The leaders in the French colonies do not reject close cooperation with France. France can count on a large fund of good will among them. But they wish to face France as equals. The French government apparently hoped not only to keep the autonomy of the colonies strictly limited but to maintain each of these new autonomous entities separated from its neighbors, so that France would have to deal with each of the 12 weak states singly. The old policy of divide and rule was to continue. At a time when the European nations rightly seek federation, such federal union or integration was denied to Arabs or Africans.

But Africa is swept today not only by the demand for an end of the colonial regimes. The African leaders know well that the boundaries between the various colonies were drawn by imperial conquest and outside arrangements. The African peoples do not wish to form small states. They see no ideal in the weak independent nation-state. They are after all not nations. They are on the way from a tribal stage of social organization to a federal stage which will include perhaps one day large contiguous areas of western, central and eastern Africa without regard to former colonial boundaries.

On January 17, 1959, representatives of four of the new autonomous territories of French West Africa, the État du Sénégal, the République Soudanaise, the République Voltaïque and the République du Dahomey, met in Dakar, the capital of Senegal, under the chairmanship of Léopold Sedar Senghor, Senegal's Prime Minister, and established the federal republic of Mali; they adopted the name of a former African state which between the eleventh and sixteenth century included most of West Africa. The preamble of the new constitution names the strengthening of "the African personality" within the *Communauté* as the principal goal. All participants in the congress of Dakar took an oath to devote themselves to missionary activities for African unity.

Two days later, on January 19, 318 delegates of the *Union Générale des Travailleurs d'Afrique Noire* met in Conakry, the capital of Guinea, and elected Sekou Touré as President. They demanded the unity of the trade unions of Black Africa and North Africa. In the same month, the Belgian government unexpectedly promised democratic reforms and future independence to the peoples of the Belgian Congo. Nigeria with 35 million inhabitants, the Cameroons, and Somalia will become independent African nations in 1960. All this represents a development which five years ago, in some aspects even one year ago, few people would have thought possible.

At the end of December, 1958, Senghor declared at a federalist conference in Bamako, the capital of the French Sudan:

> We are ready to remain in the *Communauté* as long as it opens up for us the road to the establishment of federal states in Africa and to the progressive grant of independence on the basis of an alliance with France. For that end the constitution must be interpreted in a dynamic way.

Will the Fifth Republic accept this dynamism? The African leaders, in North Africa as well as south of the Sahara, have been educated by France. They love the French language and the French civilization. But they also learned from France the importance of human dignity and equality, of cultural personality and national sovereignty. They wish to achieve these goals on the basis of federation among themselves and of cooperation with France. This is as true of the Federation of the Maghreb, which will include Tunisia, Algeria and Morocco, as it is of the Federation of West- and Equatorial Africa. In an alliance on the basis of equality among these federations and France lies not only the best hope for cooperation in the free world but also for the growth and survival of democracy in France and in Africa.

27

Western Europe and Atlantic Unity*

Cooperation between Western Europe and North America, the nations bordering on the North Atlantic, has in the last ten years changed the situation in Europe. At the end of World War II Western Europe was economically devastated and politically helpless. Communist parties exercised a great influence within the governments of France and Italy. The danger that communism might spread to the Atlantic haunted many minds. The French government, under General de Gaulle and with Georges Bidault as foreign minister, claimed France as a "bridge" or mediator between the English-speaking nations on the one hand and Eastern Europe on the other hand. In his speech before the United Nations on September 20, 1947, Bidault deplored the division of Europe into "two hostile camps" and regarded France as a third force between the two contending imperial blocs. In the fall of 1947 I heard the same said by many Czechs on the occasion of my last visit to Czechoslovakia.

The situation changed radically the following February when the Communists' coup established their exclusive control over Czechoslovakia, an event which in its consequences can be compared to Hitler's march into Prague in March, 1939. As a result, in May, 1948, France, Britain and the Benelux countries established a Western European military alliance. The following month the Soviet authorities closed all the avenues of land traffic leading to West Berlin. This blockade ended only after a successful air lift which lasted for more than ten months, in May, 1949, on the condition that a four-power conference be called to discuss the problems of Germany and West Berlin.

It was under these conditions that in 1949 two steps were taken, which were intended to prevent a further weakening of the Western European position. The Council of Europe was created, with its seat in Strasbourg, France, and in Washington, D.C., the treaty was signed which established NATO or the North Atlantic Treaty Organization. These steps marked the end of the hope which, after

* From *Current History*, September 1960. Copyright by *Current History*. Reprinted with permission.

World War II, the democratic nations of the West entertained for cooperation with the Soviet Union in continuation of their wartime partnership. It was a mistake of Western leadership, especially of United States foreign policy under President Franklin D. Roosevelt, that no alternative policy was prepared in case the Soviet leadership should refuse cooperation. In fact, any profound knowledge of Communist ideology or even of powerful trends in Russian history should have convinced American leadership of the need for being prepared. An American war correspondent wrote before the establishment of NATO that

> the nature of the alternative course of action was clear enough, and it was one of those happy alternatives which could have been prepared without endangering the success of the primary policy. It was, in effect, to create under American leadership a kind of peace federation of like-minded nations whose material strength and moral authority were so great that no one nation would long have dared to run counter to their will.[1]

The main emphasis in these words seems to lie with "moral authority." Though material strength was needed to deter totalitarianism, Fascist or Communist, from attacking the democracies, a new and decisive factor in world history emerged after 1948, the rise to sovereignty of the old and new nations of Asia and Africa and the end of the European colonial empires. From the time of Lenin on, Soviet Russia had hoped to utilize the movement for emancipation and equality among Chinese and Indians, Arabs and Africans, for the benefit of communism in its struggle against the West. In that connection "moral authority" much more than material strength is the weapon which will frustrate, and to a large extent has already frustrated, Communist hopes.

Walter Kolarz, one of the leading experts on "communism and nationalism," pointed out recently how strongly the actions of the West, endowing it with moral authority, may influence the fate of communism and its relationship with its subject peoples:

> The progressive liquidation of Western colonialism in Asia and Africa is also bound to have its bearing on the situation in the Soviet

[1] Wallace Carroll, *Persuade or Perish* (Boston: Houghton Mifflin, 1948), p. 373. Such a course of action was proposed by Clarence Streit, even before World War II, against the danger of fascist totalitarianism.

Empire. The more colonial countries acquire independence, the more does the situation in Russia become outdated, and the greater will be the moral, and ultimately even the physical pressure for a change in the status of the non-Russian peoples of the Soviet Union. It has often been said that every injustice committed in the West strengthens communism in the East and in the world as a whole. This is undoubtedly correct. But it is equally true that every wrong righted in the West, and every racial conflict successfully solved, must likewise affect the future of communist domination. It must bring nearer both the doom of communism and the emancipation of the peoples living under Soviet rule.[2]

The Council of Europe has achieved very little in the first decade of its existence. It has in no way justified the great hopes aroused by Winston Churchill in his addresses in 1946 at the University of Zurich and in 1948 at the European Congress in The Hague.[3] On the other hand NATO has shown itself on the whole a success. It has established a well functioning organization and it has kept Western Europe not only free from Soviet aggression, but in several ways has diminished the Soviet threat to the West. Nevertheless, seen from Western Europe, NATO faces today a serious test, not of its material strength but of its moral authority. The crisis is based upon the growth of nationalism, on the one hand, and the weakening of democracy, on the other hand, in Western Europe, especially among the three larger continental nations, France, Germany and Italy. It is only among the British and among the smaller nations on the continent of Europe that democracy seems well-established and grows best.

The weakening of democracy on the European continent—a weakening not in favor of communism but of a self-centered old-fashioned nationalism—has also weakened the tenuous bonds of closer cooperation and integration among the democratic European nations and in the Atlantic community. In his famous address before the *École Militaire,* General de Gaulle declared (and in view of the splendor and incisiveness of his style it might be worthwhile to quote verbatim):

[2] *The Absent Countries of Europe,* lectures held at the Collège de l'Europe Libre, Berne, Ost-Europa-Bibliothek, 1958, p. 104.
[3] See Hans Kohn, "The Difficult Road to Western Unity," *Orbis, A Quarterly Journal of World Affairs,* Fall, 1959, pp. 297-312.

Le système qu'on a appelé integration qui a été inauguré et même, dans une certaine mesure, pratiqué après les épreuves que nous avons traversées, alors qu'on pouvait croire que le monde libre était placé devant une menace imminente et illimitée, et que nous n'avions pas encore recouvré notre personnalité nationale, le système de l'integration a vécu.... Il faut évidemment que nous sachions nous pourvoir au cours des prochaines années d'une force capable d'agir pour notre compte, de ce qu'on est convenue d'appeler force de frappe, susceptible de se déployer à tout moment et n'importe où. Il va de soi qu'à la base de cette force sera un armement atomique ... qui doit nous appartenir; et puisqu'on peut détruire la France, éventuellement, à partir de n'importe quel point du monde, il faut que notre force soit faite pour agir où que ce coit sur la terre. Vous vous rendez compte comme moi de l'envergure de cette obligation ... Il faut avoir le courage de la vouloir et celui de la remplir. Dans le domaine de la défense, ce sera notre grande oeuvre pendant les années qui viennent.[4]

Democracy has been fundamentally weakened in France by the events of May, 1958, when an uprising of the French army put an end to the Fourth Republic and brought General de Gaulle to power. Though his government formally adheres to the various programs of European and Atlantic cooperation, the right spirit, the "moral authority," is absent. At a press conference held in Paris on April 7, 1954, General de Gaulle declared that it was the mission of France, without ceasing to be a member of the Atlantic alliance, to organize Europe along lines which did not prevent possible coexistence between Moscow and Washington. "Above all, let us remain French, sovereign, independent, and free."

Premier Michel Debré warned in a speech on August 15, 1959, against "bondage" to a "foreign power," and the foreign power was not primarily the Soviet Union. In the third volume of his magnificent *Mémoires de Guerre,* General de Gaulle glorifies the strong

[4] "The policy termed integration, that was inaugurated and, to a certain extent, even practiced after the trials we endured when it was believed that an imminent and unlimited menace was hanging over the free world and we had not yet recovered our national personality, has lived.... It is obvious that we must learn how to create in the years to come a power capable of acting in our behalf, that is, a striking force, that can be used anytime and anywhere necessary. It goes without saying that the basis of such power would be an atomic armament which would belong to us; since France can eventually be destroyed from any point in the world, our power must be such that it can strike anywhere on this earth. You realize as I do the scope of this obligation. ... One must have the courage to will it and to fulfill it. In the domain of our defense, this will be the great work of the years ahead."

state, the strong leader and the unique mission of French civilization. His acknowledged ambition is to make of France, which he prefers to call Gaul, "one of the three world powers and should it be necessary one day, the arbitrator between the two camps, the camps of the Soviets and that of the Anglo Saxons." [5]

To that end of making France the third world power through leadership in Europe, the European Economic Community of the six nations (France, Germany, Italy, Belgium, Netherlands, and Luxembourg) has become in the eyes of certain circles not primarily a practical step to enhance the welfare and the prosperity of the people through enlarged trade but a replica of the continental empires of Charlemagne or of Napoleon. Under the leadership of Chancellor Konrad Adenauer and of Professor Walter Hallstein, formerly Secretary of State in the foreign office at Bonn and since 1958 President of the European Economic Community, the German Federal Republic has fully supported de Gaulle. It has been one of the great European achievements of the past decade that Adenauer has put an end to the long hostility between France and Germany, a hostility which goes back to the division of Charlemagne's empire and which was intensified in the nineteenth century. But against the advice of Ludwig Erhard, Bonn's very successful minister of economic affairs, Bonn's policy has become so exclusively oriented toward Paris that it has created the impression of being fundamentally anti-British.

This is deeply regrettable. On the one hand such a policy widens the growing rift in Europe. On the other hand it weakens German democracy. Democracy in Germany is a very recent and very tenuous growth. It cannot find much encouragement in a close cooperation with the French Fifth Republic or with Franco Spain. It would find greater strength in cooperation with Britain and with the Scandinavian states, which are stable democracies, and which have proven themselves throughout the most trying periods of the nineteenth and the twentieth century during which France, Germany and Italy fell victim to nationalist intoxication and various forms of antidemocratic dictatorship. There has been lately an ominous rise of national-

[5] Charles de Gaulle, *Le Salut*, Paris: Plon, 1959, p. 179. On the occasion of his visit to Stalin, de Gaulle declared, "that there exist no objects of direct conflict (*contestation*) between France and Russia. Such conflicts we have had with Great Britain and we still have them." Pp. 68 f., 377 f. On democracy in France see Raymond Aron, "La démocratie a-t-elle un avenir en France?" in the monthly *Preuves*, Paris, July 1959. Ray Alan writes in *Commentary*, January 1960, that the RTF (Radiodiffusion-Television Française) has become so nationalistic in its commentaries that nothing similar has been heard in Western Europe, outside Spain, since 1945.

ism in Germany, too, accompanied unfortunately by some official attempts at whitewash under the pretext that an honest facing of the facts might play into the hands of communism. In fact, however, only a thorough housecleaning will really prevent the growth of fascist or Communist influences in countries where democracy is not firmly rooted.[6]

The rift in Europe between the Franco-German led European Economic Community and the recently formed European Free Trade Association under British leadership, to which the three Scandinavian nations, Switzerland, Austria, and Portugal adhere, is growing. This rift weakens the cohesion of Western Europe, weakens democracy, and thereby weakens the Atlantic community. The E.F.T.A. was formed as a protective alliance of the countries affected by the discriminatory measures of the E.E.C., but it has always been regarded by them as a possible bridge toward the E.E.C. with the principal and ultimate aim of overcoming the present conflict in European integration.[7]

Undoubtedly Great Britain committed a serious error by not assuming the leadership toward European integration in the early 1950's, when such leadership might have assured the emergence of a truly democratic Western Europe. Today Britain is afraid of any close political ties with countries which as recently as 1940, and partly even today, have given ample proof of their fundamental lack of democratic spirit and the instability of their democratic institutions. These countries, especially France, are countries in which the spirit of a rigid centralism prevails, and where little understanding exists for the pluralism and the variety of local self-government and of federalism, on which alone a democratic European and Atlantic community can be built.

The Communist bloc is also torn by conflicting national state interests and traditions. But there the commitment to a common ideology, to a common interpretation of history, a common image of man's place in society and of the power of the state, tends to overcome conflicting national interests.

The Atlantic community can show enduring strength only if it is not regarded purely as a defensive measure against Soviet aggression,

[6] See the article by Rudolf Pechel, a German conservative resistance fighter against national socialism and a staunch anti-Communist, "Überhörte Warnungen" in the March, 1960, issue of the excellent German monthly, Deutsche Rundschau.
[7] See Willy Bretscher, editor-in-chief, Neue Zürcher Zeitung, "Switzerland and European Integration," Swiss Review of World Affairs, Zurich, April, 1960.

overlooking other dangers of totalitarianism which have been deeply rooted in the recent past of continental Europe. The Atlantic community must, in order to overcome the deeply rooted nationalistic antagonisms and traditions of its members, also have a commitment to a common idea; it must be a group of like-minded nations who put their emphasis on the moral ideas of human dignity, equality and liberty everywhere. These ideas should carry a message spreading behind the iron curtain, but the message can spread there only if it is fully applied where it can be applied by the West itself, namely in the nations and the dependencies of the Atlantic community.

One of the symptoms of the uneasiness prevailing among the nations of the Atlantic community is the discussion about the invitation to Spain to join in the guardianship of democracy and human freedom. It is still well remembered by whose support and under what conditions the present government of Spain came to power. A haughty rejection of, and an utter contempt for, the democratic way of life has been voiced repeatedly by the spokesmen of the present Spanish regime.

The rise to power of General de Gaulle in France and recent actions by the governments of the United States and by the German Federal Republic have been regarded by the present Spanish regime as a justification of its anti-democratic course. The fact that the Spanish government can entertain such a view is in itself proof of the decline of democracy and moral strength in the Atlantic community. One of the distinguished United States experts on Spain, Arthur P. Whitaker, has recently emphasized in a report on "anti-Americanism in Spain" that "virtually all the opponents of the present regime, who probably constitute a large majority of the population and who represent a wide diversity of political groups and all classes of society" complain that by virtue of the bases agreement the United States has become "the ally and chief prop of the regime, without which the latter could not have maintained itself." [8]

The breakdown of the Summit Conference in May, 1960, may for a time outwardly solidify the Atlantic community. But this unity is only an outward appearance which depends on the temporary and temperamental truculence of Khrushchev. Only nations that are committed to a common ideal of representative democracy and of in-

---

[8] *Orbis, a Quarterly Journal of World Affairs*, Philadelphia, Vol. III, No. 3, p. 320. See also C. L. Sulzberger's column "Foreign Affairs" in *The New York Times*, February 9, 1959.

dividual liberty can be truly united. Unity and democracy are closely interwoven in the Atlantic community. This interconnection constitutes the distinctive character of that community, as compared with other power blocs. The single greatest obstacle to Atlantic unity and democracy is the emphasis on self-centered nationalism and imperial *gloire*. Such an emphasis is an anachronism which could lead the nations involved into great political and, above all, moral calamity. The German historian, Ludwig Dehio, pointed to this danger as early as 1953:

> Today liberty—that is the liberty of the individual, not of the state—can only be preserved as the common property of a consolidated group of nations, and any nation which draws aside to save its own [power position] will lose it. . . . It is extremely difficult for some free European nations in their changed surroundings to master the anachronistic instincts that they have formed during the centuries of the European system, and the task is hardest of all for the two great neighbors, Germany and France, in whom the continental mentality has crystallized in its most typical form.[9]

28

The Atlantic Community and the World*

The North Atlantic Community is based upon the will to defend certain common spiritual and moral values. It has to defend them today, but it had to defend them, also, before World War II against

[9] Ludwig Dehio, *Germany and World Politics in the Twentieth Century* (New York: Alfred A. Knopf, 1959), p. 138.

* An address delivered before the Conference on the North Atlantic Community, Bruges, Belgium, on September 9, 1957, and first published in *Orbis*, Vol. I, No. 4 (Winter 1958), pp. 418-427. Reprinted with permission of the publishers, The Foreign Policy Research Institute of the University of Pennsylvania.

a most perfidious attack. Then modern Western civilization—the civilization underlying the North Atlantic Community—was attacked by fascism, not only militarily but, above all, spiritually, intellectually and morally. It would be a vain effort to try to define what this Atlantic civilization and its values are. Any such effort might lead to endless and fruitless discussions. We all know what these values are, though we may express it in different ways. The dictators after World War I, Lenin and Hitler, knew very well what they rejected and what they attacked.

Modern Western civilization is a young and growing civilization. It emerged only at the end of the seventeenth century and gained shape in the course of the eighteenth century. It would be dangerous to feel—as Spengler felt and as others, especially in Europe, feel to-today—a profound *Kulturpessimismus*, a pessimism regarding the future of modern Western civilization. The feeling itself is understandable, not only in the light of the two great Europeans wars in this century but also in the light of the tensions which the rapid growth of a modern industrial mass civilization produces in societies in which many survivals of pre-industrial society still are strong. Yet Spengler's prediction of the *Untergang des Abendlandes* proved untrue. Western liberty survived the Thousand-Year Reich. Nor is present-day Western civilization old or senescent. Though rooted in the Greco-Roman tradition and in Christian piety, the Atlantic civilization, based upon the individual dignity of man, liberty of thought, and tolerance, is in its own way a new civilization, implying fundamentally new attitudes toward man and society.

No final answer can be given to the question about the geographical limits of the Atlantic civilization and Community. These limits are not fixed. This fact has nothing to do with national prejudices, though they, too, play a role. Reputedly there are some Englishmen who believe that modern civilization ends at the English Channel. There have certainly been French thinkers, like Maurice Barrès and Henri Massis, who believe that the Occident must be defended on the Rhine, that this famed river marks the border of civilization. On the other hand some Germans like to place the frontier of Western civilization on the German-Polish border. There are Poles who believe that the frontiers of the West run along the Russian-Polish border. Russians have placed the defense of the Occident along the Urals, perhaps even along the shores of the Pacific. But irrespective of these national prejudices, the frontiers of Western civilization have been shifting throughout modern history and may be shifted again. For modern Western civilization as we understand it is not a geographic term nor a national term. It is an intellectual and moral attitude.

After June, 1940 the frontier of modern Western civilization was, for a brief time, on the English channel. Almost the whole continent of Europe was then overrun or controlled by anti-Western regimes which rejected scornfully the very foundations of the Atlantic Community. Today its frontier runs along the German-Polish border or perhaps across Germany. It was not always there; it certainly will not always be there. In the nineteenth century Russia and Poland were to a growing degree members of the Western community of individual liberty and tolerance. Thus we should see clearly that the frontiers of modern Western civilization and of the Atlantic Community are geographically undetermined. One can as well say that no nation *qua* nation belongs to it and that all people potentially can join it. Italy under Mussolini, Germany under Hitler, Russia under Lenin did not belong, and did not wish to belong, to the Western community of individual liberty. Today Germany and Italy belong, and tomorrow Russia may belong. The frontiers of modern civilization run in the hearts and minds of men and not along geographic lines. Yet there is a group of nations who, not by their merit but by geographic and historic good fortune, form the core of the Atlantic Community. From this core modern Western civilization has been spreading and, by its very nature, must continue to spread.

In the world of today, a free civilization without power would hardly survive. Hitler's triumphant armies were stopped in 1940 by the military valor of the British people. If the advance of communism has come to a halt in Europe, it has been stopped by the combined efforts of the peoples united in the North Atlantic Treaty Organization. Their efforts however, would be in vain if there would not be behind the military alliance the consciousness of common values to defend. But more important even than the readiness to defend these values is the determination to live them. Only if one lives them is one willing to defend them.

This modern Western civilization is faced today not only by the challenge of anti-Western movements, like fascism or communism, but also by the perhaps more urgent task of arriving at a new relationship with the fast awakening peoples of Asia and Africa. In the last twelve years not only the political map but the moral and intellectual climate of these two continents have fundamentally changed. This change has been the result of modern Western civilization penetrating those lands. Perhaps future historians will reckon the awakening of Asia and Africa among the proudest achievements of the spirit of the Atlantic Community—I say the spirit though not always the deeds. But even the deeds of the Atlantic nations, above all of Britain, were directly involved in the awakening of non-Western peoples to a new life, and a much better life, and in laying the foundations, for the first time, of an evolving world-community. The fact that modern nations have been constituted recently in India and Ghana, that Parliaments meet in these countries according to the principles of Westminster, is a great and historical achievement of the spread of the Atlantic spirit. The Parliaments there may not always work to perfection. Parliaments nowhere do; one has spoken for a long time of "the decay of the parliamentary system" in France and Italy. The achievements of modern Western civilization in Asia, and above all in Africa, are very young and, as all human achievements are, precarious. But the rapid transformation, the rejuvenation of the two great continents, the reinvigoration of their civilizations and social life, bear witness, as perhaps nothing else does, to the vitality of the uniquely dynamic modern Western civilization. Of course these rapid and deep-reaching changes necessarily create strains and maladjustments and call for painful reappraisals and readjustments. Yet these changes are not only unavoidable and irreversible: they are a great and positive step on the road which modern Western civilization travels.

For the North Atlantic Community is by its own character an open society, the first open society in history. When Milton wrote his famous vision of the future in his *Defense of the English People,* he saw the spirit of liberty spreading from England to the farthest corners of the earth. The Declaration of Independence spoke not only for the Anglo-Americans, it spoke for mankind. The Declaration of the Rights of Man and the Citizen meant not only the French, it meant everyone. This universality of the message of the North Atlantic civilization is its great strength. It is in the true tradition of the older Western civilizations. Hellenism and the Stoic Roman Empire carried their civilization over the *orbis terrarum.* Christianity was not destined for Europe or for white men: it was a message for every soul on this globe. Modern Western civilization is not an exclusive society. If it ever tried to be that it would renege its own nature. On the other hand, it should be stressed that the North Atlantic Community does not wish to impose its civilization on anyone. If some nation feels itself the bearer of a different civilization, it has the right to be different. It is again of the essence of modern Western civilization to respect these differences, to see in them a source of potential fertile intercourse, as long as the dissenting nation does not try to destroy or undermine the North Atlantic Community and its civilization of human liberty.

Among the problems facing the Atlantic Community today is that of the integration of the underdeveloped countries into our common —hopefully common—world. It will be a difficult task, demanding the employment of all our intellectual and moral resources and a strenuous effort of rethinking and reordering familiar patterns. Yet modern Western civilization succeeded recently in a similarly difficult task. A century ago, Karl Marx expected that modern Western society would be destroyed by class war. The proletariat, the poor and the disinherited, seemed then not to form a real part of the common Western society and civilization. Not so long ago the workers in Germany were called *vaterlandslose Gesellen,* fellows without a Fatherland. All that has been completely changed—without much bloodshed or cataclysmic destruction. The workers in Britain or the United States, in Switzerland or in Norway, in the German Federal Republic or in Canada, are today an integral part of the common Atlantic Community and as ready to defend individual liberty as anyone else. The problem lying now ahead of the West may be vaster and more difficult. Yet with patience and moderation, guided by the ethical standards which form the core of the Atlantic civilization, we may succeed. We have made an auspicious start in the last ten years in India and the Philippines, in Ghana and Tunisia, in Iran and in Iraq.

* * *

The North Atlantic Community has no reason to indulge in fashionable pessimism. This pessimism contrasts with the vulgar optimism which oversimplified and coarsened much of nineteenth century thinking in the West. Both attitudes are in their extreme form untenable and dangerous. At present there exists for the dispassionate observer a strong foundation for optimism, a moderate and reasonable optimism, one that is conscious of the limits of all human endeavor, of the undeniably and fundamentally tragic character of human existence. It is an optimism, above all, which does not carry the image of a perfect or even near-perfect society here on earth. There can be no doubt that we have made great, though not unbroken, progress in the last two hundred years, not so much in technological inventions and scientific discoveries as in the humanization of our mores, in our greater consideration for our fellow-man, in the growth of social conscience and consciousness. My personal experience, during a life which began in the relatively halcyon years before World War I, has strengthened this optimism. It has been strengthened, further, by the astonishing and unexpected growth of the North Atlantic Community in recent years and by the spirit of this growth.

This spirit manifested itself time and again in the Conference on the North Atlantic Community which, co-sponsored by the University of Pennsylvania and the College of Europe, met in Bruges, Belgium, in September 1957. The intellectuals who gathered in Bruges from both sides of the Atlantic came as private individuals, each speaking only for himself and not for a nation or a party. Everyone spoke his mind freely, and opinions frequently clashed: nonconformism, after all, has been one of the elements making for the strength and resilience of our civilization. Yet, beyond this diversity, a remarkable unanimity reigned at Bruges: those who participated in the Conference were all united in a concern for the preservation and health of Free Society. Such a concern, and the desire for closer cooperation which springs from it, did not exist before the rise of fascism and communism. It exists today.

The recent progress of the idea of Atlantic unity provides cause for optimism. To the present generation this progress may appear slow and hesitant, yet one has only to think back forty years to realize how rapid and astonishing the progress has been. In 1917 Norman Angell, an Englishman who has been at home as much in the United States and in France as in his native country, called for Atlantic unity, a kind of democratic internationalism as he named it, to prevent German nationalism from re-starting the war and defeating the democracies. This Atlantic unity was then not created. In fact, each of the victorious democracies turned to isolationism. Jealousies and discord reigned among them, perhaps to a greater degree than before the war. This state of affairs, as Norman Angell had foreseen, encouraged the anti-Western dictatorships of communism and fascism to expect the imminent collapse of free society. Norman Angell proved a true prophet. Hardly twenty years after their victory the democracies found themselves threatened by the temporary alliance of the anti-Western dictatorships. Winston Churchill rightly called World War II an avoidable war. It could have been avoided if the Atlantic nations had chosen, after 1918, to follow the path which they have walked, albeit with difficulty, since 1949. Even twenty years ago, in 1937, when I pleaded for a firm alliance of the United States, Britain and France to prevent the spread of totalitarianism, the suggestion seemed entirely fantastic and outside the realm of practicability.

Now, twenty years later, the peoples of the North Atlantic Community have taken the very steps that seemed impossible a short while ago. Such an action implies a great change in the minds of men, and a new understanding of their situation. In many of the NATO institutions and colleges, men are growing into a new supranational community, losing their national prejudices, or at least some of them. There are many other and equally remarkable changes. Twenty years ago Franco-German wars were still regarded as possible; in fact their expectation has haunted my generation as it did many generations before it. Today, such a war has become unthinkable. Nor is there anyone who, in 1937 or 1940, would have believed it possible that Germany would turn to the West—not only politically but intellectually as the German Federal Republic has done, and as had never been the case under Bismarck or during the Weimar Republic. And there are very few people who would have expected, before 1956, that a youth educated for twelve years under rigid communist control would rise to reject this control and try earnestly and courageously to assert the freedom of the spirit. Thus we have witnessed in these last years many astonishing and hopeful changes in the minds of men and have seen how the idea of liberty can inspire new determination and new endeavors. There certainly is cause for optimism.

Some people are disturbed by much talk about tensions within the North Atlantic Community. These tensions undoubtedly exist. They have many causes. One of them is the growing influence of the United States—an influence which is not so much political and economic as it is moral and intellectual. Yet this growth of the American influence within the free world was foreseen long ago. Tocqueville, when he journeyed to the United States to study American democracy, came with the conviction that what was happening in America then would sooner or later happen in Western Europe. In 1902, an

English journalist, William Thomas Stead, the editor of *The Review of Reviews,* published a book called *The Americanization of the World or The Trend of the Twentieth Century.* He did not mean, by this title, America's coming political hegemony but the Americanization of European literature and art, marriage and society, habits of life and ways of consumption. He even spoke of an "American invasion" which, according to him, was then being bitterly resented by many Europeans "as if the Americans bearing gifts in their hands were bent upon doing us the greatest possible injury."

This Americanization of the Western world, foreseen by the Frenchman Tocqueville and by the Englishman Stead, as well as by many other Europeans in the eighteenth and nineteenth centuries, is not an accident. Certain trends of the modern Western world have been developed faster and earlier in this, the most modern and most Western state of the Atlantic Community, than in the more traditionbound societies of Europe. This Americanization may be inevitable and irreversible. Nevertheless, and understandably, it creates tensions and resentments the causes of which are deep-seated in human nature.

Today's anti-Americanism, which is widespread in Europe and understandably so, can be compared to the anti-Britishism which dominated many European minds in the nineteenth century. At that time Britain was, for the European continent, the most "modern" and "Western" nation in industrial development and civic liberty. At the same time, British motives were distrusted and the cry of "perfidious Albion" resounded throughout Europe. A French liberal like the historian Jules Michelet and a French reactionary like Charles Maurras—a German liberal like the poet Heinrich Heine and a German reactionary like the historian Heinrich Treitschke—all expressed, with even greater vehemence, the same arguments of dislike and hostility toward Britain which many writers from the left and the right voice today against the United States. Yet Britain survived and proved herself in 1940 the bulwark of Western civilization.

It would be a mistake to overrate the tensions within the North Atlantic Community. Tensions are an indispensable element of democratic society. There have been many and bitter tensions within the United States, and there are many and bitter tensions among the European nations. Belgium, for example, has long suffered under the conflict between its citizens of Flemish and of French language and, only recently, has passed through a violent crisis involving the question of the Royal Succession. Yet the United States and Belgium continue to exist and to flourish in spite of the undeniable tensions.

One has to be conscious of tensions and critically alert to them, but one must not overstress or overestimate them.

The Conference on the North Atlantic Community showed how little these tensions count when people are willing to face and discuss fundamental issues. The division of opinion in the discussions at Bruges was never on continental lines, not even on national lines. Americans freely disagreed with Americans and Europeans with Europeans. Complete agreement was reached on the fundamental principles of modern Western civilization. The round table charged with restating these principles performed its task brilliantly. Its success came probably as a surprise. Many books have been written in recent years on the foundations and traditions of modern Western civilization. Thus it seemed that the round table, in attempting to define the specific values cherished by the Atlantic Community, would have great difficulty in going beyond generally accepted platitudes. But the round table succeeded in stating the principles of the Atlantic Community in a refreshingly new way, clarifying some of the fundamental issues in the light not only of the tradition but also of the transformation which is taking place in Western society today. The tone of the statement is far removed from the smugness of the nineteenth century. It is the essence of modern Western civilization to be fully aware of its permanent need for critical self-examination. Even its most cherished principles have to demonstrate their worth again and again to successive generations and have to be embodied in changing social structures. Modern Western civilization is free from dogmatism. It is *"une civilisation de dialogue."* It believes in the patient discussion of differences, and this implies tolerance and the free interplay of all opinions. But tolerance has certain limits: we cannot tolerate the destruction of those institutions which make liberty and tolerance possible.

The round table stressed that the ties binding the Atlantic Community are spiritual and not racial. All men who embrace liberty and tolerance as we do are members of our Community, whatever their race, descent or origin. Therein again, the United States, which rightly has been called a melting pot, can be regarded as a prototype of the modern West. Not common descent but a common spirit has made America a nation. This spirit of an open society must be infused into the Atlantic Community as a whole. The Atlantic peoples, if they wish to remain true to their ideal and their mission, must be concerned with human dignity and liberty everywhere. The Committee of Three, which, in 1956, sought ways to broaden the scope of NATO, has rightly stressed that the Atlantic peoples, while striving to improve their own unity, must harmonize their policies in relation to other areas, taking into account the interests of the whole international community and all peoples. Nothing would be more dangerous to the idea and even the survival of the free West than a belief that the Western community is organizing for the pooling of the strength and resources of the "colonial" powers in defense of their possessions or of a Western hegemony.

This hegemony was undoubtedly a progressive factor in the nineteenth century. It was then the instrument for arousing the non-Western peoples to a consciousness of human dignity and to an effort for social and economic betterment. In the twentieth century this era of hegemony is over. The North Atlantic Community does not wish to organize against anybody. Its goal is positive, not negative: the strengthening of the cultural consciousness, of the moral vigor of the Atlantic Community, so that this strength may radiate and may be of help to all those who, under the inspiration of the Western traditions of individual liberty, seek this liberty themselves.

There is a second point in which the restatement of the principles of modern Western civilization proposed by the Bruges Conference deserves attention: it is in its reference to the great Russian writers of the nineteenth century who have enriched Western civilization. But these writers were not alone. Innumerable Russian men and women have heroically fought from 1825 on to bring Western liberty to Russia. Lenin's seizure of power in the chaos of 1917 has, for the time being, stultified their efforts. Politically Russia was a non-Western autocracy throughout the nineteenth century. Yet the spirit in Russia was relatively free, and, in continuous intercourse with the modern West, the creativeness of the Russian people has contributed considerably, and in the field of literature more than considerably, to the growth of Western civilization.

Brugge, the Flemish name for the site of the Conference on North Atlantic Community, signifies a bridge or "place of bridges." It was the task of this Conference to begin construction of a bridge of mutual understanding among nations sharing a common civilization. The participants were unanimous in the hope and the conviction that this Conference marked the beginning of a continuing and expanding dialogue, both within the Atlantic Community and with its partners in a greater community of the world.

29

United States Policy in the Cold War*

For the last twelve years United States foreign policy has largely been dominated by the fact and concept of the cold war. Three great initiatives that fundamentally changed United States foreign policy were taken under the impact of the Cold War—the Marshall Plan, the North Atlantic Treaty Organization, the resistance to Communist aggression in Korea. Each one of them implied a fundamental deviation from traditional American foreign policy. None could have been foreseen 20 years ago. They were the result of the completely changed framework of international relations as it emerged from World War II.

Yet the Cold War in itself is nothing new. It is based upon the fact that a great power's government regards itself bound by an ideology whose eventual spread all over the earth it believes salutary and inevitable. Such a situation does not lead necessarily to war in the usual sense of the word, but the government in question will try to spread its ideology through propaganda and subversion. The measures taken against Catholics in sixteenth century Britain were due largely to the fear of subversion on behalf of the great Catholic powers of that time. When Lenin came to power in Russia and when thereby the Communist ideology gained a great power basis, a new period of cold war started, such as had been unknown since the end of the French Revolutionary Wars.

The Second Congress of the Communist International at the end of July, 1920, adopted a number of theses drafted by Lenin. One of them read:

> The world political situation has now placed the dictatorship of the proletariat on the order of the day, and all events in world politics are inevitably grouped around a single central point—the struggle of the international bourgeoisie against the Russian Soviet Republic, which must gather around itself the Communist movements among the advanced workers of all countries and also all national liberation

* From *Current History*, October 1959. Copyright by *Current History*. Reprinted with permission.

movements of colonies and oppressed peoples, who have become convinced through bitter experience that their salvation lies only in union with the revolutionary proletariat and in the victory of the Soviet Power over Imperialism.

For the Russian Communist government the countries of the whole world were split into two hostile camps—the camp of Capitalism and the camp of Socialism, as a Declaration concerning the formation of the Union of Soviet Socialist Republics (1923) proclaimed. The Soviet Union was regarded not as a nation-state in the nineteenth century sense, not as a federal transformation of the former Russian empire comparable perhaps to the British Commonwealth of Nations or the *Communauté Française,* but as a decisive step on the road to the Socialist World Soviet Republic.

To the dynamic of this goal all means are subordinated. The Communist certainty of victory is based on a confidence free from all moral concepts. It starts from the conviction, to quote Engels:

> that there must be a revolution in the methods of production and distribution which sets aside all differences of class, if the whole of modern society is not to suffer dissolution. On this tangible material fact, which is forcing its way irresistibly into the heads of the exploited proletarians in more or less clear shape, on this fact and not on the conceptions of right and wrong of this or the other arm-chair theoretician, is based the certainty of victory of modern Socialism.

From the beginning the Russian Communist government was conducting a cold war against "Capitalism," "Imperialism," and "the Bourgeoisie." But between 1918 and 1940 the main target of the cold war was, for obvious reasons, Western Europe and not the United States. The British and the French empires were expanding after World War I and seemed unshaken in the 1920's. Italian and German Fascism were, in the Communist interpretation, only more vigorous forms of capitalist imperialism. The United States, which was at that time pursuing a policy of isolationism and had little involvement in Asian and African affairs, receded into the background of the international picture, as seen from Moscow. But it should not be overlooked that the cold war is always a global war, seen from the Communist point of view, in which only the chief protagonists change from time to time according to shifts in the international power context.

This context was fundamentally changed by World War II. The Communist base expanded until it reached in 1949 a contiguous territory stretching from the Elbe to Shanghai. The British and French Empires in Asia came to an end and they are coming to an end in Africa. Western Europe might gain real strength only by overcoming the nationalism and by abandoning the imperialism of each component nation. The example of France since the anti-democratic revolution of May, 1958, shows how slight the hope is for such a development. The only "capitalistic" nation which emerged greatly strengthened from World War II was the United States. Automatically it became the chief target of the Communist cold war. Without desiring such responsibility, the United States found itself the chief protagonist of the "capitalistic" or the "free" world. The United States had to adapt itself to this new situation. It should not be overlooked that basically we are not confronted with a conflict between the United States and the U.S.S.R., but with a conflict, inherent in Communist ideology, between the Communist power center and the outside world which by historical necessity is to become Communist too, though it may dislike it and resist it.

Under these conditions, what is the goal of the United States foreign policy? In the age of nationalism and of nation-states the primary goal of foreign policy is national security. That holds true, of course, even at a time when thermo-nuclear weapons may be used in a war. New technological inventions have always influenced military strategy; they cannot change the fundamental facts of the context of international relations. Even ideological powers like Communist Russia, in the context of the age of nation-states, have to pursue a foreign policy based on national security. But at a time of dynamic ideological conflict national security includes elements which it would not contain in "normal" times. Not only the methods but also the concept of national security change with the general context of international relations. The national security of the United States is not only dependent on American military posture; economic, psychological and, above all, moral factors enter the picture.

It is an undue over-simplification to reduce the relationship between the United States and the U.S.S.R. to the question of whether war will break out between the two powers. Between 1922 and 1939 the U.S.S.R. did not start a war in the usual sense of the word. Nevertheless, it conducted its cold war. It is true that at that time the U.S.S.R. was economically weak and torn by internal dissension. Today the Soviet Union is economically strong and Khrushchev's dictatorship causes probably less dissension and fear than did Stalin's blood-thirsty tyranny. On the other hand, there is more at stake for the growing ruling class in Russia today, which would be endangered by a real war, than there was under Stalin.

"Capitalist" aggression against the U.S.S.R is also an unlikely probability. Such danger really never existed after the consolidation of the Soviet regime in 1920. The Conservative British government of 1938, which had every good reason, as any free government has, to distrust the Communist regime—and especially that of Stalin who in the preceding years had ruthlessly sacrificed the Soviet peoples themselves, Communist and non-Communist—had clearly no intention to attack, directly or indirectly, the Soviet Union, as Communist propagandists at that time tried to persuade the world. By guaranteeing, in an unprecedented step, Poland's (and Rumania's) security against German aggression, Britain indirectly protected Russia against Germany. The Polish government had rejected previous German offers of a common action against Russia. It was Stalin who by his pact with Hitler in August, 1939, destroyed Poland and thereby made the German attack on Russia in 1941 possible. Nor did the United States make use of its tremendous technological superiority between 1945 and 1949 to prevent the expansion of communism.

The foreign policy of the United States vis-à-vis the U.S.S.R. must therefore be a policy which, although being prepared for war, does not regard war as probable. It is not only thermo-nuclear weapons that make wars less probable than wars were at the beginning of the century; the attitude of peoples towards war has also changed. In World War I, at least in 1914-1915, nations entered the war readily, and many people even with enthusiasm. The picture had already changed by 1939, when not only in Paris and London but even in Berlin the people (in the case of Berlin the government differed therein from the people) entered the war with much more apprehension than enthusiasm. In the 20 intervening years the disapproval of war has grown. There may be exceptions like the approval in Israel and France for the war of 1956, but the overwhelming force of disapproval expressed everywhere was a stronger indication of the general trend. It is very difficult to substantiate any statement about the feelings and reactions of the Soviet people, but it is most probable that the Soviet people are deeply apprehensive of another major war. In the case of a thermo-nuclear war, not only the Russian people and soldiers would be in grave danger, but also the Communist leadership.

Considerations like these, however, will not lead to a relaxation of the tension that is caused by Communist ideology, nor can they lead to any real disarmament so long as the tension continues. And it should not be forgotten that the tension created by communism is not the only source of unrest in this world, nor the only threat which may in the future face the national security of the United States. The bi-polarization of the world as it existed around 1950 does not exist any longer. Probably it will lose even more of its importance in the future.

The various European nations which in the late 1940's were of little account have regained ample strength. In her foreign policy the United States has to take that into consideration. In 1947, the Communist world had only one power center, Moscow. Things have since become much more complex. Peking, Belgrade and Warsaw have emerged, to a varying degree, as power centers of their own, and nobody can foresee where this unexpected (in 1947) development may lead. Above all, the whole world situation has been changed fundamentally since 1949 by the growing number of independent states in Asia and Africa and by the overthrow of dictatorships in Latin America.

The end of the colonial age has come not only for Asia but for Africa with unprecedented rapidity. There are dynamic forces at work throughout the three great underdeveloped continents which will create in the 1960's, as far as can be foreseen, a new context of international relations, within which United States foreign policy against the U.S.S.R. and against communism in general will have to be redefined. No fundamental change can be expected, but the new situation may be as different from the late 1940's as these were from the late 1920's. These are all stages in one "protracted conflict," which communism started against the non-Communist world in November, 1917. It would be as mistaken to overlook this fact as it would be to overlook the changing configurations and the different attitudes and measures demanded in each of the various stages.

For the stage of development of the "protracted conflict" which set in with the end of World War II and which is now coming to its end, United States foreign policy has, on the whole, been successful. Thanks to it, communism did not expand in Europe; and Western Europe has consolidated its position to a remarkable degree. One has to compare today's situation with that of 1946-1947, to measure the success of United States foreign policy in Europe. By strengthening the security of Western Europe, the United States has strengthened its own national security. The purpose of United States foreign policy is not only the preservation of its national security, but at least indirectly, the preservation and growth of democratic liberty everywhere. Even from that point of view the balance sheet of Europe is positive. Democratic liberty is as safe today in Britain, in Scandinavia and in the Low Countries, as it has been throughout recent times. Democratic liberties were reestablished in Germany, Austria and Italy to a degree which 20 years ago no one would have believed possible.

True, democratic liberties do not exist in central-eastern Europe, including eastern Germany. This is deeply regrettable but it is not the fault of United States foreign policy. In eastern Germany no democratic liberties existed in 1939 and even in other central-eastern European territories not democratic, but semi-dictatorial regimes were in power before these countries succumbed to Communist dictatorship. But that they succumbed to it was the fault of German policy, first by its pact of friendship with Stalin in 1939 and then by its aggression against Russia in 1941. It was German policy, and not American mistakes, which brought the Soviet army and Communist tyranny to Berlin and Prague, to Warsaw and Bucharest. In the spring of 1941, the whole of continental Europe, with the exception of two small enclaves, was ruled by four tyrannies which at that time seemed co-ordinated in their policies, the tyrannies of Stalin, Hitler, Mussolini and Franco. That was less than 20 years ago. Today, largely thanks to British courage and to United States foreign policy, a very large part of Europe has been liberated from tyranny and has grown in liberty and wealth. The "sick man" of free Europe is at present France, where political stability, national self-confidence and economic order have been restored at the expense of democracy and at the tremendous cost of extolling nationalism and imperialist pride, a most dangerous anachronism. For this development United States foreign policy is hardly responsible.

That the United States was relatively successful in Europe is understandable. There we face old established nations which, at least at present and with the exception of the Iberian peninsula, share our cultural and political traditions. But the most important event of the twentieth century is the end of the European phase of world history, a phase which has lasted for four centuries and which has created the technical and intellectual premises for the emergence of a real world history instead of a history of fragmented civilizations. The process of emancipation which is now going on irreversibly in the "underdeveloped" countries is a part of the "Westernization" of the globe, in many ways its fruit and fulfillment.

The transition from colonial or semi-colonial status—politically, economically and culturally—to self-government and equality is an immensely difficult revolutionary process, which takes place in Cuba and Guinea, in Egypt and in Vietnam. This revolutionary transition came to most people as a surprise; few in 1945 expected the situation which we are facing in 1960 and which is only the beginning of a far broader transformation.

How far has United States foreign policy been successful in the underdeveloped countries which represent the majority of mankind and whose influence is rapidly growing? Again a considered judgment will be on the whole affirmative. The transition is proceeding more smoothly, especially in the former British colonies, than any one had a right to expect. The attitude of the United States in the attack upon Egypt in 1956 went far to reassure the underdeveloped countries that the period of armed imperialist intervention is past. The attitude of the United States in that case was supported by the majority of the free European peoples. The trip of Vice-President Richard Nixon to Ghana and to other independent states in Africa in the spring of 1957 was an indication of our sympathy for the aspirations of the African people. At the same time the definite though slow progress achieved in the last years in securing for our own colored fellow-citizens, in the North as much as in the South, a full share in the life of their country is in line with the general trend of the times. The fact that there are still islands of resistance to this trend—the cruel colonial war in Algeria, the position of Africans in the Union of South Africa, our support of dictators in Spain and Latin America—weakens the position of the West in its struggle with communism. For this struggle is not only one of military might or economic efficiency, but of ideas.

What should be the principles underlying United States foreign policy in the decade ahead? First: we must recognize that though the forms of the protracted conflict may change the conflict will go on. It is grounded in the very philosophy of communism. Should this philosophy change, it would mean the end of the protracted conflict and also the end of communism. Nothing of that kind is in sight. Communism rightly feels stronger today than it was 10 or 25 years ago. Western civilization will have to face for any foreseeable future the contest with communism. This is in itself no misfortune. It forces the West not only into greater unity, into growing beyond the confines of the nation-state, but also into a new awareness of its own principles of liberty for all and an earnest effort to apply them.

The United States may be the leader of this effort not because she is the strongest of the Western nations, but because modern Western civilization found here fewer obstacles of the past to overcome. This was partly due to the fact that the United States was a British colony, and England was at that time the most modern and liberal country. These fortunate conditions did not exist in Latin America.

Second: communism is as totalitarian a regime as fascism. From the rise of Lenin to the death of Stalin, from 1917 to 1953, it has shown the same traits of brutality and of disregard of human values as did National Socialism. In a Communist regime, even if it avoids excesses of brutality, there cannot be liberty. Leninism and liberty are mutually exclusive. But that does not mean that the Soviet Union of today can be compared with the Germany of 1939. The shades of Munich confuse more than they enlighten. Khrushchev is not Hitler. He is not an impatient fanatic, but a shrewd and tough peasant-politician who knows how to bide his time. The Russian people are not the German people. Though the Russians expanded more widely than the Germans and fought many wars of conquest, glorification of war and the warrior as such has little place in their national mythology. Above all, after 1918, the Germans felt that they were a defeated people in a narrow territory in which they had no *Lebensraum* (this feeling was unjustified as proved by Germany today, which prospers with much less *Lebensraum,* but the feeling existed and was dominant in Germany before 1933).

Russia is a victorious nation, victorious beyond anyone's expectations, including her own in 1939. Russia has at present more than enough *Lebensraum* and years of hard work ahead of her, to reach the standard of living not of the United States, but that which Germany had reached before Hitler. There is no reason to expect Khrushchev to act as Hitler acted. And there is one more fundamental difference: in the 1930's Britain and the United States were disarmed and the United States had a disastrous neutrality legislation. At present, and that will be true for the future, the United States and Britain are united and are well armed.

Third: it is a great mistake to explain the revolutionary changes going on in the whole world *sub specie Communismi*. That gives much too much credit to communism and plays into its hands. Unrest in Cuba and Algeria is due to conditions in those countries, not to Communist influence. The leaders are inspired by the ideas of 1789 and by the example of the United States. Fifty years ago labor unrest in this country was attributed to "agitators," who were called anarchists or Communists according to the fashion of the times. The labor unrest ceased because the conditions which caused it fundamentally changed. United States foreign policy has to support, as far as it can, a similar change of conditions everywhere. It will thereby strengthen the Western cause and its own national security. The West, and not communism, is the advocate of human liberty and dignity, of self-government and equal justice for all. It must reassert its leadership in these fields, at least as much as in those of armaments and technology. The over-estimation of sputniks is characteristic of Communist mentality. The realization of human rights is the strong and unique Western weapon.

30

Khrushchev's Foreign Policy[*]

Late in 1959, the prospect of world peace seemed to the general public most promising. Nikita Khrushchev had visited the United States. He came with his family and showed himself as a man with a sense of humor and with a touch of the common folk. His reception, for these very reasons, had been on the whole friendly. There was no untoward incident. The summit conference was accepted as certain,

[*] From *Current History*, November 1960. Copyright by *Current History*. Reprinted with permission.

and generally the public expected some good results from it. Khrushchev talked of peaceful coexistence, and of the avoidance of World War III, and did not advance any ultimatum regarding the position of West Berlin.

By the summer of 1960, the public mood had changed. The summit conference ended in failure. While still stressing the desire for, and the need of, peaceful coexistence, Khrushchev was full of angry words, and some of the familiar accusations against the government of the United States which belonged to the liturgic formulas of former Soviet utterances reappeared in full strength.

Nevertheless, there has been no real change in the situation. No summit conference could have changed the fundamental fact that there are two opposing and mutually exclusive systems of understanding human nature and the course of history, each of which is convinced of its superiority, its final survival value, and its victory. The existence of these two opposite systems is the cause of the existing tension. There is no need to believe that this tension can be decisively lessened. There is equally no reason to believe that it will lead to war.

There are two reasons which make a war most improbable. The first one is the nature of the new armaments, the consequence of which will make war disastrous even for the victor. The second, and by no means lesser (though frequently overlooked) reason, is the growth of world public opinion as a factor indirectly influencing policy. This world opinion is not only that of the democratic and the Communist worlds. Since 1945, a third world has emerged and asserts itself more and more. This world is neither traditionally democratic nor communist; it does not wish to depend either on Moscow or Washington, and this fact has changed the world situation and altered the bipolarity which characterized it in 1945 and in the years immediately following.

Whether Khrushchev uses sweet or violent language, the cold war will go on without deteriorating into a hot war. Whenever Khrushchev uses sweet language, the continuing tension will be called peaceful coexistence. Though sweet language sounds better than violent words, it must not lull the West into somnolence which is one of the purposes of the use of the sweet language. Peaceful coexistence is only a pleasanter name for cold war. In their essence they are the same.

The tension between the U.S.S.R. and its East European friends on the one hand and the Chinese People's Republic on the other hand—a tension which was one of the most important events of 1960—clearly shows that Khrushchev is bent upon preserving the cold war as a cold war. For obvious reasons Communist China views the world situation differently from Communist Russia. China has more than three times the population of Russia. The Chinese population lives on a much lower level. The country is 30 years behind Soviet Russia. It is much more secluded, isolated and xenophobic than Khrushchev's Russia. It cares much less about world public opinion. It knows much less of the outside world and of the real strength of the United States.

In that way Communist China's attitude resembles today much more Hitler's attitude with its deep contempt for Western strength and cohesion than Khrushchev's. Khrushchev knows of the strength of the United States; he speaks frequently of overtaking the United States in various fields of production and in various aspects of the standard of living and of public welfare. In a strange but revealing way the United States is a model for the Soviet Union. China, on the other hand, is much more self-centered and apparently much more conscious of its own coming superiority.

Thus at present the wing of world communism following Khrushchev's lead maintains that communism can reach its goal without war, on the strength of its own achievements and through the disintegration of the democratic world (a view similarly held by the democratic world about its survival and final victory), whereas the wing of world communism following China's lead believes in the inevitability of war as long as democracy—called capitalism or imperialism—exists. The Chinese spokesmen regard it as a dangerous illusion to believe that democracy will disintegrate without war.

They are convinced that World War III will end with a sweeping triumph of communism all over the globe. The First World War, they say, led to the establishment of Leninism in the Russian Empire; the Second World War resulted not only in an immensely strengthened Communist Russia under Stalin but also in the expansion of its doctrine and influence over central eastern Europe to the Elbe River and the Adriatic Sea on the one hand, to China, North Korea and North Vietnam on the other hand, an expansion which in 1939 no one would have foreseen and which was bought at the cost of great suffering by the Russian people. World War III, at the expense of great suffering, will end in the final triumph of communism. Time does not work for the victory of communism; war does. Khrushchev does not share this point of view. Nor does Tito or Gomulka.

This very real difference in judging the world situation does not, however, destroy the unity and the cooperation of the Communist bloc. For the time being and for the foreseeable future the leadership in this bloc belongs to Soviet Russia. This will help to make the outbreak of World War III improbable. It is sometimes forgotten that a relatively short while ago the outbreak of a major war was threatened around the islands of Quemoy and Matsu. The war, then expected by many, did not happen.

The situation in West Berlin is not very different. In spite of all the bitter denunciations of Chiang Kai-shek as an aggressive warmonger, the Chinese Communists know well that under today's circumstances Chiang Kai-shek cannot invade the Chinese mainland. In spite of all the vituperation against Adenauer as a second Hitler preparing a war against the East, it is quite clear not only that Adenauer is in every way different from Hitler but also that power relationships in Europe have completely changed in the past 20 years, and this as a result of Hitler's criminal folly.

Germany today is much smaller and weaker than she was in 1939, and Russia today is much larger and infinitely stronger. The Germany of 1939 was defeated by the Russia of that time. A similar venture today would be outright madness. The chances of Germany in 1939 were enhanced by two facts which do not exist any longer. On the one hand, France and Britain did not enjoy the full and open support of the United States, and Germany did and could expect that the United States, voluntarily disarmed and in the throes of an economic depression, would stay out of the war. Today the United States is fortunately highly armed and in closest cooperation with Britain.

On the other hand, there were a number of weak and disunited states between Germany and Russia, which afforded to the Germans the possibility of imposing their will and domination over these states easily. At present these states, above all Poland and Czechoslovakia, are close allies of Russia and can count immediately on her full support. They are today also more industrialized and better armed than they were in 1939.

Whether or not the mind of Germany has changed in the last 15 years, there is no doubt that objective conditions and power relationships are no longer those of 1914 or 1939 and make impossible a third attempt on the part of Germany to establish her hegemony in central and east-central Europe.

Under the protective shield of NATO, Western Europe, including the Federal Republic of Germany, has made great progress toward a peak of unprecedented prosperity. So long as NATO is firmly maintained, there is no great danger of deterioration in the Berlin situation. It is to be hoped that the insistence on a fundamental revision of NATO in President de Gaulle's press conference of September 5, 1960, will have no effect and that NATO will not be weakened.

In Europe, outside France, it was generally felt that the two favorite ideas of President de Gaulle—a three power directory within the alliance, and purely national control over its military forces—would weaken the peace and security of Europe. The Athens newspaper, "Ethnos," summed up prevailing European opinion when it wrote on September 6, 1960.

> General de Gaulle's speech may flatter French national susceptibilities but can hardly be said to serve NATO. . . . If all NATO forces came under a purely national command, how could we ever ensure unity of defense and immediate reaction of a common defense system in the event of a Soviet surprise attack? . . . Unfortunately for the free world, the General seems far more interested in the grandeur of France than in present reality, the gravity of which is persistently outlined by Soviet actions.

At the time of writing—the beginning of September, 1960—it seems highly improbable that the Berlin situation will lead to serious aggravations in the near future. The government of the Federal Republic of Germany can be expected, with the support of its British and American allies, to forego all demonstrations of a prestige policy which would not change the reality. Berlin will not become again, in any foreseeable future, the Reichshauptstadt, which it was in the short time of the Second and Third Reich from Bismarck to Hitler. At the same time, Britain and the United States will not allow the liberty of the West Berlin people to be endangered. As Professor Karl Jaspers pointed out in August, 1960, the concern of the Germans cannot be primarily national unity or reunification but the maintenance and expansion of liberty.

With the broadening of the world stage, which has gone on rapidly since 1945, the center of the cold war has been shifting from Europe to Asia, Africa, and Latin America. In spite of the errors committed by the West in Egypt and the Arab lands, and in spite of the French war fought in Algeria and of recent Belgian mistakes in the Congo, the Asian and African leaders have in their vast majority clearly shown that their concern is with the independence, dignity and welfare of their peoples and that they show no inclination whatsoever to exchange Western domination for Soviet domination.

The moderation shown by the leaders of the independent African countries in the recent Congo crisis and in the United Nations has again proved this fact. Only if denied recognition of their rights—of those rights which they learned from the West—by the West, will African, Arab and Asian leaders turn for assistance to the Soviet Union.

It would be wrong for the West to respect the rights and dignity of Asians, Arabs and Africans out of fear of Soviet competition. There is some suspicion abroad that it is the fear of the potentially growing influence of communism which inspires the liberal attitudes on the part of the West. In reality, the West, and above all the United States and Britain, must show an understanding of the aspirations of the Asian, Arab and African peoples, not because the West fears communism, but because Westerners are aware of historical changes which have come about largely as a result of the penetration and the victory of modern Western ideas of human dignity and equality. In such a case, Communist hopes of turning the cold war of peaceful coexistence to communism's own advantage will be defeated.

31

The United Nations and National Self-Determination*

National self-determination and the United Nations are modern concepts of political thought. Of the two the first is older and has struck much stronger roots. Its origin can be traced back to the American and French revolutions at the end of the eighteenth century. The latter gained recognition only in the period of the First World War. Both owe their conceptual frame and their ideological content to modern Western civilization, above all to Anglo-American thought. Yet the two concepts are to a degree contradictory: the United Nations envisages an international or supranational order at a time when nationalism—the insistence on national independence, self-determination, and self-expression as supreme political values and emotional guides—has for the first time in history become a world-wide phenomenon.

Even in the great conflicts of the twentieth century the battle lines have not been drawn primarily on ideological grounds. The contests of 1914, of 1939, and those of the present day have not followed a clearcut line between parliamentary democracy and absolutism, pacificism and militarism, communism and fascism. The ideologies often have become instruments of national policy, as they were in the past—the Catholic faith for the Spain of Philip II and Greek Orthodoxy for the Russia of Danilevsky or Dostoevsky. Within each ideological camp national interests and antagonisms have continued to assert themselves. It is true that fascism as an ideology, in the service of German and Japanese nationalism, unleashed World War II, and that communism as an ideology in the service of Russian and Chinese nationalism forces the democratic powers into an armament race and into some degree of concerted action. But World War II started with an aggression of fascist Germany against semifascist Poland; fascist Italy made its independent contribution to the extension of the war by attacking an outright fascist Greece; and

* First published in *The Review of Politics,* Vol. 20 (October 1958), pp. 526-545. Reprinted with permission.

fascist Japan did not face in the China of 1937 a parliamentary democracy. Should the communist menace disappear today, nationalist hostilities in East Central Europe, between India and Pakistan, between Israel and the Arab nation, between the Algerians and France, would reappear or continue. China will cling to its imperial control over Sinkiang and Tibet, and after having acquired greater strength may put forward claims to Korea, Indo-China, and Burma, whether ruled by communist or anticommunist nationalism. Today as after 1918, nationalism is a dominant force; since 1918 its impact has widened geographically to an extent hardly foreseen in 1918. Understandably the problems caused by nationalism, by national aspirations and the demand for self-determination, played an important role in the League of Nations and play an even more important role in the United Nations.

The theory of national self-determination was put forward in and after 1848 with growing success in central and central eastern Europe as a basis for international law and democratic rights. Public opinion in the English speaking countries supported this trend. It endorsed Mazzini, Garibaldi, and Kossuth; it favored Greeks and Poles. Pasquale Stanislao Mancini, one of the great Italian jurists of the nineteenth century and, later, minister of justice and, then, of foreign affairs, of United Italy, delivered at Turin in 1851 his famous lecture *Della nazionalità come fondamento del diritto delle genti* (On Nationality as the Foundation of International Law). There he declared with words clearly intended against Austria that a state in which several nationalities found themselves forced into a union was not a political body but a monster incapable of life. "The nationalities," he wrote, "which do not possess a government issuing from their inmost life (governo uscito dalle proprie viscere), and which are subject to laws which are imposed upon them from the outside, . . . have become means for the purposes of others and, therefore, mere objects." In those words Mancini justified the ethos of national self-determination by linking it with the teachings of Locke, Rousseau, and Kant, with the Declaration of Independence and the Declaration of the Rights of Man and the Citizen.

As World War I dragged on and as its character changed after the Russian Revolution of March, 1917, and the entry of the United States into the War one month later, the rights of nationality and of national self-determination became one of the principles for which the Allies avowedly fought. Lloyd George declared on January 5,

1918, that "a territorial settlement . . . based on the right of self-determination or the consent of the governed" was one of the three fundamental conditions of a permanent peace. In the same month President Wilson declared that "an evident principle runs through the whole program I have outlined. It is the principle of justice to all peoples and nationalities, and their right to live on equal terms of liberty and safety with one another, whether they be strong or weak. Unless this principle be made its foundation no part of the structure of international justice can stand." In that way the Allied war aims in the last stage of the war took up, and tried to fulfill, the goal of the European "Spring of the Peoples" of 1848. The United States under Woodrow Wilson led the effort to make national self-determination one of the fundamental principles of the new international law. From Woodrow Wilson down to the present, the United States, more than any great power in history has believed in and tried to bring about self-determination for all peoples.

* * *

In 1918 the United States, however, was not alone in appealing to, and for, national self-determination. On the eve of the October 1917 revolution Lenin, understanding and using the trends of the time, embraced and proclaimed the principle of national self-determination, though it contradicted all the doctrinal and organizational principles of Leninsm. It was on his part a tactical move to win the cooperation first of the non-Russian nationalities in the Russian Empire which he restored on a new basis, and then of peoples outside the Empire. From the beginning his attention was directed toward Asia, where even before 1914 he had noted and understood the importance of the new nationalist movements, overlooked by most Western statesmen. In spite of the identity of the term—"national self-determination"—its meaning with Lenin had as little in common with Western usage as was the case with other terms like "peace," "democracy," or "liberty." Communist practice could not, nor did it ever, recognize self-determination, whether for individuals or for groups. To communism persons and nationalities alike were not ends in themselves but instruments to be used in various and opportunist ways for the ultimate goal, the realization of Leninism in and through a world-wide society. In his "The Law of the Soviet State" Andrei Vyshinsky re-iterated the "equality of rights of all nationalities," and the "inalienable right of nations to self-determination, including the right of withdrawal," a theoretical right guaranteed the nationalities of the Soviet Empire in the Constitution yet never realizable in a system clearly controlled from the center of world communism and where all actions were to be judged from the point of view of world communism alone.

* * *

Thanks to the leadership of the United States, national self-determination in spite of the difficulties of its concrete application and juridical definition, became part of the recognized law of nations in the peace treaties of 1919 and in the Covenant of the League of Nations, a document which owed its spirit and letter to Anglo-American ideals. In the recognition of liberalism and nationalism, of government based upon the consent of the governed, the peace treaties of 1919, incorporating the Covenant, marked the development of Europe since 1815 and its "Americanization" accomplished during World War I. The Covenant paid its tribute to the new principle also in the granting of protection, based upon the guaranties of international law, to national minorities within member states, and in the introduction of the mandate system. But the League of Nations still looked to the recent past; it was based on the traditional Europe-centered view of international relations. In 1919 Lenin was the only statesman who recognized that the "European order" was passing, that a "world revolution" was under way, a process which his dogmatic approach misinterpreted as the doom of free Western society.

Nevertheless, Lenin's recognition of the fundamental changes contained a true observation not generally seen even when the United Nations was founded. The historical transformation of Asia and Africa under the impact of the Western forces of nationalism and industrialism was by then fully under way. Among the original members of the new world body were Egypt, Ethiopia, Iraq, Lebanon, Saudi Arabia, and Syria, countries which had not been represented in 1920. In the first two years of the existence of the United Nations, Afghanistan, Thailand, Pakistan, and Yemen joined. In the following decade a number of Asian and African new nations was admitted, though this was balanced by the simultaneous admission of European nations (Austria, Bulgaria, Finland, Hungary, Ireland, Italy, Portugal, Rumania, Spain). Even in the United Nations of 1958 the European and Latin-American nations—many of whom are of relatively very small population—are heavily overrepresented in relation to their share in world population. This overrepresentation takes into account the historical role of the West in developing the present international system, and today this overrepresentation also corresponds to the military and economic power potential. It may not do so in a few decades. The future historian may regard as the greatest "revolution" of the twentieth century not Lenin's overthrow of the short-lived free regime in Russia in November, 1917, but the less conspicuous—there were no ten days or even ten years that shook the world—and, yet, more far-reaching process which brought Europe's four hundred year old dominion of the globe to an end, but at the same time spread Western principles of self-determination and nationalism to the most distant corners of the earth.

It is easily understandable that such a tremendous change which progresses with bewildering rapidity produces many serious strains, demands painful reappraisals and readjustments. The shift of gravity takes place simultaneously at several levels. In the Western world the political and economic power-center has been transferred from western Europe to North America. In the free world as a whole the influence of Asian and African nations, many of whom did not exist a few years ago, is growing. Even in the totalitarian world of communism the Asian partner, China, is fast asserting a role of leadership, as first shown by Chou En-lai's visit in 1957 to Warsaw, Budapest, and Moscow to help settle conflicts among European Communists.

In such a revolutionary situation the United Nations gains added importance as compared with the League of Nations, which operated within a seemingly still stable world. The League was unable to cope with the problems brought before it for the very reason that it took the continuation of the existing power-system for granted. The UN differs fundamentally from the League. It is conscious of the need for accommodation in a revolutionary stage of transition. Here the public opinion of the two major English-speaking nations, which form the core of modern Western civilization and have had the greatest influence in spreading liberalism and industrialism throughout the world, has on the whole, faithful to its own traditions, pointed the way.

It was Edmund Burke who, in the second half of the eighteenth century, insisted that the government of dependent territories, especially of those inhabited by less developed populations, was a sacred trust in which the interests of the native population had to be primarily considered. Thereafter this concept has dominated much of British and American thought and it has found its expression in the League of Nations and in the United Nations. The trusteeship idea, long before it was put down in legal terms, provided the rationale for British rule in India. Moritz Julius Bonn in his article on "Imperialism" in the *Encyclopaedia of the Social Sciences* summed up the reasoning about the intrinsic connection between modern Western civilization at home and self-government in the territories, where the West penetrated: "The natives were taught to believe that penetration and permeation of the alien European civilization were essential to their well being and might lead ultimately to self-government. The growth in England of liberal ideas of justice and economy and the development of democratic institutions made such alien rule appear irrational to rulers as well as ruled, and it was philosophically justified only as a sort of temporary control at the end of which stood independence or partnership."

In this spirit Macaulay introduced the Government of India bill before the House of Commons in 1833: "We are told that the time can never come when the natives of India can be admitted to high civil and military office. We are told that we are bound to confer on our subjects every benefit... which we can confer on them without hazard to our own domination. Against that proposition I solemnly protest as inconsistent alike with sound policy and sound morality. ... It may be that the public mind of India may expand under our system till it has outgrown that system; ... that, having become instructed in European knowledge, they may, in some future age, demand European institutions. Whether such a day will ever come, I know not. But never will I attempt to avert or to retard it. Whenever it comes, it will be the proudest day in English history."

The liberal British ideas of trusteeship and self-government applied to colonial territories, determined also United States policy after 1898. The United States regarded itself as trustee for the people of underdeveloped areas temporarily under its control. In his first annual message to Congress at the end of 1913 Woodrow Wilson said of the Philippines: "We must hold steadily in view their ultimate independence, and we must move towards the time of that independence as steadily as the way can be cleared and the foundations thoughtfully and permanently laid." In the Jones Act of 1916 Congress asserted that "it is, as it has always been, the purpose of the people of the United States to withdraw their sovereignty over the

Philippine Islands and to recognize their independence as soon as a stable government can be established therein." Thus the two great democracies of the West laid the foundations for a conscious and evolutionary growth of self-determination and political liberty throughout the politically and economically dependent or underdeveloped parts of mankind.

At the beginning of the twentieth century Woodrow Wilson predicted its course in an article "Democracy and Efficiency," in which he wrote:

> The East is to be opened and transformed whether we will or no; the standards of the West are to be imposed upon it; nations and peoples which have stood still the centuries through are to be quickened, and made part of the universal world of commerce and of ideas which has so steadily been a-making by the advance of European power from age to age. It is our peculiar duty as it is also England's, to moderate the process in the interest of liberty, [and to secure to the peoples thus driven out on the road of change,] the free intercourse and the natural development which will make them equal members of the family of nations.

The family of nations within which this transition could be achieved in an orderly way, was organized under Wilsonian inspiration in the League of Nations first, and, then, in the United Nations.

* * *

Both these organizations were in principle open to all nations, great and small alike, nations necessarily at various stages of development, as far as they were willing to accept the obligations of the Covenant and the Charter. Forty-two nations originally became members of the League, and another score were later admitted to membership. Only four nations never applied for membership—Saudi Arabia (the Hejaz was an original member but refused to ratify the peace treaty), Yemen, Nepal, and the United States of America. Among the members were many weak undeveloped states, such as: Liberia, Albania, Ethiopia, Afghanistan, Haiti, and the Dominican Republic. Yet it can hardly be said that these small and underdeveloped countries caused the breakdown of the League of Nations and the wars which destroyed the peace. The new and frightening barbarism, responsible for the moral and political disorder which soon was to engulf mankind, originated in powerful nations which had long been regarded as either highly civilized or as being among the leading great powers. This barbarism in its communist and fascist forms involved the rejection of the principles of the Anglo-American political tradition.

What World War I, under American leadership, did for establishing the principle of national self-determination for Central and Central Eastern Europe, World War II did for Asia and Africa. In East Central Europe itself national socialist and later Communist action—originally in cooperation in 1939-1940—destroyed the principle and reality of national self-determination, either by abolishing it entirely or by imposing upon the various nationalities forms of government and political ideology alien and often abhorrent to those nationalities. On the other hand the principle of self-determination in Asia and Africa was helped by being proclaimed as one of the goals of Anglo-American policy in the Atlantic Charter, signed by Franklin D. Roosevelt and Winston Churchill in August 1941. The effect of the Charter remained great, though its application was not clearly defined.

More influential in accelerating the movement for national self-determination in Asia and Africa than the policy statements of Western leaders were the quick and total collapse of French resistance to German aggression and the Japanese conquest and "liberation" of European colonial possessions in the Far East. These events profoundly changed the attitudes of the Asian and African masses. The war, started by European power ambitions and isolationist nationalism and by Japanese imperialism, roused the peoples outside Europe out of lethargic acceptance of their status. Soviet propaganda had little to do with it. The transformation was the work of Western influence and of examples, good and bad, set by the West. After 1945 the European empires though they did not always recognize it lacked the power to enforce a resumption of the old status.

In this changed situation a return to pre-1939 "normalcy" was unthinkable. The United States understood it well. In spite of suggestions that the date for granting full independence to the Philippines should be re-considered as a consequence of the ravages of war and the cooperation of prominent Filipinos with the Japanese, the United States kept its promise and the islands became independent on July 4, 1946. Nor did Britain, in her old liberality and realistic wisdom, attempt to restore her valuable and renowned Asian empire. From 1947 on she brought to fulfillment the work of true liberation which she had started throughout the empire before World War I. The former British India was one of the few new nations, in which thanks to British policy, in spite of great difficulty presented by differences of race, language, religion, and caste in the vast subcontinent, parliamentary democracy worked on the whole well and the democratic spirit of moderation continued to prevail. The other leading Western European power, France, however, in a resentful mood about her humiliation in World War II and in an effort to restore old imperial glory, resented Anglo-American accommodation to changing reality. Britain was held responsible for France's "loss" of Syria and Lebanon and American economic imperialism or naive innocence, or perhaps a combination of both, were suspected behind the national liberation movements in Indo-China and North Africa. Yet France was able to fight her wars in Indo-China and Algeria only with the help of American arms and money. Africa south of the Sahara seemed not to present an immediate problem of national self-determination in the late 1940's and even in the early 1950's. This changed at the end of the 1950's. Britain again took the lead in the Gold Coast which in March 1957 became the independent nation of Ghana. The question of national self-determination has since loomed larger and larger in the United Nations.

* * *

With the growth of national self-determination, the problem has become more and more an issue in the "cold war." Though the Soviet Union has tried to appear as the main defender of national self-determination, the United States has from the beginning insisted on championing that principle in the United Nations Charter. The acceptance of this United States position is one of the elements distinguishing the Charter of the United Nations from the Covenant of the League of Nations. Whereas the Covenant did not deal with national self-determination at all, the Charter, based on drafts submitted by the United States, mentions it three times. Chapter I defines as one of the purposes of the United Nations "to develop friendly relations among nations based on respect for the principle of equal rights and self-determination of peoples." Chapter XI sets forth a very broad concept regarding non self-governing territories and imposes upon member nations the duty "to develop self government, to take due account of the political aspirations of the peoples, and to assist them in the progressive development of their free political institutions." Article 76 proclaims the desirability of "independence" in accordance with "the freely expressed wishes of the peoples concerned."

Yet the United Nations Charter does not insist on independence, it insists only on self-government. Independence of small or nonviable entities may defeat its purpose. In certain cases the principle of true federation on the basis of real equality is more promising than that of national independence. National independence is not an essential element in the democratic tradition, self-government is—a government based upon consent of the governed and respect for the equality of all peoples involved.

The principle of national self-determination has nothing to do with "race" as Communist speakers often imply. It was first invoked by "white" peoples against "white" peoples in Europe and America —the Anglo-Americans and the Latin-Americans, the Irish and the Poles, the Italians and the Norwegians, the Baltic and the Balkan peoples, the Finns and the Ukrainians, and many others—later on with changing historical circumstances by Germans and Hungarians. In the twentieth century "colored" peoples following the Western examples appealed to the principle of self-determination against "white" domination in Asia and Africa. But the demand for self-determination was from the time of the awakening of nationalism in Asia also raised by "colored" peoples against non-"white" empires, by Arabs against Turkey, by Koreans against Japan. In the last few years similar demands have been voiced by non-European peoples finding themselves in a minority position in the newly created non-European states—by the Pathans in Pakistan, the Nagas in India, the Moluccans in Indonesia. As the territorial settlements of 1919, based on the principle of national self-determination, gave rise to new demands based on the very same principle, so did the settlements after World War II.

* * *

The United Nations and the United States, in view of their origin and acknowledged principles, have always favored national self-determination. But in a world situation of great tension and conflicting vital interests no principle can ever be fully applied. Here the Communists had an easier stand; they could invoke the principle of self-determination to the fullest when it suited their tactical or strategic goals and could as fully and simply deny it when it interfered with their goals, as in the case of Hungary or Tibet. The United States on the other hand had to take into consideration not only what some of its allies, rightly or wrongly, regarded as their needs or rights, but also the future of the dependent peoples themselves, whose own security or well-being might be endangered by too sudden a change in status. The United States had not only to meet the pressure of certain groups within itself—a situation unknown to countries less democratic or less heterogeneous than the United States—but had to make sometimes choices antagonizing some, though never the majority, of its NATO allies.

The admission of so many new, mostly African, nations had certainly created difficulties for the Western nations, but seen in a long-range perspective it is working out to the West's advantage. The spirit and the procedure of the United Nations has been shaped by Western democratic traditions. Representatives of peoples to whom these traditions have been alien are getting familiar with them in the discussions of the United Nations and its various agencies. Even the Communists have to adapt themselves in the United Nations, at least formally, to the ways of argumentation used in parliamentary bodies. The fascist powers, Germany, Japan, and Italy, refused a similar adaption before World War II and left the League of Nations with all signs of contempt and derision. The Communists though they are always in danger of finding themselves in a minority, frequently mustering only two or three additional votes to their own nine, stay in the United Nations understanding its value as an international forum. The United Nations is not a super-state nor an international legislative body. At the present stage of world development such a world state with legislative and executive functions would be unacceptable everywhere, also to the Congress and the people of the United States. And yet it would be a mistake to underestimate the educational value of the United Nations towards the formation of world opinion and towards a more civilized behavior on the part of those governments which have to present and defend their points of view before the United Nations.

The thinking of most Asians and Africans is obviously still warped by misinterpretation of the recent past and by indiscriminate anticolonial slogans which lack historical perspective. But formerly "oppressed" European peoples have shown the same attitude of mind, and for many decades Americans were deeply prejudiced against British rule in North America and glorified their struggle for independence as a "liberation" from oppression. In view of this general human attitude in the age of nationalism it is rather remarkable that men like Habib Bourguiba in Tunisia and others have shown a loyal understanding of the liberal Western tradition in which they were brought up during colonial rule, and of this tradition's contribution to the newly won orderly freedom of their countries.

The tensions and misunderstandings between the United States and other nations are not confined to those in Asia and Africa. The Canadians who have more in common with the United States in background and political, social and economic attitudes than other peoples show to a growing degree similar apprehensions. In 1958 a leading Canadian journalist wrote in *Foreign Affairs* that though the American threat to Canada's independence was not primarily military, "in the last century every weapon of diplomacy and commercial pressure was used by Washington against the infant Canadian nation; and it early became a deep-rooted instinct in Canadians to avoid close commercial dependence on the United States for fear of its leading to political dominance."

Revolutionary nationalism with its socialist appeal to down-trodden masses came into power first, not in Asia, but in Mexico in 1910. For many years bitter anti-capitalist and anti-imperialist resentments directed especially against the United States led to great unrest, to the rule of generals from 1913 to 1946, to the seizure of large agricultural holdings and foreign oil property, to anti-religious legislation and to open sympathy with Germany in World War I. Until the ambassadorship of Dwight Whitney Morrow who served in Mexico from 1927 to 1930, the United States opposed the Mexican revolution and interfered in Mexican affairs. In 1934 General Lazaro Cardenas radicalized the revolution. Under the slogan "Mexico for the Mexicans" economic independence was to be achieved. The masses were swayed by the slogans of Marxist class struggle. Vicente Lombardo Toledano formed his Confederation of Mexican Workers with an extreme leftist complexion. Communism gained hold of Mexican intellectuals and artists. Yet a wise and conciliatory policy on the part of the United States changed the picture. During World War II Mexico collaborated with the "colossus of the north." Revolution was turned into reform, though many of its outward trappings remained, down to the name of the Party of the Institutionalized Revolution. It rules Mexico as a one party state but on a broad basis. A strong middle class is emerging in the country. An originally violent anti-"imperialist" and anti-United States nationalism has proven a safeguard against communism.

Such was not the case in China. There the leader of the nationalist revolution Sun Yat-sen turned to Moscow for support after he failed to receive such aid from the United States. Before his death in 1925 he publicly expressed, in what may be regarded as his testament to nationalist China, his hope that the Chinese would fully cooperate with Leninist Russia in a common struggle for the liberation of mankind from imperialism. The understanding shown by the Hoover and Roosevelt administrations for the Mexican revolution was not always given to later similar movements in Asia and Africa.

In the "cold war" atmosphere, which developed in the 1950's, the United States seemed too often to regard other lands as strategic real estate instead of considering the people living there, their problems and their needs. This may not be a true interpretation of American intentions, but peoples in the underdeveloped countries where they have been accustomed for decades to being told what to do and to being used for foreign ends are suspicious and hypersensitive.

This is especially the case with the Arab people in view of their experiences from 1918 on. The Arabs regard, rightly or wrongly, Gamal Abdul Nasser as the first man to hold out a promise of a life of greater human dignity and of the end of foreign interference from which the whole region has suffered for a long time. Arab nationalism which is only part of a general movement sweeping Asia, Africa, and Latin America, a movement fundamentally for national self-determination, long predated Nasser who is its present symbol. In February 1955 Israeli armed forces attacked Egyptian positions in the Gaza strip with much superior equipment and caused many casualties. The Security Council unanimously condemned Israel as it has done on previous occasions. But when Egypt wished to re-equip her army, she turned in vain to the United States and Britain. Rebuked by the West, Egypt acquired arms from Communist lands. The growing strength of Arab nationalism induced Israel, France, and Britain to attack Egypt in the fall of 1956 to overthrow Nasser.

The overwhelming majority of the United Nations, including most European and American nations, opposed this aggression in November 1956. The United States sided with the majority, not out of sympathy for Egypt, which was even refused help to deal with the war damages it had suffered. American action was motivated by considerations for the Western position in Asia and Africa and by a realistic estimate of the consequences of the invasion. "There are those," Desmond Stewart, an English expert on the Middle East, wrote from Beirut in the March 1958 *Encounter,* the British organ of the anti-Communist Congress for Cultural Freedom, "who now argue that the Egyptian collapse was imminent, and that Eden's greatest error was not to go on. . . . One can only have an opinion, and mine is that if the Canal Zone had been successfully occupied, Egypt would have continued to fight; if the Delta had been occupied, and the Nile valley, then the arms already issued to the 'army of liberation' would have been in an underground war far more bloody and far better organized than the war in Algeria, in which the Egyptians would have been actively supported by help from outside, and inspired by the sympathy of all Asia and Africa. . . . A Suez venture continued would have been ten times more a disaster than Suez abandoned."

Militarily Nasser's armed forces might be defeated. Yet in Arab eyes his resistance was a major victory and a reason for hope. The masses might overrate Egypt's strength and believe the boastful nonsense spread by the Egyptian radio. The educated Arabs knew that Egypt was a poor country, unable militarily in open battle to stand up to trained and highly skilled Western armies. "But at Port Said a weak country refused to be weak; a people with no modern tradition of military glory fought on, and refused to surrender; a people whose government had been frequently changed on the orders of foreigners did not obey the implicit order to overthrow Nasser." France surrendered quickly in 1940; the Egyptians were determined to continue to fight; so at least it appeared to public opinion in Asian and African lands. A new pride in being Arab was born. The aggression in the old type colonial style did more for Nasser's prestige than anything he did.

* * *

It would be a mistake, directed against the very foundations of a democratic order, to assume that in an international organization any one state or group of states—so-called blocs—is entitled to control the organization. Like every democratic institution, developed under the modern Western tradition, the United Nations constitutes a parliamentry body in which various members, blocs, and pressure groups try to exercise their influence to win their point or to arrive at some acceptable compromise. When with the growth of national self-determination Asian and African nations received a better representation in the United Nations, some Western spokesmen expressed concern over the influence of an Afro-Asian bloc. The Western powers did not complain about a Western bloc nor the Communist countries about a Soviet bloc. Blocs are a democratic phenomenon of common interests, but with the exception of the Communist bloc the other blocs do not exist as rigid formations. The Soviet bloc is in a permanent and, for it, painful minority position. The Western bloc, the Latin American bloc, and the Afro-Asian bloc are fluid groups. They cooperate in various instances. Their members vote in spite of frequent pressures from within and without the "bloc" in freedom according to their interests and moral convictions. The United States can be well satisfied with the influence it exercises in the United Nations. It does not always succeed in getting everything it wants, but that is impossible in any democratic organization. No one should always "win."

The important votes on issues on which the United States and the Soviet Union disagreed during the last four sessions of the Assembly of the United Nations—from 1957 to 1960, when the number of Afro-Asian members was steadily growing—showed the strength of the United States position and at the same time the extreme fluidity of the non-Communist blocs. In 1957 the Assembly voted in favor of the United States demand to postpone a debate on the admission of Communist China by 47 to 27 votes with 7 abstentions. The nine Communist votes were naturally cast against postponement. But Denmark, Iceland, Norway, and Sweden voted also against postponement. Among the seven abstentions were Israel and Portugal. On the other hand Iraq, Jordan, Lebanon, Libya, and Malaya voted with the United States. Two years later, in 1959, the same issue was before the Assembly. Again a number of Asian and African nations joined the United States to assure a majority of 44. Other Asian and African nations voted for considering the admission of Communist China; in that, they were joined by several European nations, not only Scandinavian but also Ireland. A number of nations abstained, not only Saudi Arabia, Tunisia, and Libya, but also Portugal and Israel.

The extreme fluidity of the non-Communist blocs was also shown in two other key votes in the 1957 Assembly, on the increase of the membership of the Disarmament Conference and on the continuing support for the Middle Eastern United Nations Emergency Force.

In both votes the Communist bloc remained practically alone. In the first vote the United States was joined by many Asian nations, among them Burma and India. Among the 11 abstentions were Ireland, Israel, and Liberia. On the second vote the 9 Communist nays were joined by Chile and Ecuador. Burma, Ghana, India, Indonesia, Jordan, Pakistan, and Yugoslavia voted with the United States. Several Latin American nations and nationalist China abstained.

Questions of national self-determination which were of crucial importance were those of Hungary and Tibet. All the votes showed the isolation of the Communists. In the vote of censure against the Soviet Union concerning Hungary, 15 Asian-African nations had voted in 1956 for censure and 11 had abstained. In 1957 the number of those who censured had grown to eighteen while the abstentions diminished to nine. Among the members of the commission which drew up the indictment against the Soviet Union, Tunisia played a leading role. On the other hand no effort was made by Tunisia or other Afro-Asian nations in 1957 to press for a strong censure of French violent suppression of the Algerian demand for freedom. The influence of the United States prevailed to allow France more time to carry out a program of self-determination in the spirit of the United Nations Charter.

Yet the Afro-Asian nations were conscious of the fact that it took the Soviet Union only a few weeks to crush the Hungarian fight for independence, whereas the large French army in Algeria was unable for more than six years to break down the resistance of the Algerian fighters for freedom. It was characteristic that while the Communists claimed that the Hungarian revolt was inspired by Western "imperialism" and led by "Fascist" elements, the French ascribed the tenacious Algerian struggle for independence to the influence of Communism, of Nasser, or of Bourguiba. In both cases, of course, such influences, as far as they existed, played only a minor role in what were indigenous and genuine demands for national self-determination. There was, however, one great difference—and this difference was not lost on public opinion in Asia and Africa: in the Communist orbit no voice of protest or criticism was raised against Soviet action in Hungary, whereas in France Catholics, Liberals, and even individual officers of the armed forces spoke up, against terror and repression, on behalf of what they regarded as the true values of France and the West. Throughout the Western world sympathy for the Algerian aspirations for independence and dismay at French methods of action was voiced.

Afro-Asian nations continued to support the United States in the votes against the Communist powers on Hungary and Tibet in 1959. In both votes only the Communists voted against the resolutions. All the Asian and African nations voted either with the United States or abstained in the case of Hungary. Among the 17 abstentions were Israel and Finland. On the resolution expressing concern at the denial of human rights in Tibet 26 nations abstained, but in this case the several Afro-Asian nations were joined by Belgium, Britain, the Dominican Republic, France, and Portugal. Not one non-Communist nation voted in either case with the Communists. On October 8, 1960, some Asian and Arab nations voted with the United States not to consider Chinese Communist admission to the United Nations. Among those who voted for consideration and who remained in the minority, were the Communists, the Scandinavian nations, and Ireland, and some Afro-Asian nations. Other Afro-Asian nations abstained, together with Israel and Portugal.

The fluidity of the blocs has rather grown in the last years with the accession of more Asian and African members to the United Nations. Questions directly concerning national self-determination and the trusteeship principle involved the Union of South Africa and its position in South-West Africa, a formerly German territory put under South-African mandate by the League of Nations, and Portugal. As regards the Union of South Africa the General Assembly denounced on November 17, 1959, the apartheid policy of the Union of South Africa and its administration of South-West Africa. The texts of the resolutions were drafted by the Trusteeship Committee. The United States and most other nations voted for the resolution; Britain, France, and Portugal voted against it; and 7 nations abstained. On November 12, 1960, the Trusteeship Committee, by 45 votes in favor, 6 against, and 24 abstentions, called upon Portugal to supply information on her overseas territories. A Communist amendment to strengthen the text of the resolution was defeated. The Asian and African delegations that sponsored the motion were subjected to ridicule and pressure by the Communist bloc which regarded the resolution as too weak. They responded with open criticism of the Soviet Union. In a roll call on the resolution asking Portugal to report on her overseas territories, 28 Afro-Asian, 9 Latin American, and 8 Western European nations voted for it.

Belgium, Brazil, France, South Africa, Spain, and Portugal voted against it. Both, the Communist bloc and the United States, abstained.

The Soviet Union suffered a similar defeat, when on December 14, 1960, the General Assembly called for immediate steps toward complete independence for non-self-governing territories. Several Soviet moves for strengthening the resolution in an anti-Western sense were defeated, among them the call for a one year deadline for complete independence and the request to place the subject of colonialism on next year's agenda. By this action the United Nations, with an overwhelming majority, endorsed the principle of national self-determination. The vote was 89 to 0. Five European nations—the colonial powers Britain, France, Belgium, Portugal, and Spain—and two American nations—the United States and the Dominican Republic—abstained in addition to Australia and the Union of South Africa. Mr. James J. Wadsworth, United States delegate, declared that the United States abstained with deep regret.

* * *

Not all difficulties faced by the United States today can be ascribed to the existence of totalitarian communism. Many of them spring from the slow and painful ascent of underprivileged groups and peoples everywhere towards equality and a better life, and from their hope and determination to attain these goals, to which they were aroused by the principles and achievements of modern Western civilization. The process of ascent started in nineteenth century Europe and has since been spreading, partly thanks to the imperialism of the liberal nations, all over the globe. This process is part of the Westernization of the world which is seen too often only in its technological and material aspects.

To direct the new aspirations into constructive channels and to prevent the inevitable tensions, anxieties, and "provocations" from degenerating into bitter class and race conflicts and wars are the task of the United Nations. There, for the first time in history, all human races and civilizations—great and small, advanced and backward—can meet on a footing of legal equality and try to solve the difficult problems of world-wide accommodation to revolutionary changes by the democratic way of discussion and moral pressure.

These efforts can be facilitated by wise and generous guidance. Such an attempted guidance underlies—not always consciously—the often poorly verbalized and imperfectly carried through policy of the United States in and through the United Nations. Sometimes the United States policy creates the impression that it abandons moral principles, its own principles, for alleged considerations of strategy and that it is being too much determined by reaction to Soviet threats and by the pressure of allies and not by considerations of justice and humanity. But only a policy of positive sympathy with the forces caring for man's freedom and dignity everywhere—a policy in agreement with the message which the United States and modern Western civilization have carried—can in the long run defeat the threat of Communist or Fascist totalitarianism. The United States will be on sound ground if it will consistently favor self-determination in the true sense of the word. The United Nations should safeguard the free expression of the will of the populations involved by supervising the vote and by helping formulate the questions submitted for the vote so as to allow a true choice between real alternatives. Such a policy is the only one which will prevail in the long run without war and which combines the enlightened self-interest of the West with its appeal to the aspirations of the majority of mankind aroused to a new and better life by the West itself.

32

Germany in World Politics: 1963[*]

Germany's position in world politics, as that of any other country, depends on the constellation of world forces and on the character of world conflicts, both of them being nothing permanent but continually changing, often from decade to decade. Twenty-five years ago, Germany faced on her western border a disunited and largely disarmed West, and on her eastern border a medley of small states, none

[*] From *Current History*, April 1963. Copyright by *Current History*. Reprinted with permission.

of them nationally consolidated and all of them jealous and suspicious of each other. This constellation, which dated back to 1918— to the breakup of the Western alliance which had won the war, and the breakup of the Habsburg Empire which had presented a barrier to Germany's expansion to the southeast—allowed and encouraged Germany to undertake her second attempt, under much more propitious auspices, at establishing her hegemony over Europe and her position as a, or possibly the, leading world power.[1]

By 1963 the world political constellation has completely changed. The West is highly armed and relatively united and on the eastern border Germany faces an Eastern Europe consolidated under, and protected by, Soviet Russian power. The strength of the Soviet Union, which no one could foresee in 1938, is the direct result of German aggressiveness, of the German Drang nach Osten, in 1939 and 1941. The unity in the West, which was never achieved against German expansionism before 1914 or before 1938, is the direct result of Soviet Russia's aggressiveness manifested in Stalin's last years, from the Berlin blockade and the Prague coup to the Korean War.

Germany's fate after 1945 has been determined not only by the new reality of world forces, represented by the towering strength of the United States and of Soviet Russia, but also by the character of the new world conflict, which no longer centers, as it did in the 1930's, around German and Japanese ambitions. Now this new conflict is a result of Soviet Russian expansionism and its challenge to the situation, which the common victory of the Anglo-Americans and of Soviet Russia had brought about in Europe and the Far East. This constellation of a rapidly growing world-wide conflict between East and West made inevitable a partition of Germany, which had threatened and attacked both West and East and had been defeated by their joint effort. Each of the victorious and now conflicting power systems tried to order "its" part of Germany according to its own image and interests. There was some irony in the fact that National Socialist Germany, which with equal ferociousness and contempt had rejected and fought democracy and communism, was now in its western part organized as a democratic and in its eastern part as a Communist state. Not only the two world political forces which emerged in 1945 in their full strength as a result of German aggres-

[1] See on Germany's goals in the war of 1914 the book by the historian of Hamburg University, Ernst Fischer, *Griff nach der Weltmacht. Die Kriegszielpolitik des Kaiserlichen Deutschland 1914-18* (Düsseldorf: Droste Verlag, 1961)—perhaps the most important publication on World War I for many years, since it is based on entirely new German archival material.

siveness but also their two opposite ideologies which Germany had combatted faced each other across the new frontier established at the end of the war on German territory.

In this confrontation Western democracy has proved its economic and political superiority. There exists probably no other place on earth where this fact is as evident as in Germany. On both sides of the Elbe the people are the same in tradition and education, in industriousness and in work discipline. Yet the German Federal Republic has become one of the most prosperous and advanced political entities of the 1950's and the early 1960's, whereas the German Democratic Republic, the Communist creation in the Soviet-occupied zone, has passed in the same period through a permanent and growing economic crisis. Western Germany, with the help of the United States, was not only able to provide the highest standard of living for its inhabitants in German history but even to absorb more than nine million refugees and expellees; Eastern Germany, on the other hand, was weakened by the flight of millions of its citizens so that it had to build in August 1961 the wall across Berlin to prevent the disintegration of the Communist state. Perhaps nowhere else has American foreign policy in the last seventeen years, in spite of all inevitable minor errors and mistakes, been as successful as in Germany. The partition of Germany which German nationalists often blame F. D. Roosevelt for was not America's fault; it was the outcome of a war which Germany confidently started and ruthlessly conducted. Yet the partition of Germany has, as Golo Mann recently pointed out, a positive aspect which has made possible and stimulated a very gratifying development in West European affairs.

"Without the partition of Germany, Bonn could not have developed its highly constructive, steady, and confidence-inspiring policy towards the West, and without such a foreign policy West Germany's prosperity would not have been possible either. Without the partition of Germany, Franco-German reconciliation would not have been possible. It was achieved between Paris and Bonn, not between Paris and Berlin; between two partners of roughly equal strength, not between France and a Germany whose inhabitants would number half as many again and whose economic strength would be twice that of France." [2]

The Republic of Bonn has now lasted for about the same time

[2] Golo Mann, "Rapallo: the Vanishing Dream," *Survey*, a Journal of Soviet and East European Studies, London, October 1962, pp. 74-88. Golo Mann, son of Thomas Mann, is professor of political science at the Institute of Technology in Stuttgart.

as did the Republic of Weimar. But whereas the Republic of Weimar undermined its existence by the political passions and the anti-Western affects of a growing number of its citizens, the Republic of Bonn has shown an infinitely greater stability than its predecessor and has rightly inspired confidence in the West; the large majority of its citizens have devoted themselves to prosperity and no longer to political passions and anti-Western resentments.

This change in the German international situation and national attitude, which in 1938 no one could foresee, was not only due to American foreign policy but also to the fact that Western Germany found unexpectedly in Konrad Adenauer a great and constructive statesman. He has, which is only human, his personal and ideological limitations. He is as little a Gladstone as Bismarck was a Disraeli. In his will to power, purposefulness, and solitary authoritarianism Adenauer can be compared to Bismarck, but the Catholic Rheinlander does not share the Prussian Junker's passionate antidemocratic and anti-Western convictions. Bismarck succeeded in alienating Germany from the dominant Western trend of liberal democracy; Adenauer's achievement was greater and more unexpected—he succeeded in reversing this anti-Westernism which had grown in the Weimar Reich and had reached its climax under Hitler. Bismarck's triumph brought in its consequences great misfortune over Germany and over Europe. The Reich he created was short-lived. It collapsed partly in 1918 and definitely in 1945. The future may show that Adenauer built stronger and healthier foundations, which will help to inaugurate an era of lasting good will and peaceful co-operation for Western Europe.[3]

For thirteen years Adenauer has been identified with the consolidation, against great initial odds, of the German Federal Republic.

---

[3] On Bismarck's role, see Hans Kohn, *The Mind of Germany* (New York: Scribner's 1960); and Otto Pflanze, *Bismarck and the Development of Germany. The Period of Unification 1815-1871* (Princeton, N.J.: Princeton University Press 1963). Prof. Pflanze writes: "During the last two centuries a cultural cleavage opened along the Rhine. In the development of her political attitudes and institutions Germany followed a course largely independent of the West. . . . Because of Bismarck the gap widened still more. He compounded a new synthesis in German political attitudes between German nationalism, Prussian militarism, and Hohenzollern authoritarianism" (p. 8 f.). Adenauer tried to bridge this cleavage along the Rhine. He succeeded in considerably narrowing the gap. He was helped in it by the fortunate fact that Prussia and the Hohenzollern had definitely disappeared from the German scene. Bismarck wore the uniform of a Prussian major-general as his normal dress, and in a Christmas letter in 1872 he regretted that it had been his lot to serve the royal house as an official rather than as an officer. Such an attitude would be unthinkable in Adenauer's case.

When he was elected Chancellor on September 15, 1949, a man in his middle seventies, the future of the new state and of Adenauer's chancellorship seemed most uncertain. Both were accepted by German public opinion as temporary expediences. Yet the old man, who was then of about the same age as Bismarck was at the time of his enforced retirement, was able by his personal strength to consolidate the new state, and the two democratic and free Federal elections of 1953 and 1957 were votes of confidence in his authoritarian leadership.

Now, in 1963, the era of Adenauer is coming to its end, and this under circumstances tragic for the Grand Old Man himself. Unfortunately, at the height of his prestige and power, in April 1959, he had not the moral strength to leave the chancellorship for the quiet dignity of the Federal presidency. It was then high time for him, his great work accomplished, to withdraw, but he had no confidence in his own work; he did not believe that the German Federal Republic could continue its stability and its pro-Western orientation without him, that it could live out of its own strength. Adenauer thought himself indispensable and underestimated the democratic tide in German public opinion. The elections of 1961 no longer gave him a majority. From that time on Adenauer's administration was in a permanent crisis, which reached its climax in his and his chief ministers' mismanagement of the Spiegel Affair of October 27, 1962. Through the fault of the government the affair turned into a political scandal and used up the Chancellor's prestige, even in his own party.[5]

A few years ago Adenauer in his person represented the fountainhead and the strength of an awakening German democracy. Now his agreed-upon resignation in October 1963 will give new vitality to German democracy which has shown its power, in the parties as well as in the press, during the Spiegel Affair. The coalition of the Chancellor's party with the Free Democrats, which has governed Germany since 1961 and was re-formed at the end of 1962 after most embarrassing negotiations, is no longer a stable government. It is as much a "lame duck" as the Chancellor himself. The one promising sign of the negotiations at the end of 1962 was the attempt to form a coalition between the Christian Democrats, the Chancellor's party, and

[5] See the excellent article by Fritz René Allemann, "Hybris und Zerfall. Die Tragödie Konrad Adenauers," *Der Monat*, Berlin, January 1963; and the editorial "Uebergangsregierung in Bonn," *Neue Zürcher Zeitung*, December 16, 1962. Both the *Neue Zürcher Zeitung* and *Der Monat* have in the past strongly supported Adenauer's general line.

Germany's second strongest party, the Social Democrats whom the Chancellor had always kept out of the government and whom he had declared untrustworthy in national and international politics. Though the Federal President Lübke favored such a "great coalition," it was not realized this time. Yet a coalition between Catholic Conservatives and Social Democrats has now existed successfully for seventeen years in Austria. Adenauer's resignation will make such a coalition possible in Germany too, and thereby the conservative immobility which characterized the last years of his government will be broken. This fact will mean a further strengthening of democracy in the German Federal Republic, corresponding, to a certain degree, to the "opening to the Left," accomplished recently in Italy under Christian Democratic auspices.

"The attempt to solve the crisis by taking the Social Democrats into the government would undoubtedly have been the cleanest and most effective way to overcome the crisis of confidence in the Federal Republic," the *Neue Zürcher Zeitung* wrote, the best informed newspaper in the German language which has never shown great sympathy for the Social Democrats. "Co-responsibility on the part of the opposition would have been a guarantee for full clarity in the Spiegel Affair and against a repetition of the abuses that led to the crisis. . . . The idea of the Social Democrats' inclusion in the government has, thanks to the brief episode of coalition talks between Adenauer and Ollenhauer, grown stronger roots, and has also won the recognition, in principle, of the Christian Democratic Union. That, in any event, is an important milestone in the political development of the German Federal Republic." [6]

* * *

The end of the Adenauer era will bring a new mobility not only to German domestic policy. Germany's position in world politics, too, will experience some new vigor and change. The whole process will create a new and better atmosphere between the government and a large part of the younger generation which has looked upon the official policy as ossified, and will strengthen thereby the democratic stability of the German Federal Republic. The democratic German youth viewed in the last years the Adenauer regime with a feeling of

---

[6] From "Uebergangsregierung in Bonn," *Neue Zürcher Zeitung*, December 16, 1962, translated in *Swiss Review of World Affairs*, a monthly publication of the *Neue Zürcher Zeitung*, January 1963.

growing opposition which in its bitterness tended to overlook Adenauer's great achievements in building a more secure basis for German democracy than the Wilhelminian or the Weimar Reich ever knew. This youth lacks the historical perspective to evaluate Adenauer's great merits; it has not experienced the Berlin-centered Reich with its feeling of superiority over the Slavs, which survives in many of the older generation who have not undergone a basic change of heart.

The younger generation is eager for changing the imperialist heritage and for deepening the democratic regeneration of Germany. One finds among them "a growing realization of the need to make amends to the Poles for the treatment they suffered from the Nazis. . . . Anybody who remembers the nationalist rantings [against German eastern frontiers after the First World War] of even moderate Germans at the time of the Weimar Republic, must be truly amazed by the tremendous amount of goodwill, at least towards Poland, that is manifested in Germany today. . . . To most people of the young generation, Breslau and Königsberg, Danzig and Stettin, appear to be far-away cities irretrievably lost." [7] Adenauer's policy towards the West has been greatly successful and beneficial for Germany. Germany's Eastern European policy, on the other hand, has been characterized by immobility and sterility. The general world-political context of 1963 favors laying the foundations for a more constructive program in Germany's Eastern policy.

There are still many Germans, especially among the older generation, who pursue territorial aims. They officially demand, without pointing out how it could ever be achieved, the restoration of the frontiers of 1937 by "peaceful" means. They forget that even liberal and democratic Germany thought the eastern frontiers of Germany as they existed between 1920 and 1937 "unbearable." Some Germans go therefore even further today; they hope for the restoration of the frontiers of 1938 (which would include Austria and the Sudetenland) or those of 1914, with which Germany had not been content then and which it tried to rectify by annexations in west and east in World War I. But, as Golo Mann wrote as far back as 1950, "it is not possible to return to the past, to restore what has been destroyed; impossible to retrieve what was recklessly lost. Germany today can

[7] F. R. Allemann, "Adenauer's Eastern Policy," *Survey*, p. 35 f. See also in this magazine the article by Walter Laqueur, "Russia and Germany."

only have functional political aims—economic, moral, practical aims." [8]

Such practical aims Adenauer's Germany pursued in the West, until the romantic and reactionary fata morgana of a Western Europe dominated by a Paris-Bonn axis attracted Adenauer, after de Gaulle's "democratic" authoritarianism appeared to have established a "strong" France under a "strong" man. But outside Adenauer, West German leadership of all parties, including Dr. Ludwig Erhard, Adenauer's probable successor, and Dr. Gerhard Schroeder, his foreign minister, is opposed to de Gaulle's anti-British and anti-American policy. They know the instability of the present French authoritarian regime which depends on the life and strength of its one great man. They understand that the still delicate plant of German democracy cannot grow strong by relying preponderantly on an unstable and vacillating French democracy but only on close co-operation with Britain and the United States in that North Atlantic Community which de Gaulle so haughtily rejects. Few factors present as great a threat to the consolidation of German democracy as the hope of a domination of Western Europe by a Paris-Bonn axis under authoritarian leadership in opposition to Anglo-American democracy. Such an axis recalls international constellations in which, from the seventeenth to the twentieth centuries, continental authoritarianism in the name of Europe and its civilization proudly underestimated and fought the maritime commercial powers.[9]

---

[8] This quest for "just" eastern frontiers was one of the most potent forces to bring German nationalism to feverish heat in the Weimar Reich. Thomas Mann wrote on June 6, 1932, in a letter that nationalism was "today no more than an ugly mass passion, a barrier to world progress and a blight on our lives." He quoted Goethe as writing in 1798 that "patriotism conceived as personal bravery has outlived itself just as much as clericalism and aristocratism." Mann complained that the Germans aspired in 1932 to "restoration. Their eyes are turned backwards to a past which cannot help them; and one is filled with horror at the defeats which await them and which, it goes without saying, will involve disastrous internal struggles." There is today little of such a nationalism among the majority of young Germans, but a similar nostalgic backward-looking nationalism under de Gaulle's leadership in neighboring France harbors a danger for German democracy, too.

[9] See the important editorial by James Reston "What People Do They Think We Are?" *The New York Times*, Western edition, January 21, 1963; and the last paragraph in the editorial of "Sirius" (Hubert Beuve-Méry), *Le Monde*, weekly edition, Paris, January 10-16, 1963, which reads: "Ce qui est sûr, c'est que des affirmations de nationalisme exacerbé ne peuvent qu'engendrer le désordre et mener à l'isolement. Le général de Gaulle se complaît à ces jeux, qui effraient ou irritent ses partenaires et ne peuvent que réjouir l'adversaire. Tantôt prince de l'équivoque et tantôt risquant une mise énorme sur quelque coup de poker, il tend à imposer sa loi aux Européens et aux Américains de même qu'il a su l'imposer aux Français. Puisse-t-il ne pas avoir, comme en Algérie, à s'incliner trop tard et à trop haut prix devant les réalités qu'il se flattait de maîtriser!"

The quite successful pro-Western policy of the Adenauer era will probably be supplemented by a new Eastern policy in the post-Adenauer era. Such a policy, Golo Mann warns, and most Germans would agree, must not change Germany's faithful adherence to the North Atlantic Community, an adherence which made possible a German development much "too promising and too precious" to be allowed to be undermined either by de Gaulle's traditional nationalist ambitions or by a wrong German Eastern policy. The actual content of a new Eastern policy cannot be outlined today. Its premise is a change of fundamental attitude on the part of the official circles of the German Federal Republic. Golo Mann sums up the general terms of the possible policy as the recognition of communism as an enduring opponent with whom one will have to live if one does not want to die with him; a relaxation of tension and an understanding so far as the opponent wants it, for an understanding is inevitably a two-way affair; the recognition of the Polish Oder-Neisse frontier and of the fact that Eastern Germany lies within the Russian sphere so long as the cold war goes on; and finally concentration on the immediate aim of making conditions in Eastern Germany, in the German Democratic Republic, more tolerable, more lawful, and more free for the seventeen million Germans living there.[10]

* * *

Such a change of Germany's Eastern policy in the post-Adenauer era will be facilitated by the changed world political situation in 1963. The confrontation between the United States and the Soviet Union over the Russian missiles in Cuba has revealed both United States nuclear superiority and Khrushchev's and the Russian people's reluctance to wage a nuclear war. Today the United States possesses, according to Hanson W. Baldwin, "the strongest military force in the world. . . . The chief elements of this superiority are a powerful and increasingly invulnerable nuclear delivery capability, many times greater than Russia's, and with sufficient power to destroy the USSR as a military or political entity, and a Navy greatly superior to Rus-

---

[10] See Golo Mann, *Survey*, pp. 87 f. See also Gerald Freund, *Germany Between Two Worlds* (New York: Harcourt, 1961), p. 253. On the change in Western Germany regarding a more active Eastern policy see Klaus-Peter Schulz, "Grenze von Gestern, Brücke von Morgen. Gedanken über die Aussichten einer deutsch-polnischen Verständigung," (The Frontier of Yesterday, the Bridge of Tomorrow. Thoughts about the Prospects of a German-Polish Understanding), *Der Monat*, Berlin, January 1963, pp. 42-54; and the articles of Rolf Schroers, Hartmut von Hentig, and Margret Boveri in *Merkur*, Munich, April and October 1962.

sia in over-all strength." The new budget proposed by President Kennedy in January 1963 will "lengthen the United States lead over Soviet Russia in numbers of inter-continental missiles, both landbased and sea-based. In fact, this lead now appears to be so great that there is no immediate prospect that Russia can overtake it numerically." [11]

The new attitude of Khrushchev in favor of "peaceful co-existence," an attitude apparently shared by the peoples in the USSR and in the European satellites, found its expression in his rapprochement with Yugoslavia, in the growing rift with China, and in the speeches at the Sixth Congress of the Communist Party of the German Democratic Republic held in East Berlin in mid-January 1963. The representatives of Yugoslavia who participated for the first time at a party congress in the satellite countries were warmly welcomed. A very different reception was given to the Chinese delegate Wu Hsiu-chuan, who bitterly attacked the Yugoslavs—meaning thereby Khrushchev—as "usurpers of the title of communists" who had "surrendered to the imperialists." Khrushchev came in person to the East Berlin Congress but not to renew his ultimative demand about West Berlin delivered more than four years ago, in November 1958. His speech was, naturally within the ritual framework of Communist incantations, surprisingly void of threats and aggressiveness. "Premier Khrushchev's speech in Berlin today," Max Frankel reported from Washington on January 16, "was regarded here as milder towards the Western powers . . . than anyone has expected it to be. Administration analysts read the Soviet Premier's address as notice that the Berlin crisis was over for the foreseeable future. They had felt it to be so but had not dared to anticipate a candid admission of the collapse of the major Soviet diplomatic drive." [12]

The confrontation over the missiles in Cuba and the firmness of the Kennedy administration over West Berlin have, at least for several years, turned back the Soviet offensive against West Berlin in the same way as the Anglo-American airlift did fifteen years ago. West Berlin's inhabitants have on both occasions remained determined to continue their democratic freedom. In addition, West Berlin is being developed with the help of the Ford Foundation into one of the leading intellectual and artistic centers of the democratic West. With the growing antiauthoritarian vigor and vitality in the German Fed-

---

[11] *The New York Times*, Western edition, January 19, 1963.
[12] *The New York Times*, Western edition, January 17, 1963, p. 1.

eral Republic there exist good prospects that the post-Adenauer era will broaden the basis of democracy and will help to make the German Federal Republic, by its faithfulness to the North Atlantic Community and by its constructive and no longer backward-looking Eastern policy, a stabilizing factor in European and world politics.

Bibliography

Books by Hans Kohn from 1922 to 1963
(In Chronological Order)

Nationalismus, Ueber die Bedeutung des Nationalismus im Judentum und in der Gegenwart. Wien: R. Löwit Verlag, 1922. 130 pp.

Sinn und Schicksal der Revolution. Wien: E. P. Tal & Co., 1923. 105 pp. Czech translation, Prague: Var, 1926.

Die Politische Idee des Judentums. München: Meyer & Jessen, 1924. 68 pp.

A History of the Arab National Movement (in Hebrew). Tel Aviv: Hapoel Hazair, 1926.

Zionistische Politik. (Together with Robert Weltsch). Mährisch-Ostrau: R. Färber, 1927. 292 pp.

In Memory of Gustav Landauer (in Hebrew). (Together with Hugo Bergmann). Tel Aviv: Hapoel Hazair, 1929.

Am-Adam. Manifestations of Human Conscience (in Hebrew). (Together with Hugo Bergmann). Jerusalem: Am-Adam, 1930.

Chapters from the History of Zionist Thought (in Hebrew). Warsaw: Biblioteka Jesodoth, 1929, 1930. 2 vols.

Geschichte der Nationalen Bewegung im Orient. Berlin-Grunewald: Kurt Vowinckel Verlag, 1928. 378 pp. English translation, *A History of Nationalism in the East,* tr. by Margaret M. Green. London: George Routledge & Sons, 1929. 476 pp.

Martin Buber. Sein Werk und seine Zeit. Hellerau: Jakob Hegner, 1930. 415 pp. A second edition with an epilogue, 1930-1960, by Robert Weltsch was published with a new introduction. Köln: Joseph Melzer, 1961. 484 pp.

L'Humanisme Juif. Quinze Essais sur le Juif, le Monde et Dieu. Paris: Editions Rieder, 1931. 276 pp.

Nationalismus und Imperialismus im Vorderen Orient. Frankfurt a.M.: Societäts-Verlag, 1931. 456 pp. English translation, *Nationalism and Imperialism in the Hither East,* tr. by Margaret M. Green. London: George Routledge & Sons, 1932. 340 pp.

Orient und Okzident. Weltpolitische Bücherei, Vol. 24. 95 pp. Berlin: Zentral-Verlag, 1931. English translation *Orient and Occident.* New York: The John Day Company, 1934. 140 pp.

Der Nationalismus in der Sowjetunion. Frankfurt a.M.: Societäts-Verlag, 1932. 150 pp. English translation, *Nationalism in the Soviet Union,* tr. by E. W. Dickes. London: George Routledge & Sons; and New York: Columbia University Press, 1933. 162 pp.

Die Europäisierung des Orients. Berlin: Schocken Verlag, 1934. 356 pp. English translation, *Western Civilization in the Near East.* London: George Routledge & Sons; and New York: Columbia University Press, 1936. 330 pp.

Force or Reason. Issues of the Twentieth Century. Cambridge, Mass.: Harvard University Press, 1937. 168 pp. Third printing, enlarged by a new preface, XXIV pp., 1938. Fourth printing, 1942.

Revolutions and Dictatorships. Essays in Contemporary History. Cambridge, Mass.: Harvard University Press, 1939. 438 pp. Third enlarged and revised edition, 1943.

Not By Arms Alone. Essays on Our Time. Cambridge, Mass.: Harvard University Press, 1940. 162 pp. Second printing, 1941.

The World Must Federate. Isolation Versus Cooperation. Privately printed. New York: Press of the Wooly Whale, 1940. 28 pp.

World Order in Historical Perspective. Cambridge, Mass.: Harvard University Press, 1942. 352 pp. Second printing, 1943.

The Idea of Nationalism. A Study in Its Origins and Background. New York: The Macmillan Co., 1944. 735 pp. Eighth printing, 1960. Macmillan Paperbacks Edition, 1961. Spanish translation, *Historia del Nacionalismo.* Mexico: Fondo de Cultura Economica, 1949. German translation, *Die Idee des Nationalismus.* Heidelberg: Lambert Schneider, 1950. Revised edition, Frankfurt a.M.: S. Fischer Verlag, 1962. Italian translation, *L'Idea del Nazionalismo nel suo sviluppo storico.* Florence: La Nuova Italia, 1956.

Prophets and Peoples. Studies in Nineteenth Century Nationalism. New York: The Macmillan Co., 1946. 213 pp. Fourth printing, 1957. Italian translation, Turin, 1949. German translation by Hugo Knoepfmacher and Therese Treuenfels. 250 pp. Bern: A. Francke, 1949. Japanese translation, Tokyo, 1954. Paperback edition, Collier Books, 1961.

The Twentieth Century. A Mid-Way Account of the Western World. New York: The Macmillan Co., 1949. 252 pp. Third printing, 1952. New enlarged edition, *The Twentieth Century. The Challenge to the West and Its Response.* 312 pp. New York: The Macmillan Co., 1957. Second printing, 1961. German translation, Zurich, 1950. Korean translation, Seoul, 1958. Spanish translation, *El Siglo XX. Reto a Occidente y su respuesta.* 344 pp. Mexico: Editorial Reverte, 1960. Portugese translation, *O Seculo Vinte, um desafio ao homem.* Rio de Janeiro: Editora Fundo de Cultura, 1960. 360 pp. Italian translation, Florence: La Nuova Italia, 1963.

Pan-Slavism, Its History and Ideology. University of Notre Dame Press, 1953. 356 pp. Second revised edition, 480 pp. New York: Vintage Books, 1960. German translation, tr. by Helge Pross, *Die Slawen und der Westen. Die Geschichte des Panslawismus.* Wien: Verlag Herold, 1956. 360 pp. French translation, Paris: Éditions Payot, 1963.

German History. Some New German Views. Edited by Hans Kohn. London: Allen & Unwin; and Boston: The Beacon Press, 1954. 224 pp.

The Mind of Modern Russia: Political and Social Thought of Russia's Great Age. Edited by Hans Kohn. New Brunswick: Rutgers University Press, 1955. 300 pp. Second printing, 1957. Paperback edition, Harper's Torch Books, 1962.

The Making of the Modern French Mind. An Anvil book. Princeton, N.J.: D. Van Nostrand, 1955. 192 pp.

Nationalism, Its Meaning and History. An Anvil book. Princeton, N.J.: D. Van Nostrand, 1955. 192 pp. Indonesian translation, Djakarta, 1959. Spanish translation, Buenos Aires, 1963. German translation, Freiburg i.B. Herder Verlag, 1963.

Nationalism and Liberty. The Swiss Example. London: Allen & Unwin; and New York: The Macmillan Co., 1956. 134 pp. German edition, *Der schweizerische Nationalgedanke. Eine Studie zum Thema Nationalismus und Freiheit.* Zurich: Verlag der Neuen Zürcher Zeitung, 1955. Japanese translation, Tokyo: Asaki-Sha, 1962. 259 pp.

Basic History of Modern Russia. Political, Cultural, and Social Trends. An Anvil book. Princeton, N.J.: D. Van Nostrand, 1957. 192 pp. German translation, *Das Moderne Russland. Grundzüge seiner Geschichte,* tr. by Heddy Pross. Freiburg i.B.: Karl Alber Verlag, 1961. 232 pp.

The Future of Austria. Headline Series. New York: Foreign Policy Association, 1955.

American Nationalism. An Interpretative Essay. New York: The Macmillan Co., 1957, 272 pp. Paperback edition, Collier Books, 1961. 286 pp.

Is the Liberal West in Decline? London: Pall Mall Press, 1957. 74 pp. German translation, *Ist die Freie Welt zum Untergang verurteilt?* Köln: Westdeutscher Verlag, 1959. Italian translation, *Valori e Prospettivi della Civiltà Occidentale.* Rome: Opere Nuove, 1958. Japanese translation, Tokyo: Keiso Shobo, 1960.

West Germany: New Era for German People. Headline Series. New York: Foreign Policy Association, 1958.

Heinrich Heine, The Man and the Myth. New York: The Leo Baeck Institute, 1959.

The Mind of Germany. The Education of a Nation. New York: Charles Scribner's Sons, 1960. 370 pp. Third printing, 1962. Revised British edition, London: Macmillan & Co., 1961. German translation, *Wege und Irrwege. Zur Geistesgeschichte des bürgerlichen Deutschland,* tr. by Wilhelm Pferdekamp. Düsseldorf: Droste Verlag, 1962. Dutch translation, Amsterdam, 1963. Italian translation, Milan, 1963.

Die Welt der Slawen. Edited by Hans Kohn. Frankfurt a.M.: Fischer Bücherei, 1960, 1962. 2 vols.

The Habsburg Empire, 1804-1918. An Anvil book. Princeton, N.J.: D. Van Nostrand, 1961. 192 pp.

Karl Kraus, Arthur Schnitzler, Otto Weininger. Aus dem Jüdischen Wien der Jahrhundertwende. Tübingen: J.C.B. Mohr, 1962. 72 pp.

The Age of Nationalism. The First Era of Global History. New York: Harper & Brothers, 1962. 170 pp.

The Modern World. 1848 to the Present. Readings in European Intellectual History, ed. by Hans Kohn. New York: The Macmillan Co., 1963. 362 pp.

Living in a World Revolution. My Encounters with History. New York: Simon and Schuster, 1963. 200 pp.